The Comparative
Perspective on Literature

The Comparative
Perspective on Literature

APPROACHES TO THEORY
AND PRACTICE

EDITED AND WITH AN
INTRODUCTION BY

Clayton Koelb AND *Susan Noakes*

CORNELL UNIVERSITY PRESS

ITHACA AND LONDON

First published 1988 by Cornell University Press.

International Standard Book Number (cloth) 0-8014-2031-8
International Standard Book Number (paper) 0-8014-9477-X
Library of Congress Catalog Card Number 87-25062
Printed in the United States of America
Librarians: Library of Congress cataloging information
appears on the last page of the book.

The paper in this book is acid-free and meets the guidelines for
permanence and durability of the Committee on Production Guidelines
for Book Longevity of the Council on Library Resources.

Contents

Contents

Acknowledgments

We are grateful to the Division of Humanities of the University of Chicago, the Department of French and Italian at the University of Kansas, the departments of English and Foreign Languages at Purdue University, and the Department of Germanic Languages at Princeton University for supporting this project with secretarial assistance, mailing and telephone costs, and other courtesies. Thanks are also due to Jonathan Monroe and an anonymous reader for Cornell University Press for making suggestions that substantially improved the book. Several scholars who were not able to contribute essays assisted us with suggestions, encouragement, and criticisms. Anthony C. Yu took time out of a leave of absence to help find appropriate contributors. SunHee Kim Gertz and her colleagues at Clark University kindly listened to our presentation of some of the material in the Introduction and sharpened our awareness of a number of issues.

We owe a particular debt of gratitude to our editor, Bernhard Kendler of Cornell University Press, who probably spent more time, effort, and gnashing of teeth on this than on any three other books. His experience and patience with projects like this more than once helped to keep us from going astray. We are also grateful to Kay Scheuer, who shepherded this complex project through the production process, and to our superb copy editor, Judith Bailey.

Finally, we acknowledge a number of special permissions. *The Second Tongue* by Edwin Thumboo, *Time and Its People* by Muhammed Haji Salleh, and *Myths for a Wilderness* by Ee Tiang Hong are published by Heinemann Publishers Asia. We thank Heinemann for allowing us to quote from these works in Woon-Ping Chin Holaday's essay "Hybrid

Blooms." Robert Frost's "Spring Pools" is reprinted in Jonathan Culler's "The Modern Lyric" with permission of the publisher, Henry Holt.

CLAYTON KOELB AND SUSAN NOAKES

Chicago, Illinois and Lawrence, Kansas

PART ONE

Comparative Literature
Today

CLAYTON KOELB
SUSAN NOAKES
WLAD GODZICH
LOWRY NELSON, JR.
FRANK J. WARNKE
SAMUEL WEBER

*not a prescriptive book—
but examples—
an exemplary me*

[1]

Introduction:
Comparative Perspectives

CLAYTON KOELB AND SUSAN NOAKES

The idea for the present volume arose from the curiosity of its editors about the current state of Comparative Literature studies in North America. Both having been trained about fifteen years ago in Comparative Literature programs that were at the time relatively strong (at Harvard and Yale, respectively) and, by faculty example if not precept, conveyed an identifiable notion of what the discipline was, we shared a sense that the last decade and a half had brought considerable change. We were hesitant, however, to describe this change on our own, for the field is broad and we were acutely aware that, despite divergence in our backgrounds and interests, we had, as colleagues and friends for almost ten years, developed a certain homogeneity in disciplinary outlook.

In addition to our shared curiosity about the development of a field of which we both felt ourselves to be a part, we were also concerned about the continuing problem of conveying to those in other disciplines and especially to students beginning the study of Comparative Literature the nature of the field as it presently exists. It was our sense that earlier studies designed to provide an introduction to the discipline[1] no longer accurately represented what people associated with the field are currently doing. We felt, however, that what was needed was not yet another prescriptive book enumerating the kinds of study in which comparatists engage. More interesting and useful, it seemed to us, would be a volume exemplifying what comparatists actually do.

We therefore began to contact colleagues in the field throughout the country, asking them if they would be willing to contribute essays that

---

1. Many are listed by François Jost, *Introduction to Comparative Literature* (Indianapolis: Bobbs-Merrill, 1974), 308–10.

[3]

Clayton Koelb and Susan Noakes

would be not *about* Comparative Literature but *examples* of work in the field. Our only rule was that the work must be previously unpublished.[2] We steadfastly refused to say what we meant by Comparative Literature, though several potential contributors asked. We acted on the assumption that everyone we asked to contribute knows, in practice, what Comparative Literature "is," in the sense that each has an operative model, a set of goals and practices which, even if not articulated as a disciplinary prescription, makes it possible for the individual scholar trained or employed in a Comparative Literature program to write and teach.

We strove for as much diversity as possible, trying not to let our own critical preferences and network of professional contacts shape the list of contributors and thus distort the mirror of the field we hope to provide. Clearly, we realized, the projected single volume would not permit invitations to all the leading names in the field—nor would we have wished to slant the volume toward the already well established, leaving out just those younger scholars whose work is most likely to point the way to new directions in the field. We tried, as best we could, to choose contributors from a variety of age groups, a range of geographic locations, and, most important, a spectrum of critical and scholarly tendencies. Inevitably, a number of significant areas of research failed to find representation in the volume, despite the best efforts of both the editors and the publisher. We regret, for example, the lack of an essay treating Hispanic literature, an area swiftly becoming more and more prominent in comparative studies—in striking contrast to the situation of the sixties and early seventies. We also miss the presence of an explicitly Marxist voice. Finally, we recognize that the spectrum of essays represents to some degree the limitations of the editors' training and linguistic competence, as well as the history of the discipline in this country. It is skewed heavily toward Europe and indeed toward the canonical writers of a few particularly well studied European languages. As a number of essays included here demonstrate, one of the current goals of some comparatists is to break through what many believe has been a Europe-centered tunnel vision on the part of almost all Comparative Literature programs. It is clearly a process that is only beginning.

When the essays we had solicited began to reach us, we noticed almost immediately that our initial expectations as to the shape of the volume were not being met. We had expected that contributions would fall into the by now well-known kinds of generic categories set forth in standard accounts of the field (for example, studies of influence, of genre, of

2. We have made exceptions in a couple of cases for essays that have appeared in languages other than English or in publications not readily available to our intended audience.

Introduction: Comparative Perspectives

theme) and that literary theory would be one—a large and distinguished one—among these categories. Instead, we found that most of the essays elude standard scholarly taxonomies and that hardly any of them are theoretical contributions plain and simple. The great majority address theoretical concerns, suggesting that theoretical reflection is pervasive in Comparative Literature today. But they do so almost always in the context of "something else": for example, historical interpretation or rhetorical analysis.

The Comparative Perspective on Literature is similar in purpose to two collections of essays brought together during the period in which we were trained: Stephen G. Nichols, Jr., and Richard B. Vowles, *Comparatists at Work: Studies in Comparative Literature* (Waltham, Mass.: Blaisdell, 1968) and A. Owen Aldridge, *Comparative Literature: Matter and Method* (Urbana: University of Illinois Press, 1964). It is instructive to compare the contents of this book to that of the earlier two. Of the ten contributors in the Nichols and Vowles book, two address broad disciplinary concerns, one deals with recent trends within a particular school of criticism, three have to do with theory of the novel, one treats the "sister arts," and one each is devoted to an international approach to an individual author, a problem in historical periodization, and a chapter in the history of ideas. Of the seventeen essays in the Aldridge volume (excluding the editor's introduction), four concern themselves with the history of criticism, two with periodization and movements, two with themes, three with genres, and six with international and cross-disciplinary literary relations. Our book contains twenty-one essays (in addition to this Introduction), of which four treat general disciplinary concerns, four fit—somewhat loosely— within the domain of international literary relations, one deals with women's literary history, one with educational history, five address aspects of the relations of literature to other disciplines, and six treat theoretical problems (primarily, as we mentioned earlier, in the context of other matters).

The earlier collections show an interest in the study of movements, literary periods, and the history of themes and ideas, none of which is the central concern of any of the essays published here. Our contributors also show diminished interest in the history of criticism. The level of interest in international literary relations and the relationship of literature to other arts or disciplines remains steady, but there is greater variety in these related disciplines and a slightly greater interest in oriental thought and literature. Theoretical investigation of questions of genre remains a central concern, but there now appears to be more attention paid to what might earlier have been considered marginal matters: "minor" genres such as biography and theoretical margins such as the intersection (or lack of it) between generic categories in Western and Eastern criticism.

Clayton Koelb and Susan Noakes

There is considerably more interest in the analysis of Comparative Literature as a discipline. Several entirely new areas make an appearance here
for the first time in such a collection: women's studies, the history of
education, theory of reading, and semiotics.

Our contributors show, in other words, no special interest in areas that
have in the past formed the center of such theoretical concern among
comparatists, such as the history of criticism, nor are many of them
disposed toward the abstract discussion of such widely used period/ movement designators as romanticism or symbolism. Many, however, are interested in the theoretical implications of diverse literary phenomena that
might, a decade or two ago, have seemed marginal. There is, by and large,
a kind of decentering in progress, both in terms of notions of reading and
of canons prescribing what is to be read. One can discern a tendency to
move away from matters that have been considered essential to the understanding of the history of literature as a great and unified cultural
enterprise (movements, themes, periods, the history of ideas) and toward
issues that range around the frontier ("emergent" literatures, relations to
other disciplines, women's studies, marginalized forms of reading: "prereading," "female-reading," and "lethetic reading"). This general movement away from the traditional center of critical discourse is, of course, a
feature of much of today's literary scholarship and is not in any way
special to Comparative Literature.

One thing that is special, perhaps, is how contemporary comparatists
use literary theory. Of all the changes in emphasis revealed by comparing
this anthology to earlier ones, the one that is perhaps most telling and
thus in most need of explanation is the relative decline in the number of
"purely" theoretical essays and the increase in those that are theoretically
oriented. In looking through the essays presented here and discovering
the near ubiquity of theoretical concern, one might well be reminded of
Jonathan Culler's contention, aired in various contexts over the past few
years, that the whole of what the French call the human sciences is being
more or less rapidly transformed into something called theory, which
encompasses not only literary criticism but also philosophy, history, art
history, musicology, architecture, psychology, and social and political
theory as well. Thus one could conceivably find in a single department—
very possibly called Comparative Literature—scholars interested in
Marx, Freud, Lacan, Luhmann, Nietzsche, Wölfflin, Adorno, Derrida,
Heidegger, Abraham and Torok, Louis Sullivan, and so on, as well as
Dante, Shakespeare, Goethe, Flaubert, and the other canonical writers of
Western literature. Culler's observation would seem to be borne out in
microcosm by the contents of the book we are now introducing. One
wonders, however, just why this transformation has come about and why

Introduction: Comparative Perspectives

it is so particularly visible among practitioners of Comparative Literature in North America.

Certainly Comparative Literature has always had a certain tendency toward theoretical discourse, a result no doubt of the discipline's urge to move from the particular (national literatures) to the general (an international literary community); but until recently that tendency had been checked by a widely shared belief that the central task of Comparative Literature has been historical, in the broadest sense of that term. One can see an effort to hold this course in a famous address delivered by Harry Levin to his comparatist colleagues at a convention in the late sixties:

We spend too much of our energy talking—as I am now—about comparative literature, and not enough of it comparing the literature. We have too many programs and not enough performances, too many drum majors and not enough instrumentalists, too many people telling us how to do things they have never done. We put too much stress on setting up, or knocking down, apparatus. . . . Hours that might better be devoted to reading and contemplation are expended, like this one, at meetings and conferences. . . . After all the preliminaries, the propaedeutics, the estimates, the surveys, and the self-questionings, after reassessing the state of our union, the comparatist should advise himself: *Nunc age.* Now proceed: compare the literature.[3]

Levin's remarks were, of course, pointed particularly at theorizing about Comparative Literature and not at theorizing in general, but the direction in which they marshal us is certainly not toward more literary theory but toward more acts of literary history, more investigations of the interactions between texts.

Levin himself, like the other great lion of midcentury North American Comparative Literature, René Wellek, is principally a literary historian. Wellek has always been very interested in literary theory, to be sure, but he is above all a historian of criticism. Both Levin and Wellek exemplify a particular ideal centered upon denationalizing our conception of literary history. They reacted not only against the barriers of traditional (that is, German-style) national language and literature departments but also against a nation-centered concept of Comparative Literature developed mainly in France. (We are speaking now of the period when Comparative Literature in the United States was almost always defined between the poles of Harvard and Yale.) Jean-Marie Carré had explained, for example, that "comparative literature is a branch of literary history," meaning

3. "Comparing the Literature," delivered as the presidential address at the meeting of the American Comparative Literature Association at Indiana University in 1968, cited here from the rpt. in *Grounds for Comparison* (Cambridge: Harvard University Press, 1972), 74–90.

Clayton Koelb and Susan Noakes

particularly French literary history, and had pointed out further that "the discipline is mainly concerned with the transformations that each nation, each author imposes upon what has been borrowed."[4] Levin and Wellek both rejected this model, which essentially saw Comparative Literature as the customhouse of European literature, stamping the appropriate visas on documents as they crossed national boundaries. They felt more at home with the view of Matthew Arnold, who in 1865 had envisioned "a criticism which regards Europe as being, for intellectual purposes, one great confederation, bound to a joint action and working to a common result; and whose members have, for their proper outfit, a knowledge of Greek, Roman, and Eastern antiquity, and of one another."[5]

They, like Erich Auerbach and a number of other influential scholars trained in the universities and classical *Gymnasien* of pre-Nazi Europe, saw themselves as conservators of a great and coherent body of material, a unified cultural heritage whose *défense et illustration* was their particular calling. Wellek named this calling "true criticism" and specified that such criticism "means a concern for values and qualities, for an understanding of texts which incorporates their historicity and thus requires the history of criticism for such an understanding, and finally, it means an international perspective which envisages a distant ideal of universal literary history and scholarship."[6] It is significant that Wellek, coauthor of the most widely read book on literary theory in this century, saw as his ideal, however distant, not a universal "theory" of the kind Culler sees emerging today but a universal literary *history*. The great goal was to account for, classify, and interpret the world's literary texts in the context of a coherent cultural development.

While Levin and Wellek remained always sensitive to what Wellek called the "vitality of the different national traditions"[7] and therefore never challenged outright the existence of the established national literature departments, other comparatists saw in the goal of "universal literary history" a notion so compelling as to render the very concept of national literature obsolete. François Jost stated the case as aggressively as could be:

Comparative literature represents a philosophy of letters, a new humanism. Its fundamental principle consists of the belief in the wholeness of the literary phenomenon, in the negation of national autarkies in cultural economics, and, as

---

4. Carré, Foreword to Marius-François Guyard, *La Littérature comparée* (Paris, 1951), 5–6. The English translation is Jost's in *Introduction to Comparative Literature*, 25, 255.

5. *Essays in Criticism*, 1st series.

6. "The Name and Nature of Comparative Literature," in his *Discriminations: Further Concepts of Criticism* (New Haven: Yale University Press, 1970), 36.

7. Ibid.

a consequence, in the necessity of a new axiology. "National literature" cannot constitute an intelligible field of study because of its arbitrarily limited perspective: international contextualism in literary history and criticism has become a law. Comparative literature represents more than an academic discipline. It is an overall view of literature, of the world of letters, a humanistic ecology, a literary *Weltanschauung*, a vision of the cultural universe, inclusive and comprehensive. . . . Comparative literature is the ineluctable result of general historical developments.[8]

It was in a sense inevitable that what Wellek cautiously put forward as a "distant goal" would become the center of an aggressive, totalizing internationalism like Jost's. It is part of the nature of Comparative Literature, given its history of opposition to literary studies subdivided according to language, to prefer the general to the particular. But it has become clear since the mid-1970s that the urge toward totalization could not be carried out in the field of international literary history, at least not in any satisfactorily short period of time. We have learned all too well that Wellek was correct in his caution and that literary studies in North America, as well as in most European universities, will continue to be conducted for the most part in departments organized according to the model generated by nineteenth-century German philology. We have also learned that "universal literary history" is much harder to practice than perhaps we thought. "Universal" is an unforgiving concept: it will not let us stop, for example, with "the whole Western tradition" or even with "all the major literatures." It insists, as Wlad Godzich points out in his contribution to this book, that we take into account "literatures" that did not exist, or that we did not know existed, only a few years ago.

One of Comparative Literature's greatest ambitions has thus been frustrated or, at the least, deferred. In the meantime, other forces, themselves partly generated by Comparative Literature, have altered the scene of literary criticism in North America. For one thing, the national literature departments have responded to the challenge of Comparative Literature by becoming much more international in their approaches. It is unthinkable today, for example, that a student writing a dissertation on Coleridge's literary criticism would be allowed to remain ignorant of the German philosophical tradition that so influenced Coleridge's aesthetic ideas, even if that student happens to be enrolled in an English department. English departments regularly offer courses on such topics as symbolist poetry and continental romanticism; their faculties can teach them and their students need them. Along with this internationalizing of the study of national literatures has come a recognition of the importance of "theory" (in Culler's sense) and a desire, sometimes mixed with no little

8. *Introduction to Comparative Literature*, 29–30.

anxiety, to have one or more theoreticians in the house. Where can one find scholars, especially beginning young scholars, who might be thought to be specialists in theory?

They emerge, though perhaps somewhat ambivalently, from programs in Comparative Literature. The ambivalence arises because, though they are probably flattered to be thought of as particularly knowledgeable about theory, very few of these young scholars actually think of themselves as specialized theoreticians. For very practical reasons, nearly all Comparative Literature programs leading to the doctorate require some training in literary theory and the history of criticism. So, too, do many programs in French, English, German, and so on, it is true, but Comparative Literature has felt an urgent need to develop these requirements and to give them a place of special importance within the discipline. The need arises because of the very heterogeneous nature of students in the field: this one is studying rhetoric in Arthurian romance, that one the semiotics of objects in early twentieth-century novels, another the imagery of organic growth in classical Chinese and eighteenth-century French poetry. If "Comparative Literature" is to be more than a name on the door of an office where someone signs enrollment forms, the curriculum will have to have something in it that *all* such students can study together, and that something has been theory. Students in Comparative Literature have, moreover, had to become conversant with more than just whichever single critical school dominates the study of a single national literature at a given moment (for example, structuralism in French studies, reception theory in German); they have had to learn to participate in an international community of theoretical exchange.

Over the past two decades Comparative Literature departments have made this necessity into a mark of distinction. What began as a curricular imperative is now the intellectual center for many comparatists, no matter what their official field of specialization may be. No matter what else they study, *all* students of Comparative Literature study at least some, usually more than some, literary theory, and they are encouraged or even required to make their theoretical assumptions evident in their other work as well. Comparatists trained since the mid-1960s have as a group been systematically taught to attend to the theoretical issues in their work, starting with that first seminar in the first year of graduate study, and they carry that concern with them into their work as mature scholars. At the same time, however, they rarely work entirely within the domain of "pure" literary theory; they continue, rather, to maintain an interest in a certain group of texts or set of historical problems. They continue, in short, to "compare the literature."

Both theoretical concern and relative theoretical sophistication have become the trademarks of the latest generation of comparatists. Formerly, the distinguishing mark of the student of Comparative Literature had been a knowledge of several foreign languages and of the history of more than one national literary tradition. While this aspect of the comparatist's training has not been eliminated or even diminished in most Comparative Literature programs, it no longer seems to hold the center, which is now conspicuously occupied by theory. More and more programs even offer the alternative of a specialization in literary theory itself, although the number of students actually completing degrees with such a specialization does not appear to have grown dramatically. But while few declare themselves to be specialists in theory, all have more and more exposure to it.

Whether we think of Comparative Literature as characterized most centrally by its concern with the languages and literatures of several different traditions or with the mastery of more than one theoretical approach to literature, we find in Friedrich Schlegel's aphoristic definition of the literary critic an even better characterization of those committed to the comparative perspective: "A critic is a reader who ruminates. He should therefore have more than one stomach."9

We have divided the volume into four major sections. These divisions are not intended to represent anything like a taxonomy of current comparative literary studies; they merely provide a reasonably convenient structure for the collection. The reader will quickly come to realize that even the very broad and simple framework offered by our section headings establishes boundaries that our contributors regularly cross. There is hardly an essay in the group that could not have been placed in more than one of these niches, and for a few we had to choose among more than two. This uncertainty of category is in itself significant. It shows perhaps a certain maturing of Comparative Literature as a discipline, a confidence among its practitioners that one can combine, say, historical, theoretical, and "extraliterary" concerns in approaching a particular text or sets of texts. Comparative Literature today seems to be less a set of practices (e.g., comparing texts in different languages, comparing literary and "nonliterary" texts, comparing literature and the other arts) and more a shared perspective that sees literary activity as involved in a complex web of cultural relations.

The division offered here has nonetheless a usefulness apart from opening the question of its own inadequacy. The essays do tend to cluster in a few recognizable areas and to sort themselves out into a number of distinct—if closely related—centers of interest. It is no surprise that the

---

9. From the *Kritische Fragmente*: "Ein Kritiker ist ein Leser, der wiederkäut. Er sollte also mehr als einen Magen haben." Our translation.

first of these to strike our attention was the set of essays devoted to the consideration of the state of Comparative Literature itself. Here are four contributions all devoted to a discussion, often pointedly critical, of our current practice in the field. Although their individual concerns vary considerably, taken as a group they represent a challenge to comparatists to continue rethinking the field. Indeed the notion of "field" figures prominently in the opening piece by Wlad Godzich. Within the context of the broad question of how the academic disciplines as institutions make it possible for society to contain the crisis brought about by the instability of knowledge, Godzich asserts that Comparative Literature is currently "at risk" and that this crisis presents comparatists with an important opportunity. He illustrates the nature of this opportunity by reference to the work of the black South African writer Ezekiel Mphahlele and the Angolan writer Manuel Rui. Godzich's notion of "emergent literature"[10] can be understood as pushing Comparative Literature toward a very different relationship with the academic institution than the one it has regularly had.

Lowry Nelson, Jr., also views literature as an institution, but within a Kantian framework that, for Nelson, excludes practical, moral, logical, or metaphysical goals. He too finds literary study in a state of crisis, but he has quite a different conception of how Comparative Literature might work its way through it, seeing the best solution in a return to the setting of boundaries for an aesthetic realm and an aesthetic faculty. Nelson has a clear idea of what the "field" of Comparative Literature should be, and it differs sharply from Godzich's. The question of field comes up again in Frank Warnke's contribution, in which the canon of works studied in Comparative Literature programs provides the topic. Warnke accuses comparative literary scholarship of a pervasive provincialism, evidenced in a general ignorance of non-Western literatures, an almost complete ignorance of the "minor" Western literatures, and a spotty knowledge of the "major" Western literatures.

Samuel Weber returns to the same Kantian ground traversed by Nelson, but maps it in an entirely different way. Weber understands Kant to be questioning the possibility of any such entity as "the aesthetic realm" by insisting upon the practical and individual nature of aesthetic judgments. Kant's conception of aesthetics precludes the possibility of founding criticism upon scientific discipline, and according to Weber, aesthetics is therefore permanently "foundering." But the absence of such a foundation might also be what makes contemporary Comparative Literature

10. One might want to compare this notion with the "minor literature" of Gilles Deleuze and Félix Guattari in *Kafka: Toward a Minor Literature* (Minneapolis: University of Minnesota Press, 1986).

possible. If the practice of Paul de Man is taken as emblematic of what Comparative Literature tries or wishes to be, <u>the impossibility of a foundation for aesthetics is in a sense the enabling moment for this discipline</u> "<u>which is not one.</u>"

The other three divisions of this book correspond to a structure of past pedagogical experience perhaps more than they do to any internally generated principle. This is said without apology and with no little skepticism toward the notion of "internally generated" ordering principles. The editors, thinking as much of their experience with the organization of Comparative Literature doctoral programs as of recent published work in Comparative Literature, see the contributions as clustering in areas corresponding to the alternatives chosen by graduate students—obviously at the advice of supervisory faculty—writing dissertations in recent years. As a rule we have found that most students tend to focus on topics involving some problem coming out of their study of literary history in more than one language, that is, a problem defined by history or by international literary relations. A minority is attracted to problems involving the relationship of literature to other disciplines, and a still smaller minority attempts to deal with a distinctly theoretical or methodological question. We suspected, then, that we might get contributions in areas roughly corresponding to these categories, and indeed we did.

The topic of Part 2, "Historical and International Contexts," was therefore the one we believed—correctly, as it turned out—would contain the largest number of essays. That it is only slightly larger than the others demonstrates how the discipline has changed. While we could have made it look bigger still (for example by transferring Robert Magliola's essay from Part 3 to Part 2), we thought it best to leave it as is. Its place in the collection and its relative weight show that historical and international contexts still represent the core activity of comparatists but that the place of such work at the core is by no means so secure as it once was. It is evident that, within this broad category, many very different sorts of critical practices are taking place. We also see that the critiques of the discipline such as those voiced by the contributors to Part 1 are being heard.

A. Owen Aldridge responds to the call for increased study by comparatists of non-Western literatures by tracing the resemblances between Natsume Sōseki's *Kokoro* and J. W. Goethe's *Die Leiden des jungen Werther*. He finds that these resemblances are more significant than those between *Werther* and the Japanese novel to which Japanese critics have more often compared it, Noichi Nakagawa's *Moonflower Heaven*. Two other critics examine non-Western literature in this section as well. Woon-Ping Chin Holaday highlights the efforts of Malaysian and Singaporean poets who write in English to develop indigenous forms and locate indigenous themes. She shows how these efforts illustrate the problems all writers inevitably face in expressing an imaginative consciousness in terms that resemble to varying degrees those more widely employed by the writer's immediate audience and by the broader potential global audience. To complete the discussion of East-West literary relations, Pauline Yu addresses the fundamental difficulties facing the comparatist who would transfer the conventions of genre or criticism across cultural boundaries. Primarily treating the Chinese short poem (*shi*) and the Western lyric, she argues that these two forms only appear to be analogous in nature and in fact have different roots which give rise to rather different sets of critical concerns. Reluctant to believe that significant intercultural discourse is impossible, she nonetheless argues that comparatists must not take fundamental critical vocabulary and notions as givens; they must make themselves aware of the contexts that have given rise to them.

Margaret W. Ferguson responds in a different way to the call to open Comparative Literature to new areas of inquiry. She offers a new assessment of the situation of women readers and writers in the period roughly from 1400 to 1750. Taking as her theoretical point of departure the fundamental poststructuralist notion that social discourse constructs the individual, she shows how these early modern women struggled with the words written about their sex by men. In a study of Renaissance education, Aldo Scaglione seeks to open Comparative Literature in yet another way. He champions cultural history as a model for comparatists, particularly that branch of cultural history which integrates the history of education into the study of the intellectual formation of the writer. He argues that Comparative Literature can contribute to the study of cultural history what no other discipline can: the identification of the ideological, social, and economic circumstances that make possible the creation of a given literary work.

Right in the middle of this book is a piece of scholarship of the kind long associated with the heart of Comparative Literature. Melvin Friedman offers a classic example of the study of international literary relations, locating William Styron's place within the modernist movement by tracing its particular character to Styron's French sensibility. Specifically, Friedman sees the defining feature of Styron's contribution in his strong commitment to public life, which makes him more Gallic than American and helps explain the great interest Styron's work elicited in France.

Part 3 contains a selection of essays in which literary criticism is applied to or illuminated by the study of disciplines and practices ordinarily thought of as nonliterary: philosophy, religion, psychoanalysis, the law, and the visual arts. The trend of this group is to argue in favor of closing the gap between the literary and the nonliterary to show how much literary criticism needs and is needed by these other disciplines. By means

Introduction: Comparative Perspectives

of an analysis of the key concept of *cogito* in Jean-Paul Sartre's *La Nausée*, W. Wolfgang Holdheim demonstrates how criticism of the novel has failed to grasp its structure and significance because of a failure to come to grips with this concept. He goes on to urge that an understanding of the integral relationship between philosophy and literature in Sartre's novel prepares the way for a reading of the work as a whole which could in turn provide a foundation for assessing the impulse behind postmodern theory.

Robert Magliola's contribution suggests that the discussion of literary and nonliterary phenomena naturally coalesces when one is dealing with major cultural processes. Magliola studies the imagery of female and male consorts in the Buddhist tantric and European Renaissance traditions. He finds that this imagery expresses, through the notion of a nuptial liaison, a kind of deconstructive process he calls abrogation. He views its inscription of androgynous form into social discourse as a necessary strategy for the maintenance of an unstable relationship between opposing value systems. Ulrich Weisstein also demonstrates such a coalescence, this time between the discourse of literary criticism and art criticism. Weisstein's essay treats an expressionist play which turns crucially on its presentation of a fictitious painting by Cranach. He examines several of Cranach's actual works and those of certain of his contemporaries to show how visual evidence may lend support to literary criticism.

Susan Rubin Suleiman questions the possibility of a narrative practice untouched by the characteristic problems of literary narrative. Reexamining Freud's narrative of his unsuccessful treatment of the patient known as Dora, she discovers in his failure to discriminate his role from Dora's in the generation of the narrative a slippage that reveals much about the impulse that both underlies and limits narrative activity. Richard Weisberg also deals with the question of narrative stability but in the context of legal rather than psychoanalytic discourse. He illustrates the growing interchange between literary and legal studies with an analysis of certain novels published between 1860 and 1960 which centrally depict legal investigation. These novels focus attention not on the resolution of conflict but on the generation of successive narratives of anterior events, effectively calling into question the ethical value of rhetoric.

The final section of the volume presents "Comparative Perspectives on Current Critical Issues," a rubric under which are gathered essays of a more assertively theoretical cast, especially those that do not fit readily under one of the earlier headings. It is not difficult to see, however, that a couple of leading themes figure prominently in the concerns of this group. They are, in brief, reading, rhetoric, and intertextuality.

Stanley Corngold announces the major theme by focusing his essay on reading, specifically a phenomenon he calls prereading, the shaping of the act of reading by what has been read previously. He contends that the novelistic genre takes as one of its principal goals the focusing of attention on this phenomenon and supports his contention through analysis of Gustave Flaubert's *L'Education sentimentale* and Franz Kafka's *Der Prozeß*. Clayton Koelb is also interested in the theory of reading, particularly in how writing is generated out of reading. He proposes that new versions of classic old stories can be produced in two distinct ways, out of two radically different modes of reading, the "lethetic" and the "alethetic." He takes as his chief example the story of the Sirens from Homer's *Odyssey*, as represented in a poem by Rainer Maria Rilke and a story by Franz Kafka. Rilke's and Kafka's versions of the story look superficially similar, since both make the Sirens silent when Odysseus approaches, but they are fundamentally different. Koelb shows how Rilke's alethetic reading, which assumes that Homer's text contains a meaning that it is the reader's duty to preserve, remains faithful to that meaning in spite of substantial revision of the myth, while Kafka's lethetic reading deliberately ignores it.

Jonathan Culler's examination of the lyric genre also turns upon questions of reading. Culler proposes that the readability of a Western lyric poem depends on certain generic assumptions unconnected with the poem's content. To read a poem as a lyric, he points out, presupposes a focus on a speaker and a view of the poem as a "drama of attitudes." The prevailing model of the lyric thus excludes from central consideration anything that is neither speaker nor consciousness. He concludes that the lyric genre, like other genres, provides a model of intelligibility which neutralizes the potentially disruptive role literary texts might more often play if such controlling generic models did not have the force they continue to possess. Juliet Flower MacCannell also treats the issue of the relationship between cultural models and the practice of reading, but she moves in an almost opposite direction. Instead of understanding a practice of reading as based upon a cultural model, she understands cultural models as in a sense derived from acts of reading. She finds in Walter Benjamin's concept of allegory and Mikhail Bakhtin's of intertextuality powerful alternative models to the concepts of communication and evaluation provided by formalism. She sees these two theorists not only as neo-Marxists but also as "proto"-deconstructionists, who offer a reevaluation of rhetoric and its role in creating a community of values.

Susan Noakes offers a contribution to the history of the theory of reading that argues for a semiotically informed feminist hermeneutics. Tracing the evolution of hermeneutics out of the discourse of a priestly elite that has excluded women from the role of interpreter, she argues that the opposition created between the notion of woman as superficial and man as deep reader has been an important strategy permitting Western hermeneutics to avoid the difficult issue of temporality as an

Introduction: Comparative Perspectives

essential component in semiotic and hermeneutic processes. Michael Riffaterre, too, in his characteristic fashion combines semiotics and hermeneutics. He analyzes three different sign systems that function in biography, a hero-making system that focuses on the extraordinary character of the subject, a humanizing system that makes the subject seem close enough to the rest of us to keep our interest, and a moral system that presents the biographer and his story as legitimate authorities. He concludes that biography is not so much the record of a life as the record of a reading of a life which always refers to an intertext, a "model" that the subject is understood as having imitated.

It is telling that so many of these concluding essays are concerned with intertextuality, with the relation between old text and new text, between reading and writing. If there is one principle that Comparative Literature in all its forms has stood for over the years, it is the necessity to understand literary texts in relation to other texts, whether belonging to other languages and cultures, other disciplines, other races, or the other sex. That necessity continues to inform the comparative perspective today.

three sign systems

hero-making of the subject

humanizing the subject

moral system - biographer + story as leg. auth.

intertextuality above all

[2]

Emergent Literature and the
Field of Comparative Literature

WLAD GODZICH

It is in the nature of knowledge to be unstable: on one hand, it must ensure its continuance by the preservation of the achievements of the past; on the other, it must not let them stand in the way of new advances and discoveries. The precarious equilibrium and the resulting tensions between the reproduction of existing knowledge and the production of new knowledge are not allowed to propagate their instability in society at large; they are contained within the apparatus of knowledge and especially in its institutional forms, which, in our day, means the academic disciplines. Any crisis that may affect these disciplines should thus be limited in scope, or at least in impact, and should not threaten either the edifice of knowledge or society itself; at worst, a discipline may collapse— a most unlikely happenstance given the power of endurance provided by its institutional setting—necessitating a new realignment in the division of intellectual labor. Since the logic of modern societies requires ever greater specialization, that is, division of labor, it is more likely that a discipline in some form of trouble will in fact be subdivided into two or more new ones, as, for instance, seems to be happening to biology recently under the stress of its own development. Disciplines are generally quite resilient, though, as befits the institutions they are. Were one to threaten implosion—as opposed to subdivision—the resources of the entire apparatus of knowledge could be counted upon to be mobilized in a rescue, for the collapse of any discipline poses a threat to the entire organization of knowledge, not least by disclosing its constructed and malleable character.

Under what circumstances is a discipline at risk? There appears to be scant literature on the subject. It is acknowledged that various disciplines have, at different times, undergone rather profound changes, but such changes, having been internally negotiated and contained, are seen as part of the normal instability of the entire knowledge enterprise. Four conditions, it seems to me, must obtain in order to put a discipline in jeopardy. (My readers, being cognizant of the context in which this essay appears, will rightly conclude that I shall presently argue that these conditions prevail in Comparative Literature, though I shall further argue that this danger represents a major opportunity for all of us.) The four conditions derive from the four basic constitutive elements of a discipline: (1) a normative object of study; (2) a defined field within which this object obtains or is constituted; (3) a determinate set of theories and methodological procedures that are applied to the object in the field (these theories and methodologies need not be at all unified or even dovetail with each other, though there must be a sense that they are limited in number); (4) a set of individuals who are recognized and identify themselves as practitioners of the discipline and some of whom are engaged in, among other things, the training of those who will succeed them in this practice.

Comparative Literature is doing very well as far as the fourth element is concerned, at least in North America. The number of programs and departments has grown considerably in recent years, and there is a sense that comparatists, alongside feminists and scholars of ethnic studies, represent what is most progressive and most interesting in the teaching of literature. Some disagreement still obtains as to who is a properly trained and qualified comparatist, but it tends to be obscured in the relative success of the enterprise at large.

In recent years, it is the third element that has received the most attention. When even such mass-media instruments as the *New York Times* and *Newsweek* begin to write about the theoretical and methodological disputes that have agitated our domain, it is clear that this agitation must have reached a threshold beyond which a more direct societal interest begins to assert itself. We have all been involved in these disputes, frequently shifting ground as the issues became defined and redefined. As yet, however, we have little understanding of what precipitated the whole brouhaha in the first place. And in the absence of such understanding, there proliferate two unreflecting reactions: one that seems characteristic of the times, namely a recourse to some version of conspiracy theory, with its heavy-handed insistence on foreign importation and then concentration in unlikely loci of subversion (Johns Hopkins! Yale!), the other more in keeping with a predominant mode of comparative inquiry (though not entirely incompatible with the first), the search for influence, with its explanations by means of locating the *origin* of some theory or methodology. It matters little that everything that originates somewhere does not exert an influence and that if the notion of influence is to have any value

Wlad Godzich

at all it must not only identify the original material but must also account for the receptiveness it encounters in its new setting. In any case we must acknowledge that we do not presently have any consensual view for the success of Russian formalism, French structuralism, deconstruction, semiotics, reception aesthetics, the work of the Bakhtin group, or the current vogue of what some have taken to calling the new historicism; thus, we have left ourselves open to the charge that we are given to faddish fluctuations and have no standards by which to evaluate our theories and methods.

We may not have much understanding of what lies behind the theoretical agitation of recent years, but we know what some of its consequences have been. Indeed, these have figured prominently in the controversies. One of the foremost has been the sudden uncertainty surrounding the very object of our study. Until quite recently it was the work, and the work was taken to be a given of our discipline. But disciplines do not have givens; as constitutive parts of the apparatus of knowledge, they have objects that are constructed by and for them. Students of literature discovered slowly that the work, by which we frequently meant the masterpiece, was a notion located at the intersection of a periodizing concept with a generic one and defined by literary history. Even the retheorization of the work as text, while attentive to dimensions explicitly excluded by the notion of work, remained beholden to literary history for the production of the texts to be studied. However removed they may have been from its assumptions, theoreticians of diverse stripe found themselves governed by the parameters of a literary history that they mistakenly assumed to be either obsolete or so discredited as no longer to warrant any examination.[1] As they found themselves forced to focus their attention upon it, they discovered that the very definition of the object of the entire discipline had to be rethought. In the present division of labor, academic departments that deal with "national" literatures hold on to previously elaborated canons of texts that must be taught if for no other reason than to maintain the institutional identity of their department. To be sure, these canons are challenged, especially by feminist critics, but it is interesting to observe that this challenge takes place within previously defined national boundaries, somehow intimating that, whatever the status of gender, it either comes after nationhood—an eighteenth-century concept—or is significantly altered by it.[2] Comparatists have never had any

---

1. Cf. Wlad Godzich and Nicholas Spadaccini, eds., *Literature among Discourses: The Spanish Golden Age* (Minneapolis: University of Minnesota Press, 1986).

2. I raise this matter not in order to point to a contradiction within current feminist concerns but rather to wonder at the wisdom of a strategy that takes the route of canon revision. Were this strategy to be successful, one of its consequences would be the reinforcement of national boundaries inasmuch as these would be further legitimated by women

such canon, as even a conservative conception of the discipline made clear.[3] Instead, <u>we have either maintained the definitions of object that obtain in the "national" literatures or have attempted to develop our own on the basis of some specific theoretical and methodological orientation.</u> Those who are inclined to pursue the project of a general poetics thus focus on general processes that are presumed to obtain in literary works, regardless of period or national origin; others, more inclined to the elucidation of cognitive or epistemological problems, look at literary texts as privileged examples for the staging of such problems; still others bring a social dimension to bear upon their studies. But all view the material support of their object rather unproblematically: it is a text that has been defined somewhere as literary. It is precisely this privilege of the literary text that is challenged in some of the most promising methodological approaches today, which, for the sake of convenience, we could label discourse analysis.

Here the object is defined in a completely novel way, one that partakes of the preoccupation of the poetician, the epistemologist, the sociologist of literature, and indeed many others. For the discourse analyst there is, strictly speaking, no literary discourse. <u>There are only multiform discourses that together are the web and woof of the prevalent social discourse, of which literature is a socially defined use.</u> It is at this juncture that the discourse analyst encounters the greatest difficulty: having redefined the object of inquiry in such a way that it would not be tainted by any of the social privileges granted to literature, discourse analysis finds it very difficult to reconnect with the literary phenomenon. It can deal with discourse about literature but is stymied when it comes to the discourse of literature. Some practitioners in this area ultimately give up on literature altogether. It must be noted, however, that, in spite of its global pretensions, discourse analysis accepts the dominant framework of the nation-state as its geographical boundary and generally follows the periodizations set in literary history.[4]

The reasons for the difficulties of discourse analysis are instructive: having set its sights on the whole of the universe of discourses, discourse analysis cannot internally generate the differentiations it needs in order to specify an entity like literature. The recourse to pragmatics, which is the preferred strategy under such circumstances, does not solve the prob-

---

writers. One needs to ask oneself, though, what is the wisdom, if not the validity, of a selection that seeks to fit women writers within a canon previously defined on the basis of masculinist traits.

3. Werner P. Friederich, with the collaboration of David Henry Malone, *Outline of Comparative Literature from Dante Alighieri to Eugene O'Neill* (Chapel Hill: University of North Carolina Press, 1954).

4. Cf. the writings of Pierre Bourdieu as a telling example of these problems.

lem, which is one of *field*. Objects must have fields in which they are either found or constituted, and fields cannot be conceived of as the totality of the phenomena construable under the object if the approach is to have any success in analytic differentiation. The predicament is not unique to discourse analysis, far from it. It is inherent to the problem of literary study today. Yet the problem of field is the one that has received the least attention, even among comparatists, for whom it is absolutely central.

To comparatists the problem of field presents itself as a challenge to the historical construction of the discipline. It was constituted to compensate for the orientation of literary studies along national lines, but, we must acknowledge, from the outset we have privileged certain literatures, notably the German, French, and English. We have granted very limited status to such others as the Italian, Russian, or Spanish, and except in the newly developing area of East-West studies, we have remained firmly Eurocentric, even when dealing with texts from the Americas.[5] Even in East-West studies, that is in the area where developments in Chinese, Japanese, and, less frequently, Indian, or even Arabic, literatures are studied by comparison with those in European literatures, it is always the latter that have provided the terms of reference, so that we have had considerations of symbolism in Chinese poetry, in which, for example, the Chinese phenomena were described in terms of their congruence, or divergence, from French and German ones.

What we are dealing with here is a long-standing pretension and implicit assumption of Comparative Literature: despite the diversity and multifariousness of literary phenomena, it is possible to hold a unified discourse about them. This pretension is the heir to the old project of a general poetics which was challenged and ultimately brought to a standstill by the European turn to nationalism in the eighteenth and nineteenth centuries. Comparative Literature is the haven in which the idea of this project has been preserved. The challenge posed by the establishment of distinct French, German, and English literatures is nothing, however, in comparison with that which issues today from the emergence of all sorts of new literatures: in Africa, Asia, Latin America, Canada (with its two "national" literatures), Australia, as well as black literature in the United States, women's literature in many parts of the world, native people's literature in the New World, and so on.[6] The project of a general

5. For a discussion of these issues in the constitution of Comparative Literature, see Claudio Guillén, *Entre lo uno y lo diverso: Introducción a la literatura comparada* (Barcelona: Editorial Crítica, 1985), especially the first 121 pages.

6. Blacks, women, Chicanos, and native people have been writing for quite some time, of course, but the notion that their writings constitute distinctive traditions and bodies of literature is recent. It is in the name of this notion that the older writings are being reclaimed either from a forgotten past or from other constructs to which they seemed to belong.

Emergent Literature and Comparative Literature

poetics could move in the general direction of the complementary study of ethnopoetics on one hand and of universals of literature on the other, incidentally recapturing Herder's conception of literary study,[7] and thus could institutionalize the division of labor between Comparative Literature and the "national" literatures along lines often suggested in the debates during our period of theoretical development: theory in Comparative Literature and analysis and criticism in the "national" literatures.

Such a division of labor is ultimately untenable, whatever appeal it may have had or may still hold. There is no atheoretical approach to literature; *yes* there are only more or less consciously held theoretical tenets. The present "decline" of theory in Comparative Literature is due in great part to the fact that many of the theoretical developments of the past twenty years have become part and parcel of literary analysis. When a certain theoretical hegemony—that of New Criticism in North America—was challenged, Comparative Literature provided an institutional setting from which this challenge could be mounted. Today we have a much more heightened theoretical awareness in all areas of literary scholarship, and one cannot draw an institutional separation by means of theory, even if one wants to. And there are excellent reasons for not wanting to, not the least of which is the implied autonomization of theory.

One of the criticisms most frequently addressed to those working in the *criticism of theory* area of theory is precisely their tendency to detach themselves from the study of literary works and to operate exclusively in the world of concepts. This criticism cuts across political lines: conservatives, such as Denis Donoghue, interpret this detachment as arrogance and a turning of one's back upon the tradition, which for him clearly means the institution of literary studies; progressives, like Edward Said, see it as a refusal to carry out the critical function of the intellectual in the social world, as a retreat into a form of religiosity. This is not the place to rehearse the controversies surrounding these arguments, but it must be acknowledged that a speculative tendency was very much in evidence in the theoretical enterprise, propelling it toward ever greater autonomization.

It is important to understand the nature of this propulsion, for it is *theory is deconstructive by nature* doubly articulated. To begin with, the theoretical impulse originated in an operation of demystification: it sought to bring back to light the constructed and institutionally determined character of the objects of literary study, something that the institution of literature, like all the other institutions within the apparatus of knowledge, prefers to gloss over, though, in all fairness, without denying its factuality. Institutionalized knowledge practices—another name for disciplines—have

7. Johann Gottfried von Herder, *Journal meiner Reise im Jahr 1769*, in his *Gesammelte Werke*, ed. B. Suphan (Berlin, 1807).

rules and protocols for the determination of their objects; once some entity is constituted as such an object, its constructed character is left out of consideration, and it functions for all practical purposes as a given. It is precisely the function of methodological and theoretical debates to delimit the parameters of object construction. Such debates serve, then, as reminders that what a particular discipline takes to be a given is actually a construct. Furthermore, the debate over the redefinition of object-construction parameters accentuates the constructed character of the discipline as a whole and therefore its autonomy from any external object, from any givenness. To put it more simply: the entire apparatus of knowledge—and, a fortiori, the disciplines—functions on the premise that objects are available to or given for the cognitive operations specified within the apparatus; at the same time, this apparatus constructs these objects, that is, determines conditions of givenness. The two parts of this operation are not incompatible but they do not admit of simultaneous consideration: one must be carried out before the other. The discomfort caused by theory stems from its attempts to maintain both aspects of the cognitive operation at the same time. The result is that theory appears to be at a further remove from the object—in this instance, the work—than the atheoretical approaches practiced within the institution, and thus it tends to be perceived as functioning autonomously.

The second part of this doubly articulated propulsion toward autonomy is to be found in the very relation of the cognitive to the given, constitutive of the prevailing apparatus of knowledge. In terms borrowed from the history of philosophy, one could describe it as the permanent temptation of Hegelianism within Kantianism, that is the passage from the realm of the empirical to that of the conceptual. The cognitive model constructed by Kant acknowledges the given but grants it the status of an otherness, that is, as both constitutive of and a challenge to the knowing instance.[8] This model places all knowledge in a painful predicament: it ultimately depends upon something that it does not control but must accept as it finds it. The predicament is a historical one, however: it affects only the conception of knowledge that we find underpinning modernity. The ancients, notably Aristotle, accepted this initial givenness through theories of being; modernity rests upon the forgetfulness of being, as Heidegger reminds us, and it cannot readily accept anything the provenance of which it can neither control nor account for. In Heidegger's terminology, the totalizing and all-embracing pretension is a characteristic of *tekhne*, by which he means the specific cognitive orientation of modernity, in which the knowable must be reduced to the status of an

---

8. Martin Heidegger, "Die Zeit des Weltbildes," *Holzwege* (Frankfurt a.M.: Vittorio Klostermann, 1950), 69–104.

object upon which a knowing subject can perform specified cognitive operations.[9] From the outset of modernity, givenness is a problem, since for modernity everything must be brought within the orbit of the subject, and yet givenness cannot be accounted for by the sustaining role (in the sense of the Greek *hypokeimenon*) of the subject; on the contrary, it is precisely that which escapes the subject; the object is but a poor substitute for it. Hegel's solution was to hold out the hope, to be fulfilled in the fullness of time, of all givenness being invested by the Spirit—his designation for the knowing instance—so that ultimately given and known would coincide in Absolute Knowledge. It is this drive toward the reduction of the distance between given and known that constitutes the second element of the double articulation we have been examining.

Combined with the first, it leads to a heightened sense of the importance of the constructed in all knowledge and to a powerful urge to turn one's back upon all givenness. Givenness appears to be superfluous, since, at best, it is but a purport for the constructs with which one really works. Furthermore, since all the models for implementing *tekhne* require the sort of internal coherence that can be made answerable to logic or to mathematical variations of it, the forgetfulness, or rather the deliberate pushing aside, of the given does away with its logically irreducible character in favor of constructs conceived along logically acceptable lines. The theoretical enterprise is thus both structurally and historically propelled toward greater autonomy: knowledge becomes more conceptual in modernity, and theory, in a first stage, partakes of its movement.

There is a second movement as well, however, which is also staged in Kant, though hardly in Kantianism if by that one means the body of doctrine extracted from Kant's writings. In the first two *Critiques*, Kant indeed provided the underpinnings of the model of knowledge that prevails in modernity, but thorough thinker that he was, he did not turn his back on the problem of givenness; he returned to it in the *Critique of Judgment* where the long analytics of the beautiful, and especially of the sublime, constitutes, among other things, a lengthy reflection upon the given as the other of knowledge. In the space available here, suffice it to note that this otherness, which challenges and defies our cognitive ability, is precisely what forces Kant to conceive of aesthetic judgment as content-less and as beyond the purview of either reason or the understanding: in the aesthetic experience, that which offers itself to our sensory apparatus neither possesses the form characteristic of reason's object nor grants a

9. There is an attempt to recuperate this free-standingness by means of the purposiveness of nature, but a careful reading of the text shows that it is not accomplished. Such a reading cannot be attempted here. For a discussion of the third *Critique* along the lines suggested here, though with different objectives in view, cf. Samuel Weber's contribution to this volume.

Wlad Godzich

hold to the law making of the understanding; it merely, but irreducibly, is.[10] Incidentally, this is the phenomenon that Paul de Man sought to apprehend by the phrase "the resistance to theory."[11]

It has often been remarked that the third *Critique* entertains a strange relationship to the previous two; it starts as a continuation of their effort to provide a solid ground for the operations of knowledge, but, in the process of argumentation it snatches that ground from under them in order to claim as foundational the results of the reflections it undertook on their basis, thus casting some doubt upon the notions of ground, primacy, base, and upon the entire architechtonics of the three *Critiques*. We are at one such juncture in the argument here. What is revealed as mere being (in the sense of existing) in the operation of aesthetic judgment cannot be collapsed back into some newfangled ontology, given the thrust of the previous *Critiques*. To begin with, it gives itself in the sphere of experience and thus cannot be reduced to any of the transcendental instances previously examined. To say that it is in the sphere of experience is to acknowledge that it exists in time and space, yet given the treatment of these two categories in the first *Critique*, one must go farther and recognize that this givenness, inaccessible to either reason or the understanding, conveys no other content but the fact of its being in space and time. This givenness is what Paul de Man came to call inscription.[12] It corresponds to the formal definition of the chronotope in Mikhail Bakhtin's reflection on this subject.[13] What is thus given to experience is what the first *Critique* established as the very condition of experience, experientiality itself. And since experientially defines subjecthood, the experience of experientiality constitutes subjects.

Thus, whereas the first two *Critiques* appear to derive their propulsion from the sovereign position of the subject, the third addresses the constitution of the subject itself and rests on that which resists the cognitive ("theoretical," in Kant's terminology) pretensions of the subject and eventually leads the subject to recognize itself as a historical being, that is, as a being that counterposes its own activity in space and time to the givenness it encounters. This activity and its products constitute the realm of cul-

10. This is not an ontological assertion, but it could lead to an inquiry along ontological lines, although this is not the course that will be followed here. The ontological line would have to come upon the discursive through the category of *deixis*, which cannot be touched upon here. Cf. Wlad Godzich and Jeffrey Kittay, *The Emergence of the Prose* (Minneapolis: University of Minnesota Press, 1987).

11. For a discussion of this notion, see my Foreword to de Man's *The Resistance to Theory*, Theory and History of Literature, 33 (Minneapolis: University of Minnesota Press, 1986), 3–20.

12. Ibid., 27–53.

13. "Forms of Time and of the Chronotope in the Novel: Notes toward a Historical Poetics," in his *The Dialogic Imagination* (Austin: University of Texas Press, 1981), 85, n. 2.

ture, although the provenance of culture cannot be accounted for in the terms I have put forward so far, since culture is never an individual project but a collective one.

It will be recalled that when he speaks of aesthetic judgment Kant is very insistent that the maker of this judgment must intimately feel that others would make the same judgment were they in her or his place. Insofar as this insistence has received attention, it has been interpreted in the light of the categorical imperative of the *Critique of Practical Reason* as reaffirming human universality. If we take it that, among other things, the third *Critique* is concerned with the constitution of the subject, then this reading has to be modified in the light of earlier findings. Faced with the givenness that constitutes it as subject in a punctual moment of space and time, the subject, insists Kant, feels very strongly that others would make the same judgment were they in his or her place. Since the subject has just experienced experientiality and has come to see itself as subject, Kant's insistence means that the subject acknowledges that the encounter with givenness will equally constitute others as subjects.

This notion has far-reaching consequences, one of which is of immediate interest to me here: for the newly constituted subject to make this step, it is necessary that she or he not only imagine that others locate themselves in the very site she or he is occupying—tantamount to the reduction of others to same—but that this new subject occupy, in principle if not empirically, a number of different loci in space and time which others may occupy and that the subject experience experientiality there, that is, verify that subjects are constituted there. This is not some sort of conversion of same to other, as one might wish to conclude, but rather the delimitation of a field of experientiality—that is, of subject constitution—which is not reductive to sameness since, it will be recalled, all of this is content- and formless. In other words, what takes place in the aesthetic judgment is not a singular event—as seems to be the case in H. G. Gadamer's reconstruction of hermeneutics on a Heideggerian ground—but the demarcating of a field within which subjects are constituted as entities inhabiting a given set of spatiotemporal conditions, in such a way that these conditions define their commonality or, as Heidegger would put it, their destiny. It is in a concretely delimited field that both community and society are elaborated, the first by establishing a relation between all who are constituted into subjects in and by the field, and the second by means of the relations that are established with respect to the givenness that gave rise to the field.[14]

14. I elaborate upon the relationship of society to givenness in "The State, Religion, and Post(al) Modernism," Afterword to Samuel Weber, *Institution and Interpretation* (Minneapolis: University of Minnesota Press, 1987).

Wlad Godzich

Defined in this way, the notion of field takes priority over the notions of cognitive object and subject, let alone theory. It is an enabling condition for the elaboration of these notions, which then interact to form the cognitive dimension of the culture delimited by the field. It is within this culture that the apparatus of knowledge is constructed and the disciplines are assigned their roles. We had seen earlier that the notion of "field" is one of the four elements of a discipline, but the term "field" was used in a different sense from the one that I have just elicited from Kant. In relation to disciplines, "field" refers to a parcel of the culturally constructed domain of knowledge as it is subject to the operations of the apparatus of knowledge, whereas field (without quotations marks) is the enabling condition of cultural elaboration. At this juncture, I would like to put forward the following claim: the "field" of Comparative Literature is field. In other words, I take it that, within the prevalent organization of knowledge, it is incumbent upon comparatists to inquire into the relationship of culture to givenness, to its other.

 If a culture is formed by the cognitive operations performed within a field, its internal economy stands in a particular relationship to the givenness that led to the constitution of the field in the first instance. This givenness is not part of the culture, since it precedes it, yet it pervades the culture, since it could be said to animate it inasmuch as it determines not only the conditions of its emergence but the dimensions of the field within which it evolves. It is thus an active principle rather than a passive one, as the term *givenness* may have connoted. It should be clear that it does not manifest itself as such within the culture, for culture is a construct in response to it. If it has any existence within the culture, it is figural, although it may be better to view it as the operator of certain effects. The following example provides a good instance of such effect production and may help us understand this operator.

Ezekiel Mphahlele is a contemporary black South African writer who has been very much concerned with problems of cultural identity in both his fictional and his critical writings. It does not take a great effort of the imagination to see that the lived experience of any South African, let alone that of a black writer forced into exile and banned both personally and in his writings and yet eventually returned to his land, will require reflection upon issues of cultural inclusion and exclusion, identity and empowerment, that is, a theory of culture. Mphahlele's work marks the various stages in the elaboration of such a theory, from his early autobiographical writings to the two versions of his first collection of essays and to the later critical writings.[15] For our immediate purposes, one strand in this ongoing reflection bears closer examination.

15. Ezekiel Mphahlele, *The African Image* (London: Faber and Faber, 1st ed., 1962; 2d ed., 1974); *Voices in the Whirlwind* (London: Macmillan, 1972). I have profited from M. Chabani

Emergent Literature and Comparative Literature

The young Zeke Mphahlele, having been raised in the slums of Pre-
toria, suddenly got the opportunity to receive a Western education that
would eventually take him to England. Like many other Africans before
him, indeed, like anyone who did not belong to the class whose culture
was set as the norm of Western education, Mphahlele felt doubly alienated: from his milieu, which could not provide him with the nurturing
support he needed in—and which was presupposed by—the education
he was receiving, and from the culture he was assimilating in the course of
this education. After having made an attempt to assimilate this culture,
notably in his senior thesis devoted to English romantic poetry, Mphahlele turns his attention to the question of cultural assimilation itself and,
for his master's thesis, studies the representation of blacks in Western
literature. Predictably, he finds such representations far from perfect, but
he is not content with remarking their distortion; he is far more concerned with the claim of universality and totalization that he finds in
Western knowledge, which trips upon the problem of blackness. Taking it
as an ideological problem, he turns his attention to *négritude*, which he
rejects for its elitist and attentivist orientation, and determines to rethink
the problem, which, for him, is an existential one in the personal dimension and a political one as far as the collectivity of black South Africans is
concerned.[16]

It is not surprising, then, that his initial formulation should follow
Sartrean lines or, more accurately, Franz Fanon's version of Sartre's
existential psychology,[17] though in terms of inside versus outside. Because of his education, his language, his frame of literary reference,
Mphahlele is white inside while on the outside, he is black—and this
outside can never be forgotten in the land of apartheid. Mphahlele could
have followed the Sartrean path at this juncture, but his distrust of
individualism and his commitment to a nonelitist stand took him in a
slightly different direction that has far less to do with the personal dimension of Sartrean psychology. He discovers, and therefore knows, that he is
white inside, but this knowledge does not bring him any closer to whites,
not because of his external blackness but rather because whites, even in
South Africa, know that they are white only in a casual way. It is the way in
which he knows that he is white on the inside that differentiates Mphahlele from whites. At this juncture he is tempted to conclude that it is the
knowing instance, namely his consciousness, that makes for this difference, that is, that his consciousness of being white is different from the

---

Manganyi, *Exiles and Homecomings: A Biography of Es'kia Mphahlele* (Johannesburg: Raven
Press, 1983).
16. I follow South African antiapartheid usage in calling all nonwhite South Africans
black, rejecting the apartheid-dictated distinction between "blacks," "coloreds," and "In-
dians."
17. Franz Fanon, *Peau noire, masques blancs* (1954, rpt. Paris: Maspéro, 1969).

Wlad Godzich

fact that is so known and that this consciousness is precisely where his blackness resides. Conjuncturally, this conclusion translates itself into the impetus animating the Black Consciousness movement of the sixties and seventies, which Mphahlele provides. Mphahlele is nothing if not rigorous however, and he quickly realizes that to establish such a divergence between the knowing and the known would make it impossible to bring being black within the sphere of the known and thus to make such knowledge casual knowledge. The result would be that he would know that he is black casually, the way whites know they are whites, and therefore would confirm his being white by the mode of this knowledge, characteristic of whites. At this juncture, Mphahlele is struggling with the mechanism of the dialectic into which he has been drawn and which seems to drag him inevitably through all the stages of the Hegelian master-slave interplay. There is no turning back once one is drawn in, and Mphahlele understands that the dialectic must be played out till it overcomes itself. In other words, whites must learn to know that they are whites in a noncasual way. The Black Consciousness movement, like the Black Power movement in the United States or in the Caribbean, had attempted to do just that, but it had done so from the position of blackness, thus choosing as a ground the very instability upon which the dialectic was being played. Mphahlele understands the dangers of such positioning—he had already seen it in *négritude*—and distinguishes between the fact that whites must be challenged to know that they are white in a noncasual way and to associate this challenge, and knowledge, with blackness, on one side, and the fact that the consciousness of sameness and therefore of difference is not only consciousness but a locus from which a reinscribing of black-and-white relations can be launched. This locus is experienced as consciousness by the individual but is not thereby either contained or defined by consciousness.[18] Mphahlele attempts to address this through the notion of a double stream of consciousness,

18. White South African writers have struggled to the first part of this realization. In *July's People* (London: Jonathan Cape, 1981), Nadine Gordimer has her white heroine understand the black July only at the end of the novelette when he addresses her in his own language, which she does not understand. Similarly André Brink in his earlier *A Dry White Season* (London: H. Allen, 1979) has his white hero understand that his effort to identify with Gordon Ngubene was scandalous to all blacks and that he must see himself as they see him in order to espouse their cause, as he wishes to do. Mphahlele comes upon this problem through a consideration of the modern African writer's relationship to tradition. He seeks to describe this relationship through temporal, structural, and eventually political terms (cf. *Voices in the Whirlwind*, esp. 144). The terminological lability points toward a discursive dimension that Mphahlele alludes to but does not develop in his critical writings, though it is very much in evidence in his fiction. For a superb thematization of this terminological motility that ends in the identification of the discursive as a battleground, cf. the extraordinary novel by the Zairois writer M. a M. Ngal, *Giambatista Viko; ou, Le Viol du discours africain* (Lubumbashi: Alpha-Oméga, 1975).

Emergent Literature and Comparative Literature

which is a way of acknowledging that consciousness is not the producer but the product of an operativity that remains unknowable, since there is no consciousness to know it.

Mphahlele's reflection brings us to the same point we had reached in reflecting upon givenness, with this difference: we must understand givenness not as a passive (or a resultative, in the linguistic sense of the term) but as an active principle. Givenness is agency. As such it never gives itself but is figured in that which is given, and it is knowable only through its figurations: god, nature, history, consciousness, the state, language are some of those that have historically been proposed. Yet it is accessible, as Mphahlele's working out of a noncasual way for whites to know that they are whites demonstrates. In dialectical terms, this new knowledge that whites have should be called black knowledge in opposition to the casual white knowledge, but what matters beyond the dialectic here is that this knowledge is not produced through a play of negativity and sublation; it is not because one negates the casual that one reaches what, for lack of a better term, I have been calling the noncasual, nor is it because of a dialectic of self and nonself in which the latter is positioned as other. The casualness of white knowledge is the result of its univocity, of its reliance upon a stable and fixed positionality. When, under Mphahlele's questioning, it is thrust to the ground of its production, it comes upon the fact that this ground is not a position but a field that determines positionality. Mphahlele was no longer interested in playing the positional games that are still to be found in the writings of even such anti-apartheid writers as Nadine Gordimer, André Brink, or Molefe Pheto.[19] His commitment to a social and revolutionary role for the writer required an understanding of the rules of this positional game, of how they control moves, and of the interest of the game itself.

The question of the "field" of Comparative Literature can be asked again, but it cannot be answered in the theoretical or methodological way in which it was reached, since the field we have uncovered is the ground upon which the theoretical gaze is formed and is thus conditioned by it. We must attempt to address this field by means of the givenness that animates it. The work of another writer, also from austral Africa, may prove of some help. It is a short story written in Portuguese, titled "O relógio" (The watch), by the Angolan writer Manuel Rui.[20] This short story contains a double narrative: the story of a watch and the story of the telling of the story of the watch, a structure that makes any paraphrase or summary perilous. In an area under the control of the Movimento Popu-

---

19. Molefe Pheto, *And Night Fell* (London: Allison and Busby, 1983). Pheto is a good representative of the Black Consciousness movement.

20. Manuel Rui, "O Relógio," *Sim Camarada!* (Luanda: União dos Escritores Angolanos, n.d.), 19–55, but see in the text for a discussion of publication data. The translation is mine.

Wlad Godzich

lar para a Liberação do Angola (MPLA) prior to its final victory over the Portuguese, there lives a veteran comandante of the rebel forces. Having lost a leg on a Portuguese mine, he is now retired and spends much of his time with children. A ritual has developed whereby the story of the watch is recounted every Sunday. The children are by now quite familiar with the plot of the story, yet they continue to coax it out of the comandante, who thus functions as traditional storyteller and priest substitute in this Sunday ritual. The storytelling is far from straightforward. The children interrupt with questions, remind the comandante of details he gave previously, seek new precision, and store in their memory the new elements as they are being elaborated. In fact, the story provides one of the best descriptions of the collective labor involved in the production of an oral tale. At first, only the comandante is aware of what is going on. Progressively, the children become emboldened and grow more secure in their role as coauthors of this story, so much so that the particular telling that is the focus of the written tale has them elaborate a new ending to the story. This complex creative process, at once traditional and revolutionary—in all senses of the term—is constantly redefining the boundaries of the historical and the fictional, with an attention to aesthetic, cognitive, and political significance.

The story of the watch is itself quite simple. The beginning gives a flavor of the whole:

O Comandante abria sempre da mesma maneira: —O relógio foi fabricado na Suiça e a marca era Omega. —E onde está a Suiça? —Muito longe. Não é uma pessoa. E um país, muito longe, na Europa e là faz muito frío. Era o costume. A garotada interrompía. [22]

The Captain always began in the same way: "The watch was Swiss-made and its brand was Omega." "And where is this Swiss?" "Very far. I don't mean a person. It's a country, very far, in Europe, and it's very cold there." That is the way it went. The kids would break in.

Through the give and take between the comandante and the children, we learn that this Swiss watch was sold to a Portuguese dealer, who shipped it to the capital of Angola, Luanda, where it was sold in a shop called Paris Jewellers. This telling takes quite some time because the children want to know why watches are not made in Angola (which provides raw materials) or even in Portugal and what are the advantages of naming a jewelry store after the capital of France. Eventually the story progresses to the point where a major in the Portuguese expeditionary forces sent to put down the MPLA purchases the watch. This very major is sent in pursuit of the comandante and his troop and is killed in an ambush they set. One of the rebels makes the comandante a gift of the plundered watch. In the subsequent pursuit by the Portuguese seeking to avenge the ambush, the comandante and his squad are forced to cross into neighboring Zaire, where they have to use the watch to ransom themselves from a corrupt Zairois police official about to turn them over to their pursuers. This is the basic story told by the comandante every Sunday. The account purports to be historical, though subject to the embellishment and the greater precision demanded by the children. But on this particular Sunday one of the children suggests the story need not end there. Let the Zairois assist an anti-MPLA (and United States and South African-supported) group and enter Luanda and establish a base, then let the watch be recovered by daring MPLA pioneers who seize the Zairois prisoner. Finally let the watch be returned to the children of the Portuguese major with an account of its peregrinations in the form of a song sung by the children and carried to Portugal in a conch. Such is the story. Although it calls for a full analysis, a few remarks may suffice for our purposes.

It would be tempting to read the story as an allegory of one sort or another: temporality is clearly one of the stakes; the brand name of the watch suggests an ending, if not the end, of Western domination; a new epoch is foreshadowed both in the return of the watch to Europe and in the collective elaboration of the tale, which renews ties with traditional modes of African storytelling which presumably were endangered by colonization. Such a reading, or variations thereof, would depend on the treatment of the watch as either a symbol or the objective correlative of one. The story lays such stress on the material aspect of the watch, its provenance, its process of fabrication, and its circuitous deambulations as to intimate a resistance to this type of reading. The watch does not stand for anything; it is, and by just being, it forces readerly reactions in the direction of symbolic interpretation.[21] It brings the various protagonists within the measure of the time that it marks. The distant Swiss watch-maker, the Portuguese import-export agent, the colonial shopkeeper with dreams of grandeur, the imperialist military agent, the revolutionary, the neocolonial stooge, the rising generations of liberated Africans and postimperialist metropolitans—all are brought within its orbit; all share the same chronotope, the measure of which it punctuates in accor-

---

21. There is reference to another watch in the story. It appears on the wrist of one of the two famous young heroes of the Angolan war of national liberation, as depicted in a revolutionary poster. The poster is clearly symbolic of revolutionary struggle and the watch depicted therein overtly partakes of the symbolism. The comandante is reticent with respect to it; he begins by describing a watch not depicted on the poster, which belongs to the other hero, and ends by cutting the children's questions short. There is also a reference to his own watch which is described in purely functional terms. The watch of the story is neither functional nor symbolic, that is, it is there neither to tell time nor to appeal to an immediately identifiable set of explanatory referents or signifieds. Its function is to force a textual circulation, the economy of which requires re-marking in the form of a critical discourse.

dance with the workings of its inner mechanism. It organizes a discursive space, the very space that an interpretative reading will attempt to fill, the dimensions of which are already adumbrated in the children's relentless questioning. This interdiscursive space is its field, and it must be the "field" of Comparative Literature, in the sense not so much that we must fill it as that we must be attentive to the mode of its constitution and indeed must participate in it as do the children of the story, who eventually wrest away the comandante's command over the story in order to send it in a circulation that is not necessarily different from that of the watch though with a rather different set of themes attached to it.[22]

It is not irrelevant to a consideration of this story to note that Manuel Rui's book was not actually printed in Angola, even though Luanda is given as its place of publication, and that no date of publication appears. The book was actually printed in Portugal by Edições 70 for the Union of Angolan Writers at a time when such printing presses as could operate in Angola were still fully mobilized in the revolutionary effort that followed independence. Manuel Rui's manuscript had traveled to Lisbon, where, following the April revolution, it was printed on postimperial Portugal's presses and then returned to Angola, thereby adding a further twist to the production of the story and preventing anyone from determining its temporal end. This is far more than a critical conceit as a quick return to the story shows.

At one juncture, the comandante compares his own stainless steel utilitarian watch with the watch of the story and characterizes the latter as a "relógio de burguês"—a bourgeois watch. The insistence on the process of fabrication and, even more so, on the various trades the watch was subject to takes on additional meaning. The circulation of this bourgeois commodity reveals the existence of a world economic system that recognizes national boundaries only when it finds it suitable to its own ends. So pervasive is such a system that even a war of national liberation begins to look dubious: the nation-state it will result in is likely to become but one more relay in the circulation of commodities. To this world order built on the relationship to the commodity and punctuated by the limits of nation-states and the rhythms of linear time, the story counterposes a field of discursive creativity that is repetitive, endless, and articulated around the relationship among those who are engaged with the givenness within it. To a world socioeconomic order of commodity production and circulation across national boundaries, it opposes the dialogic community of the

22. I use the term *interdiscursive* in the sense given to it by Jurgen Link, *Elementare Literatur und generative Diskursanalyse* (Munich: Wilhelm Fink, 1983). esp. 48–72. Link analyzes a mode of social existence granted to semiotic objects in which they animate a number of diverse and frequently divergent discourses to constitute a space of interdiscursivity within which these objects are granted reality.

comandante—the children, the Portuguese major's children, Angolan writers, Portuguese publishers, North American readers and critics, etc. This may appear to be a binary opposition but only because a third term is occulted. Much is made in the story of the children's slow determination to send the watch, and its story, back to Portugal. The crippled comandante, firmly committed to a realistic mode of storytelling, following perhaps the ideological and aesthetic orientations of his chief, Augustinho Neto, head of the MPLA and eventually president of Angola as well as an internationally renowned poet, had never imagined this eventuality. Like Neto he was involved in building the nation and attempting to endow it with a literature worthy of it, an Angolan literature. The children see other boundaries than those of the state and seem wary of the state's institutions. Their form of creative realism recognizes that state institutions, if not the state itself, are at best inadequate protection from and perhaps willing accomplices of the world system and that the discursive creativity they employ must not be contained within obsolete structures. For their story they want the agential power presently harnessed on behalf of the commodity in late capitalism against the petrified and monumentalizing approach of national literature.

It is my claim that it is precisely this hegemonic and monumentalizing view of literature which is challenged by emergent literatures. "Emergent literatures" are not to be understood then as literatures that are in a state of development that is somehow inferior to that of fully developed, or "emerged," literatures—our own disciplinary version of "underdevelopment" or "developing" literatures, if you wish, with attendant "Third-Worldist" ideologies—but rather those literatures that cannot be readily comprehended within the hegemonic view of literature that has been dominant in our discipline. In this view, emergent literatures will include writings by racial and ethnic minorities in countries such as the United States; literature by women in, let us say, Italy, France, or Australia; as well as much of the new writing from Africa, Asia, and Latin America, including the Caribbean.

Emergent literatures represent a different conception of field and of object than that represented by the often used expression "emerging literatures." The latter reflects a Hegelian conceptualization according to which the new literatures are viewed as representing less-mature stages of canonical literatures, which we as theoreticians and analysts of literature should have little difficulty in understanding—so little, perhaps, that they may not warrant the commitment of our time and may well be left to others, such as students writing dissertations. It is not difficult to see that this attitude seeks to perpetuate existing theoretical hegemonies. If my notion of emergent literatures as literatures that challenge these hegemonies is to be retained, we could readily conceive that a contemporary writer from a Third World country could write in a nonemergent way. And in fact this happens even in the career of a single individual. Witness the case of V. S. Naipaul. His early novels, such as *A House for Mr. Biswas*, are good examples of emergent literature, with their attempt to record the discourse of everyday life in colonial Trinidad and especially the features of what Mervyne Alleyne has called "post-creole English."[23] But the later novels—such as *The Guerrillas*, which is also set in Trinidad— with their standardized diction and their representation of different speech as alienatingly distant from the norm implicitly shared by a North Atlantic reader and writer, are not emergent literature. It is no accident that at this juncture Naipaul should become the favorite Third World writer of the *Times Literary Supplement* and the *New York Review of Books* and that a powerful lobby should seek the Nobel Prize for him. And yet even then Naipaul remains problematic. Where will the institution of literature as presently constituted put him? Doesn't part of the exceptional treatment being accorded him go beyond ideological convergence and mark the fact that he must be treated exceptionally if the prevalent division of labor in literary studies is to be preserved. Otherwise, where will we teach him? in British literature? in West Indian or East Indian literature? His very prominence occults these questions, and yet it indelibly inscribes them and the problems they represent within the field of Comparative Literature.

23. "A Linguistic Perspective on the Caribbean," in *Caribbean Contours*, ed. Sidney W. Mintz and Sally Price (Baltimore: Johns Hopkins University Press, 1985) 155–79.

[3]

Defining and Defending
Comparative Literature

LOWRY NELSON, JR.

I

In the simplest and best formulation, Comparative Literature is nothing other than the study of literature. My notion of literature is that it is an art; that its productive human faculty is conveniently called imagination; that its works must be considered in their individual integrity and also in groupings by national and international traditions, movements, periods, and genres; and that its theory and mode of existence belong under the philosophical heading of aesthetics. In Aristotelian and Kantian terms, to which I largely subscribe, literature is purposive without purpose, that is, it is goal seeking (to fulfill its wholeness, form, or the implications of its subject matter) and yet does not have its goal in practical or moral activity or in the proofs of logic, epistemology, and metaphysics. Such a view avoids the triviality of art for art's sake and also the grandiosity of literature as world saving and inclusive of all verbal discourse. Likewise, the prime effect of literature is "disinterested pleasure"—a complex of both thought and feeling which a text arouses by its artistry and not by its practical, partisan, or historically illustrative usefulness. Once the prime object and the prime attitude toward it are established—and only then— it is possible to view literature as an institution and its study as one of the many human pursuits that by their humanity are all intricately interrelated. Literary works can be seen as documents in history, psychology, anthropology, and philosophy; they are often made to be part of music, social doctrine, and even propaganda and ritual. Or conversely, those nonliterary disciplines may, with care, use literary works as subsidiary texts or as documents or as evidence. Such interchange can often be illuminating all round, so long as literary scholars keep their grasp on

Lowry Nelson, Jr.

their own object of study and maintain a reasoned concept of its wholeness or integrity. What in my own work I have found indispensable, along
with primary aesthetic response, is a continually hard-won sense of history and social context. But history is not simply what we know of the past;
it is also how our living in the present—as part of continuing history—
clarifies and "perspectivizes" the past. Similarly, to read a previously
unread work of literature also deepens or even changes our sense of
literary art and its possible classifications. A lifetime is insufficient for
reading and knowing enough. What is essential is to keep a double
perspective in these matters: to know all one humanly can of the past and
to see history as including one's own necessary and inescapable present.
For me the best lesson is that in Greek mythology the Muses are the
daughters of Memory.

In this straight summary fashion I express my views concerning the
study of literature at the risk of seeming peremptory or simplistic. I can be
blunter in the negative. Comparative Literature is *not* a specialty; it is
simply a convenient traditional designation for the whole study of the
whole of literature so far as one's mind and life can stretch. True, the
word *literature* in the phrase *Comparative Literature* refers to the *study* of
literary works, but that is a now archaic meaning that can be tolerated in
conventional usage. It is far simpler, of course, to say that one reads
literary works as a prime or an adopted or a chosen purpose in life. The
academic, professional, or private terminology may well follow from that
direct statement, yet it must be scrutinized often for adventitious connotations. For instance, I would insist that a critic is not a special species; any
experienced and reflective reader who renders a coherent judgment is
thereby a critic. The purpose of literary study is not immediately to relate
literature to some other pursuit but rather, first and foremost, to understand and appreciate, to perceive, enjoy, and evaluate works of literature
in their artistic integrity and aesthetic interrelatedness. Such an emphasis
does *not* presume to deny social, national, temporal, biographical, or even
private associations that may prove interesting, instructive, provocative,
illuminating, or personally precious. It merely seeks to assert a first principle or essential priority that would seem almost self-evident if there were
not currently so clamorous a bazaar in which, competing for attention, are
many celebrity egos, the familiar isms in newfangled garb, an assortment
of panaceas and aporias, any number of peccadillos and perversions that
bear watching, and uncountable pages coming prematurely into print.

As this decade begins to slope toward the next, a seeming turn in time
may be sufficient pretext for reflecting on the general state of literary
study (a phrase equivalent, for my purposes, to Comparative Literature)
and for asserting some perspectives in the current welter. Literature,
literary study, and literary theory have an intertwined genealogy, such

that the lone reader may welcome reassurance that poets and fiction writers do indeed make art works and not velleitous swatches of texts, that those who discourse *about* art perform a different function (unseemly if it is exploitative or competitive), and that good and original theorists of literature are historically very much rarer than fine poets and fiction writers. In saying that literature is an art and not merely a semiotic product, one sets it in the realm of aesthetics and not epistemology or logic or metaphysics. Yet the shortcomings of traditional aesthetics may discourage the amateur literary philosopher, who often ends up as a frantic loner, an impulsive joiner, an eclectic, or a purveyor of vigorously misplaced rigor.

II

What is now institutionalized as Comparative Literature has, of course, a pedigree that can be variously traced—back to Aristotle, perhaps, who considered all there was in the way of tragedy and derived a theory of a "perfected" or fulfilled genre; back to the Alexandrians, who preserved and treasured their ancient past and made a strangely new literature on the foundations of the old; back to the Romans, who then had two venerable traditions to experience and from which to make literature even more strangely new in their own way; back to the middle Middle Ages when the remote classical past was only spottily known and when its casual or respectful teaching could conveniently be assimilated to rhetoric and at the same time become a model (Walter's *Alexandreis*), a subtext (Henric van Veldeke's *Eneit*), or even perhaps an antimodel (new Latin and newer vernacular poetry) in a momentous process to continue in barely charted ways into the Renaissance. All along, such preceptors or theorists as Aristotle, Horace, Longinus, Geoffroi de Vinsauf, and Dante considered literature, in effect, to be what there was to hand, irrespective of language or nationality, and even more, the practitioners of literature, for the most part silently, chose their array of inherited exemplars to "imitate" (the least understood of terms) in an international process of making over into something else, as the German Wolfram refashioned the French Chrétien or the English Chaucer refashioned the Italian Boccaccio. In this respect Dante, with his survey of the known "national" literatures in the *De vulgari eloquentia* emerges as the broadest "comparatist" up to his time. Yet what is most momentous is not theoretical pronouncement but the continuing practice of practicing authors in constituting for themselves a creatively chosen and multifarious tradition without any prescribed or predictable bounds. And that practice will of course continue through subsequent ages.

Lowry Nelson, Jr.

An intensely explicit or self-conscious program was created by the theory and practice of the romantics (from the Schlegels and Mme de Staël to Franz Bopp, Friedrich Schelling, Coleridge, and Hegel), who collectively founded a vast canon of literature, a general science of "philology," and, almost paradoxically, a basis for a *national* literature seen in its separate development from primitive roots to luxuriant foliage. In effect the old system of genres was overturned, and especially prized were the romance and the novel and the subjective meditative poem; "exotic" literatures were explored and smaller national literatures were founded; by "imitation," translation, and reportage (especially in the great magazines of the time) a new sense of the vastness and variety of world literature became possible. On the model of the natural sciences and of all-explaining philosophical systems, some pioneers of literary history and literary theory, basing themselves on the enormous continuing labors of antiquaries and scholars, were emboldened to write sweeping histories of national or regional literatures (Simonde de Sismondi, George Ticknor, Hippolyte Taine, Francesco De Sanctis) and to essay general propositions about literature as a whole and its differentiation according to national character, tradition, taste, and even climate. Such a situation made it possible to sketch theories of literatures compared, or, on the analogy of *anatomie comparée*, *littérature comparée* and eventually Comparative Literature, *vergleichende Literaturgeschichte*, etc. The terms had various fates which have been informatively explored, yet only in the last two generations has some concept of Comparative Literature been institutionalized, practiced, and propagated. That concept or focus of attention is rightly under constant discussion and in dispute; at the same time, by apparent paradox, it is taken for granted as a field.

One plausible way of simplifying the state-of-things-now is to declare that literature (in the sense of imaginative or artistic literature) needs no qualifying adjective, that standing by itself it can, like physics or economics or philosophy, be understood as a field of study corresponding to a certain human activity or realm of experience and restricted only by the degree of skill, sensibility, and longevity of the student. The skills would be those of an attentive and thoughtful reader who habitually reads and reflects on many texts in several languages. The sensibility required is harder to characterize summarily and uninvidiously. Surely it should include an open and responsive mind, a capacity to exercise a "willing suspension of disbelief . . . that constitutes *poetic* faith," and an experienced aesthetic taste. Because of its medium, language, literature of all the arts is most subject to distortion and misapprehension. The blind and color-blind are unfortunately incompetent to experience painting, the deaf and tone-deaf to experience music; yet many with analogous disabilities undertake to study and judge literature and to construct theories that pervert its nature. Literature occasionally attracts those who lack skill and sensibility and those who wish above all to *do* something with it, that is, to use it for some nonaesthetic purpose without being able to understand its nature. Attention is thereby drawn away from the literary or imaginative aesthetic object and is brought to focus on external typologies, general intellectual history, linguistics, and various philosophical or political or religious schemes and systems of belief. Thus the object or subject matter of literary study becomes diffuse and obscured, and in keeping with the spirit of now superannuated modernism, literary study seems stymied by being displaced to its farthest frontiers, which vaguely border on an infinity of other human or humane pursuits. One may indeed sense that any connection is possible and that anything goes if it gets attention.

Through its very medium the integrity of literature in general or of a particular work is precarious. A text, like a fabric, can be pulled apart and made to serve other than "intended" purposes. A lovely fabric can be used as a rag or incorporated into pulp for making paper. A literary text, given that all words are to some extent polysemous, may be perversely made to bear any meaning of any word or may be used to "document" some ideological or philosophical point. The analogy of literary work to fabric is limited because of the latter's necessary materiality and can be made only by a prevalent misuse of etymology. More to the point would be an analogy to painting or to music or to other works of art. A painting may be retouched or even destroyed and a piece of music may be transposed, played slower than indicated, or cast from a "classical" into a "popular" style. Indeed, a painting or a score may have a cultic or even propagandistic origin. Yet even within such changes of functionality or intention, some works and versions may be judged better than others and may be said to possess aesthetic qualities perceivable even by those unaware of the original or its original function. The sorting out of motives and uses is clearly a difficult matter: the same objects may be perceived and discussed under greatly differing aspects. Yet, the *literary* study of literature must obviously be grounded in some fundamental acknowledgment of aesthetic or artistic or imaginative qualities. It is based upon certain capacities of the human mind which, for some or for many, possess central experiential importance. Such capacities and their exercise and gratification, even if, unfortunately, not universal, seem to me the essentials of literary study and, therefore, the foundation and prerequisite of Comparative Literature. Otherwise the jig is up and it's better to go into some other line of business.

Upholding the aesthetic integrity of the literary work of art may seem either obvious or untenable: obvious and therefore to be taken for granted or untenable in that aesthetics as a whole is suspected of lacking

Lowry Nelson, Jr.

rigor or proof, in that Comparative Literature has so often or even traditionally been occupied with matters external to art, in that literary scholarship does not officially require a capacity for appreciative aesthetic response. But literary studies are always perilously exposed to assimilation to such other pursuits as philosophy or politics or psychology and to the ancillary activities of establishing texts or constructing typologies or illustrating rhetorical terms. If the essential value of literature is abandoned because it seems difficult to defend, then its appreciators are depreciated and its prestige, so often meretriciously traded on, diminishes for all concerned, including the traders. Indeed, for many, the very value of life is involved. For some, no calamity would ensue, and in fact an obscenely egalitarian urge might be satisfied. It is unlikely, however, that no more authors would aspire to create further fictions on which they and their readers set aesthetic and even moral value.

III

One looks to modern philosophy for aid, if not comfort, in sorting out the issues of art. My impression is that philosophers for some time now have been most successful in logic; in social, political, and legal theory; in ethical speculation; and in discourse about the physical world (philosophy of science). Two large realms where it is difficult for me to see successful activity are hermeneutics (including philosophy of language) and general aesthetics. In hermeneutics, the territory staked out is impossibly vast, covering as it does the whole subject matter of the three Kantian *Critiques* (not to mention a whole library of quick fixes), and the method is excessively dependent on restricted and inexpert language theory. In general aesthetics, since Ernst Cassirer, Suzanne Langer, and Nelson Goodman, little attempt has been convincingly made to incorporate and accommodate literature in a system or theory of the arts. The large systems most common currently seem to be the familiar derivatives of Marxism, psychoanalysis, and linguistics—often combined in varying admixtures or wholly housed under the capacious circus tent of semiotics. Such arrangements have the effect of degrading or dismissing the aesthetic function and value especially of literature, which, as a language art, can be insidiously assimilated or exploited to serve other than aesthetic purposes. In comparison, artistic expression in stone or metal, in paint, in body movement, or in consciously produced and modulated sound, is much less "common" and is generally restricted to a situation of assumed aesthetic expectation. If we were to pursue an evenhanded aesthetics of all art, we might be justified in considering literature, despite its highly diffuse medium of language, as also existing in an integral or circumscribed condition that presupposes aesthetic expectation. Then, just as we would not turn over sculpture to the geologist, painting to the interior designer, or music to the acoustician, so we would not surrender literature to the ideologue, the psychologist, the preacher, the linguist, the rhetorician, the cultural historian, or the antimetaphysical meta-metaphysician.

My plaint or complaint concerns general aesthetics and literature's place within it along with the other arts. Most attentive readers, I presume, make aesthetic assumptions: coherence, purposiveness or "form," correctness (in grammar and idiom according to tone or level), interest, pleasure, and a whole list of other qualities that may or may not be present or fulfilled in a given work. At the same time there are those nowadays who nurse an exacerbated sense that we should question such qualities and lay them bare by attempting to demonstrate their imperfect or even impossible fulfillment, by adducing extreme or borderline cases or exceptions to disprove any rule or norm, and by transferring interpretation from the realm of art to biographical or ideological or general linguistic explanations. In the process, the notion of text becomes almost as generic as the notion of textile, the notion of literary performance or enactment becomes diluted in Noam Chomsky's elementary contrastive set of competence/performance (a version of Saussure's *langue/parole*), the notion of prosody is swallowed up in the phonetician's study of the intonation of anyone's ordinary speech, narrative structure is assimilated to anthropological and psychoanalytic models that by their very hypothetical nature, are reductive. All too often the purpose and experience of literary art are stretched on a scale not of aesthetic value but of utilitarian or ideological expediency.

I would adduce two chief reasons why the nature or status of the literary work of art seems peculiarly contested and embattled. First, over the past century there have been so many departures in great art from traditional norms, so many splendid and justly celebrated special or marginal cases, that the reader-spectator may be baffled or buffaloed into an acceptance of disorientation as normal or of obscurity as indispensable. He or she may perforce become an adept, an initiate, a hierophant, indeed a critic in some specious sense. Difficulty and novelty come to be prized for their own sake. The self-capitalizing Critics initiate or intimidate the reader and thereby aggrandize themselves. The second general reason for contesting or neglecting literary aesthetics is a common desire to pursue some sort of unified field theory in the humanities (*les sciences de l'homme, die Geisteswissenschaften*) that will, in academic jargon, bring about, by transnational and interdisciplinary means, a consummate cross-fertilization. Such an ambition has a serious history from Aristotle to Wilhelm Dilthey. Yet clearly it has, on lower levels, the danger of trivializing and homogenizing intricately different fields, modes of thinking, assumptions, and subject matter. On the one hand, literary texts may come in handy as documents for historians, psychologists, philosophers, and linguists. On the other hand, presumptive students of literature may eclectically and arbitrarily borrow from any number of other pursuits, laying out for themselves a whole cafeteria of "approaches" to literature. On both sides there may often be a confusion of motives, not necessarily the elucidation of a subject matter but rather its hoped-for justification from the outside (practicality in getting ahead, therapy in getting one's head straight, service to some modish ideology).

In its current exposed state, literature (along with the theory proper to it) has been buffeted by the winds of doctrine. Thirty years ago was the heyday of existentialism, Sartre's version or reinterpretation of Heidegger and Husserl, with roots more in Hegel the ideologue than in his master Kant the aesthetician. Indeed, the watchwords had a distinctive Marxian tone: absolute necessity or determinism of choice, political commitment (engagement), and social utility. It was a heady time for thousands of academic devotees. Where are they now? In the late 1960s there arose a vogue for "structuralism" that has since preoccupied many literary scholar-critics. Like existentialism, it required crash programs of homework. Only gradually did some knowledge of the genealogy that stretched from outmoded eighteenth-century speculation on language and Saussure's *Cours de linquistique générale* to the Prague Linguistic Circle, the phonology of Nikolai Trubetskoi and Roman Jakobson, the anthropology of Franz Boas and Ruth Benedict, and the popular latter-day works of Claude Lévi-Strauss (who in his fashion synthesized American anthropology and Jakobson's version of linguistic theory). This enterprise has led in so many directions that one can only summarize by naming neo-Freudian psychoanalysis, semiotics, and neorhetoricism. At least for a while the word *paradigm* (made current by Thomas Kuhn) seemed to sum it all up. If one adds the belatedly "discovered" Russian so-called formalists (along with the recently "recuperated" Bakhtin), one can account for the widespread preoccupation with linguistics and with "devices," to the extent that much of the attraction seems to lie in the elevation of linguistics to something like an exact science and in the succinct neatness of equating literary success with the employment of discrete devices (*priëmy*). Even more recently we witness the surprising success of a philosophical project to treat literary tests as objects of deconstruction (deconstrual? misconstrual?) in order to lay bare their pretentions to integralness and finality—in effect, to expose the inner workings of illusionism and the presumed slipperiness of language and therefore of any linguistic construct. Indeed, any text should do as object of deconstruction. The method is a kind of philosophical rhetoricism or rhetorical philosophy; it is close reading made closer than close, and it has about it the dissolving aura of Jacques Derrida's suprametaphysical attempt to overturn the whole of Western philosophy.

If one assumes that these widespread modes of thought or ideologies or methods are important and effective, one must also reflect that they leave the specifically literary text undefined or perhaps that they render it categorically nonexistent. Another way of putting the matter is to say that implicitly literary study becomes coextensive with philosophy. Yet philosophy here is most restricted indeed; it is a matter of words with no argued relation to reality. Thus, meanings can be produced from texts by fair means or foul, and any producible meanings whatsoever are somehow valid. The traditional endeavors of philosophy—logic, ontology, epistemology, theory of perception, metaphysics—may still be operative, but their levels and boundaries can be trespassed at will and their arguments and goals jumbled. Figures of rhetoric, for example, in *themselves* are taken to have large epistemological or even metaphysical meaning. A casual passage or word may suddenly be isolated and subjected to misplaced rigor. It is not easy for the amateur to know in what realm he is meant to be situated and what rules and controls can possibly govern the incessant flow of speculation.

IV

Beginning with Plato's, many aesthetics have subordinated art to other, apparently more momentous concerns. For Plato, art is either an unrational and divine gift (*Ion*) or a potentially dangerous stimulus to unruly emotions (*Republic*). Forms of Neoplatonism generally divinize beauty and trace its manifestations in art to a transcendental emanation. Aristotle's answer would recognize art as humanly crafted, shaped in various media available to the senses and to the mind, and related in some way to a concrete reality that is immanent and common in human experience. I would argue that Aristotle's concept of mimesis states in a word that mysterious, experiential, complex relationship between art and reality. With Lucretius and Horace begins the notion of art as instructing through pleasure, which has a long career stigmatized by Benedetto Croce as "art the meretrix" and "art the pedagogue." What Croce undertakes to do is to break from that view, to resolve antinomies of form and content, to dispense with classificatory systems like rhetoric and external histories in order radically to assert, as did Vico, the existence of a special and crucial human faculty, the imagination (*fantasia*). But once again the specificity of art gets lost in a general theory of intuition as expression. I sympathize with the motive of asserting the authentic existence of the aesthetic faculty and object. There are other attempts to salvage art by assimilating it to experience (John Dewey), to a general pleasure principle (George Santayana), or to symbol formation (Ernst Cassirer)—all considered essential aspects of human life and not merely leisure-time indulgences.

My own inexpert urge is to get back to a Kantian, ultimately Aristotelian view—at least to a recognition of the limits of human four-dimensional knowledge and of the need to argue consistently and systematically. Kant's attempts at formulating a concept of taste that is not mere whim or physiology, a concept of pleasure in art, and the relatively autonomous relation of art to practical and ethical pursuits are perhaps unstable attempts. I myself do not think so. That they are vulnerable is certainly true. That aesthetic pleasure is *interesseloses Wohlgefallen* or that art exhibits *Zweckmässigkeit ohne Zweck* may seem refutable or deconstructable or merely old-fashioned among the current counterclaims. Such formulations are hard won in Kant's context and, like any grand generalizations, require at least provisionally sympathetic consideration in a full awareness of the intrinsic and abiding difficulties they attempt to resolve.

Whatever the merits and interests of the various fashions of argument over the last thirty years—meaning those that are highly publicized and popular—they seem to lack concern for defining an aesthetic realm or acknowledging an aesthetic faculty. Yet the attraction and pleasure of a novel, a poem, a painting, a movie, a piece of music, a ballet remain central and essential for many of us. As with some of the more dithyrambic and hieratic notions of art among the romantics, insufficient attention is paid to the *differentiae* or the *specifica* of literary art in particular, again because of its medium in words, which start so many hopping hares. Whole books are written on poetry with no attention to what makes it poetry. Novels are treated as social tracts or psychological case histories. Plays are discussed without regard to their existence in performance. Such complaints are not new, and their implied demands are difficult to fulfill. When is a rhyme successful? What are the norms of nonmetrical verse? How does a novel imaginatively "convince"? How do we know that an actor has not fully realized or perhaps has misunderstood a character? What kind of "justice" can a translation do?

Clearly, in my view, a critic of literature should have some elementary aesthetic views or convictions and should be able to state them even if defending them may be hard for a nonphilosopher. The critic is primarily a reader, in the sense that all good readers are critics. The critic is concerned with valuable and evaluable works, whose art is part of the indispensable life of the imagination.

Defining and Defending Comparative Literature

V

By its very scope Comparative Literature as here discussed is a presumptuous study. It requires not only knowing many things but also knowing about many more. Obviously a deep knowledge of, say, four or five or more languages and their literatures would be a goal of the mature comparatist. Fundamental questions of literary theory and literary history have to be understood in their proper settings and arguments—not in pure abstraction but in circumstantial detail. One could continue. What is crucial is that all this must be happening, be present, in a single mind, in a single aesthetically aware sensibility. It is utterly illusory to think that by putting together a set of specialists one can create an enterprise or department of Comparative Literature. From the point of view of the study of literature in general such a grouping would in fact be less than the sum of its parts. It is also illusory to assume that the mere cultivation of literary theory makes one a comparatist or that Comparative Literature is the special repository of literary theory. That Comparative Literature has currently a certain adventitious modishness is as much an embarrassment as an advantage. Curiously, as theoretical activity has vastly expanded, the active canon of literary works seems to have narrowed. This is surely not a stable situation. One may quite easily surmise that few current theoreticians will have made a permanent mark, that gifted readers will continue to face the supposed perils and indeterminacy of polysemy and semiosis, that poets and fiction writers will continue at times to write masterpieces, and that the faculties of imagination, taste, and judgment will continue to be exercised by those who possess their gift in sufficient measure.

[4]

The Comparatist's Canon:
Some Observations

Frank J. Warnke

The canon of Comparative Literature—to the extent that such a thing exists—is even stranger and more arbitrary than the canons accepted in the various national literatures that make up our Western literary community.[1] The scholar specializing in an individual literature will usually have some disagreements with its commonly accepted roster: he or she may privately drop a few figures from that august list and add a few more. And the national canon itself changes over the centuries, though the rate of such change is generally glacial. In English, for example, Longfellow has vacated the place he held in the canon during the late nineteenth century, Donne has taken a place in its higher reaches, and recently such figures as Frederick Douglass and Kate Chopin have found their niches therein as the consciousness of the literary community has been slowly raised. Nevertheless, within any given literature there is substantial agreement at least as to the major figures of the canon. To choose once more an example from English, the attempt to dislodge Milton, conducted in some quarters in the earlier twentieth century, failed utterly, and that worthy remains securely seated at the right hand of Shakespeare.

The comparative canon presents a far murkier picture. All comparatists have, by definition, four separate or at least separable canons: that of the literature of their mother tongue (or, in some cases, tongues), that of

---

1. My terminology here is potentially misleading, but since the terms have established themselves firmly in the discourse of comparatists, more would be lost than gained by any attempt to replace them with less ambiguous terms. By "national literature" I mean not the literature produced by citizens of a given nation-state but rather the literature of a given language (i.e., English includes British, Anglo-Irish, American, etc.; German includes German (East and West), Austrian, Swiss-German, etc.). "Literary community" is not parallel in usage to the linguists' "language community" but designates, rather, the entire community of national literatures deriving from a shared cultural tradition.

[48]

The Comparatist's Canon

the other languages with which they are professionally involved as specialists, that of the remaining languages of the literary community (the Western, for example), and that of world literature in its broadest definition. In practice, few comparatists have the cosmopolitan range that such a formulation suggests. One may be, for example, professionally involved with materials in English, French, and German, and have a pretty clear sense of what is canonical in each of those literatures. In this case one would, beyond a doubt, also know that Dante, Boccaccio, and Petrarch are canonical in Italian, Cervantes and Lope de Vega in Spanish, and Pushkin, Tolstoi, and Dostoevski in Russian, but one's awareness might not extend much further than that. Very often—unless the hypothetical *one* happens to be Romanian or Dutch—all of literature in Romanian or Dutch or whatever else remains terra incognita. As for the non-Western literatures, those belonging to any of the other literary communities, one has heard some names—perhaps Li Po, Shikibu Murasaki, Yukio Mishima, Firdusi, Rabindranath Tagore, a few others—and that is all.

Even in the case of the larger Western literatures, many a comparatist has a curiously tilted frame of reference. The Western comparatist who does not happen to have Italian as an area of special competence will, as I have suggested, certainly know something about Dante, Petrarch, and Boccaccio but may have only the foggiest notion of Ariosto and Tasso and may know nothing whatsoever of Ugo Foscolo, Giacomo Leopardi, Alessandro Manzoni, Giovanni Verga, or Cesare Pavese.

What I am suggesting is that literary scholarship, even comparative literary scholarship, suffers from a bad case of provincialism, the symptoms of which are a widespread ignorance of non-Western literatures, an almost total ignorance of the smaller Western literatures (unless one happens, oneself, to be a product of one of those smaller language areas), and a selective and eccentric knowledge of the major Western literatures that lie outside one's areas of specialization. The question of integrating a knowledge of non-Western literatures into the awareness of the cultivated Westerner is currently being addressed by qualified specialists, that is, those with a professional's knowledge of one or more languages and literatures of either the East Asian, the South Asian, or the Middle Eastern literary community. It is likely that within a couple of generations Western provincialism will have been at least modified. The provincialism of the larger Western literatures with regard to the smaller may well prove to be a more stubborn problem. Before considering it, however, I'd like to make a few observations about the canon of the larger Western literatures as it exists in the mind of the nonspecialist.

Since the shape of the problem will differ according to the point of departure, let me posit, again, a comparatist formed initially by Anglo-American literary culture and concerned professionally with literature in

Frank J. Warnke

English, French, and German. Such a scholar will, as earlier noted, certainly be aware of the canon generally accepted in those three literary cultures. Beyond that, however, his or her knowledge of the canon of even the other large Western literatures is likely to be capricious, <u>for the circumstances affecting casual canonization are various, disparate, and sometimes frivolous</u>. One factor is, of course, sheer, undeniable stature: the nonspecialist knows of Dante and Cervantes, of Tolstoi and Dostoevski. But another factor is cosmopolitanism, or apparent cosmopolitanism: the possibly excessive eminence of Camus in the English-speaking world may result from the fact that he is more readily accessible than Mauriac, who does not, in general, have such eminence. A third factor, quite different from the second, is congruence with the national mirage: Federico Garcia Lorca and Antonio Machado are both great poets, but the former is much more likely to be familiar to the non-Hispanist literary scholar, perhaps because writing about gypsies and bullfighters and amorous ladies is what the Anglo-American imagination unconsciously expects from a Spanish poet. (Similarly, Colette's position in the general English canon of Western literature may be the result, in part, not of her great gifts as a novelist but of her characteristic subject matter and her own myth-image as the sexy Frenchwoman.)

There are other factors as well in the process of casual canonization. Scandal is one: Ibsen, one of the very few figures from the smaller literatures to achieve the breakthrough into the general Western canon, did so initially not because of his artistic greatness but because of his shock effect. <u>Ideology, politics, and religion are other frivolous factors affecting literary canonization.</u> Still other factors are sheer difficulty or other obstacles to exportability: Friedrich Hölderlin is less well known in English-speaking intellectual circles than is Heinrich Heine in part because he is more difficult[2] (and in part because he did not write poems that, like Heine's, lend themselves superbly to settings in the universal language of music).

One curious feature of the canonization in one literature of authors and works from another is the apparent irrelevance of the author's position within his or her own literature: students of English or comparatists for whom English is one of their areas rightly regard Wordsworth as a towering figure in English poetry; others are unconvinced. They would rather read Byron, who has proven as exportable as Wordsworth is unexportable. La Fontaine occupies in the French mind a position of unique centrality; he has made little impression on the English sensibility and does not figure in our anthologies of world literature in translation (the story is different in Eastern Europe, where his prestige has long been

2. Cf. Richard Unger, Preface to *Friedrich Hölderlin* (Boston: Twayne, 1984).

high). Manzoni—especially his masterpiece, *I promessi sposi*—is revered in his native Italy, but his name is scarcely a household word among comparatists who do not have an Italian emphasis.

The author who is securely canonized within his own culture but largely ignored by the international canon poses a nice problem for the student of Comparative Literature. Does the international indifference— or relative indifference—not result from the fact that such an author is so fully, so intensely expressive of that particular culture? Who could be more English than Wordsworth, more French than La Fontaine? And Manzoni is virtually a key to Italian civilization. If there is any merit in this suggestion, a further question presses itself upon us: Ought we, as comparatists, to focus our attention exclusively on that which seems familiar in the foreign or that which feeds our mirage of what a given foreignness ought to be like? I would suggest that the various national canons, in their specificity and in what may sometimes seem their eccentricity, might well be accorded more authority, more of a leadership role, than the international community of comparatists has generally been prepared to grant. The comparatist is by definition a cosmopolitan, but he or she need not be a rootless cosmopolitan. The study of roots is perhaps the base of our discipline, a discipline that should be concerned not merely with the delighted (and sometimes superficial) noting of similarities among texts but also with the unavoidable differences—of culture, of language itself—that we ignore only at the peril of sinking into the dreaded quagmire of dilettantism.

If in foregoing paragraphs I have often employed the terms *ought* and *should*, I hope their incidence does not give these remarks the flavor of a sermon or an admonitory lecture. Scholars should—forgive me, scholars *must*—concern themselves only with those phenomena that arouse their enthusiasm, and they are under no obligation to deal with anything else. But I believe that scholars will do more excellent work, whatever the object of inquiry, if they approach it equipped with a broader awareness, with a literary culture more cognizant of the particular national canons and more cognizant, also, of the smaller literatures of the literary community. The international canon, whether the lopsided one we currently work with or the more inclusive one I'm unrealistically arguing for, may be seen as affecting three separate but interrelated areas of our professional life: research, teaching, and general cultural awareness. With a broader awareness one *might* find new matters for research and one *might* find new texts for teaching, but one would surely have gained in general sophistication.

There are some practical problems related to teaching less-familiar texts. On the undergraduate level, where some use of materials in translation is surely justified, the texts have to be available for adoption, and

Frank J. Warnke

publishing houses are in business to make a profit, not to serve our cultural aspirations. (One can find, for example, any quantity of Brecht in English translation but precious little Giraudoux; lots of Camus or Sartre, but no Hofmannsthal except in expensive hardback.) On the graduate level, where texts are studied in the original, the problem is less acute: with a little lead time one can order from abroad, and the libraries of the larger universities provide us with God's plenty. At the very least, however, the teacher can make students aware of the existence of eminent authors, canonized within their own cultures, who have yet to make it into such collections as the *Norton Anthology*—in itself a quite estimable work but one which perpetuates the lopsided canon.

Such problems are dwarfed by those attendant on any attempt to expand the comparatist's canon by the inclusion of great writers from the smaller European literatures (I use the term *smaller* in order to avoid the pejorative implications of *minor*). The comparatist's canon, as it exists in the English-speaking area, gives scant recognition to any literature outside of English, French, German, Italian, Spanish, Russian, and, of course, Latin, Ancient Greek, and the Hebrew of the Bible. There are a handful of breakthrough figures from the smaller literatures: Ibsen (as already noted), August Strindberg, Knut Hamsun perhaps, and—for brief tenures of international acceptance after the Nobel Prize has been awarded—Nikos Kazantzakis, Pär Lagerkvist, Halldor Laxness, George Seferis, Ivo Andrić, etc. Latterly some contemporary writers from Eastern Europe—Milan Kundera comes to mind, and Czeslaw Milosz—have been available in English, to a certain extent exemplifying canonization for ideological reasons. But in general, one might get the impression that there are no Dutch plays, no Hungarian epics, no Serbo-Croatian novels, no Portuguese short stories, or anything else from the smaller literatures. Dialect literature poses a related problem. Since it is difficult to digest the Viennese of J. N. Nestroy into High German, the tendency of international, of comparative literary scholarship has been to ignore him.[3] (I shall not attempt here to address the question of what makes the difference between a language and a dialect. As a wise person—a linguist—once remarked, "There are no languages; there is only language.")

To exemplify the predicament of the smaller Western literatures, I should like to choose Dutch, for the simple reason that it is the only smaller Western literature with which I have some substantial familiarity. The points could be made with equal salience with reference to Danish, Swedish, Hungarian, Romanian, or a good many other literatures. Dutch,

---

3. There is one selection of Nestroy's plays available in English translation: J. N. Nestroy, *Three Viennese Comedies*, trans. and ed. Robert Harrison and Katharina Wilson (Baltimore: Camden House, 1986).

however, may recommend itself particularly because of the great length of its literary history, the rich productivity of some of its literary periods, and the incredible neglect it has experienced at the hands of its more populous neighbors, not just the English-speaking world but also the French-speaking and, most particularly, the German-speaking.

To begin at the beginning, the earliest Dutch poet is the Fleming Henric van Veldeke (fl. 1170). The most recent study of him bears the title *Heinrich von Veldeke*, as if he were a German poet, and the author thus follows a well-established precedent. It is a defensible precedent, in view of the fact that van Veldeke's major work has come down to us only in a Middle High German recension of the original Middle Dutch text. Less comprehensible is the inclusion, in an anthology entitled *Deutsche Geistliche Dichtung*, of a generous selection of lyrics by Guido Gezelle.[4] The small print gives us the name of the translator of Gezelle's Dutch original into German, but the print is very small. Even less comprehensible is Malcolm Bradbury and James McFarland's ambitious and wide-ranging *Modernism*, with its almost total omission of any reference to modernist literature in the Netherlands and Dutch-speaking Belgium.[5] Although this volume deals with all the larger Western literatures and many of the smaller, there is no mention of Paul van Ostaijen, the great Flemish experimentalist; of Hendrik Marsman, the Dutch expressionist poet; of Simon Vestdijk, the incredibly prolific novelist, poet, and essayist, whose fiction some critics rank with that of Proust, Joyce, and Mann; of Gerrit Achterberg, whose lyric cycles are comparable to the best modernist poetry in the larger languages.

The neglect of Dutch letters on the international scene extends even to a widespread and appalling ignorance of the language in which it is expressed—even among those who ought to know better. One hears it asserted that there is no Dutch language, that it is a "dialect" of German, although even a native speaker of German who has not studied Dutch will be incapable of understanding it in either its written or its spoken form. One hears that it is a "corruption" of German, an accusation that will not withstand even minimal historical scrutiny. On the other hand, some otherwise cultivated literary people are under the strange impression that Dutch and Flemish are different languages. As is often the case, ignorance is accompanied by absolute certainty. At a dinner party some years ago the widow of an eminent American poet assured me, with a confi-

---

4. Friedhelm Kemp, ed., *Deutsche Geistliche Dichtung aus Tausend Jahren* (Munich: Kösel, 1958), 436–40, 526.

5. *Modernism* (Hassocks, Sussex: Harvester, 1978). The only reference I noted is to the literary journal *Van Nu en Straks*, inaccurately identified as a journal published in Holland rather than, as it actually was, in Flanders (203).

dence bordering on smugness, that there existed no poetry in the Dutch language.

This vacant space in literary awareness, exacerbated by the paucity of translations (at least into English), deprives the non-Dutch reader of many valuable experiences, as it deprives the non-Dutch literary comparatist of some useful historical insights. Among the Dutch masters there are at least eight of world format, or at least of general Western format. The greatest figure in Dutch literature, Joost van den Vondel, who flourished in the seventeenth century, wrote lyrics, satires, epics, and especially verse dramas that place him on the level of such baroque giants as Milton and Corneille. Eduard Douwes Dekker, who wrote under the pseudonym "Multatuli," created in *Max Havelaar* (1860) a satirical novel of extraordinary power, which uses the abuses of colonialism as a stick with which to bash bourgeois hypocrisy, conformity, and materialism vigorously and inventively. Louis Couperus, early in our century, wrote a number of novels that retain their considerable value; I've already mentioned Vestdijk and Achterberg. In Flanders the poet Guido Gezelle and the novelist Stijn Streuvels produced masterful work in the nineteenth century, and the versatile man of letters Hugo Claus dominates the contemporary scene.

Others could be cited as at least possible candidates for the canon of Western literature: the thirteenth-century Flemish female mystic Hadewych; Vondel's seventeenth-century contemporaries P. C. Hooft, G. A. Bredero, Constantijn Huygens, and Jan Luyken; the symbolist poets J. H. Leopold and P. C. Boutens in the Netherlands and Karel van de Woestijne in Flanders; the aforementioned Paul van Ostaijen; and the modern Dutch novelists Anna Blaman, W. F. Hermans, and Harry Mulisch. There are others as well.

Such writers are worthy of attention, and it is regrettable that so little is available in translation.[6] Some knowledge of Dutch letters would also, as I have suggested, round out one's picture of general European literary history. In the seventeenth century, for example, Dutch literary culture performed an important role as transmitter, even as intermediary, be-

6. The meager store of work available in English translation has recently been augmented by the publication of two important contemporary Dutch novels: Cees Nooteboom, *Rituals* (Baton Rouge: Louisiana State University Press, 1983), and Harry Mulisch, *The Assault* (New York: Pantheon, 1985), as well as an anthology of modern poetry, *Dutch Interior*, ed. James S. Holmes and William Jay Smith (New York: Columbia University Press, 1984). Egbert Krispyn of the University of Georgia is currently engaged in directing an ambitious project in which a team of translators will produce six volumes drawn from seventeenth-century Dutch literary classics. E. M. Beekman has published translations of Multatuli (*The Oyster and the Eagle* [Amherst: University of Massachusetts Press, 1974]) and has, since 1981, been editing Library of the Indies, a series of volumes in English translation of Dutch classics dealing with the former colonial empire in that region.

tween the literatures of the Romance languages and those of the German-speaking world; German poets and dramatists of the baroque learned many of their lessons first from Dutch masters. Much later, Nietzsche, Freud, and D. H. Lawrence all expressed their admiration of Multatuli, whose satiric vitality and extravagant romantic irony may have had some impact on their own imaginative visions.

The appropriate assessment of the contribution of the smaller literatures to the formation of the larger has, in general, received nothing like sufficient attention. To shift the focus from Dutch letters, one might, for example, consider the special relationship to the Scandinavian literatures entertained by two of the giants of twentieth-century German literature—Thomas Mann and Rainer Maria Rilke. Mann, who pays tribute to Scandinavian letters in a notable passage of "Tonio Kröger," may well have derived his familial myth of the son formed by a conflict between the southern/artistic/Bohemian mother and the northern/commercial/bourgeois father from a reading of the Scandinavian texts of the Dane Jens Peter Jacobsen (especially *Niels Lyhne*) and the Norwegian Jonas Lie.[7] Significantly, Rilke, who studied Danish to be able to read Jacobsen in the original, imagined the protagonist of his *Aufzeichnungen des Malte Laurids Brigge* as a young Danish nobleman. Some knowledge of the Danish and Norwegian masterpieces is a desirable precondition for a sufficiently thorough response to the imaginative creation of these German artists. And a truly adequate study of the Nordic elements in the poetry of W. H. Auden remains to be made.

What I have been suggesting is that the canon of comparative literary studies is in need of both correction and expansion: correction to take more notice of figures canonized in their own, major, literatures but curiously ignored by the comparatist community and expansion to include the good, and great, figures from the generally ignored smaller literatures.

To these desiderata should be added the necessary expansion of the Western comparatist's canon to include, as something other than novelty, the masterpieces of the non-Western literary communities. And those of our number who possess one or more of the smaller languages, whether through birthright or through eccentric acquisition, would do the entire profession (and its students) a service by drawing attention—insistently and, if need be, rudely—to overlooked merit. To be hopelessly idealistic about the whole thing, one might even suggest that the comparatist whose point of departure is one or more of the major Western literatures might well consider the desirability of acquiring at least one of the smaller Western languages (or one of the larger *or* smaller non-Western lan-

7. For Lie, see Sverre Lyngstad, *Jonas Lie* (Boston: Twayne, 1977).

Frank J. Warnke

guages) and its literature—to combat the provincialism that threatens even comparatists and to help us claim a heritage that is, perhaps, larger and richer than any of us realize. Only thus can we achieve a literary study that is truly comparative; only thus can we begin to accomplish the imperative that Goethe gave us so many years ago—the furthering of *Weltliteratur*.[8]

8. Goethe's conception is expressed in the *Gespräche mit Eckermann*. See François Jost, *Introduction to Comparative Literature* (Indianapolis: Bobbs-Merrill, 1974), 14–20.

[5]

The Foundering of Aesthetics:
Thoughts on the Current State
of Comparative Literature

SAMUEL WEBER

The whole enterprise of aesthetics and art is being challenged today: the distinction between the good, the true, the beautiful, and the useful known to the Greeks but most clearly elaborated by Kant, the whole concept of art as one of the distinct activities of man, as the subject matter of our discipline, is on trial. [. . .] Whatever the merits of these criticisms [. . .] may be [. . .] the abolition of art as a category, seems to me deplorable in its consequences both for art itself and for the study of art and literature.[1]

These words of René Wellek, written some two decades ago, indicate both how little has changed since then, and also: how much. The immediate occasion of Wellek's alarm was an article, "Beyond a Theory of Literature," in which Ihab Hassan had suggested that "perhaps the function of criticism . . . is to attain to the difficult wisdom of perceiving how literature is finally, and only finally, inconsequential." To see how little—and how much—has changed in twenty years, we need only juxtapose the following words of Paul de Man:

The Triumph of Life warns us that nothing, whether deed, word, thought or text, ever happens in relation, positive or negative, to anything that precedes, follows or exists elsewhere, but only as a random event whose power, like the power of death, is due to the randomness of its occurrence. It also warns us why and how these events then have to be reintegrated in a historical and aesthetical system of recuperation that repeats itself regardless of the exposure of its fallacy.[2]

1. René Wellek, "Comparative Literature Today," in his *Discriminations* (New Haven: Yale University Press, 1970), 48–49.
2. "Shelley Disfigured," in de Man, *The Rhetoric of Romanticism* (New York: Columbia University Press, 1984), 69.

Samuel Weber

One would be tempted to see the "history" of Comparative Literature, at least at Yale, as a kind of test case of de Man's assertion: the discontinuity, or gulf, that separates the two quotations, the sequence of Sterling Professors of Comparative Literature at Yale, appear both random and yet also not without a certain consistency. For both Wellek and de Man have done much to transform and to extend the meaning of the discipline of Comparative Literature, and in ways that are not entirely unrelated. Wellek's work has undoubtedly been decisive in broadening "the subject matter of our discipline" so as to include nothing more or less than "the whole concept of art" and of literature. In the *Theory of Literature*, first published in 1949, Wellek and Austin Warren advocated the establishment of departments of Comparative Literature, "which should then become, we said, 'Departments of General and International Literature, or simply Literature'," something that has in the meanwhile become reality at a number of universities, both in North America and in Europe. But this identification of "literature," or more particularly, of the "work of literature," as the authentic object of literary studies, and hence, a fortiori, of "comparative literature," was supported by a constant reference to the "theory" and "history" both of literary criticism, and of literature itself.

In this perspective, the sequence Wellek—de Man does not appear quite as random as de Man's statement, in quite a different context to be sure, seems to suggest. For Wellek, too, sought to problematize a certain notion of literary history as continuity, whether of motifs, of influences, or of national traditions. His effort to extend the scope of Comparative Literature so that it would become a study of literature in general, rather than a comparison of particular cases, has helped make the discipline a focal point for theoretical discussion in the broadest sense.

This development has determined the process by which Comparative Literature has progressively demarcated itself from the study of national literatures. To the extent that it no longer understands itself as a composite product of those literatures, as a study of influences, parallelisms, or divergences of the one upon, with, or from the other, Comparative Literature finds itself confronted by a twofold exigency, which might also be described as something of a double bind. On the one hand, it is obliged to construct or at least to clarify the concept of literature in general; on the other, it must also seek to defend the *specificity* of literature and thus assure its own raison d'être. The solution to this problem, for Wellek, lay in the reconciliation of "both literary history and criticism" within "the wide perspective which only comparative literature can give." And yet, both Wellek's own practice and his theoretical statements make it clear that, in the marriage of criticism and history, the latter calls the shots: "Criticism means a concern for values and qualities, for an understanding of texts which incorporates their historicity and thus requires the history of criticism for such an understanding, and finally, it means an international perspective which envisages a distant ideal of universal literary history and scholarship."[3] It is in this sense, then, that the differences between the programmatic statements of Wellek and de Man, quoted above, reassert their significance. For the one, literary criticism "means a concern for values," which in turn is informed, ultimately, by the ideal, however distant, "of universal literary history." For the other, such a concern appears as the more naïve aspect of the inevitable self-delusion of criticism, an aspect that its reception of Shelley's *The Triumph of Life* exemplifies, particularly in its treatment of the poet's death and the manner in which it interrupts the poem:

For what we have done with the dead Shelley, and with all the other dead bodies that appear in romantic literature [. . .] is simply to bury them, to bury them in their own texts made into epitaphs and monumental graves. They have been made into statues for the benefit of future archeologists "digging in the grounds for the new foundations" of their own monuments. They have been transformed into historical and aesthetic objects. Such monumentalization is by no means necessarily a naive or evasive gesture, and it certainly is not a gesture that anyone can pretend to avoid making. It does not have to be naive, since it does not have to be the repression of a self-threatening knowledge. [. . .] What *would* be naive is to believe that this strategy [. . .] can be a source of value and has to be celebrated or denounced accordingly.[4]

What is naïve in the strategy by which criticism monumentalizes texts—i.e., historicizes and aestheticizes them—is not the strategy as such, which de Man regards as inevitable, but the estimation of itself as a "source of value." This in turn entails repressing "a self-threatening knowledge": knowledge of the ineluctable randomness of mortality.

On the other hand, if it is the randomness of mortality that threatens the self, what does it mean to "know" such randomness? De Man's response is that such knowing is inscribed in a process it cannot comprehend, which we call by the deceptively familiar name of reading: "To read is to understand, to question, to know, to forget, to erase, to deface, to repeat—that is to say, the endless prosopopoeia by which the dead are made to have a face and voice which tells the allegory of their demise and allows us to apostrophize them in our turn."[5] Inasmuch, then, as the discipline of Comparative Literature is defined by the kind of aporetical reading and rewriting that de Man here is both describing and practicing, its status and standing become far more problematic and elusive. De Man,

3. "The Name and Nature of Comparative Literature," ibid., 36.
4. De Man, "Shelley Disfigured," 67–68.
5. Ibid.

no less than Wellek, does not refrain from eliciting judgments of value from the situation he has just delineated. One such judgment—and it is implied in the very notion of reading itself, however value-free it may seem—is that some readings are better than others: "Whenever this belief occurs [the belief that reading can be a source of value]—and it occurs all the time—it leads to a misreading that can and should be discarded. [. . . Such a belief] functions along monotonously predictable lines, by the historicization and the aesthetification of texts, as well as by their use, as in this essay, for the assertion of methodological claims made all the more pious by their denial of piety."[6] To practice "reading as defiguration," in the way de Man's essay reads Shelley's *The Triumph of Life*, would therefore "be to regress from the rigor exhibited by Shelley, which is exemplary precisely because it refuses to be generalized into a system."[7]

Yet is it sufficient to conclude, as de Man's text—and perhaps his work—does, by affirming that the exemplarity of this sort of reading consists precisely in its refusal to generalize itself "into a system"? It is clear enough that de Man's own rhetoric does not hesitate to generalize and, indeed, that some such generalization is inevitable, even if it consists in the refusal of *systematic* generalization. The question that remains, however, is: what might such generalization entail for the practice, or practices, of Comparative Literature? To relate this question to what preceded it, thus both violating and confirming de Man's argument, one might reformulate it as follows: To what extent can, or should, Comparative Literature become general?

The following remarks will attempt to introduce certain elements of a possible response, by returning to the work of a thinker who, for both Wellek and de Man, marks a decisive turn in the emergence of modern criticism. It is to this philosopher that Wellek, in the passage quoted at the beginning, refers when he seeks to describe what he takes to be at stake and in jeopardy today, namely, "the distinction between the good, the true, the beautiful, and the useful known to the Greeks but most clearly elaborated by Kant, the whole concept of art as one of the distinct activities of man." In another essay, published in the same volume, Wellek lauds Kant as "the first philosopher who clearly and definitely established the peculiarity and autonomy of the aesthetic realm. [. . .] The idea of the autonomy of art was not, of course, totally new with Kant [. . .] but in Kant the argument was stated for the first time systematically in a defense of the aesthetic realm against all sides."[8] Kant might have been surprised to hear himself cited in this way and, in particular, to learn that he was

6. Ibid.
7. Ibid., 69.
8. "Kant's Aesthetics and Criticism," *Discriminations*, 124–25.

regarded as the first systematic defender of "the aesthetic realm." He would have doubtless held such a defense to be both vain and superfluous: to defend a realm one must have a realm to defend. Here, as elsewhere, Kant had some rather precise ideas about what constitutes a realm and what does not:

Concepts, insofar as they are related to objects, and independently of whether or not a cognition of these objects is possible, have their field[. . . .] The part of this field, wherein cognition is possible for us, is a territory for these concepts and for the cognitive capacity they require. The part of the territory in which these concepts lay down the law is the realm [*Gebiet, ditio*] of these concepts, and of the corresponding cognitive capacities. [. . .] Our entire cognitive capacity has two realms, that of natural concepts, and that of the concept of freedom.[9]

Although it may seem uncharitable to insist on what might appear to be a rather minor detail, one need only recall that Wellek's entire use of Kant depends precisely upon being able to attribute to him the notion of an aesthetic realm, ruled by its own laws, as autonomous as the discipline Wellek feels obliged to defend "against all sides" if need be. To characterize Kant, as Wellek does in the conclusion of his essay, as "the founder of modern aesthetics," makes sense only in this perspective.[10] And yet, such a perspective ignores what is most obvious in Kant—his refusal to acknowledge aesthetics as a discipline capable of being "founded." To reread "the founder of modern aesthetics" might, on the other hand, allow us to understand a bit better just why the discipline, and indeed the very term *aesthetics*, has never entirely been able to stop foundering and why this foundering might constitute its chance, rather than simply an external danger against which it should or could be defended.

To put Kant back in perspective, then, let us begin by citing the long and well-known note from the beginning of *The Critique of Pure Reason*, where Kant justifies his use of the term *transcendental aesthetic* as the title to the first section of the *Critique*:

The Germans are the only ones who currently use the word *aesthetics* to designate what others call the critique of taste. Underlying this use there is the fallacious hope, first conceived by the excellent analyst Baumgarten, of being able to bring the critical evaluation [*Beurteilung*] of the beautiful under rational principles, and of elevating their rules to a science. This effort, however, is futile. The rules or criteria conceived derive above all from empirical sources and can therefore never serve as a priori laws that our judgment of taste would follow; rather, it is the latter that constitutes the authentic test of the correctness of the former. This is why it is

9. I. Kant, *Kritik der Urteilskraft* (Critique of judgment), Einleitung (Introduction) (Frankfurt a.M.: Suhrkamp, 1981), 81–82 (sec. 2), my translation. Henceforth cited as KU.
10. "Kant's Aesthetics and Criticism," 142.

our judgment of taste should come first; after, comes our finding empirical rules

Samuel Weber

advisable to allow this designation either to perish, and to reserve it for that doctrine which is a true science [. . .] or to share the terminology of speculative philosophy, which takes "aesthetics" partially in a transcendental sense, partially in a psychological one.[11]

Although Kant obviously changed his mind about the relation of the term *aesthetics* to the beautiful, the point on which he never wavered was his conviction that aesthetics could never be or become the name of a systematic area of study. Since "no objective principle of taste [is] possible," as section 34 of the *Critique of Judgment* is titled, the subject matter of criticism can only be the interaction of imagination and understanding "in a given representation," and it can only be studied in two ways. Either it can seek to derive the possibility of such evaluation from the nature of the cognitive faculties involved, in which case Kant allows that it would be "scientific" but also insists that the result would be no different from the *Critique of Judgment* itself; *or* criticism can attempt to elaborate the rules of such interaction by examining "examples," in which case such criticism would be an *art*: "Criticism, as art, seeks merely to apply the [. . .] empirical rules by which taste effectively operates to the manner in which it judges its objects; it criticizes the products of beautiful art, just as the former [i.e., scientific, transcendental criticism] criticizes the ability to judge itself."[12] The tendency to identify criticism and art, we see, is by no means a recent invention. To be sure, what Kant means by art here is something very different from the connotations that term has today. If Wellek seems to have no qualms about equating aesthetics and art, arguing, for instance, that for Kant "art accomplishes a union of the general and the particular, of intuition and thought, of imagination and reason,"[13] *The Critique of Judgment*, by contrast, insists from beginning to end upon the importance of distinguishing art from aesthetics: "Every art presupposes rules, the establishment of which alone makes it possible to construe a product as something that can be called artistic. The concept of beautiful art, however, does not permit the judgment of the beauty of artistic products to be derived from any rule based upon a concept."[14] In a Kantian perspective, then, we should distinguish between three activities: art, aesthetic judgment, and criticism. Of the three, aesthetic judgment and criticism turn out, perhaps surprisingly, to have the least in common. Art, for Kant, is still conceived as a form of technique, that is, as a practice governed by objective rules, concepts, and representations. If beautiful

11. *Kritik der reinen Vernunft* (Critique of pure reason) (Hamburg: Felix Meiner, 1960), 64–65 (sec. 1), my translation.
12. Ibid., 216 (sec. 34).
13. "Kants Aesthetics and Criticism," 130–31.
14. *KU*, 242 (sec. 46).

Criticism and art Investigating examples

art (*schöne Kunst*) is less "theoretical," it is because it is beautiful, not because it is art. So much for the "autonomy" of art, at least for the "founder of modern aesthetics," as Wellek calls him.

But what then of aesthetics? If we mean the practice of aesthetic judgment, aesthetics is at the other extreme: it operates in the absence of predetermined rules or concepts, working by "flair," as it were, and in any case, is inextricably bound to the individual case without any possibility of objective generalization. Aesthetic judgment, in short, is *demonstratively undemonstrative*: forgoing rational argumentation, which in any case would be utterly ineffective (*de gustibus non disputandum est*), it is apodictically deictic, pointing adamantly at the "this" of "this rose is beautiful" and insisting intractably that everyone else share "this" particular pleasure. Aesthetics as a form of judgment, in short, is closer to what Kant calls practical reason than to theoretical cognition.

As to criticism, as we have seen, either it can be transcendental and "scientific," in which case it is limited to demonstrating the general conditions under which particular aesthetic judgments take place, or it can study individual aesthetic judgments themselves, and then it will be more a description of what has occurred than an explanation of why it has happened. Criticism, in this sense, will be an "art" of investigating examples, rather than a scientific theory. The knowledge it yields will be based on empirical concepts, extrapolated from experience and therefore lacking universal validity.

We thus arrive at a curious, if preliminary, conclusion: the very thinker to whom Wellek attributes the foundation of modern aesthetics, conceives aesthetics—whether as aesthetic judgments of taste or as the critical theory and history of taste—to be defined precisely by its lack of foundation, in the transcendental sense at least. All that can be founded, according to Kant, is the impossibility of founding aesthetics as a scientific—that is, as an objective, cognitive—discipline. If this idea constitutes the foundation of modern aesthetics, it is in a very different sense from that envisaged by Wellek, for it founds aesthetics as that which resists and eludes foundation. Let us therefore take a closer look at what might therefore be called, the *foundering of aesthetics* in Kant.

To begin with, it will be useful to recall the context in which aesthetics imposes itself upon Kant. What is almost always emphasized in this respect is the mediating function that Kant attaches to aesthetics, hoping to find in it a bridge spanning the gap separating nature from freedom, theoretical cognition from moral practice, phenomena from things-in-themselves. What, however, is thereby almost always overlooked—in Anglo-American literary theory at least—is what leads Kant to discuss aesthetics in the first place. It is as though the prestige attached to the study of art sufficed to explain why *The Critique of Judgment* should consist essentially of an analysis of *aesthetic* judgments, rather than of any other kind.

It is not entirely surprising that those concerned with either defending or attacking the discipline of aesthetics or of literary studies, whether comparative or general, would readily equate Kant's interest in aesthetic judgment with a concern for the thing itself, whether this thing is understood as art or as the aesthetic realm. Nor is it surprising that these same readers seem hardly bothered by the inconsistency of this view with Kant's insistence that the beauty or sublimity that constitutes the subject matter of aesthetic judgments is to be found in its purest form not in art but in what he calls nature. Everyone knows, after all, that the romantics were nature lovers and that Kant was one of the first romantics.

All the more surprising, however, is the discovery that nature, in the third *Critique*, entails something very different from what we generally understand by the term. In this text, what nature signifies is not anything reassuringly familiar but rather something impenetrably opaque. Nature names the place where judgment encounters its "other," a heterogeneity and diversity which resist subsumption under general concepts. Nature, in short, could be designated as the realm of the particular, if the radically particular could be said to have a realm (which for Kant, no less than for Hegel, it cannot). Nature is thus something very different from what it was in *The Critique of Pure Reason*, which was concerned with it in general; and it is also something quite different from what it will become for Hegel: the exteriorization of the thinking spirit. Nature, then, is that which resists conceptualization, not simply in a provisional fashion to be surmounted dialectically but in an antinomial manner, which no theoretical concept can hope fully to comprehend.

This is the aspect of nature that interests *The Critique of Judgment*. In its efforts to discover the transcendental principle peculiar to judgment as such, the third *Critique* must identify an area where judgment can be examined as such, that is, as something independent of the mere application of existing knowledge. For in the latter case, Kant argues, the very applicability of given knowledge makes such an examination impossible. If we understand judgment, as Kant does, to be the "capacity of thinking the particular as contained under the universal,"[15] the question of whether or not it possesses its own specific principle can only be answered if we are able to observe it so to speak *in statu nascendi*, i.e., in the act of establishing the relationship *of* the particular *to* the universal.

It is for this reason that Kant seeks to distinguish, at the very outset of the third *Critique*, between those forms of judgment in which the particular is already—from the start, as it were—contained under the universal,

15. *KU*, Einleitung, 87 (sec. 4).

The Foundering of Aesthetics

those cases, in short, where "the universal . . . is given" and those where "only the particular [is] given," for which the universal must first be found. It is only where the universal must first be found that judgment can be made the object of a transcendental critique. Otherwise, it functions as an element of theoretical cognition, applying given laws and rules rather than finding its own.

Judgment, therefore, occupies an intermediary position not only between nature and freedom but between the universal and the particular. But that position does not imply either symmetry or reversibility: in cases where the universal is "given," judgment merely applies the law or concept in what Kant calls determinative judgment. In those cases where only the particular is "given" and the universal remains to be found, judgment acts on its own, without the support of existing knowledge. Kant calls this type of judgment reflective, because it represents the effort or the attempt to reach the universal rather than the universal itself. It is reflective because it reflects an effort of judgment itself—Kant calls this the judging subject—rather than a cognition of the object. And yet it is only in its reflective form that judgment can be studied as such, since only here does it attempt to "think" its way, as it were, from the particular *to* the universal.

This "movement to," or more precisely, "toward," the universal is what interests Kant in the third *Critique*. Should judgment actually arrive at its goal, should it produce valid knowledge, the particular would henceforth be contained within the universal, and judgment would have become determinative, cognitive, and part of theoretical thinking. It is only where this movement *toward* the universal is, in a certain sense, perpetuated and held in suspense that judgment reflects its own operation.

Only in this context does the aesthetical realm impose itself on and in *The Critique of Judgment*, for it is above all in those judgments called aesthetical, Kant remarks, where we predicate beauty and sublimity of objects, that the movement of judgment from the particular toward the universal is to be found in a pure form, that is, in a form that cannot be subsumed under an objective concept. In judging things to be beautiful or sublime we do not and cannot know what we are talking about. We speak as though we were talking about objects, in particular and in general, whereas in reality what we are talking about is our ability to represent: the other, the different, the heterogeneous, the unknown, the unnameable. It is this ability to represent that is at stake, and at work, in the critique of aesthetic judgment.

Even to begin anything like a systematic or comprehensive discussion of these stakes would far exceed the limits of this essay. I will therefore limit myself, more or less at random—without being certain just what *random* here or elsewhere might actually mean—to indicating just a few of the issues raised by the Kantian notion of reflective judgment, under which he subsumes aesthetics.

Let me begin with the distinction between reflective and determinative judgment. Kant defines it in such a way as to suggest that it concerns forms of judgment that are mutually exclusive: either the universal is "given" with or before the particular, or it is not, and "only" the latter is "given." The implication is that whereas the particular is always "given"—the data of sensory experience, for instance—the universal is not: it may have to be "found." Aesthetic judgment is occupied with "finding" the universal, which is not given in the particular case. To found aesthetics, in this sense, is to found a certain effort to find the universal. Aesthetical judgment, therefore, finds, but what it finds can never be founded, if by this we mean justified, legitimated, demonstrated, or falsified. The judgments of aesthetics are irrefutable, and hence, devoid of scientific or cognitive value. From the standpoint of science, then, aesthetics founders upon the unfounded and unfoundable character of its findings. What it finds are forms, beautiful or sublime, but never what those forms "contain," their content.

Form and content thus are radically separated in Kant's "aesthetics," so it has been charged,[16] and so it would seem. But such a semblance depends upon a reading of Kant's text which takes its statements at face value without bothering to reflect upon their implications. Let us consider for a moment the distinction between determinative and reflective judgments. Kant writes of them as though they were mutually exclusive: either the universal that corresponds to and contains the particular is given, or it must be found. What, however, does it mean for a universal not to be given? The particular case, as I have suggested, is, for its part, always given, that is, judgment always finds itself confronted with a particular—an object, event, work, etc. In describing a situation in which "the universal (the rule, the principle, the law)" is not given but must be found, Kant does not mean that *no* universals are given but that those which are do not suffice to subsume the particular case at hand. When we say "the rose is beautiful," we appeal to a universal—the notion of rose—in order to identify the particular that we call beautiful. What Kant means, therefore, is that the concept "rose" is not what constitutes the beautiful object but rather something *else*. It is not the fact that no universals are available, therefore, that defines the situation of reflective judgment but rather that those which are available do not suffice to "determine" the particular object (by subsuming it). On the other hand, if they are not sufficient,

16. Most recently by Frank Lentricchia, for instance, who traces what he considers to be the impasse of contemporary "formalist" criticism back to its Kantian "origins." See his *After the New Criticism* (Chicago: University of Chicago Press, 1980).

such universals are nonetheless necessary elements of any judgment, including reflective ones, for without them, no particular could be identified as such, that is, particularized. If it is true, according to Kant, that judgments of beauty are always singular in form; if they necessarily always relate to individual objects or, more precisely, to individualized representations, the process of individualization itself is unthinkable without reference to universals. We do not and cannot say that X is beautiful but rather that *this* X—rose, tulip, work—is beautiful. The generic name, a universal, is required to distinguish the particular, singular case precisely as one that is *not* subsumable under the available universal laws or concepts.

What is not given, then, in reflective judgment is not the "universal" as such, but the particular universal required to subsume the particular case; the particularity of this case, therefore, is defined, not by the absence of universals but by a relationship to those universals that are given but do not suffice to subsume or determine it. To use de Man's terminology, the condition of reflective judgment is a certain "randomness," since what "follows"—the particular case at hand—is not the logical consequence of what preceded it; it cannot be explained, predicted, or derived from what came before. And yet, this "randomness," this discontinuity, is by no means equivalent to a nonrelationship. It defines itself, to begin with at least, precisely in and through this demarcation from its antecedents.

If we extend this argument to the subspecies of reflective judgment constituted by aesthetic judgments of taste, we can see that what Kant designates as form does not stand entirely outside of a relationship to concepts—i.e., to universal laws or rules—but discloses itself, initially at least, by resisting subsumption under those universals. Since the universals themselves will always be determined as a particular set of universals and not universals as such, the resistance of form will be equally particular and hence relatively determinate.

Form, therefore, must be construed not as the sheer absence of objective concepts but as that which resists their subsuming power. Such resistance, to be sure, is not static, does not occur once and for all; it marks both a disruption of given universals—i.e., of established knowledge— and at the same time the *transformation* of this knowledge. Form, then, entails far more than merely the spatial-temporal unity of apprehension brought about by the imagination, acting, Kant suggests, as though it were free and yet in conformity with the understanding. Rather, form implies a process of disruption and of transformation: the categories and concepts available to us fail to grasp, comprehend, and "contain" that which is "given" to us; this gift takes away, as it were, our conceptual framework and so is closer to a process of deformation, or "disfiguration," as de Man calls it, then to one of formation.

Samuel Weber

In this perspective, Kant's analysis of the sublime, which he refers to as a mere appendage of the analytics of the beautiful, is in fact already prescribed by the very notion of reflective and, hence, aesthetic judgment. To judge a particular for which the universal is not and cannot be "given" is to engage in a process of deformation that merely becomes manifest in and as the analytics of the sublime. The "unform" of the sublime is the consequence of the incapacity of the beautiful form to subsume the singular, since any such subsumption would entail as its unifying principle a reference to an objective universal.

In one sense, then, the analytics of the sublime repeat the inconsequentiality of the analytics of the beautiful. Yet such repetition involves more than the recurrence of the same. As *The Analytics of Aesthetic Judgment* proceeds, there is a shift in how the process of representation is construed: the initial but problematic focus upon the individual object ("this rose is beautiful") is increasingly supplanted by a concern with processes that entail conflictual relations of forces. This culminates in the discussion of the dynamical sublime, which begins with the definition of *Macht*, "power," as the "ability [*Vermogen*] to overcome great obstacles."[17]

What changes in and through such repetition, then, is the very status of the text of the third *Critique*: beginning as a theoretical attempt to articulate the transcendental principle of aesthetic judgment, which it tends to portray as midway between a constative and a performative speech act— "this rose is beautiful"—Kant's text is forced increasingly to associate the beautiful form with the object and to seek the alterity of the singular in the nonobjective conflictuality of the sublime. The sublime appears as the heir of what the beautiful form could not accomplish: subsumption of the singular under a nonobjective universal.

The same oscillation can be traced with regard to the role of the imagination. This role, Kant insists, must be construed not as "reproductive, as when it is submitted to the laws of association, but [as] productive and autonomous."[18] And yet this autonomy is in turn not simply free play, since it depends upon the particular, individual object that confronts it, the representation of which, as form, must conform to the demands of the understanding. It is this difficulty of construing form on the one hand as conformity (of imagination and understanding) and on the other as deformation or transformation in regard to existing concepts that causes Kant's argumentation in the third *Critique* to oscillate, continually turning back upon itself, caught, as it were, between the conflicting demands of a *singularity* that defines itself by virtue of its resistance to

17. *KU*, 184 (sec. 28).
18. "General Remark on the First Section of the Analytic," ibid., 160.

conceptualization and the *uniformity* of a form that inevitably entails reference to some sort of concept in order to assure its unity. The result is that *The Critique of Judgment* finds itself increasingly embroiled in what it sets out merely to describe and to analyze. It is progressively drawn into what turns out to be an unresolvable struggle, one in which each new attempt at a solution reveals itself to be merely a displacement of the problem it seeks to resolve.

In the time and space remaining, I can only briefly indicate two aspects of this struggle. The first involves what Kant calls the transcendental principle of reflective judgment: the fact that, confronted with the irreducible heterogeneity and diversity of nature, the judging subject inevitably approaches the singular event *as though* it were the product of an intelligence like its own (i.e., capable of "giving" laws and concepts) and yet precisely unlike ours, since it can give these laws not only in general but also in the particular case that escapes subsumption through the universals available to our understanding.[19] The "assumption" of this other intelligence or intentionality—the problematicity of which I have discussed elsewhere[20]—seems very similar to what de Man refers to as the "historicization and aestheticization" of texts and their "monumentalization." To "assume" what can only be called an authorial intentionality is to posit just the continuity of universal and particular whose absence necessitates reflective judgment. It is, of course, for this very reason that Kant calls this type of judgment reflective, since it reflects its own desire, rather than the object it ostensibly judges.

What Kant's argument suggests is that such a projection is necessary, even if it is highly problematic. We "assume" such an authorial intelligence, although we "know," or should know, that this is "only" an analogy without objective value.

It is this kind of gesture, and "knowledge," that marks the writing of Paul de Man, who, in an interview given toward the end of his life, discussed the "assumption" that underlies much of his interpretive strategy: "I have a tendency to put upon texts an inherent authority[. . . .] I assume, as a working hypothesis (as a working hypothesis, because I know better than that), that the text *knows* in an absolute way what it's doing. I know this is not the case, but it is a necessary working hypothesis."[21]

The argument of the third *Critique* suggests that the apparently untenable position here formulated by de Man is a necessary assumption of

19. *KU*, Einleitung, 88 (sec. 4).
20. S. Weber, "Ambivalence: The Humanities and the Study of Literature," *Diacritics* (Summer 1985), 23.
21. Stefano Rosso, "An Interview with Paul de Man," in Paul de Man, *The Resistance to Theory* (Minneapolis: University of Minnesota Press, 1986), 118.

Samuel Weber

reading wherever texts elude subsumption under given cognitive concepts. If this is the case, however, it is no wonder that readers have rarely dwelled upon this assumption, which makes a most inhospitable "dwelling" in view of the prevailing—although not necessarily accurate—norms of cognition.

One of the consequences of such an assumption would be to raise a question that science has generally sought to avoid: the question of *desire* and its relation to cognitive practice. This brings me to my second and concluding remark. This question is posed at the very beginning of the *Critique of Judgment*, albeit only to be deposed almost immediately, or rather to be relegated to the margins of the text in what turns out to be the longest note of the book. This note is found in the section of the Introduction in which Kant presents the third *Critique* "As a Link Making the Two Parts of Philosophy a Whole." In order for the *Critique of Judgment* to accomplish this task of linking understanding and reason, cognition and freedom, the faculty of judgment must be distinguished from the two other faculties that correspond to the two authentic realms of philosophy, the theoretical and the practical. Since the subjective faculty to which judgment, according to Kant, corresponds, is "pleasure and displeasure," *Lust* and *Unlust*, what must be established is how the pleasure of judgment distinguishes itself both from objective cognition and from what Kant calls the *Begehrungsvermögen*, the faculty of desire.

It is the mention of this term, *Begehrungsvermögen*, that ushers in the note to which I would like to call attention here, however briefly. In it, Kant explains the "use" of attempting to give "transcendental definitions" of concepts in order to demarcate them from others with which they might be confused. In this particular case, Kant is concerned to defend the definition of desire he had formulated in the Preface to *The Critique of Practical Reason*. In view of Kant's conception of the "disinterested" quality of aesthetic pleasure and of the importance of this argument for the whole of the third *Critique*, the subject matter of this note can in no way be considered incidental, despite its marginal place in the text. To establish that the pleasure of aesthetic judgment has nothing to do with desire one must first determine more or less unequivocally just what desire "is."

Kant's note, however, testifies to the fact that his initial attempt to delineate desire has not been an unequivocal success: "I have been criticized for attempting such a [transcendental] definition of the capacity of desire as a capacity to be the cause, through its representations, of the reality of the objects of these representations: because [it was argued] mere *wishes* are also desires, and everyone agrees that wishes alone cannot produce their objects."[22] Kant's response to this objection is that this

22. *KU*, Einleitung, 85 (sec. 3).

incapacity of wishing "to make it so" demonstrates only "that there are also desires through which human beings stand in contradiction with themselves." In short, he acknowledges the content of the observation, but denies that it constitutes an objection to his definition: "Although in such fantastic desires we are aware of the insufficiency of our representations (or of their inadequacy) to be *causes* of their objects, nevertheless the fact remains that the relation of these representations, as cause, and hence the representation of their causality, is contained in each wish, and this is eminently visible when this wish is an affect, namely longing, yearning [*Sehnsucht*]."[23] In responding to the objection, Kant, you will have noticed, has shifted his ground: the indisputable link of desire to a certain unfulfillment; and indeed, the obvious existence of wishes that in some sense presuppose the impossibility of realizing their object, are invoked by Kant as proof of his definition. But this defense is only plausible if we forget that he has silently shifted ground. In *The Critique of Practical Reason* he speaks of desire as the capacity "*to be* the cause of the reality of the objects it represents"; in the *Critique of Judgment* wishes entail not the being but only the representation of such causality. This difference may seem subtle, but it is decisive for the third *Critique* and also perhaps for the modern aesthetics it is said to found. For in the former case, desire can be excluded from the pleasure of aesthetic judgment insofar as it is deemed the cause of the existence of what it represents (as desirable) and thus to be interested, in Kantian terms, in reality. In the redefinition, by contrast, desire is said to entail merely "a relation" (*eine Beziehung*) of representations to their realization; to desire is not "to be" the cause of reality but rather to represent oneself as that cause.

In short, desire is still interested, but this interest is now suspended between representation and reality. Desire is interested not simply in reality or realization but in the capacity of representations to cause reality, to become reality. In this sense, desire contains a reflexive element: it is the representation of the causality of its representations in respect to their objects. It is the "other side" of reflective judgment, which is also suspended between reality and representation, between the reality of the particular, individual event or object and the effort to grasp it in and as a representation.

Kant's first definition of desire is thus not merely a description of desire but a discourse *of* desire. Desire is described as the faculty that "is" what it would like to be: the cause of the reality of its objects. His second, revised

23. Ibid., 86. The beginning of the German sentence here is so equivocal that I will cite the text: "Ob wir uns gleich in solchen phantastischen Begehrungen der Unzulänglichkeit unserer Vorstellungen (oder gar ihrer Untauglichkeit), *Ursache* ihrer Gegenstande zu sein, bewußt sind: so ist doch die Beziehung derselben, als Ursache, mithin die Vorstellung ihrer *Kausalität*, in jedem *Wunsche* enthalten."

version redefines desire, this time as a reflexive mode of representation, representing itself not as object but as the representation of a relation of representations to an object.

In this second sense, desire, far from being excluded, is at work throughout the third *Critique*, or rather, the *Critique of Judgment* can be read as the constant effort to demarcate itself from the desire it begins by excluding but which, as excluded "background," gives the "work" its "form." That form, as I have suggested, is one of increasing oscillation, *beginning* with Kant's effort to describe the "principle" of reflective judgment and reaching a certain culmination in the discussion of the sublime, as a movement of ambivalent attraction and repulsion involving the impossibility of representations to comprehend or contain the objects they seek to represent.

It would require a prolonged and patient rereading of the third *Critique* to explore the consequences of this intrusion of desire into the nondomain of aesthetics. Although such a reading cannot be attempted here, perhaps these all too sketchy remarks will suffice both to suggest its necessity and also to indicate why the generative force of Comparative Literature may not be synonymous with what Wellek and Warren called general literature.

PART TWO

Historical and
International Contexts

A. OWEN ALDRIDGE *Japanese novel, theme*

MARGARET W. FERGUSON *theme of women as readers/writers — treated by them as women*

MELVIN J. FRIEDMAN *Hyman in France*

WOON-PING CHIN HOLADAY *English-making in poetry*

ALDO SCAGLIONE *liberal arts in post Ren, pre enlight France*

PAULINE YU

not mimesis but stimulus response as underlying ethic of Chinese poetry — idea of lyric

[6]

The Japanese Werther of
the Twentieth Century

A. Owen Aldridge

Long before the epoch of structuralist criticism, Western scholarship succeeded in perceiving a geometrical pattern in one of the most common situations in life and literature, that is, the circumstance of two rival lovers competing for the affections of a person of the opposite sex. It is not strange that the love triangle should occupy Japanese as well as Western writers, for it is a classic situation in all levels of life which readily lends itself to the artistic exploitation of tragic or sentimental elements. In the domestic literary triangle, the intervening lover or the spoiler of the marriage may be either a man or a woman. In two of the most famous novels in Western literature, Flaubert's *Madame Bovary* and Tolstoi's *Anna Karenina*, the faithless spouse is a woman. An earlier novel, from the eighteenth century, *Les Liaisons dangereuses* by Choderlos de Laclos, presents a wide variety of combinations, including a man intervening in one marriage and a woman in another and a man and a woman uniting to seduce in turn a married man, a young virgin, and a virtuous married lady. The most notorious of masculine intruders into domestic tranquility in Western fiction is the protagonist of Goethe's *Die Leiden des jungen Werther* (1774).

Early in the twentieth century (1914) Natsume Sōseki, the Japanese writer who first imparted a Western flavor to Japanese fiction, published a psychological novel, *Kokoro*, with many resemblances to *Werther*. *Kokoro* is one of Sōseki's most treasured novels, a classic of Japanese fiction. Its parallels with *Werther* are significant whether or not Sōseki knew the work of his German predecessor, but the evidence is conclusive that he did. Sōseki studied English literature at the University of Tokyo and later received private instruction in London from the Shakespearean scholar, W. J. Craig. His first novel *I Am a Cat* (1905), drawing extensively upon

A. Owen Aldridge

European sources, satirizes both literature and society, particularly character types in middle-class urban Japan. His other works, including *Kokoro*, reveal the more somber side of his vision of life. In general, Sōseki pursued a middle course between the sordidness of naturalism and the idealism of romanticism.

Strangely enough, the twentieth-century work Japanese critics have compared to *Werther* is one with considerably less similarity than *Kokoro*. This is a *Moonflower in Heaven* (1938) by Noichi Nakagawa, one of a group of neosensualists. In this study of resignation and tenacious loyalty, a young man falls in love with a married woman seven years his senior. She admits that the feeling is mutual but insists on preserving her marital fidelity. For twenty years, the lovers meet at rare intervals but exchange no more than a single kiss. The man lives for a time as a hermit on the top of a snowy mountain in order to worship his idol in purity; he promises not to approach her for a period of five years. Then, on the eve of the day when the period of renunciation would have come to an end, she dies. Nakagawa refers in his story not only to Goethe and Marianne's betrayal of Wilhelm Meister but also to Emma Bovary and Anna Karenina. A Western work this novel more closely resembles is the seventeenth-century psychological romance *La Princesse de Clèves* by Mme de Lafayette, the story of a respectable married lady who is suddenly smitten with an overwhelming affection for another man. Although she commits no breach of marital fidelity, the princess is driven by an innate sense of honor to reveal her feelings to her husband. Dramatic tension is created by having the other man overhear the confession while chancing to pass beneath a window. The husband dies in a state of chagrin, and the wife is kept by her notions of honor from accepting the other man as a lover after her husband's death. Although Nakagawa's novel was praised by André Gide for its subtle simplicity and translated into French and English, it is not a masterpiece. It is spoiled by the same kind of saccharine idealism or romantic fantasy that led Mishima to call his *The Sound of Waves* "that joke on the public."[1] *Kokoro* has much more in common with *Werther* not because of any flavor of romanticism or neoromanticism but because of similarities in theme and structure.

Although Sōseki does not refer to Goethe in *Kokoro*, he mentions the character Werther four times in his humorous novel *I Am a Cat*, and he has one of his own characters refer to one of the others in this novel as "Werther of the twentieth century." The latter personage is only lightly sketched, however, in contrast to the protagonist of Kokoro, who is subtly and profoundly delineated and for this reason could indeed be appropriately described as a modern Werther.

---

1. John Nathan, *Mishima: A Biography* (Boston: Little, Brown, 1974), 229.

The Japanese Werther

Both *Werther* and *Kokoro* are short, and their effectiveness depends more upon the atmosphere and characters created by each writer than upon the action or series of events narrated. In a broad sense both novels could be considered as belonging to the genre of epistolary fiction, in which the action is communicated by letters between the various characters, though in the rigorous sense, an epistolary novel must consist of nothing else but letters, and neither *Werther* nor *Kokoro* conforms to this rigid requirement. *Werther* is divided into three major segments, the third of which is titled "The Editor to the Reader." This section consists for the most part of third-person narrative in which occasional passages from letters of the protagonist are quoted. *Kokoro* also contains three parts. The first two are first-person narratives, and the third a single letter, or testament, also in the first person, written by the major character of the preceding two parts. The use of letters does not in itself establish a significant relationship between the two works. Although Goethe was clearly following a major tradition of Western literature, developed earlier in the eighteenth century, in which plot is narrated and characters delineated by means of a series of letters, Sōseki was following a much older and completely independent tradition, the Japanese technique of creating atmosphere by means of entries in a diary. To be sure, the third part of *Kokoro* is not a genuine excerpt from a diary, a record by one person of intimate concerns not designed to be communicated to any other reader, but is instead a statement written by one person intended to be seen by another. Yet it resembles the intimate style of the diary. Sōseki also follows the Japanese tradition of a "suicide letter," designed to absolve the writer of his faults, to leave a moral lesson behind, and to justify his suicide to the world. Sōseki was indubitably aware of the resemblance between the narrative techniques in his long letter and those developed by the masters of the epistolary style in the West. In a sense, he was exploiting both his native Japanese tradition and more modern Western trends.

In the first part of *Kokoro*, the narrator, a young student, describes the development of a relationship with an older man whom he encounters at a bathing beach and later addresses by the conventional term of respect *Sensei*, meaning master. Throughout the novel Sensei is portrayed as neither strong nor weak but somewhere in between. He and his wife seem on the surface to be ideally matched, but the narrator suspects, without knowing why, that some flaw exists in the domestic scene. The narrator conveys the impression that some tragic event has taken place in Sensei's past, something connected with his wife. The fact that she cannot bear children could possibly be interpreted as divine punishment. Sensei himself, although completely normal in his behavior, seems weary of the world; he expects nothing from it and distrusts the whole of humanity.

A. Owen Aldridge

His loneliness and seclusiveness perhaps represent the source of the strong attraction he exerts upon the narrator.

After an extended period of time, during which the narrator acquires a basic knowledge of Sensei's philosophy but is still puzzled by his character, the narrator is called back to his parents' home in a smaller community because of the imminent death of his father. While there, he receives a long communication from Sensei, indicating that the latter has probably already committed suicide and explaining the reasons for taking this action. These reasons date back to the period before his marriage. As a student in Tokyo with an independent income, Sensei had rented two rooms in a home occupied by a widow and her daughter, who enjoyed comfortable financial circumstances. Shortly thereafter Sensei insisted on sharing his quarters with a fellow student who is identified merely by the letter *K*. The student K. had a somewhat morose disposition, professed a philosophy of religious self-denial, and had no income and almost no money. Neither student openly declared himself to the daughter, Ojosan, as interested in marriage, but both were attracted to her and pursued a subdued courtship. Eventually K. confided to Sensei that he was in love, and Sensei, driven by jealousy, asked the widow for her daughter's hand and was accepted. Two days after, Okosan, the mother, revealed this circumstance to K., and he committed suicide. Sensei, nevertheless, proceeded with the marriage, lived an apparently normal life for a number of years, but privately suffered from feelings of guilt brought about by his having failed to attain complete honesty in relations with his student friend. He felt that he had betrayed K. in much the same way that he had earlier been betrayed by an uncle who had cheated him of his inheritance. He thought to himself, "Through cunning, I have won. But as a man, I have lost."[2] These feelings, combined with an inherent distrust of humanity, led him to take his own life.

Goethe's work will be more familiar to Western readers. The title character, Werther, a young amateur painter from a middle-class family, has taken up residence in a picturesque countryside, following his habitual inclination of settling in small cottages in the midst of rural scenery. He makes the acquaintance of a young woman, Charlotte, whose beauty, gentle disposition, and natural charm immediately kindle his emotions. In her late teens, she is the eldest of seven orphaned children and guardian of the other six. Werther describes her as the most lovable of women, an angelic character. He learns that she is engaged to marry a worthy young man of means, Albert, who is at the time on a journey concerned with his inheritance. Werther realizes that he has fallen in love with

2. Natsume Sōseki, *Kokoro*, trans. Edwin McClellan (Tokyo; 1975), 228, hereafter cited parenthetically in the text.

Charlotte and engages in fantasies that she may be persuaded to recipro-
cate his feeling. When Albert returns, Werther, almost against his will,
recognizes that his rival is likable, worthy, and even noble. On his side,
Albert respects Werther for his good sense and apparently does not object
to his interest in Charlotte. Werther then learns that Charlotte's mother
on her deathbed had given her blessing to the projected union of her
daughter and Albert, and he thereupon decides to abandon his own
hopes and pretensions. He accepts a minor diplomatic post in another
district, attempts to distract his thoughts from Charlotte by dissipation,
but eventually starts writing letters to her. Learning through correspondence that Albert has married Charlotte, he is nevertheless unable to
banish her from his mind. He resigns from his diplomatic post and
returns to Charlotte's village in order to be near her but with no other
fixed goal. He encourages himself with the reflection that Albert, for all
his noble qualities, is not the man to satisfy Charlotte's needs, particularly
because he lacks sensibility, a quality that, of course, Werther possesses to
a high degree.

Werther is received hospitably by both Albert and Charlotte and visits
them regularly, even at times when Albert is away from their home. He
begins to drink excessively, and Charlotte reproves him. On one occasion
he is tempted to take her in his arms but solemnly resolves never to give in
to his impulse, calling in the aid of religion to assist him in his resolution.
He becomes morose and irritable and attempts to interfere between
Albert and Charlotte. At the same time he acquires a secret dislike for
Albert, and Albert, for his part, asks his wife to see less of Werther in the
future. After many allusions to suicide throughout his narrative, Werther
finally resolves to take his own life and communicates his decision in a
message to the friend who has received all his other letters. Charlotte,
believing that she is merely one of several causes contributing to Werther's ungovernable passion, informs him that their relations cannot
continue as they have in the past. Werther writes a letter to Charlotte
justifying his intended suicide, which he leaves to be delivered after his
death. When he visits her for a final time, he completely loses control of
his emotions, takes Charlotte in his arms, and kisses her. She orders him
away forever, and he takes his life, but does so in a contented frame of
mind under the belief that Charlotte had been unable to refrain from
returning his kiss. Werther had borrowed Albert's pistols for his suicide,
and Charlotte herself had put them in the hands of the servant who
delivered them to Werther.

In neither novel is it absolutely certain that the man who marries the
coveted woman is actually the one who attains the highest place in her
affections. Werther, the unsuccessful suitor, believes that Charlotte at the
bottom of her heart really prefers him, and Sensei, whose proposal of

A. Owen Aldridge

marriage is accepted, has strong suspicions that his fiancée would have been better satisfied with his rival. This ambiguity is perhaps deliberate on the part of Goethe and Sōseki, and it may be in some measure responsible for the universal appeal of both works.

In the genre of autobiography, the Western world has developed a subclassification known as the confession. Typical and most famous of these in early Christianity is the *Confessions* of Saint Augustine, matched in modern times by Jean-Jacques Rousseau's. Life histories that emphasize the violation of norms of social conduct, in which admission of guilt and desire for expiation are often elements, are considered to be confessional literature, whether the story told is based on actual life or is purely fictional. Both *Werther* and *Kokoro* belong to this genre of fictional confession. Sensei actually compares his self-revelation to the cutting open of his heart, or ritual suicide (129).

Apart from this identity of genre, obvious parallels in the two novels consist in the tripartite division, the triangular relationship of the characters, the use of diaries and letters, and the theme of suicide. *Werther* begins as an amorous triangle in which two men compete for the favors of a woman but changes in the second part to a domestic triangle in which two of the participants are married. The structure of *Kokoro* is somewhat more complex, comprising three triangles, only one of which involves amorous feelings. In the first, the narrator makes the acquaintance of a husband and wife and becomes intimate with the husband without having any effect upon the marriage. In the second, told in flashback, the narrator learns of a close friendship the husband had established with a young man in his youth. The third triangle, also part of the flashback, consists of the conventional amorous situation in which two men are rivals for the hand in marriage of a young girl. In both works, the first section establishes relationships but has relatively little action and moves slowly. The subsequent parts pick up speed as crucial events take place.

In neither *Werther* nor *Kokoro* is the epistolary or diary form essential to the development of character and atmosphere or to the advancing of the plot. In the most sophisticated examples of the epistolary novel, such as *Les Liaisons dangereuses*, the letters written by all the principal characters are not mere narratives of events but constitute in themselves essential elements in the unfolding of the plot. In *Werther* every one of the letters is written by the protagonist, most of them to a single friend, Wilhelm, who performs no other function than to receive the letters, edit them, and write an editorial narrative, confined primarily to the third division of the novel. Here Wilhelm describes in detail scenes and events of which he could logically have had no knowledge. He depicts, for example, a scene in which Werther reads aloud to Charlotte a number of emotional passages from Ossian, a favorite author of the romantics; when she breaks into tears, Werther seizes her hand and also weeps bitterly. In *Kokoro*, Sensei and the narrator carry on a correspondence, but nearly all of it is from the pen of the narrator. He receives in return only two letters, one of which is the long first-person testament that makes up the third section of the book. The element of verisimilitude is greater, nevertheless, in *Kokoro* than in *Werther*.

The prologue to *Werther*, ostensibly written by Werther's confidant and executor, Wilhelm, could be applied with equal success and relevance to *Kokoro*, with merely the substitution of the name Sensei for Werther.

I have carefully collected whatever I have been able to learn of the story of poor Werther, and here present it to you, knowing that you will thank me for it. To his spirit and character you cannot refuse your admiration and love: to his fate you will not deny your tears.

And thou, good soul, who sufferest the same distress as he endured once, draw comfort from his sorrows; and let this little book be thy friend, if, owing to fortune or through thine own fault, thou canst not find a dearer companion.[3]

The only word in the title of Goethe's novel which would not apply equally to Sensei is the adjective young, for his trials and sufferings last from his youth throughout maturity. Other passages in Goethe also remind us of Sōseki. Regarding the relative importance of intellect and feeling, for example, Werther remarks that the prince he serves "values my understanding and talents more highly than my heart, but I am proud of the latter only. It is the sole source of every thing—of our strength, happiness, and misery. All the knowledge I possess everyone else can acquire, but my heart is exclusively my own" (66). This is the sentiment that permeates Sōseki's masterpiece and is reflected in the simple but revealing title *Kokoro*, which is the Japanese word for heart.

There are, of course, certain differences between *Werther* and *Kokoro* which should be indicated before the similarities are further elaborated. The primary difference is that of tone: *Werther* reflects the mood and perspectives of youth; *Kokoro*, those of maturity. Goethe published *Werther* at the age of twenty-five; when *Kokoro* came out, Sōseki was almost twice that age, not an old man but well past his literary apprenticeship and already considered a major author in Japan. Sōseki's subdued tone undoubtedly reflects the solemn and spiritually significant atmosphere in Japan consequent to the death of the Emperor Meiji in 1912, which marked the passing of the era of the "Meiji spirit." In regard to *Werther*, however, the author's personality is more important than the spirit of the age. Highly autobiographical, the novel reflected a traumatic failed court-

---

3. Goethe, *The Sorrows of Young Werther*, trans. William Rose (London, 1929), hereafter cited parenthetically in the text.

A. Owen Aldridge

ship that Goethe had himself recently experienced. Whether or not *Kokoro* is related to any events in Sōseki's life, his attitude is so detached that it conceals any emotion he may have had during the process of composition. One might almost say that everything in *Werther* is exaggerated and overdrawn, and everything in *Kokoro* is understated or underplayed.

Werther was published in 1774 during the earliest years of the European romantic movement, and it remains one of the classics of that turbulent literary period. Goethe's novel was in many ways a prototype of romantic fiction, possessing many of the characteristics the romantics came to prize, including subjectivity, unbridled portrayal of emotional states, distrust of reason, description of natural scenery, association of external nature with human character and behavior, and rapturous outpourings over the cosmos, considered as either sublimely perfect or as somehow the source of incalculable suffering for the writer. There is no comparable period or movement in Japanese literature, however. *Kokoro*, moreover, was published in 1914, well into the twentieth century and more than a century after *Werther*. Yet there existed in Japanese fiction at this time a tendency to present heroes and heroines of such nobility and purity of character that they transcended the world of actuality. This romantic idealism was balanced by the contrary forces of Western naturalism, which often went beyond the bounds of realism to portray the crude, the vulgar, and the ugly. Sōseki pursued a middle path, portraying characters aware of their physical urges but keeping them under control by the application of firm moral principles. The prevailing contemporary technique for the novel in the West was still realism, although the movement had passed its height and was soon to receive strong competition from impressionist and experimental trends epitomized by Proust and Joyce. Many realists believed that human behavior could be explained as the reaction to the forces of biology and chemistry, and they incorporated a deterministic philosophy in their fiction. In *Kokoro* one realist section of Sensei's testament concerns the theory that biological functions have a decisive influence over human conduct. Sensei particularly stresses that "the development—or the destruction—of man's body and mind depends upon external stimuli" and that "unless one sees to it that the intensity of the stimuli is gradually increased, one will find too late that the body, or the mind, has atrophied" (177). The impersonal detachment of Sōseki, which has already been mentioned, is another major aspect of realism.

These differences between *Werther* and *Kokoro* in expression and approach may also be partly explained by variations in culture. *Werther's* exuberance and emotional outpourings are alien to the mainstream of Japanese culture, which even today closely reflects the formality and restraint of Sōseki's style. Sōseki, moreover, believed that traditional Japanese reticence required that the emotional aspects of love be kept subordinate in literary portrayals. In his "Study of Literature," he remarked, "We regard love as important, but at the same time we always try to suppress it. If we fail to suppress it, we feel as if we have lost the dignity of an educated man. If we yield to the clamorous demands of passion, a sense of sin must inevitably follow."[4]

In contrast to Sōseki's principles of reticence and regulation, Goethe early in *Werther* argues that rules, decorum, and the laws of society "destroy the genuine feeling of nature as well as its true expression" (16). He advises the pouring forth of affection in amorous relationships and the expression of individual genius in art rather than the control or repression of either affection or individuality.

Many of the writers of Western romanticism deliberately stressed the therapeutic value of releasing the passions in contrast to the elevation of reason in the preceding period of the Enlightenment, and *Werther* was one of the most powerful works of fiction to portray the unchecked display of the affective emotions. It is not part of Sōseki's purpose in *Kokoro* to establish a contrast between passion and reason. Although in the passage I have already quoted concerning external stimuli he strongly suggests that reason should be the major arbiter in life, elsewhere he reveals strong distrust of the rational faculties. It is significant that both the young Werther, an example of total surrender to the emotions, and Sensei, an exponent of living according to clearly defined philosophical principles, experience a tragic end.

Both novels are rich in symbols or symbolic descriptions, suggesting the dependence of human behavior upon external nature, a commonplace theme in both Western and Japanese literature. In the first of Werther's letters he describes a landscape designed not according to scientific plans but according to the impulses of a sensitive heart. In the next letter, he feels the presence of the Almighty in the tall grass by the side of a trickling stream. The influence of the earth upon him is described as comparable to that of the form of a beautiful mistress upon her lover. Later he describes the wastefulness of nature in providing untold numbers of flowers, few of which mature into fruit (49). He believes that the system, although wasteful, is fundamentally salutary. His own passion for Charlotte may in this way be vindicated as a normal attitude in tune with the procedures of the universe. Midway through the novel the vicar's wife in Charlotte's village orders a clump of walnut trees in the vicarage to be felled, and Werther finds the destruction unpardonable. He uses the

4. Matsuo Sakuko, *Natsume Sōseki as a Critic of English Literature* (Tokyo: Centre for East Asian Cultural Studies, 1975), 114.

incident to reflect upon the perversity of people who are unable to appreciate the few things in life which possess real value. The symbolic meaning of these trees is not apparent until the end of the narrative, when it becomes clear that they represent the enduring quality of Werther's sentiment for Charlotte, which is destroyed by his own death, a direct result of the conventions of society which could not condone his infatuation. Finally, in his farewell letter to Charlotte, he begs her to intercede with her father to allow him to be buried in the corner of the churchyard under two linden trees. These probably represent in his tortured mind the classical story of Baucis and Philemon, a husband and wife whose love for each other was so great that at their death they were changed by one of the gods into intertwining oak and linden trees. Just before the reference to the trees in the vicarage, Goethe introduces a passage fraught with traditional erotic symbolism. Charlotte holds a pet canary to her mouth to peck and kiss her. The bird performs this function with such fervor that Werther speculates on the amount of bliss it must feel. At this point, Charlotte holds the canary toward Werther and allows the bird's beak to move from her mouth to Werther's. The latter, although enjoying the symbolic pleasure of the contact, remarks that the bird may have been disappointed by these kisses and would have preferred solid food. Charlotte immediately replies that the canary does in fact eat out of her mouth and exhibits seed on her lips to prove it. Werther is then capable only of turning his face away, divided between blaming her for exciting his imagination and excusing her because of her heavenly innocence.

The symbols in *Kokoro* are less obvious. Early in the novel Sensei remarks that a ginkgo tree which he passes every month will in the fall become a beautiful mass of yellow leaves. At a later point in the novel, the narrator reflects on a bushy osmanthus tree in Sensei's garden, which has in his mind become inseparable from Sensei's house. He thinks of the beautiful flowers this tree will bear in autumn. Presumably these passages represent the passage of the seasons or the evanescence of beauty. They may also reflect the rosy attitude toward the future which the narrator exhibits as a foil to the pessimism of Sensei, or they may represent the satisfaction both men derive from nature rather than human beings. In a later passage the sound of cicadas inspires melancholy feelings in the narrator. These are fall cicadas which have replaced those of the summer, and they foreshadow not only the change of seasons but also loneliness and the sadness of approaching old age. They inspire the narrator to associate his aging father with Sensei.

Character portrayal is not remarkable in either novel, and it transcends the superficial only in regard to the male characters. The women are almost colorless with the exception of Charlotte, but even she is so incredible in her apparent naïveté that she does not come to life. In *Kokoro* the widowed mother is described as a woman of some understanding, but she reveals no evidence of possessing even social graces out of the ordinary. All her efforts seem to be devoted to showing off her daughter Ojosan to best advantage. The latter is cast in the role of a coquette, but since her speech is rarely recorded, the impression she makes on Sensei is not convincing. Her chief function consists in alternately favoring Sensei or his fellow student with her company and thereby stimulating the rivalry between the two. Ojosan has pretensions to culture, specifically a certain familiarity with music and the art of flower arranging, but she is deficient in the practice of either one. Sensei's fellow student is not even named in the narrative. Everything we know about him is contained in Sensei's testament, in which K. is first portrayed as an interloper, almost a villain. Then, toward the end, the perspective changes and he appears righteous, almost a martyr. The reader is forced to make a complete turn about. K.'s adopted parents think he is studying to be a doctor, but he is secretly preparing for the priesthood. When he finally reveals the truth to his parents, they are furious, and he is obliged to look for work. He possesses Zen and Christian notions of the mortification of the flesh, but at the same time is aware of the more liberal theology of Swedenborg. The suggestion is of a certain intellectual shallowness resembling the limited extent of Ojosan's artistic abilities. The reasons for his suicide are not stated or forcefully suggested, but since it follows almost immediately after Sensei's engagement to Ojosan, we conclude that it may have something to do with hurt pride, disappointment in human nature, or even religious fanaticism.

Next to Sensei, the narrator himself is the character who is most fully delineated. Although all his attention seems to be devoted to Sensei, he reveals considerable information about himself, particularly in relation to other members of his family. He has received a university education but does not place a high value on it. His father is both proud and resentful of his son's graduation. He welcomes the distinction it would give the family but is apprehensive that it might make his son argumentative and vainglorious. The father also emphasizes the economic value of a university degree, while the narrator himself is indifferent, almost antagonistic to the thought of using his academic background as a means of obtaining employment. The narrator is aware that his father's health is so bad that his death is imminent, but his reactions vary from sentimentality to indifference. He returns home when his father lies on his deathbed but frequently allows the image of Sensei to take the place of the image of his father in his thoughts (105). When his father seems on the verge of breathing his very last, after a period in a coma, he receives the letter from Sensei containing the latter's testament, and without giving further thought to his father or his grieving family, he boards a train for Tokyo,

A. Owen Aldridge

reading the testament en route. This behavior can only be interpreted as callous disregard for the feelings of his family—even though it may be motivated by honorable motives of friendship and respect for a revered master. It certainly illustrates the hold a superior mental force may have on another human being. By either Japanese or Western standards, this behavior cannot be accounted honorable except on a symbolic level. The narrator may have felt duty bound to try to save the one father figure in his life after realizing that his real father was all but dead. At this point the narrator and his problems fade completely out of the novel. We are never told anything further of the circumstances of his father's death or its aftermath.

The character of Sensei is the only one that can be said to be fully drawn. Sōseki reveals his character gradually and with great skill, indeed creating in the process a certain suspense. Several Western critics of *Kokoro* have pointed to its resemblance to the detective story in withholding vital information until the denouement. In the first two parts of the novel, Sensei is seen entirely through the narrator's eyes; in the third part, through his own. At the outset we are told that he is cold and aloof and that he rejects intimacy with others because of his low self-opinion. At first his guilt feelings seem to be associated with the inability of his wife to have children, which he ironically describes as a divine punishment (17). He even insists to the narrator that there is guilt in loving another person (26). It is suggested that there is somewhere in the background a frightening tragedy, inseparable from his love for his wife (24). At the very end of the novel we learn that Sensei seeks expiation in caring for his mother-in-law and treating his wife with gentleness; Sensei also confesses that he has acquired a strong feeling of the sinfulness of man, perhaps in some measure because of his encounters with Western religions (241). It is this feeling that has impelled his monthly visits to K.'s grave. His sense of sin is so strong that it borders upon masochism, his desire for punishment so great that he imagines welcoming being flogged, even by a complete stranger (142). Indeed his sense of self-abnegation has become so strong that he has determined to go on living as if he were dead, presumably merely keeping himself alive but obstinately refusing any activities that might afford him pleasure or satisfaction. Although the narrator acquires a tremendous admiration for him, placing him in his regard even above his own father, we are not given a satisfactory explanation of the reasons for this esteem (20). It may be that the narrator is attracted by Sensei's indifference; he expects nothing from life (22) and is "weary of the world" (37). His wife even suspects that she may have been responsible for this weltschmerz (40), but why she feels this way remains an enigma for the reader until the end of the book. Sensei indicates that he would take the place of the narrator's bedridden father if it were possible (46). This self-

abnegation could possibly be interpreted as a sign of generosity or nobility of spirit, but it might equally be nothing more than a reflection of his
melancholy. Despite his air of philosophical detachment, Sensei allows
himself to become excited when he is reminded of disagreeable events in
the past, and he admits that he has a vindictive nature, unable to forget
past injuries and indignities (65). He confesses, moreover, that he had
reacted emotionally when K. informed him of his interest in Ojosan (204).
The mental pain was so great that cold sweat seeped through his clothing.
In the years after K.'s suicide he did everything possible to control his
emotions or at least not to reveal them by outer signs. The heart may have
continued to dominate understanding in his daily life, but the narrator, to
his disappointment, is allowed to see only Sensei's detachment. Sensei's
other major characteristics, his misanthropy and his sense of loneliness,
are also themes in the novel, and I shall treat them subsequently under
these headings.

There are only three characters of importance in *Werther*, as in *Kokoro*.
Ojosan and Charlotte are parallel catalysts inspiring the emotional reactions of the protagonists Sensei and Werther, who are also parallel figures. K. and Albert, however, have little in common, and their roles are
quite different. Albert seems to have almost no personality except a
pervasive nobility or purity, and he serves little function except to represent traditional morality and to provide an obstacle to Werther's infatuation with Charlotte. K., on the other hand, possesses strong, if not necessarily admirable, traits of character, and his personality and his fate
exercise a strong influence upon the protagonist Sensei.

There are two ways of looking at Albert. In one sense, his politeness,
discretion, unruffled demeanor, and general nobility are so unfailing that
he seems almost naïve. Even after his marriage and after Werther's atten-
tions to his wife became obviously physical in intent, Albert deliberately
retires from Charlotte's apartment during Werther's visits. From another
perspective, Albert seems to be intended as a foil to Werther, that is, to
illustrate completely contrary characteristics. Albert is a man of reason or
understanding; Werther a man of passion or heart. This antithesis is most
striking in a conversation in which the two men discuss the role of the
passions in behavior. Albert takes the position that "a man under the
influence of violent passion loses all power of reflection, and is regarded
as intoxicated or insane" (43). As a spokesman for this attitude, Albert has
much in common with Sensei, and those who admire the latter's stern
principles will find much to praise in Albert as well. Werther takes an
opposite position, which he bases on his own experience. He admits that
he has frequently been intoxicated, that his passions have always bor-
dered on extravagance, and then he maintains that "all extraordinary
men, who have accomplished great and astonishing actions have ever

A. Owen Aldridge

been decried by the world as drunken or insane." Werther even associates human passions with the destructive power of nature, describing the universe as a horrible monster that is forever devouring its own offspring (48).

Charlotte, on the surface, possesses many of Albert's noble traits. She is adored by her dying mother and younger brothers and sisters and when necessary assumes the responsibilities of head of the family. If her sentiments and reactions are all genuine, she is exceeded in naïveté only by Albert, but a modern reader, at least, is likely to have some doubts of her ingenuousness. In other words, she behaves very much like a sexual tease. I have already cited the passage in which Charlotte allows a canary to peck her on the tongue and immediately transfers the bird to Werther to perform the identical gesture. She encourages him in other ways. After he has repeatedly asked for a pink ribbon she had worn in her dress on the day of their first meeting, she sends it to him on his birthday (49). Both before and after her marriage, she receives him privately almost on demand. They engage in joint activities, moreover, walking in the country and gathering fruit from the orchard. Ojosan, in contrast, so far as we are told, seems to be indifferent to both Sensei and K. She visits both men in private, but we can only guess at the degree of physical contact, and Sōseki does not suggest there was any. Another major difference between the two women is that Charlotte inspires a passionate ardor in Werther from the moment of their first meeting; whereas Sensei becomes attracted to Ojosan only slowly and then presumably because of contiguity or availability rather than any inherent qualities. For this reason at least, she is a more realistic figure than Charlotte, paradoxically so, for Goethe based Charlotte upon a real woman with whom he had a similar frustrating experience. Presumably he felt that a real woman would seem real to his readers.

Whatever similarities exist between Sensei and Werther depend upon circumstances or events rather than on traits of character. Both men enjoy independent means, enabling them to support a life of idleness, and both are deceived in financial matters, but superficially at least, they are almost indifferent to their losses. Both appreciate the merits of their rival, but subconsciously resent him as well. The two men are possessed of broad culture and are more concerned with art and philosophy than with a career or social position. Although Werther is nominally a Christian, he has no pervading sense of sin or guilt. He is driven entirely by erotic impulses and self-pity. Sensei, to the contrary, has a strong sense of personal guilt and responsibility, but his behavior is also inspired by selfish motives. Neither Sensei nor Werther shows true friendship, charity, or concern for humanity.

Three dominant themes are common to both novels, and these themes are associated, moreover, with the character of the protagonists: misanthropy, loneliness, and suicide. The theme of general disgust with humanity is pervasive in *Kokoro* but subliminal in *Werther*. Sensei early in the novel tells the narrator that he does not trust himself and, therefore, has no confidence in others. Indeed he declares that he distrusts "the whole of humanity." This suspicious attitude has been triggered in his youth by an uncle who had deceived him financially, and he turned it against himself when he realized that he also had been capable of dishonesty and disloyalty in the K. affair (30, 29). Even the narrator at one point shares this ill nature and admits that he wanted to humiliate his idol Sensei. In regard to the relatives who had taken financial advantage of him in the past, Sensei indicates that he has come to hate not only them but the human race in general (66). He later reveals that even as a child he not only suspected the motives of individuals but also doubted the integrity of all human beings (130). Sensei particularly emphasizes the importance of this revelation and indicates that all similar passages of his testament should be read in this light (130). When he left home for the final time, he declares, he was already a misanthrope (149). Sensei recognizes that his hatred of humanity is linked to his own feelings of guilt, and he expresses a desire for punishment. In other words, he is both a masochist and a misanthrope.

The strain of misanthropy is much less obvious in *Werther*, but it is unmistakable. In a commentary on the weather, Werther admits that he has resented the visits of anyone in the neighborhood. He even prefers bad weather so that he can be sure that nobody will intrude upon his privacy (59). Not only does Werther receive no solace from religion, but he uses the language and symbols of Christianity to underscore the wretchedness of human beings. Human destiny, he declares, is to fill up the measure of suffering and to drink the allotted cup of bitterness (77). He predicts that at the moment of death he will be a creature oppressed beyond all resource, deficient and appalled at his lack of strength. On the surface this is not misanthropy at all, but since this intense bitterness is not alleviated by any feelings of pity or concern for the sufferings of others, it certainly approaches universal hatred. In behavior and demeanor, neither Werther nor Sensei reveals any sign of this misanthropic attitude; it is communicated entirely by their own words. In *Werther*, moreover, the pessimistic mood blends strangely with the personal optimism that keeps Werther's hopes of eventually winning Charlotte constantly fresh until the very end.

The associated theme of the evil of solitude is particularly noticeable in *Kokoro*. The narrator is imbued with loneliness, symbolized for him by the sound of summer cicadas. He imagines that sorrow creeps into his heart with the cry of the insects as he remains motionless, thinking of his

A. Owen Aldridge

solitary state (99). But it is Sensei, the protagonist, who is the greater victim. At the outset of the novel he is portrayed as always alone and suffering from weariness of the world (13, 37). What is never made clear, however, is whether Sensei's loneliness is the result of his personal past, particularly the episode with K., or of his disillusionment with modern life as a whole. It is strongly hinted that his financial misfortunes and poor treatment at the hands of his relatives are also possible causes. He specifically declares that "loneliness is the price we have to pay for being born in this modern age, so full of freedom, independence, and our own egotistical selves" (30). The narrator tries to find an explanation for Sensei's pessimism. At first he imagines that it may have been the result of a passionate involvement between Sensei and his wife during their youth which has ended in disappointment, but he quickly abandons this hypothesis. He then concludes that Sensei's misanthropic views are "applied to the modern world in general" (32). There may be a connection between Sensei's feeling of guilt over the episode involving K. and his notion of the pervasive egotism of modern life, but these two strands are never specifically brought together. A similar confusion exists in *Werther*. The protagonist cannot in any sense be considered the victim of loneliness, but his attitudes toward solitude are contradictory. As we have already seen, he once expresses a preference for remaining completely alone rather than dealing with obtrusive visitors, but in another extended passage he deplores the evils of solitude and remarks that he has forced himself to associate constantly with other people and is all the better for it. In his words, "Nothing is more dangerous than solitude. . . . [Because the imagination works in solitude] we continually feel our own imperfections, and fancy we perceive in others the qualities we do not possess" (57).

Both *Werther* and *Kokoro* end with the protagonist taking his own life. Suicide is a major theme, however, not because of this denouement in itself but because the concept of voluntary death is introduced early in each work and continually reappears until the conclusion. There are, of course, different cultural views of suicide at work. In the period of Roman antiquity at least, stoic philosophy not only accepted but extolled suicide, much in the manner of some Japanese traditions. In Western literature in general, however, suicide is considered an unusual event. Many Western tragedies, including those of the great dramatists, incorporate one or more voluntary deaths, and many Western novels, including *Madame Bovary* and *Anna Karenina* end with the protagonist taking his or her own life. There is a difference, however, even in individual novels in which suicide occurs, between the Japanese and the Western treatment. In a Japanese novel several different suicides are likely to be involved, for example, whereas the Western novel is usually limited to one, that of a main character, and it usually provides an important or indispensable part of the action.

The references to suicide leading up to the conclusion of both *Werther* and *Kokoro* are so many that I am able to mention only a few of the most obvious. Soon after Werther meets Charlotte he confides to Wilhelm that sometimes when he is contemplating the deed, he hears her sing and instantly his gloom is dissipated (34). Up to this point, however, no suggestion has been made that his sorrows have reached the point where he would contemplate taking his life, and no adequate reason for his suffering has been give apart from his temperament or disposition. While he is serving in the diplomatic post, he is embarrassed to learn that a group of the nobility had been displeased by his presence at a function his own lower birth did not entitle him to attend. He confides to Wilhelm that in the aftermath he had contemplated plunging a dagger into his breast, and he draws a parallel with a breed of horses that, when heated and exhausted, instinctively use their teeth to open a vein in order to breathe more freely (63). Werther adds that he is frequently tempted to open one of his own veins in order to procure eternal liberty for himself. In the discussion between Albert and Werther on the relative merits of passion and understanding to which we have already referred, Albert condemns suicide as a weakness on the grounds that it is easier to die than to bear a life of misery. Werther angrily repudiates this attitude as "a wretched commonplace" (44). He argues that the question is one not of strength or weakness but of the ability to endure extreme suffering, whether physical or mental. He affirms that it is no more just to call a man who destroys himself a coward than so to label someone who dies from a malignant disease.

In *Kokoro* two suicides are part of the action and are also interwoven with the actual historical suicide of General Nogi. Sensei and the narrator discuss suicide as an example of death brought about by unnatural violence, but neither considers the action a mark of either nobility or cowardice (53). The reader is not prepared for K.'s suicide, nor are his reasons by any means clear although several possible motives present themselves: disappointment at losing the landlady's daughter to a rival, the discrepancy between his ideals and the reality of daily life, or the need to escape from a feeling of loneliness. When Sensei commits suicide he seems to have been driven to the act by a sense of guilt and a nagging desire for punishment (part of his masochism). His wife in jest suggests *Junshi* as the solution to his problem, and he gratefully follows her hint. He delays, nevertheless, until he has completed his confessional narrative, citing as a parallel the painter Watanabe Kazan, who postponed his voluntary death for a week in order to complete a painting. A parallel in more recent times is the novelist Yukio Mishima, who sent the manuscript of his final novel to the publisher on the morning of his suicide.

We are now back once more to the problem we have already discovered in *Kokoro*—whether Sensei's psychological dilemmas are caused by his

A. Owen Aldridge

personal circumstance or by the difficulties of adjusting to the historical period in which he is living. His motives for suicide seem manifold, comprising escape from the complications of modern life, a release from loneliness, a need to expiate his shameful conduct toward K., and generalized expiation or punishment. Werther's motives are far less complex. Having been ordered by Charlotte never to see her again, he has without question lost all hope of possessing her for his own. Superficially he seems to be driven by chagrin or disappointment, but he maintains in his letters that he dies happy. He victoriously affirms that Charlotte actually loves him, and he even speaks of being reunited with her in another world. One cannot very well maintain, therefore, that it is the sorrows of Werther which have driven him to his desperate action. In some ways his suicide, like Sensei's, possesses an element of ritualistic honor; in others it conforms to the opinion of Albert and Sensei that it is the easiest way out.

One may point to a parallel in the status of Charlotte and Albert after the death of Werther and that of Ojosan and Sensei after the death of K. Both couples face the future with the knowledge that their marriage rests to a certain degree upon the failed life of another human being, but both husbands have had good reason to resent that person's obtrusion into their own orbit. In Goethe's words, "We may observe from the character of Werther's correspondence, that he had never affected to conceal his anxious desire to quit this world. He had often discussed the subject with Albert; and, between the latter and Charlotte, it had not unfrequently formed a topic of conversation" (104).

Sensei and Werther, the two protagonists, despite their many differences—almost contrasts—are brought to a common end, suicide. It does not matter that Sensei goes to his grave as a pessimist with no faith in himself or his fellow man and that Werther cherishes the optimistic belief that despite apparent failure he has emerged as a victor over impossible odds. Sensei takes the trouble to write the letter in which he exposes his inner life, and he does so with the faith that his young friend will profit from it and carry on as his successor. In this manner, he completes his function as *sensei*, or teacher.

Somber as Sensei may be, Werther's attitude is even more gloomy, superficially at least, as the title, *The Sorrows of Young Werther*, underscores. It has frequently been said that Goethe's intention was to combat the notion of the eighteenth-century Enlightenment that all is right with the world. Sōseki delivered the same message over a century later, utilizing in the process the literary techniques of realism and neoromanticism. The two novels are related, therefore, by a triangular structure, a dominant emotional crisis in the protagonist, and a somber perspective toward life.

[7]

A Room Not Their Own: Renaissance Women as Readers and Writers

Margaret W. Ferguson

> Sexuality is to feminism what work is to marxism: that which is most one's own, yet most taken away.
>
> —Catherine A. MacKinnon,
> "Feminism, Marxism, Method, and the State:
> An Agenda for Theory"

The title and initial inspiration for this essay came from observing an odd parallel between two women writers' descriptions of an alienating experience of reading what men have had to say about the female sex. The first passage occurs in Virginia Woolf's 1929 essay *A Room of One's Own*; the second comes from Christine de Pizan's *The Book of the City of Ladies*. That text, which was written in 1405, has still never been published in book form in its original language; it was published in English, however, during Henry Tudor's reign, and it has recently been republished in a new English translation, no doubt because the social movement known as women's liberation is having effects on the interconnected institutions of higher education and academic publishing.[1]

For their generous help with earlier versions of this essay, I would like to thank Mary Anne Ferguson, David Kastan, Joseph Loewenstein, and Mary Poovey. I am also grateful for comments from the members of a colloquium on feminist literary theory held at the Johns Hopkins University in November, 1986, at which a draft of this paper was discussed.

1. Pizan's *Livre de la cité des dames* was translated in 1521 by Brian Ansley (*Boke of the Cyte of Ladies*) and was retranslated by Earl Jeffrey Richards (New York: Persea, 1982). Richards's translation, from which quotations in the body of this essay are taken, is based on the manuscript in the British Library, Harley 4431, one of some twenty-five manuscript versions of the text. The only printed version of the French original is based on the Bibliothèque Nationale Fonds français 607 codex and is available, unfortunately, only in the form of a University Microfilms International dissertation (Ann Arbor, Mich.) by Maureen Cheney Curnow, "The *Livre de la cité des dames* of Christine de Pisan: A Critical Edition," 3 vols. (Ph.D. diss., Vanderbilt University, 1975). Curnow's French text, therefore, does not always correspond exactly with Richards's translation.

Margaret W. Ferguson

Virginia Woolf did not know Christine de Pizan's book or that this French contemporary of Joan of Arc, after being widowed at twenty-five, supported herself by her pen; paradoxically, however, Woolf's very ignorance of Pizan's work supports the general argument both authors make about the suppression or misrepresentation of women in the accounts of history constructed by men. As a prelude to their efforts to rewrite such accounts, both authors describe an experience of feeling themselves expropriated by a misogynistic discursive tradition. Woolf recalls a morning when she sat in her room looking at "a blank sheet of paper on which was written, in large letters, Women and Fiction, but no more."[2] Oppressed by that blank page, she leaves the room and goes to the British Museum, a larger but, as it turns out, even more oppressive space. Entering it, she stands for a moment stupefied beneath the vast dome, feeling, she says, as if she "were a thought in the huge bald forehead which is so splendidly encircled by a band of famous names" (26). She goes to the catalogue, and after being nearly overwhelmed by the number of titles to be found under the heading "Woman," she chooses some dozen volumes and spends the next four hours, isolated in her stall, taking notes on them. By lunchtime, she is in a state of listless depression. All the contradictory jottings she has made coalesce suddenly into an image she finds herself sketching on her notebook page, an image of a heavily built, great-jowled, small-eyed man named Professor von X who is writing a monumental work to be titled "The Mental, Moral, and Physical Inferiority of the Female Sex" (31).

Christine de Pizan describes a similar experience in the first section of her *Book of the City of Ladies*. Sitting alone in her study, "surrounded by books on all kinds of subjects" and dwelling on "the weighty opinions of various authors" whom she has studied for a long time, Pizan seeks to relax for a moment by reading something light. "By chance," she writes, "a strange volume came into my hands, not one of my own but one which had been given to me"; seeing that the volume is by one Maltheolus, she smiles, for she had heard that it "discussed respect for women."[3] Before she can read through it to amuse herself, however, her mother calls her to supper, and she is able to return to the book only the next morning. Again seated alone in her study, she peruses Maltheolus's book. The result of her morning's reading is that "a great unhappiness and sadness welled up in my heart, for I detested myself and the entire feminine sex, as though

---

2. Woolf, *A Room of One's Own* (1929; rpt. New York: Harcourt Brace Jovanovich, 1957), 25. All quotations are from this edition.

3. Richards, 3; Curnow, 2:616–17: "Un jour comme je fusse seant en ma celle avironnee de plusieurs volumes de diverses mateires, mon entendement a celle heure aucques travaillié de reccuillir la pesenteur des sentences de divers aucteurs par moy longue piece estudiés. . . . entre mains me vint d'aventure un livre estrange, non mie de mes volumes. . . . [C]elluy parloit bien a la reverence des femmes."

we were monstrosities in nature."[4] The cause of her grief is not just Maltheolus's book, which has turned out to be a bitter satire on women, but the realization that Maltheolus's opinions are shared by philosophers, poets, and orators. "It seems," she laments, "that they all speak from one and the same mouth. They all concur in one conclusion: that the behavior of women is inclined to and full of every vice."[5] Pizan's book-filled study becomes, in this passage, a prisonlike space, an echo chamber in which the woman writer and reader falls into a state of lethargic anomie as she hears a chorus of authoritative male voices anatomizing the faults of her sex:

I was so transfixed by this line of thinking that it seemed as if I were in a stupor. Like a gushing fountain, a series of authorities . . . came to mind, along with their opinions on [the] topic of [woman]. And I finally decided that God formed a vile creature when He made woman, and I wondered how such a worthy artisan could have deigned to make such an abominable work which, from what they say, is the vessel as well as the refuge and abode of every evil and vice.[6]

More than five hundred years separate Christine de Pizan from Virginia Woolf; the parallel between their autobiographical accounts of being textually defined by men serves, first of all, to indicate the historical continuity in certain aspects of the Western sex-gender system.[7] The parallel also serves to ironize the title of Woolf's essay and the well-known proposal to which that title refers: the proposal that a woman must have a room of her own and five hundred pounds a year to be able to write freely. But Woolf herself was unable to write that morning when she went to the British Museum, despite her possession of her own room and the relative

---

4. Richards, 5; Curnow, 2:620: "me sourdi une grant desplaisance et tristesce de couraige en desprisant moy meismes et tout le sexe feminin, si comme ce ce fust monstre en nature."

5. Richards, 4; Curnow, 2:618: "[Il] semble que tous parlent par une meismes bouche et tous accordent une semblable conclusion, determinant les meurs femenins enclins et plains de tous les vices."

6. Richards, 4–5; Curnow, 2:619–20: "En ceste pensee fus tant et si longuement fort fichiee que il sembloit que je fusse si comme personne en etargie, et me venoyent audevant moult grant foyson de autteur[s] ad ce propos que je ramentevoye en moy meismes l'un aprés l'autre, comme se fust une fontaine resurdant. Et en conclusion de tout, je determinoye que ville chose fist Dieux quant il fourma femme, en m'esmerveillant comment si digne ouvri[e]r daigna oncques faire tant abominable ouvrage qui est vaissel, au dit d'iceulx, si comme le retrait et herberge de tous maulx et de tous vices."

7. Feminist anthropologists use the notion of the sex-gender system to describe how a given culture transforms the fact of anatomical sexual difference into a system of ideologically coded meanings and practices. See Gayle Rubin, "The Traffic in Women," in *Toward an Anthropology of Women*, ed. Rayna R. Reiter (New York: Monthly Review Press, 1975), 156–210, esp. 150, 161; and also Louis Montrose, "*A Midsummer Night's Dream* and the Shaping Fantasies of Elizabethan Culture: Gender, Power, Form," in *Rewriting the Renaissance*, ed. Margaret W. Ferguson, Maureen Quilligan, and Nancy Vickers (Chicago: University of Chicago Press, 1986), 70.

economic independence it symbolizes. Although she, like Pizan, belongs to that historically small and privileged group of women who have actually had a room of their own, neither can find therein a refuge from her culture's definitions of her sex; nor can either escape the historically specific socioeconomic arrangements to which the apparently transhistorical discourse of misogyny indirectly points.

My specific focus in this essay is on how certain literate women in the era between 1400 and 1700 both reproduced and contested social constructions of female nature which alienated them not only from their sexuality but also from that special form of productive activity which is writing. The phrase "social constructions" refers to a complex of social processes—some discursive, some not—which work to transform anatomical sex difference into concepts of gender that have distinct effects on one's economic status, one's status in the system of law, and one's general range of behavioral options. Such processes of social construction, and the relations of mutual determination among them, are very difficult to reconstruct analytically; not only do they vary over time and according to geographical region, but the evidence we have for them is inherently problematic, consisting as it does chiefly of coded representations—pictorial and textual—and of highly incomplete documentary material from such sources as court records, parish registers, company account books, and guild ordinances.[8]

In this essay I shall be concerned chiefly with the effects of discursive modes of social construction and, even more narrowly, with the effects, on specific women writers, of patently ideological discourses that construct an "ideal" of womanhood on the (flawed) ground of female nature as it was culturally defined. Those texts that overtly prescribe certain kinds of female behavior make up a small segment of the broader discursive territory that scholars have named the *querelle des femmes* and traced in legal, medical, political, educational, and literary works (among others).

---

8. There is a large and heterogeneous body of scholarship on the changes that occurred in the sex-gender system, particularly the structure of the family, during the early modern era. Lawrence Stone's monumental *The Family, Sex and Marriage in England, 1500–1800* (London: Weidenfield and Nicholson, 1977), which advances, among other theses, the idea that the Protestant Reformation in England saw a "new emphasis on the home and on domestic virtues," has been challenged on many counts but remains central to scholarly debate. For a discussion of Stone's work in the context of recent scholarship, see R. B. Outhwaite, Introduction to his edition of *Marriage and Society: Studies in the Social History of Marriage* (New York: St. Martin's Press, 1981). For bibliographic information on the documentary sources available for studying women in the Renaissance, see Joan Kelly, "Did Women Have a Renaissance?" *Women, History, and Theory: The Essays of Joan Kelly* (Chicago: University of Chicago Press, 1984), 49–50; and the essays on women's work by Merry E. Wiesner and Judith C. Brown, in *Rewriting the Renaissance*, 191–205, 206–24. That volume also contains an extensive bibliography on recent research on women in the early modern era.

Such works were produced and disseminated in many languages from the fifteenth through the seventeenth centuries in Europe.[9] The overtly prescriptive segment of this general discursive territory provides particularly interesting, if always partial, evidence about the economic and institutional structures that shaped women's social being during this period. The evidence is partial not only in the general sense of being incomplete but also in the specific sense of being more incomplete with respect to lower-class women than to women of the middle and upper classes. Although the set of prescriptions about female behavior I shall be examining arguably had significant, if uneven, effects on women of all social classes—on their very access to literacy, for instance—it is clear that the prescriptions were mainly articulated by educated men and aimed at controlling the behavior of relatively privileged women.[10] Such prescriptive texts—comprising, among other things, conduct books, sermons, and educational treatises—were often reprinted and translated into several vernacular languages; this "international" body of textual material worked, Peter Stallybrass has argued, to produce "a normative 'Woman' within the discursive practices of the ruling elite."[11] That woman was defined as a private rather than a public being, and the three "especiall vertues" she was most insistently required to possess—as Robert Greene epitomizes them in his book on "faeminine perfection," *Penelope's Web* (1587)—were chastity, silence, and obedience.[12] Of these three, by far the most important from a socioeconomic point of view was chastity. But for Renaissance women writers, as we shall see, the issue of chastity was intricately bound up with the problem posed by the (ideological) logic that made silence an equivalent of bodily purity. To see how women writers were affected by that strange equation, we need first to examine the "fetish," as Virginia Woolf called it, of female chastity.

"Chastity," Woolf writes in the section of *A Room of One's Own* devoted to the tragic biography of an imagined sixteenth-century woman named Judith Shakespeare, "may be a fetish invented by certain societies for unknown reasons," but she adds, "it had then, it has even now, a religious

9. See, for a useful survey of the discussions of women in various disciplinary discourses, Ian Maclean, *The Renaissance Notion of Woman* (Cambridge: University of Cambridge Press, 1980).

10. See Peter Stallybrass, "Patriarchal Territories: The Body Enclosed," *Rewriting the Renaissance*, 123–42, for a discussion of the prescriptive literature on women in the context of the larger Renaissance discursive project of "behavior modification" analyzed by Norbert Elias in *The History of Manners*, vol. 1 of his *The Civilizing Process*, trans. E. Jephcott (New York: Pantheon, 1978). See also Suzanne W. Hull, *Chaste, Silent & Obedient: English Books for Women, 1475–1640* (San Marino: Huntington Library, 1984).

11. Stallybrass, "Patriarchal Territories," 127. For information on the translation of books addressed to female readers (who were presumed to be unable to read foreign tongues), see Hull, *Chaste, Silent & Obedient*, 25–28 and passim.

12. Greene's treatise is cited in Hull, *Chaste, Silent & Obedient*, 173.

Margaret W. Ferguson

importance in a woman's life, and has so wrapped itself round with nerves and instincts that to cut it free and bring it to the light of day demands courage of the rarest" (51). For Woolf, the fetish of chastity was a major obstacle, perhaps *the* major obstacle, to women's ability to work as writers. Her use of the term *fetish* is fascinating, as is her airy suggestion that this particular one was "invented" for "unknown reasons": she knew, of course, that two major nineteenth-century male theorists had appropriated the notion of the fetish from its original religious context and used it in their elaboration of strong (and strongly incompatible) theories of causation. Freud's concept of the fetishization of the phallus, and Marx's concept of the fetishization of the commodity, are indeed suggestive for an understanding of the problem of female chastity.[13] Marx's concept is directly relevant insofar as female chastity was a commodity bought and sold on the marriage market during the early modern era. Nonetheless, neither psychoanalytic nor Marxist theory has to date done much to explain the fetish of female chastity; nor have many feminist scholars gone deeply into the problem, though it would seem to be a major historical instance of that "alienation" of female sexuality which Catherine MacKinnon takes to be the prime object of feminist theory.[14]

It is, of course, easy enough to provide a functionalist sociological rationale for the requirement of chastity in the era of the transition from feudal to capitalist social formations in the West. As Angeline Goreau remarks in the Introduction to her collection of writing by and about seventeenth-century women, the "insistence" on female chastity had its roots

in concrete economic and social circumstance: under the patriarchal, primogenital inheritance system, the matter of paternity could most emphatically *not* be open to question. . . . As the aristocracy's chief means of consolidating and perpetuating power and wealth was through arranged marriage, the undoubted chastity of daughters was a crucial concern. To be of value on the marriage market, girls had to deliver their maidenheads intact on the appointed day: a deflowered heiress could be disinherited, since her virginity was an indispensable part of her dowry; by its loss, she would deprive her father of the possibility of selling her to a husband whose family line she could perpetuate. Legally, a woman's chastity was considered the property of either her father or her husband.

13. See Freud's essay "Fetishism" (1927), *The Standard Edition of the Complete Psychological Works of Sigmund Freud*, ed. James Strachey et al., 24 vols. (London: Hogarth Press, 1953–74), 21:149–56; and, for a useful discussion of the development of his theory of fetishism and its role as a "proof" of the castration complex, Juliet Mitchell, *Feminism and Psychoanalysis* (New York: Random House, 1975), 84–85. On Marx's theory of fetishism, see *A Dictionary of Marxist Thought*, ed. Tom Bottomore (Cambridge: Harvard University Press, 1983), 165–66.

14. The quotation from MacKinnon's article is from *Feminist Theory: A Critique of Ideology*, ed. Nannerl G. Keohane, Michelle Z. Rosaldo, and Barbara C. Gelpi (Chicago: University of Chicago Press, 1982), 1.

A Room Not Their Own

A father could sue his daughter's seducer for damages; a husband could sue his wife's lover for trespassing on his property—and many did, with success.[15]

This is a succinct and useful account of the socioeconomic rationale for chastity in women of the upper classes and even in the middle classes that were emerging during this era in the countries of Western Europe and in England; still, the economic rationale does not fully explain why chastity was required so insistently of *all* women, irrespective of their class status; nor does it explain the psychological and ideological logic according to which female silence was prescribed as a necessary sign of the (invisible) property of female chastity. It was that chain of signification which Renaissance women had to examine and challenge in order to write at all, much less to publish their words and thereby enter—albeit not with their bodies—that "public" realm in which the property of their chastity was felt to be most at risk.

Let me further set the stage for their drama of transgressive utterance, as it might be called, by citing first some relatively simple and then some more complex examples of how the equation between silence and chastity was formulated in the prescriptive literature of the Renaissance. "It is proper," Francesco Barbaro wrote in "Speech and Silence," a chapter of his treatise *On Wifely Duties* (1417), "that not only the arms but indeed also the speech of women never be made public; for the speech of a noble woman can be no less dangerous than the nakedness of her limbs."[16] If one accepts the logic of this argument, which is bolstered by a citation of Plutarch's *Coniugalia praecepta*, Barbaro's paradoxical conclusion will not be surprising: women, he says, "should believe they have achieved [the] glory of eloquence if they will honor themselves with the outstanding ornament of silence."[17] The formulation is by no means unique to Barbaro. In England over two centuries later, in Richard Braithwait's *The English Gentleman; and the English Gentlewoman*, for instance, a similarly paradoxical formulation appears: "Silence in a woman is a moving rhetoricke, winning most when in words it wooeth least. . . . More shall we see

15. *The Whole Duty of a Woman: Female Writers in Seventeenth-Century England* (Garden City, N.Y.: Doubleday, 1985), 9–10.
16. Quoted from Francesco Barbaro, *On Wifely Duties*, trans. Benjamin G. Kohl, in *The Earthly Republic: Italian Humanists on Government and Society*, ed. Kohl and Ronald G. Witt, with Elizabeth Welles (Philadelphia: University of Pennsylvania Press, 1978), 205. The original, from the chapter "De verbis ac taciturnitate," is in *De re uxoria*, ed. A. Gnesotto, *Atti e memorie della R. Accademia di scienze, lettere ed arti di Padova* (Padova: Tipografia Giovanni Battista Randi, 1915–16), 6–105: "Unde non modo lacertos, sed ne sermones quidem mulieris publicos esse conveniet. Nec enim minus hujusmodi feminae vox quam membrorum nudatio verenda est" (76).
17. Kohl, 206; Gnesotto, 77: "Itaque bene dicendi gloriam se assecuturas existiment, si praecipuo silentii ornamento scipsas honestaverint."

fall into sinne by speech then silence."[18] The sin Braithwait has in mind, we may presume, is lust; as Peter Stallybrass observes, the "connection between speaking and wantonness was common to legal discourse and conduct books. A man who was accused of slandering a woman by calling her a 'whore' might defend himself by claiming that he meant 'whore of her tonge,' not 'whore of her body.' "[19]

So far, the cultural equation between chastity and silence (which defends against the perception of a "natural" equation between female sexual desire and loquacity) seems fairly straightforward. One can grasp easily enough the economic and psychological rationales for construing a woman's closed mouth as a sign for that vaginal closure which secured her as a man's private property. As the English translator of Benedetto Varchi's *Blazon of Gelousie* put it, a wife was a "high-pris'd commoditie of love"; when that "commoditie chanceth to light into some other merchants hands, and that our private Inclosure proveth to be a Common for others, we care no more for it."[20] Shakespeare's Othello articulates a similar sentiment:

> O curse of marriage,
> That we can call these delicate creatures ours,
> And not their appetites. I had rather be a toad
> And live upon the vapor of a dungeon
> Than keep a corner in the thing I love
> For others' uses.[21]

Matters become more complex, however, when we note that some passages in the prescriptive literature valorize silence over "literal" chastity. The English translator of Varchi's *Blazon*, for instance, adds this marginal gloss to his text:

> Maides must be seene, not heard, or selde or never,
> O may I such one wed, if I wed ever.
> A Maide that hath a lewd Tongue in her head,
> Worse than if she were found with a Man in bed.[22]

18. Braithwait's treatise (London, 1641) is cited in Catherine Belsey, *The Subject of Tragedy: Identity and Difference in Renaissance Drama* (London: Methuen, 1985), 179. Belsey also cites (180) John Dod and Robert Cleaver, *A Godly Form of Household Government* (London, 1641): "Now silence is the best ornament of a woman, and therefore the law was given to the man, rather then to the woman, to shew that he should be the teacher, and she the hearer."

19. Stallybrass, "Patriarchal Territories," 126.

20. The quotation is from one of the supplemental notes Richard Tofte added to his translation of Varchi's *Lezione su la Gelosia* (Lyons, 1550). Tofte's translation was published in London in 1615. Stallybrass, "Patriarchal Territories," 128, quotes the passage.

21. Quoted from *The Tragedy of Othello*, ed. Alvin Kernan (New York: NAL, 1863), 102–3 (3.3.267–72).

22. Cited in Stallybrass, "Patriarchal Territories," 126.

A Room Not Their Own

Reversing the hierarchy that underpins the legal defense in which the phrase "whore of her tongue" is a lesser slander than "whore of her body," this little quatrain opens a problematic space between literal and figurative modes of unchastity. That space is opened in a different way by a passage in Richard Allestree's *The Ladies Calling*, which construes female loquacity as a "symptom" not of physical wantonness but rather of an error Allestree seems unable to define except by a series of odd metaphors. "[T]his great indecency of loquacity in women," he writes, is "a symptom of a loose, impotent soul, a kind of incontinence of the mind." Allying loquacity to curiosity (through their shared association with "indecency"), he suggests that a metaphorical form of unchastity somehow *causes* physical defilement: "Every indecent curiosity . . . is a deflowering of the mind, and every the least [*sic*] corruption of them gives some degree of defilement to the body too."[23]

Such formulations open a Pandora's box of questions about how literate Renaissance women themselves perceived the nature of the transgression they committed when they engaged in that *figurative* mode of speech which is writing. Among those questions—which translate and simplify the moments of oblique and often anxious interrogation I shall shortly examine in texts by Renaissance women—are the following: What are the symbolic equivalences between acts of speech and acts of writing? Could not writing be construed in opposition to public speech rather than in conjunction with it?[24] Why—to rephrase that question in words borrowed from an anonymous seventeenth-century "defender of her sex"— do "censuring critics . . . measure [a woman's] tongue by [her] pen, and condemn [her] for a talkative by the length of [her] poem"?[25] Just how like a penis *is* a woman's tongue? Did authoritative classical and early Christian injunctions against women's public speech, especially Saint Paul's oft-invoked stipulations that women should "keep silence in the

---

23. *The Ladies Calling* (London, 1673), quoted in Goreau, *The Whole Duty*, 55, 11.

24. Leonardo Bruni, for instance, insists that rhetoric "in all its forms . . . lies absolutely outside the province of women" but later in the same educational treatise recommends that women study great classical orators in order to learn eloquent expression in their *writing* (*De studiis et litteris*, a letter to Battista da Montefeltro Malatesta written in 1405 and translated in W. H. Woodward, *Vittorino da Feltre and Other Humanist Educators: Essays and Versions* [1897; rpt. ed. E. Rice, New York: Bureau of Publications, Teachers' College, Columbia University, 1963], 126, 128). Writing, for Bruni, appears to be somehow excluded from the category of "rhetoric in all its forms," but as Margaret L. King and Albert Rabil, Jr., observe in their introduction to *Her Immaculate Hand: Selected Works by and about the Woman Humanists of Quattrocento Italy* (Binghamton, N.Y.: Center for Medieval and Early Renaissance Studies, State University of New York at Binghamton, 1983), women were in fact barred from those forms of writing employed by humanists in their capacity as public officials, secretaries, or diplomats.

25. The quotation, from *The Female Advocate: or, An Answer to a Late Satyr Against Pride, Lust and Inconstancy of Woman*, Written by a Lady in Vindication of Her Sex (London, 1686), is in Goreau, 13.

churches" (1 Cor. 14:34) and "learn in silence" (1 Tim. 2:11), clearly
define a woman's act of writing (especially for a "private" audience) as
sinful? And how did the injunction against female public speech apply to
women's relation to an institution unknown to Saint Paul, namely publication through print? Finally, and most generally, in what way does
female utterance—oral, written, or printed—constitute a threat to the
"rights of men"?

That last question underlies the moments of defensive rhetoric that
appear in almost every text I have found by a Renaissance woman. Some
lines by the English poet Anne Finch, Countess of Winchilsea (1667–
1720), can serve to illustrate the gesture whereby women writers defen-
sively anticipated being criticized for writing and warded off such criticism by disclaiming an intent to publish:

> Did I, my lines intend for publick view,
> How many censures, wou'd their faults persue.
>
> . . .
>
> True judges, might condemn their want of witt,
> And all might say, they're by a Woman writt.
> Alas! a woman that attempts the pen,
> Such an intruder on the rights of men,
> Such a presumptuous Creature, is esteem'd
> The fault, can by no virtue be redeem'd.
> They tell us, we mistake our sex and way;
> Good breeding, fassion, dressing, play
> Are the accomplishments we shou'd desire;
> To write, or read, or think, or to enquire
> Wou'd cloud our beauty, and exaust our time,
> And interrupt the Conquests of our prime;
> While the dull mannage, of a servile house
> Is held by some, our outmost art, and use.[26]

The New England poet Anne Bradstreet (1612–1672) makes a similar
gesture of apologetic self-defense in the prologue poem of her book *The
Tenth Muse Lately Sprung Up in America*, a collection of lyrics published—
ostensibly without her consent—in London in 1650:

> I am obnoxious to each carping tongue,
> Who sayes my hand a needle better fits,
> A Poet's Pen all scorne, I should thus wrong;
> For such despite they cast on female wits:

---

26. "The Introduction," *The Poems of Anne, Countess of Winchilsea*, ed. Myra Reynolds
(Chicago: University of Chicago Press, 1913), 4–5.

A Room Not Their Own

If what I doe prove well, it won't advance.
They'l say its stolne, or else, it was by chance.[27]

I cite these passages by Finch and Bradstreet to illustrate the most obvious—but by no means the least interesting—way in which female writers reacted to the cultural ideal of the chaste, silent, and obedient woman. In such passages—and they are legion—we see the author herself at once reproducing the ideological injunction against female public expression and querying it by the very fact that she *is* writing and imagining public criticism, even in works that disclaim her intent to publish.

In what follows I shall examine in somewhat more detail two other modes of reaction on the part of women writers to the ideologeme of female chastity, silence, and obedience.[28] The first and apparently more conservative reaction, most common among highly religious women writers of the upper classes, involves an anxious effort to justify female self-expression, a certain disobedience to (secular) male authority, without challenging the supreme value of female chastity. In the course of interrogating the extension of the rule of chastity to the question of female speech and obedience, however, such women writers often expose significant contradictions in the rule itself, or rather, in its articulation by different social groups for different institutional purposes. In particular, as we shall see, a theological concept of female chastity, an institutional equivalent of which was the Catholic convent, could be deployed against the concepts of chastity required—for secular purposes even when they were formulated as theological ones—by the institution of marriage.

In contrast to those women writers who accepted the value of female chastity even if they did so in ways that had potentially subversive social implications, a few Renaissance women overtly defied social and literary conventions alike by celebrating female erotic passion. Such women generally lived and published in urban centers and were, significantly, *not* nobly born or nobly married. Membership in the landed gentry was seldom conducive to women's writing about their sexual experience.

27. *The Complete Works of Anne Bradstreet*, ed. Jospeh R. McElrath, Jr., and Allen P. Rabb (Boston: Twayne, 1981), 7. See Patricia Crawford, "Women's Published Writing, 1600–1700," in *Women in English Society, 1500–1800*, ed. Mary Prior (London: Methuen, 1985), 214, 218, for information about the circumstances of the publication of Bradstreet's poems; her British publisher, as if acting out the male role of skeptical critic sketched in the Prologue, wondered whether Bradstreet's poems were truly her own work.

28. I adapt the term *ideologeme* from Fredric Jameson, *The Political Unconscious: Narrative as a Socially Symbolic Act* (Ithaca: Cornell University Press, 1981), 87–88 and passim. Jameson uses the term to denote minimal ideological "units" that manifest themselves "either as a pseudoidea—a conceptual or belief system, an abstract value, an opinion or prejudice—or as a protonarrative." Although he deploys the term to analyze conflicts among social classes, it seems equally appropriate for analysing gender conflicts.

Margaret W. Ferguson

To illustrate that mode of justifying female self-expression which proceeds without (overtly) challenging the value of female chastity, I shall adduce two examples, one French and one English: Christine de Pizan and Elizabeth Cary. Throughout her *Livre de la cité des dames* but especially in the concluding section devoted to the stories of female martyrs, Pizan challenges the idea that women's chastity is signified by silence; in so doing, she obliquely justifies her own act of writing as a "legitimate" form of disobedience to that masculine authority represented by secular patriarchal rulers and even by Saint Paul. Her book, which revises Augustine's *City of God*, Boccaccio's *De claris mulieribus*, Ovid's *Metamorphoses*, and (for the saints' lives) Vincent of Beauvais's *Speculum historiale*, among many other sources, both represents and enacts a challenge to Saint Paul's injunction against female teaching. She derives her revisionary authority, within her fictional frame of a dream vision, from the three allegorical virtues, Reason, Rectitude, and Justice, who encourage her to rectify men's false accounts of women by constructing her "city"—both the text itself and the imaginary place it represents.

Many of Christine's portraits of female martyrs stress the heroines' learning and powers of speech. Saint Catherine, for instance, is so well versed in "the various branches of knowledge" that her arguments for the existence of God render a hostile pagan emperor mute with admiration. He summons a host of philosophers to debate with her; in a clear allusion to the gospel account of the boy Christ's questioning of the teachers in the Jerusalem temple (Luke 2:45–48), Catherine confounds the philosophers with her questions, dispelling her interlocutors' initial scorn about being gathered for an occasion so trifling as a debate "with a maiden." Her eloquent reasoning persuades the philosophers to convert to Christianity; the emperor, however—another figure for a male audience—not only remains unpersuaded by Catherine's words but is so enraged by them that he initiates a series of tortures that eventually lead to her death along with those she has converted.[29]

An even more striking and disturbing narrative of powerful but ultimately self-destructive—though soul-saving—female eloquence occurs in the story of Pizan's own patron saint. Her name, a female version of Christ's, assumes special significance in a narrative that not only has strong autobiographical overtones but also works a telling revision on the New Testament. Saint Christine is presented as a beloved daughter of God and also, like the Church and the allegorized bride of the Song of Songs, a spouse of Christ; as the narrative progresses, however, with Christine actively performing miracles and enduring torments, she becomes a sister to or even a female substitute for the Son. The story begins

29. The story is in Richards, 219–22; Curnow, 3:978–82. The French versions of the passages I quote are: "comme grant clergesce et aprise es sciences que elle estoit" (979) and "pour disputer a une pucelle" (979).

with her smashing her cruel earthly father's gold and silver idols; after undergoing horrendous tortures at his hands, she is delivered to a trio of equally cruel male judges. Rescued several times by God, Christ, and various angels, she performs miracles that include walking on water and raising a man from the dead. Her most notable power, however, seems to be her ability to convert thousands of men by what the text calls her "words and signs" (238); and it is no accident that her final torture, which occurs after she has been accused of witchcraft, consists of having her tongue cut out not once but twice—a vivid emblem for the censoring of female speech. The censorship, however, miraculously fails: after the first mutilation, she continues to speak "even better and more clearly than before of divine things and of the one blessed God," who responds to her prayers with the gift of his voice, saying, "Come, Christine, my most beloved and elect daughter, receive the palm and everlasting crown and the reward for your life spent suffering to confess My name" (239). Hearing this voice, the pagan judge orders the executioners to cut Christine's tongue even shorter so she "could not speak to her Christ." The second mutilation provides the martyr with an astonishing instrument of revenge: she "spat this cut off piece of her tongue into the tyrant's face, putting out one of his eyes. She then said to him, speaking as clearly as ever, 'Tyrant, what does it profit you to have my tongue cut out so that it cannot bless God, when my soul will bless Him forever . . . ? And because you did not heed my words, my tongue has blinded you, with good reason'" (239–40). The tongue, through divine authority, acquires the license to disobey and wound those earthly father figures who would censor it. But the price of this license is high, both in Christine's story and in the others Pizan tells of women beheaded, racked, and debreasted for their devotion to God.[30] If, on the one hand, the martyr stories suggest that powerful female speech need *not* be associated with the idea of sexual sin, they suggest, on the other hand, that the female body itself must be sacrificed in exchange both for divine grace and for eloquence.

Elizabeth Cary (1585?–1639) in her play *The Tragedie of Mariam, the Faire Queene of Jewry* (1613) provides another exemplary meditation on the vexed relationship between female speech and chastity. Like Pizan, Cary both interrogates and in some sense affirms the ideological link between unruly female bodies and unruly tongues. Some of the parallels between their ideological positions derive, no doubt, from the fact that

30. Saint Christine's story is in Richards, 234–40; Curnow, 3:1001–10. The originals of the passages cited are: "les parolles et signes" (1006); "mais mieulx que devant et plus cler parloit ades des choses divines et beneyssoit Dieu" (1008); "Viens Christine, ma tres amee et tres elitte fille et reçoy la palme et la couronne pardurable et le guerdon de ta passionable vie en la confession de mon nom" (1008–9); "si luy couppassent si pres que tant ne peust parler a son Crist" (1009); "Tirant, que te vault avoir couppee ma langue adfin que elle ne beneysse Dieu, quant mon esperit a tousjours le beneystra. . . . Et pource que tu ne congnois ma parolle, c'est bien raison que ma langue t'ait aveuglé" (1009).

Margaret W. Ferguson

Cary, the daughter of a wealthy lawyer, secretly converted to Catholicism early in what proved to be an unhappy arranged marriage to a Protestant aristocrat. Scholars surmise that she wrote *Mariam* in the first years of her marriage; her choice of plot, drawn from Josephus's *Jewish Antiquities*, would seem to have autobiographical significance, since the story involved an unhappy interfaith and cross-class marriage between the royal Jewish woman Mariam and the less nobly born and non-Jewish Herod.[31]

Cary's closet drama, the first original play to be published in English by a woman, is indebted not only to *Jewish Antiquities* but also to Mary Sidney's translation of Robert Garnier's *Marc Antoine*; it bears, moreover, such striking resemblances to Shakespeare's *Othello* that it may well have either influenced or been influenced by that tragedy.[32] In the opening scene, Mariam soliloquizes about her ambivalent reactions to the (rumored) death of Herod in Rome. She hates Herod for having murdered her brother and grandfather to acquire the Judean throne through marriage to her, but she also loves him enough to regret his death. Brooding on the parallels between her current situation and that of a male hero, Mark Antony, when he lamented Pompey's death, she recalls, in particular, her prior "public" speech act of criticizing Antony for hypocrisy:

> How oft have I with publike voice run on?
> To censure Rome's last Hero for deceit:
> Because he wept when Pompeis life was gone,
> Yet when he liv'd, hee thought his Name too great.
> [1.1.1–4]

31. Cary's play was written sometime between 1603 and 1612, when it was licensed in the Stationers' Register; it appeared in quarto in 1613, printed by Thomas Creede for Richard Hawkins, and bore on the title page the statement "Written by that learned, vertuous, and truly noble Ladie, E. C." This edition, of which there are several copies extant, was reprinted by the Malone Society (London, 1914) with an introduction by A. C. Dunstan. He explains the evidence for identifying the "E. C." of the title page with that Elizabeth Cary (or Carey or Carew) who was the daughter of Lawrence Tanfield and Elizabeth Symonds and the wife of Sir Henry Cary, after 1620 Viscount of Falkland. My quotations are from Dunstan's edition, which is full of textual problems I have not sought to correct. The autobiographical resonance of the play is obvious when one reads it in conjunction with the *Life* of Cary by one of her daughters, who became a nun in a French convent after her mother's separation from Sir Henry in 1525. The relationship between the *Life* (printed for the first and last time in an edition by Richard Simpson [London: Catholic, 1861]) and the play is discussed by Elaine Beilin, "Elizabeth Cary and *The Tragedy of Mariam*," *Papers on Language and Literature* 16 (Winter 1980), 45–64.

32. The uncertainty about the dating of both *Mariam* and *Othello* makes it impossible to say which influenced which; I could make a plausible case, however, for *some* direct influence. The parallels in plot and phrasing are more extensive than critics have noticed. The topic has indeed hardly been discussed, though it's hinted at by Theobald in his editorial gloss on the famous "base Indian" or "base Iudean" crux (*Othello* 5.2.421); arguing for the latter reading he cites Cary's Herod, who, lamenting his killing of his wife on a false charge of adultery, berates himself for throwing his precious "Jewell" away (5.1.2061). See *A New Variorium Edition of Shakespeare*, ed. Horace Howard Furness (Philadelphia: J. B. Lippincott, 1886), 327.

These lines immediately link the idea of female speech with transgression ("run on") and with punishment ("censure"). The question mark after the first line seems at first glance merely an oddity of seventeenth-century rhetorical punctuation. The question itself, however, voiced at the threshold of the play by a heroine whose "unbridled speech" (3.3.1186) eventually plays a major role in provoking Herod to kill her on the grounds of adultery, is by no means simply rhetorical. Note first that to construe it as a rhetorical question at all, we must "run on" over the line's end and its punctuation. The structure of the verse creates for the reader a slight but significant tension between pausing, to respect the seemingly self-contained formal and semantic unit of the first line, and proceeding, according to the dictates of the syntactic logic that retroactively reveals the first line to have been part of a larger unit. The verse thereby works to fashion a counterpoint between formal and semantic strains: we pause on the theme of running on, we run on to encounter the theme of censure. Deploying the strategy of the "pregnant" beginning most famously used in *Hamlet,* Cary's opening lines epitomize a dilemma of "choice" that recurs, for the heroine and others, throughout the play: the irony is that such choices frequently turn out, in retrospect, not to have involved genuine ethical alternatives at all.

A key example of such a nonchoice is provided at the end of the Chorus's speech in act 3, a speech that builds its ethical injunction for Mariam by articulating an abstract doctrine of wifely duty. The doctrine entails an extraordinarily strict definition of the wife's duty to remain in the private sphere and a correspondingly extreme definition of woman's "publike language" as a phenomenon equivalent to prostitution:

> Tis not enough for one that is a wife
> To keepe her spotles from an act of ill:
> But from suspition she should free her life,
> And bare herself of power as well as will.
> Tis not so glorious for her to be free,
> As by her proper selfe restrain'd to bee.
>
> . . .
>
> That wife her hand against her fame doth reare,
> That more than to her Lord alone will give
> A private word to any second eare,
> And though she may with reputation live.
> Yet though most chast, she doth her glory blot,
> And wounds her honour, though she killes it not.
>
> When to their Husbands they themselves doe bind,
> Doe they not wholy give themselves away?
> Or give they but their body not their mind,
> Reserving that though best, for others pray?

No sure, their thoughts no more can be their owne,
And therefore should to none but one be knowne.

Then she usurpes upon anothers right,
That seeks to be by publike language grac't;
And though her thoughts reflect with purest light,
Her mind if not peculiar [one's private property] is not chast.
For in a wife it is no worse to finde,
A common body, then a common minde.

[3.3.1219–25, 1231–48]

This speech constructs the wife as a property of her husband no less absolutely than does the common law doctrine of coverture, which holds that "the very being or legal existence of the wife is suspended during marriage, or at least is incorporated and consolidated into that of the husband: under whose wing, protection and cover, she performs everything."[33] The play, however, works in many ways to question the logic of this view of the wife, a view that clearly condemns female authorship (figured as an illicit desire for "glory" and "fame"), and by implication denies this very play-text's right to exist.[34]

One way in which the play interrogates the censoring authority of the Chorus is by defining the heroine's dilemma as one not adequately "covered" by the ethical rule the Chorus defines and applies to Mariam in its final stanza:

And every mind though free from thought of ill,
That out of glory seekes a worth to show:
When any's eares but one therewith they fill,
Doth in a fort her purenes overthrow.
Now Mariam had, (but that to this she bent)
Been free from feare, as well as innocent.

[3.3.1249–54]

These lines suggest that Mariam could have avoided her tragic fate had she refrained from speaking her mind to anyone other than her husband.

33. Sir William Blackstone, *Commentaries of the Laws of England, Book the First* (Oxford, 1875), 442, quoted in Mary Poovey, *The Proper Lady and the Woman Writer* (Chicago: University of Chicago Press, 1984), 6–7.

34. Angeline Goreau errs, I think, in taking the speech as a simple expression of Cary's own beliefs and an illustration of "the social hegemony of 'modesty'"; the oversimplification arises in part because Goreau considers the speech out of its dramatic context (she defines it as "a poem") and without reference to Cary's own activity of writing. See her essay "Two English Women in the Seventeenth Century: Notes for an Anatomy of Feminine Desire," in *Western Sexuality: Practice and Precept in Past and Present Times*, ed. Philippe Ariès and André Béjin, trans. Anthony Forster (from the French ed. of 1982) (Oxford: Blackwell, 1985). For a provocative discussion of the speech see Belsey, *The Subject of Tragedy*, 171–75.

A Room Not Their Own

The ethical choice the Chorus presents is between speaking publicly to many or speaking privately to one. But this construction of behavioral options doesn't fit Mariam's situation, since, as subsequent plot developments show, it is partly *because* she speaks freely to her husband that she loses her life. "I cannot frame disguise, nor never taught / My face a looke dissenting from my thought," she says to Herod, refusing to smile when he bids her to (4.3.1407–8). It is, however, not only her habits of speech that bring her downfall. The problem is that she both speaks too freely and refuses to give her body to Herod: she swears an oath, in fact, never to sleep with him again after she learns that he has commanded her death in the event of his own during an absence from Judea (3.3.1136–37).

The problem of her sexual withholding is only indirectly addressed by the Chorus in the form of the (apparently) rhetorical question, "When to their Husbands they themselves doe bind, / Doe they not wholly give themselves away?" By the end of its speech, the Chorus has evidently suppressed altogether the crucial issue of Mariam's denial of Herod's rights to her body, focusing instead, as we have seen, on the condemnation of public speech. The Chorus thus anticipates the logic of Herod's own condemnation of his wife: "Shee's unchaste / Her mouth will ope to any stranger's ear" (4.7.1704–5). This powerful (and anatomically bizarre) way of equating physical and verbal license casts Mariam's fault as one of double excess or openness, whereas what the play actually shows is that her verbal openness is linked to sexual closure. Her behavior entails a property crime in certain ways more threatening to the institution of marriage than adultery because she takes to a logical extreme, and deploys against the husband, the ideal of female chastity. As the Chorus later says, she refuses to "pay" her marriage debt (4.8.1935).

Inadequate as it is to cover the complex facts of Mariam's situation and ethical stance, the Chorus's "law" against female public speech seems nonetheless to be partly upheld by the final unfolding of the plot. Mariam is represented, through a messenger's account of her last moments, as a woman who has finally learned to bridle her tongue. Taunted by her mother on the way to her death, she remains silent, and she dies after saying "some silent prayer" (2026). The wickedness associated with the female tongue is now symbolically transferred from Mariam to her mother, who takes Mariam's place as the object of Herod's censoring wrath: "Why stopt you not her mouth?" Herod asks the messenger, referring to the mother's taunts (1979). We remember that he has just exercised his power to stop Mariam's mouth.

In what seems the play's most complex and ambivalent irony, Herod begins to value Mariam's eloquence immediately after her death. "But what sweet tune did this faire dying Swan / Afford thine ears: tell all, omit no letter," he says (5.1.2008–9). Frantically interrogating the messenger who has witnessed the execution, Herod asks—in words that resemble those of another patriarchal tyrant, King Lear—"Is there no tricke to make her breathe again?" (2031). Again he asks the messenger to repeat every precious word she said. "Oh say, what said she more? each word she sed / Shall be the food whereon my heart is fed" (2111–12).

It is significant that Cary imagines Herod valuing Mariam's eloquence only when her body—site of unresolvable ideological conflicts—has been removed from the scene. "Her body is divided from her head," the messenger announces, and with this detail and others Cary adds to Josephus's narrative, the play constructs Mariam's death as an allegorical Christian martyrdom. It is possible to read the play's ending as a symbolic act of authorial self-punishment that affirms the value of female silence even as—and partly because—it deploys the discourse of theology to exalt Mariam as a martyred innocent. On this interpretation, the play would "repent," as it were, for its various moments of mimetic transgression, its representations of not only Mariam's "unbridled" thoughts and speech but also those of other female characters (most notably Herod's sister Salome) who variously question the logic—and justice—of the patriarchal social system. It is, however, also possible to see in the play's ending—particularly in its handling of the scene of Herod's remorse—a wishful reformation of the tyrannical patriarchal power he represents, a reformation that draws on those currents in contemporary theological and political thought which contested the absolutist doctrine of sovereignty and that "strengthening" of patriarchal ideology which attended it.[35] Mariam's defiance of Herod's authority as both king and husband should be understood, I am suggesting, in the context of those discourses of "minority dissent," both Catholic and Protestant, that justified resisting a sovereign (or a husband) if his commands conflicted with God's. "Your husbands over your soul have no authority and over your bodies but limited power," states a Catholic *Treatise on Christian Renunciation* addressed to women readers.[36] Mariam enunciates a version of the same

35. See Lawrence Stone, "The Reinforcement of Patriarchy," chap. 5 of *The Family, Sex and Marriage*; and Jonathan Goldberg, "Fatherly Authority: The Politics of Stuart Family Images," in *Rewriting the Renaissance*, 3–32. See also his *James I and the Politics of Literature: Jonson, Shakespeare, Donne, and Their Contemporaries* (Baltimore: Johns Hopkins University Press, 1981). If Cary's play does indeed reflect as well as obliquely criticize a form of patriarchal ideology specific to James's reign, then it would be worth exploring the parallels between Mariam and two historical queens whose images posed problems for James: Elizabeth Tudor and Mary Stuart.

36. Quoted by Marie Bowlands, "Recusant Women 1560–1640" in *Women in English Society*, 165. Cf. the radical Protestant Katherine Chidley's statement in her *Justification of the Independent Churches of Christ* (London, 1641): "I pray you tell me what authority the unbeleeving husband hath over the conscience of his beleeving wife. It is true he hath authority over her in bodily and civill respects but not to be a Lord over her conscience" (26). See also Sandra K. Fischer, "Elizabeth Cary and Tyranny," in *Silent But for the Word*, ed. Margaret P. Hannay (Kent: Kent State University Press, 1985), 225–37.

argument: "They can but my life destroy, / My soule is free from adversaries power" (4.8.1843–44).

By drawing on contemporary discourses of minority religious dissent for her characterization of Mariam, Cary, like Christine de Pizan, ambivalently sanctions a certain disobedience and freedom of speech for women; in so doing, both authors implicitly interrogate the idea of woman as the "property" of men: both, indeed, show women taking possession of their bodies insofar as they refuse to give them to (earthly) fathers or husbands. Neither, however, does more than hint, under the sign of an ethical negative, at the possibility that women might take *positive* possession of their sexuality. Pizan, for instance, justifies an illegitimate incestuous love on the grounds that the pagan queen in question, Semiramis, lived at a time when "there was still no written law, and people lived according to the law of Nature, where all people were allowed to do whatever came into their hearts without sinning";[37] and Cary has her wicked character Salome, who plays an Iago-like role in shaping Mariam's downfall, voice the "sinful" idea that women ought to have the same legal privilege men have to divorce an unloved mate when a new passion arises.[38] As if to counter the potentially subversive implications of such textual moments, however, both Pizan and Cary present their readers with images of valued heroines whose freedom to speak is bought, as it were, by their willingness to relinquish their (chaste) bodies to a paternal God.

A more overt challenge to the ideologeme of female chastity, silence, and obedience is offered, as I have suggested, by those few Renaissance women writers who, by virtue of their nonaristocratic birth and unconventional marital status, were unusually well positioned to question social as well as literary rules of proper female behavior. Veronica Franco, a Venetian courtesan; Louise Labé, a Lyonnais ropemaker's daughter whose marriage to another ropemaker did not prevent her from having a notorious love affair (for which, among other things, she was denounced by Calvin); and Aphra Behn, an English woman of obscure birth who, after the early death of her Dutch merchant husband, supported herself by writing poems, novels, and plays (which were produced on the London stage) and by working as a spy. All three of these women wrote and oversaw the publication of love poetry that revised Petrarchan conventions to create a lyric "I" capable of articulating female passion. As Ann R. Jones wryly observes of Labé's *Oeuvres* (1555)—and the comment applies as well to Franco's *Terze rime* (1575)—a female beloved who says, "I am

37. Richards, 40; Curnow, 2:680: "adonc n'estoit point de loy escripte: ains vivoyent les gens a loy de nature, ou il loisoit a chacun sans mesprendre de faire tout ce que le cuer luy apportoit."

38. See Salome's soliloquy in *Mariam*, 1.4, where she eloquently queries the sexual double standard and vows to be the "custome breaker" who will "shewe my Sexe the way to freedomes doore" (319–20).

here; I too burn and freeze; I am yours," offers a disconcerting challenge
to that poetry of "male deprivation and fantasy" generated by Petrarchan
lovers addressing their silent ladies.[39]

I have space here to comment only on Behn, whose poem "The Disappointment" can serve to illustrate the kind of challenge Jones has in mind,
which she and other feminist critics have begun to analyze in the works of
Labé and Franco.[40] Behn is of particular interest to English-speaking
readers because, as Virginia Woolf remarked, she was the first English-
woman to earn her living by her pen (*Room of One's Own*, 67). She remains,
however, relatively unknown except to specialists: a late eighteenth-century edition of the *Dictionary of National Biography* excoriated her as one
whose wit, "having been applied to the purposes of impiety and vice,
ought to be . . . consigned if possible to eternal oblivion."[41] That judgment, which prevailed during most of the eighteenth and nineteenth
centuries, was repeatedly voiced during Behn's own lifetime as well,
provoking her to defend herself in the Preface to her play *The Lucky
Chance* with words that provide an interesting gloss on "The Disappointment." In the prose passage, Behn seeks to vindicate her right to write
after proclaiming her innocence of the "crime" of immoral representation:

All I ask, is the Priviledge for my Masculine Part the Poet in me (if any such you
will allow me) to tread in those successful Paths my Predecessors have so long
thriv'd in, to take those Measures that both the Ancient and Modern Writers have
set me, and by which they have pleas'd the World so well; If I must not, because of
my Sex, have this Freedom, but that you will usurp all to your selves; I lay down
my Quill, and you shall hear no more of me, no not so much as to make Comparisons, because I will be kinder to my Brothers of the Pen than they have been to
a defenceless Woman. . . . I value Fame as much as if I had been born a Hero; and
if you rob me of that, I can retire from the ungrateful world and scorn its fickle
Favours.[42]

What is fascinating about this passage, to my mind, is that Behn here
defines the poet in her as her masculine part and seeks freedom for "him"

39. Jones, "Assimilation with a Difference: Renaissance Women Poets and Literary Influence," *Yale French Studies* 62 (1981), 135–53; quotation 146.

40. See, e.g., Ann Jones, "City Women and Their Audiences: Louise Labé and Veronica
Franco," in *Rewriting the Renaissance*, 299–316; Margaret F. Rosenthal, "Veronica Franco:
The Courtesan as Poet in Sixteenth-Century Venice" (Ph.D. diss., Yale University, 1985);
and François Rigolot, "Gender vs. Sex Difference in Louise Labé's Grammar of Love," in
Rewriting the Renaissance, 287–98.

41. Cited by Fidelis Morgan in her Introduction to Aphra Behn, *The Lucky Chance*, ed.
Morgan (London: Methuen, with the Royal Court Theatre, 1984), n.p. For the history of
Behn's reputation, see Angeline Goreau, *Reconstructing Aphra: A Social Biography of Aphra
Behn* (New York: Dial, 1980).

42. Quoted from *The Works of Aphra Behn*, ed. Montague Summers, 6 vols. (1915; rpt. New
York: Benjamin Blom, 1967), 3:187.

in language that strikingly reproduces—in the form of the wounded threat to "retire" from the world and be silent—her society's vision of a woman's proper role. Behn's prose self-defense thereby presents an ideologically confusing argument for the woman's right to write: she should have this freedom not because she intrinsically merits it but because the masculine part in her deserves to tread those paths that "his" literary predecessors have successfully trod. In her dramatic and poetic practice, however, Behn frequently constructs a less contradictory and theoretically bolder argument for a public female voice. She often does so not by simply following in her male precursors' footsteps but rather by parodically revising conventions, both social and literary, from a perspective explicitly defined as "female." This is what she does in "The Disappointment," a poem that tells the story of a pastoral Petrarchan lover who pursues his bright-eyed lady in the time-honored fashion but finds himself in an embarrassing situation when, after she has properly repulsed his advances, his mistress suddenly steps out of her conventional role and faintingly offers herself to him. The male lover is, however, unable to rise to this surprising occasion:

> In vain th'enraged youth essayed
> To call its fleeting vigor back;
> No motion 'twill from motion take;
> Excesse of love his love betrayed.
> In vain he toils, in vain commands:
> The insensible fell weeping in his hand.

The nymph is understandably confused by this turn of events and, reviving from her amorous trance, reaches out her hand to touch "that fabulous Priapus / That potent God, as poets feign."[43] These lines suggest that the object of Behn's irony is the tradition of male love poetry—which includes the French and English subgenre of the impotence or "Imperfect Enjoyment" poem[44]—as well as the body of the imagined lover. And in stanza 12 Behn comically undermines the tradition by making her nymph reassume the conventional female attributes of disdain and blushing shame. (Her blushes are described with bawdy pseudoanatomical precision as displacement of blood upward from the "hinder place.") In

---

43. "The Disappointment," *Works*, 6:178–82, quotations 180 (stanza 11).

44. There is much irony in the fact that Behn's poem was originally printed as the Earl of Rochester's; his "The Imperfect Enjoyment," like other poems in this subgenre (which goes back to Ovid's *Amores* 3.7), treats impotence from a purely male point of view. On Behn's revisionary strategies in this poem see Judith Kegan Gardiner, "Aphra Behn: Sexuality and Self-respect," *Women's Studies* 7 (1980), 67–78; and for a discussion of the Restoration "obsession" with impotence, see Jay Arnold Levine, "The Dissolution: Donne's Twofold Elegy," *ELH* 28, 4 (Dec. 1961), 303.

Margaret W. Ferguson

this poem, however, the Petrarchan mistress comes to resemble Daphne, who flees Apollo only because she has suffered a disappointment, not because she wishes to resist. Resistance to eros, prescribed for women by the codes of both society and Petrarchan poetry, is subversively relocated in Behn's little drama onto the male body itself.

In the poem's final stanza, an authorial "I" emerges from the third-person narration and deliberately reveals itself as a gendered consciousness:

> The nymph's resentments none but I
> Can well imagine or condole:
> But none can guess Lysander's soul,
> But those who swayed his destiny.

By indicating her special knowledge of and sympathy for the nymph, the author coyly implies that she and her heroine are one. The moment of gendered authorial "unveiling" acquires, however, a special ironic force in Behn's poem, which not only unveils the authorial "I" as a female but also unveils—exposes in a comic light—the very idea and even the anatomical instrument of male potency, biological and literary. Instead of retiring into the silent private space culturally defined as the woman's proper room, Behn writes eloquently and loquaciously of a man's most private secret—and of how a woman felt about it. The poem offers a witty protest against—and an unconventional analysis of—the normative Renaissance definition of woman as chaste, silent, and obedient.

In so doing, Behn's poem dramatizes a danger envisioned by many male humanist writers: the danger is that simply by being exposed to "humayne letters," by acquiring the ability to *read* the works of men, women may well "learn to be subtile and shameless lovers, connying and skilful Writers, of Ditties, Sonnettes, Epigrames, and Ballades." The text I am quoting here is Giovanni Bruto's *La institutione di una fanciulla nata nobilmente*—an educational treatise that paradoxically (but also symptomatically) advises against educating women at all: "It be not mete . . . for a Maiden to be . . . trained up in learning of humayne arts, in whome a vertuous demeanor and honest behaviour, would be a more sightlier ornament than the light or vaine glorie of learning."[45] Bruto's argument exposes a problem that lies at the heart, I think, of the general Renaissance discursive project of prescribing (and proscribing) female behavior, verbal and sexual. The problem has to do with female literacy itself, a phenomenon defined and assessed in highly contradictory ways by male

---

45. Bruto's treatise (Anvers, 1555) was translated by Thomas Salter (London, 1579); the quotation is from Jones, "City Women," 300.

A Room Not Their Own

writers—servants of churches and states—who sought to shape readers' behavior through textual instruction and also to prevent their readers from using their literacy for "unlicensed" ends. One such end was usurping the authority claimed by members of the emerging international group of male intellectuals whose work as diplomats, courtiers, and educators played an important role in the transition from feudal to capitalist societies in the West.[46]

Literacy was a double-edged sword, and it is no accident that humanist and Protestant propaganda for the value of literacy was "pitched less enthusiastically," as David Cressy remarks, toward women than toward men—and more toward men of the upper classes than toward those of the lower ones.[47] It is also no accident that our knowledge of literacy rates in the early modern period is severely hampered by the fact that reading was frequently taught separately from writing. French synodal regulations and episcopal ordinances of the Counter-Reformation Church, for instance, often insist that girls, unlike boys, should be taught not to write but only to read (and to sew).[48]

In the larger study for which the present essay is a preliminary sketch, I hope to explore the ways literacy, in theory and in practice, constituted a major site of social conflict in the early modern period (as it still does today in the relations between "First" and "Third" World countries). Believing that the topic is as important for students of Comparative Literature as it is for our fellow comparatists in the field of social anthropology, I shall define literacy not as a self-evident phenomenon but—in John Guillory's formulation—as a "complex of social facts that corresponds to all of the following questions: who reads? who writes? in what determinate circumstances? for whom?"[49]

Defining literacy thus, I shall hope to come to a better understanding of the role that our precursors in the field of education played in constructing, and representing, that "complex of social facts." Consider, for example, the following passage from Richard Allestree's *The Ladies Calling*

---

46. See Antonio Gramsci, "The Intellectuals," in his *Selections from the Prison Notebooks*, ed. and trans. Quintin Hoare and Geoffrey Nowell Smith (New York: International, 1971), 5–23. See also, on the humanist intellectuals as servants of the emerging nation states of the early modern period, Wlad Godzich, "The Culture of Illiteracy," *Enclitic* 8 (Fall 1984), 27–35.

47. Cressy, *Literacy and the Social Order* (Cambridge: Cambridge University Press, 1980), 128.

48. See François Furet and Jacques Ozouf, *Lire et écrire: L'Alphabétisation des français de Calvin à Jules Ferry*, 2 vols. (Paris: Minuit, 1977), 1:85. Cf. also Margaret Spufford, *Small Books and Pleasant Histories: Popular Fiction and Its Readership in Seventeenth-Century England* (Cambridge: Cambridge University Press, 1981), 25.

49. Guillory, "Canonical and Non-canonical: A Critique of the Current Debate" forthcoming in *ELH*.

Margaret W. Ferguson

(1675), which translates, for new social purposes, Saint Paul's injunctions against female public speech. The apostle, Allestree remarks,

expressly enjoins women *to keep silence in the church*, where he affirms that it is a shame for them to speak: and though this seems only restrained to the ecclesiastical assemblies, yet even so it reaches home to the gifted women of our own age, who take upon them to be teachers. . . . But besides this, he has a more indefinite prescription of silence to women . . . *Let women learn in silence.* . . . The Apostle seems to ground the phrase, not only on the inferiority of the woman in regard of the creation and the first sin, but also on the presumption that they needed instruction, towards which silence has always been reckoned an indispensible qualification. . . . If some women of our age think they have outgone that novice state the Apostle supposes, and want no teaching, I must crave leave to believe, they want that very first principle which should set them to learn, i.e. their knowledge of their own ignorance.[50]

Allestree's passage shows that men as well as women were able to interrogate the logic of extending Paul's ancient prescription to a different historical situation. The passage also suggests, however, that the male writer's investment in his own authority helps shape a new rationale for the necessity of female silence. Recognizing that the Pauline prescription is "indefinite," Allestree at once opens and seeks to close that Pandora's box of questions to which I referred earlier in this essay—a box in which truths that seem self-evident are revealed, if only intermittently and partially, to be (one hopes) contestable.

50. Quoted from Goreau, *The Whole Duty*, 55.

[8]

William Styron's Fiction and Essays:
A Franco-American Perspective

MELVIN J. FRIEDMAN

William Styron, more nearly than any American of his generation, has glided gracefully from the classical harmonies and mythical constructs of modernism to the disruptions of postmodernism. He has never needed to resort to the extreme visual tricks and displacements of certain of his contemporaries who have effectively tied typesetters' hands up in knots. His central text has always been *Madame Bovary* while theirs seems to have been *Tristram Shandy*.[1] Styron's masters have been the modernists who looked back over their shoulders at Flaubert, he who virtually invented the notion of a *roman pur* but also believed he would eventually write *un livre sur rien*. Among these modernists are Joyce, Faulkner, Fitzgerald, Hemingway, and their younger contemporary Robert Penn Warren. In an accustomed nostalgic moment in *This Quiet Dust* (1982), Styron looks back: "And so the other fathers also quickly took possession. I was soon reading *Gatsby* and *In Our Time* and *The Sound and the Fury* with the same devouring pleasure that I had read Wolfe. Perhaps I sound too idolatrous. . . . Yet I think it has to be conceded that rarely has such a group of literary figures had the impact that these writers have had upon their immediate descendants and successors."[2]

1. Styron remarked in his 1954 *Paris Review* interview, "As for Flaubert, *Madame Bovary* is one of the few novels that moves me in every way, not only in its style, but in its total communicability, like the effect of good poetry." He echoes this somewhat in a 1968 exchange with Charles Monaghan: "Also Flaubert. He brought me back to the idea of discipline. It's dangerous for any American not to read Flaubert." In a 1981 interview with Michel Braudeau he commented, "I write little and slowly, like my master Flaubert." For these interviews see *Conversations with William Styron*, ed. James L. W. West III (Jackson: University Press of Mississippi, 1985), 12, 111, 254. All subsequent references will be to this edition.

2. *This Quiet Dust* (New York: Random House, 1982), 90. All subsequent references will be to this edition.

Melvin J. Friedman

Styron, from the very beginning, seems to have been haunted by these modernist "fathers." *The Sound and the Fury* especially, as many critics have pointed out, appears to have informed his earliest moments as a novelist. Indeed, one might from our present vantage point suggest that *The Sound and the Fury* stands in somewhat the same relationship to *Lie Down in Darkness* (1951) as *The Odyssey* to Joyce's *Ulysses*, offering something of a literary scaffolding. Just as Joyce seemed to be acknowledging his lifelong fondness for Homer in using the *Odyssey* parallel so Styron was staking out his position as a southern writer, Faulkner style, when he persistently and creatively echoed *The Sound and the Fury*. It is not too farfetched, I think, to suggest that Styron perhaps uses something akin to T. S. Eliot's "mythical method" in structuring *Lie Down in Darkness*. Warren, another southerner, offered him the inspiration for the second-person beginning for this first novel, which clearly echoes the opening pages of *All the King's Men*.

Even in the more modest *The Long March* (1952) Styron was able, in typically modernist fashion, to enlarge the possibilities of a forced march in the Marine Corps, turning it into a tragedy of almost Sophoclean dimensions. He managed this transformation partly through language: "In the morbid, comfortless light they were like classical Greek masks, made of chrome or tin, reflecting an almost theatrical disharmony."[3] The ordinary, the quotidian, is expanded by symbol, myth, and a dexterous use of poetic allusion.

The scaffolding is more elaborate in *Set This House on Fire* (1960). The theme of the ingenuous American abroad, which we associate with Mark Twain, Henry James, and F. Scott Fitzgerald, is one of several myths explored. Vibrations from *The Great Gatsby* are sounded intermittently through Styron's text, especially toward the end; and the rhythms of *Gatsby* are unmistakably caught, for example, in: "Then you know, something as I sat there—something about the dawn made me think of America and how the light would come up slowly over the eastern coast, miles and miles of it, the Atlantic, and the inlets and bays and slow tideland rivers with houses on the shore."[4] The modernist poet E. E. Cummings also makes a fugitive appearance: "He moved through dooms of love, through griefs of joy, in his lonely seeking" (13). There is even something of a running parallel between Styron's text and Sophocles' *Oedipus at Colonus*, which has been explained persuasively by another novelist who has skillfully cultivated myth, Michel Butor.[5] Butor, interestingly, was

3. *The Long March* (New York: Modern Library, 1956), 29.
4. *Set This House on Fire* (New York: Random House, 1960), 499. All subsequent references will be to this edition.
5. See Butor's preface, "Oedipus Americanus," to William Styron, *La Proie des flammes*, trans. Maurice-Edgar Coindreau (Paris: Gallimard, 1962), vii–xx.

one of the prime movers among the *nouveaux romanciers* who brought a new kind of experimental novel to France in the 1950s, which seemed to anticipate the postmodernists' acknowledgment of the limits of the technological world and its dehumanizing consequences. Styron, in *Set This House on Fire*, appears tuned into the *nouveau roman*'s playful irreverence in the matter of myth and its mocking circumventions of detective fiction formulas. Thus the "hero" of *Set This House on Fire*, Cass Kinsolving, is allowed to go free and to return to his native South Carolina even though the Italian policeman Luigi knows that he is the murderer of Mason Flagg. This is the kind of mock-detective twist we find in such *nouveaux romans* as Butor's *L'Emploi du temps*, Alain Robbe-Grillet's *Les Gommes*, or Nathalie Sarraute's *Portrait d'un inconnu*—which Sartre called (in his preface to the Sarraute novel) "un anti-roman qui se lit comme un roman policier."[6]

Set This House on Fire might be said to suggest the first signs of Styron's passage from modernist to postmodernist strategies; there is something mildly disruptive about its texture, its concerns, and its accommodation to French modes.

Styron calls *The Confessions of Nat Turner* (1967) "a meditation on history" in his Author's Note. The novel mingles poetic statement with historical fact as it offers the same sort of hybrid assemblage we find in works like Norman Mailer's *The Armies of the Night* and *The Executioner's Song*, E. L. Doctorow's *Ragtime* and *World's Fair*, and Truman Capote's *In Cold Blood* and *Handcarved Coffins*. Styron enters the frame of his novel by giving his own voice to Nat Turner—the language of the confessions is Styron's language, rather than that of an antebellum slave. Biblical quotations occur frequently in Nat's almost hymnal confession; they are drawn especially from the prophetic books of the Old Testament, including Ezekiel, Isaiah, and Jeremiah. These act as almost subtexts as they enlarge the contours of Styron's novel.

Sophie's Choice (1979) removes all the masks and disguises. The novel is narrated by a young Virginian named Stingo who is hard at work on his first novel. In a sense it is a modernist *Künstlerroman* of the order of Joyce's *A Portrait of the Artist as a Young Man*, but it is also something much more contemporary. Stingo writing his first novel is quite transparently William Styron undergoing his own literary baptism with *Lie Down in Darkness*. There is no need for subterfuges of any sort as memoir and fiction intersect. This kind of thing happens regularly among our most experimental contemporaries, such as Ronald Sukenick and Raymond Feder-

6. See my "William Styron and the *Nouveau Roman*," in Melvin J. Friedman, *William Styron*, Popular Writers Series, 3 (Bowling Green: Bowling Green University Popular Press, 1974), 19–36, 64–66.

Melvin J. Friedman

man; witness, for example, *Up*, in which Ronald Sukenick, the narrator and main character in his own novel, has as his principal concern the fleshing out of a novel. *Sophie's Choice* clearly does not resort to the visual displacements, typographical eccentricities, and verbal dislocations of *Up*, but it has in common with it certain self-reflexive qualities.

Sophie's Choice departs from modernist practice as it avoids the tidily finished and mythically ordered frame in favor of a more open-ended design. This large-limbed, oversized novel contains within it the seeds of the urban Jewish novel with a nod to Philip Roth and Saul Bellow, the southern novel with frequent glances back at Faulkner, Wolfe, and Warren, even the European novel of ideas of the kind written by Thomas Mann and André Malraux. Woven into the literary text is an elaborate series of documentary subtexts. Styron, for example, culls from the formidable literature on the Holocaust bits and pieces from such works as George Steiner's *Language and Silence*, Richard Rubenstein's *The Cunning of History*, and Rudolf Höss's *Commandant of Auschwitz*—which he reinforces at every turn with his own elegant commentary.

The disruptions of *Sophie's Choice* are quite different from those that Jerome Klinkowitz finds in the work of contemporaries like Federman, Sukenick, Donald Barthelme, Kurt Vonnegut, Jr., and Gilbert Sorrentino. Terms frequently used about these writers—metafictional, surfictional, self-apparent, for example—simply do not apply to Styron.[7] Yet perhaps we are wrong in thinking that the postmodern necessarily brings with it an irreverence and uncertainty about everything in the fictional text, even the function of print on the page. It seems clear to me that Styron has gracefully negotiated the passage from modern to postmodern in the years separating *Lie Down in Darkness* from *Sophie's Choice*, without having recourse to anything visually or verbally unsettling. He has gone the way of *Madame Bovary* rather than that of *Tristram Shandy*, even though he has never aspired to write *un livre sur rien*.

When Styron gathered his essays together and published them as *This Quiet Dust* in 1982, he was doing something quite different from most of his American contemporaries, possibly excepting William Gass. First of all, he was allowing his raw nerves to be placed on display. Second, he was worrying aloud about the literary, political, and social dilemmas of the age; he was confronting major issues like the military, the Holocaust, and the uncomfortable heritage of slavery in the spirit of *engagement* so familiar to the French nurtured on Sartre, Malraux, and Camus.

This Quiet Dust acts as a kind of vade mecum for the later fiction. It is something of a parallel text that must constantly be measured against *The*

---

7. See Klinkowitz, *Literary Disruptions: The Making of a Post-Contemporary American Fiction* (Urbana: University of Illinois Press, 1975).

Confessions of Nat Turner and *Sophie's Choice*. Tzvetan Todorov has always thought of the critical act as being the *double nécessaire* of literature. It is precisely that with *This Quiet Dust*.

Styron gave his voice to Nat Turner, his voice and his growing pains as a writer to Stingo. But he still maintains a distance, surely less marked in *Sophie's Choice* than in *The Confessions of Nat Turner*. The distance disappears in *This Quiet Dust*.

Styron makes clear in his "Note to the Reader" that "I have applied as much effort and have spent as much time, proportionately, to the crafting of these pieces as I have to the writing of the novels" (ix). This is no idle claim. And Styron is not content merely to have his essays of almost three decades stand, with their assured and settled knowledge, as they were originally written; he appends introductions and aftermaths to guarantee that things are up-to-date and to indicate any changes in his own thinking. There is something *en train de se faire* about this enterprise. *This Quiet Dust* has a restlessness and urgency about it which is never noticeable in the neatly packaged collection of essays that is usual from the poet or novelist who doesn't take the critical function very seriously.

Mallarmé imagined Hamlet in a famous image, which Joyce quoted in the library scene of *Ulysses*, "Il se promène, lisant au livre de lui-même." Indeed, one has the feeling with *This Quiet Dust* that Styron is reading the book of himself. As he does so, he uncovers things about himself, his social and political commitments, his career as a novelist. His admiration for other writers—Faulkner, Warren, Fitzgerald, James Jones, and Peter Matthiessen—is expressed with selfless genuineness and conviction. His outrage at Lieutenant William Calley, General Douglas MacArthur, and Mayor Richard Daley brings forth an anger tempered only by words. Calley's position, for example, is elegantly clarified when he is said to possess "rancid ordinariness," "stupefying vacuity" and "dwarfishness of spirit." We now better understand his disquieting presence on the depressing Vietnam scene. Styron's fondness for the Virginia landscape of his childhood and young manhood, his being quite taken with the seductions of the Nile River, which "I could go back to . . . over and over, as if in mysterious return homeward, or in quest for some ancestral memory" (171), reveals a passion about place quite as poignant as his intense feelings about people. *This Quiet Dust* abounds in this rhetoric of commitment and responsibility. It ends up offering us codes of artistic, moral, and political behavior.

The first section of the book, titled "South," may be said to have an intertextual relationship with *The Confessions of Nat Turner*. In an introduction to this section Styron enters in propria persona, examines once again the controversy that surrounded his novel, and offers a reasoned response to the blacks and historians who undermined his enterprise.

Melvin J. Friedman

"South" is an important document in its own right but gains appreciably when read as a parallel text, as a kind of self-reflexive gloss to *The Confessions of Nat Turner*.

This Quiet Dust is even more essentially involved with *Sophie's Choice*. In his latest novel Styron flashes back and forth through fact and fable, blurring, in postmodern fashion, all distinctions between the two, on the way to diagnosing the ills of a sustained period in Western history which accommodated such atrocities as American Negro slavery and the Nazi concentration camps. *This Quiet Dust* is the ideal companion volume to this novel. So many of the elements from one reappear in the other. Thus Richard Rubenstein's *The Cunning of History*, for example, is discussed in both texts. Robert Penn Warren's *All the King's Men* as source for the opening pages of *Lie Down in Darkness* is mentioned both in the novel and in the collection of essays. The following sentence from Styron's testimonial to Philip Rahv in *This Quiet Dust* should have a familiar ring to readers of *Sophie's Choice*: "At a time when the urban Jewish sensibility was coming to the forefront of American literature, and the writing of Southerners was no longer the dominant mode, I shared some of the resentment of my fellow WASPs over what we construed as the self-conscious chauvinism often displayed by the literary establishment" (265). Nathan Landau says something of the same thing to Stingo in *Sophie's Choice*, when he suggests that "Jewish writing is going to be the important force in American literature in the coming years," replacing the southern.[8] The list of overlappings is appreciably longer than this, but the point of the vital kinship between *This Quiet Dust* and *Sophie's Choice* should be apparent.

The blurring of genres is very obvious in a novel like *Sophie's Choice*; bits and pieces of essay, diary notation, and letter intrude to break up the text and impede the development of the story line. Narrative, history, literary and social criticism all come together to unsettle readers who are accustomed to a greater purity of novelistic design. Such readers might also be disturbed by the irregularities of *This Quiet Dust*, which would fail to satisfy their expectations about essay collections by practicing novelists. Styron enters into conspiratorial relationships with the people and places he encounters, as he thrusts his *self* into the essayistic frame. He seems never able to resist the confessional urgency even when commenting on a book about Vietnam experiences, Philip Caputo's *A Rumor of War*: "[I] experienced from the very first page a chilling sense of déjà vu. Caputo and I are separated in age by approximately twenty years, and although there were significant differences in his Marine Corps experience and

---

8.*Sophie's Choice* (New York: Random House, 1979), 116. All subsequent references will be to this edition.

mine, I was struck immediately by the similarities" (209). And Styron goes on with this counterpointing for several sentences. This is his accustomed mode of discourse throughout *This Quiet Dust*: his self-awareness is enlarged by his confrontations with people, places, and books. He himself is the constant subject of this collection. It sounds almost as if he were heeding Montaigne's famous warning to his reader before the beginning of the first chapter of his *Essais*: "Ainsi, lecteur, je suis moy-mesmes la matiere de mon livre." Styron seems to be following in a line of memoirists of decidedly French temperament which began with Montaigne and carried through Saint-Simon and Rousseau down to Sartre and Malraux. *This Quiet Dust* belongs in this company as it also functions as a parallel text for his later, more postmodern fiction.

The key to all this may be found in what might be called Styron's French temperament and sensibility. Almost two decades ago the Sorbonne professor Roger Asselineau ended an influential essay on *The Long March* by speaking of its author as "un écrivain plus français qu'américain."[9] French commentators have been making similar judgments about American writers for more than a hundred years. Indeed, the French have performed miracles of taste and interpretation when they have flirted with a succession of American poets and novelists since Edgar Allan Poe. Many of these writers, interestingly enough, were either southerners by birth or spent a considerable period in the American South. The case of the Virginian Edgar Poe is legendary in the annals of literary appropriation. The French took him over, gave him (according to Patrick Quinn) a "French face," and transformed him into a symbolist poet. Baudelaire's translations of Poe strike one as superior to the originals. Mallarmé and Valéry treated him with a special awe and reverence (quite unlike his contemporary Emerson, who spoke of him disparagingly as "the jingle man," or Sidney Lanier who later remarked that Poe "did not *know* enough to be a great poet"). The hermetic words and cadences of Mallarmé's "Le Tombeau d'Edgar Poe" suggest it all. Debussy struggled for long periods, mostly in vain, to musicalize Poe. For the symbolist generation Poe became a kind of *umbilicus mundi*.

The instance of William Faulkner is, if possible, even more astounding. He was taken up vigorously and creatively by the French—even before he was properly appreciated in his native country—and, on occasion, was deemed to be an inheritor of the French symbolists. Maurice-Edgar Coin-

---

9. Roger Asselineau, "En suivant *La Marche de nuit*," in *Configuration critique de William Styron*, ed. Melvin J. Friedman and August J. Nigro (Paris: Lettres Modernes, 1967), 82. It is interesting to note that this French collection of criticism on Styron is the first volume devoted to an assessment of his work in any language. A fine essay in the area I am covering here is Harry Levin, "*France-Amérique*: The Transatlantic Refraction," *Comparative Literature Studies* 1 (1964), 87–92.

dreau introduced the Mississippi writer into France with a perceptive essay in the June 1931 *Nouvelle Revue Française* and went on to translate into French *As I Lay Dying* (1934), *Light in August* (1935), and *The Sound and the Fury* (1938). By this time, three influential French writers had begun to take up his cause, Valery Larbaud, André Malraux, and Jean-Paul Sartre.

Two of Faulkner's contemporaries who lived for a time in the South and fared well at the hands of the French were John Dos Passos and Sherwood Anderson. Indeed, Coindreau's first gesture as a translator of American fiction was to turn Dos Passos's *Manhattan Transfer* into French in 1928.

He continued his good offices into our own time with translations of such southern contemporaries as Truman Capote, Flannery O'Connor, Reynolds Price, and Styron himself. While Coindreau did not officially introduce Styron's work into France—Michel Arnaud's 1953 translation of *Lie Down in Darkness* as *Un Lit de ténèbres* deserves this distinction—he firmly established Styron's reputation with sensitive renderings of *Set This House on Fire* (*La Proie des flammes*, 1962) and *The Confessions of Nat Turner* (*Les Confessions de Nat Turner*, 1969). The canon is now virtually complete in French, thanks to Michel Mohrt's translation of *The Long March* (*La Marche de nuit*, 1963) and Maurice Rambaud's of *Sophie's Choice* (*Le Choix de Sophie*, 1981) and *This Quiet Dust* (*Cette paisible poussière*, 1985).[10] Styron enjoys the privileged status of seeing his novels and his collection of essays all appear under the revered imprint of Gallimard, France's most prestigious publisher. In a 1983 interview with Stephen Lewis, Styron remarked about *Sophie's Choice*: "In France, it is now the best-known serious American novel since World War Two." In a May 1984 conversation with Georgann Eubanks, he reported that French sales of the novel were running "over 200,000 copies."[11]

Thus Styron seems to have joined Poe and Faulkner in the enviable process of being Gallicized. As early as 1968 he was able to comment unhesitatingly to a French interviewer: "La France est mon foyer spirituel. De tous les pays du monde qui ont traduit mes livres, je crois que c'est ici qu'on les comprend le mieux."[12] He has reaffirmed this position many times since then, as France has increasingly become his adopted homeland. *Lie Down in Darkness* was placed on the *Agrégation* list in En-

10. Rambaud, a professor at Paris IX, appeared on a panel with Styron at the Third International Conference on Translation at Barnard College of Columbia University on November 9, 1985.

11. *Conversations with Styron*, 263, 270.

12. Thérèse de Saint Phalle, "William Styron: 'En U.R.S.S.—et en France—je suis chez moi,'" *Le Figaro Littéraire* (28 October–3 November 1968), 26. See Valarie M. Arms, "William Styron in France," in *Critical Essays on William Styron*, ed. Arthur D. Casciato and James L. W. West III (Boston: G. K. Hall, 1982), 306–15.

glish literature for the academic year 1973–1974, thus making the author's first novel required reading for all English *agrégatifs*. Styron followed this honor with a tour of four French universities, Nantes, Paris, Rennes, and Bordeaux, in April 1974.[13] When I lectured at Nantes myself, two years after Styron's visit, my hosts seemed more eager to discuss *Lie Down in Darkness* than the subject of my visit, Flannery O'Connor's *A Good Man Is Hard to Find*, which had then joined the *Agrégation* list.

In 1981 Styron attended the inauguration of François Mitterrand at Mitterrand's invitation and described the event in an article revealingly titled "A Leader Who Prefers Writers to Politicians" in the July 26 *Boston Globe*. The following year he wrote the introduction to Mitterrand's *The Wheat and the Chaff* (the English translation of two of his books), in which, among other things, he commended the French leader's sensitivity to writers, several of whom, including Julio Cortázar and Milan Kundera, were granted French citizenship immediately following the inauguration. This was an accommodation, duly noted by Styron, which would never be possible in Reagan's America.

Some day there will be the need for a book with the title *William Styron en France*, which would be something of a companion volume to S. D. Woodworth's 1959 study, *William Faulkner en France*. But for the moment it might be more profitable to consider in what ways Styron's work is "plus français qu'américain." Reviewers of his novels, especially *Set This House on Fire* and *Sophie's Choice*, have pointed to the European nature and range of his enterprise, which is nowhere more evident than in his only work of nonfiction, *This Quiet Dust*.[14] This volume of essays seems to belong on the same shelf as the critical writings of Thomas Mann, Camus, Sartre, Malraux, and Butor; it is markedly different from recent collections by American contemporaries, say, John Updike's *Hugging the Shore* or John Barth's *The Friday Book*. Perhaps the work it most nearly resembles is the gathering of Camus's nonfiction, which Alfred A. Knopf brought out in 1961 as *Resistance, Rebellion, and Death*. Both books seem strategically located at that Gallic intersection between public discourse and art. Styron and Camus both emerge from their collections quite as committed to public life as to literature and the arts. One turns to their essays as much for a certain moral guidance as for literary insights. One theme which the two have hauntingly in common is capital

13. See the interview that came out of the tour: Ben Forkner and Gilbert Schricke, "An Interview with William Styron," in *Conversations with Styron*, 190–202. In their introductory remarks the interviewers comment revealingly, "It should be mentioned that the French gave Styron one of the warmest receptions accorded an American writer in recent years" (190).

14. See my "The 'French Face' of William Styron," *International Fiction Review* 10 (Winter 1983), 33–37.

punishment. Indeed, Styron at one point in *This Quiet Dust* refers to Camus's classic discussion of the subject: "Camus's great essay 'Reflections on the Guillotine' was alone almost enough—in its persuasive logic and eloquence—to make me an enemy of capital punishment" (111). That "persuasive logic and eloquence" is nowhere more evident than in this passage about the 1957 Burton Abbott case: "Any other penalty, even the harshest, would have left him that chance. The death penalty left him none. This case is exceptional, some will say. Our lives are exceptional, too."[15] While Camus's rhetoric doubtless *indirectly* saved lives, Styron's writing on the subject was crucial in sparing the life of a black man convicted of murder in Connecticut, Benjamin Reid. The spirit of *engagement*, on which the French seem to hold a monopoly, is surely part of the texture of *This Quiet Dust*. Just as Styron flirted with certain *nouveau roman* strategies early in his career as a novelist, so he seems to have taken a decisive Gallic turn in his nonfiction, especially in supplying that unmistakable link between the fiction and the criticism I spoke of earlier in this essay.

The French literary landscape stretches across *This Quiet Dust* as Styron delights in invoking his French masters. His "master Flaubert" offers a parallel text for Styron's own vivid descriptions of his trip down the Nile, as he allows the French writer's reactions to break in upon his own: "In benign hypnosis I sit on deck for hour after hour, quite simply smitten with love for this watercourse, which presents itself to the gaze in many of its aspects exactly as it did five thousand years ago. 'Like the ocean,' Flaubert wrote, 'this river sends our thoughts back almost incalculable distances.' Beyond the fertile green, unspooling endlessly on either bank, is the desert" (166). Styron splendidly counterpoints his own reactions with those of Flaubert.

Two other French "fathers" seem dominant figures in Styron's later writing, although they are not central to *This Quiet Dust*. One is André Malraux, who provides Styron one of two epigraphs he uses for *Sophie's Choice*: "Je cherche la région cruciale de l'âme, où le Mal absolu s'oppose à la fraternité." This quotation from *Lazare*, according to Styron, was suggested to him by the Mexican writer Carlos Fuentes.[16] But the connection between Styron and Malraux seems to go deeper than this. Styron mentions him admiringly in his introduction to Mitterrand's *The Wheat and the Chaff*, especially his relationship with Charles de Gaulle. Indeed it is not too farfetched to imagine a similar relationship between Styron and

15. Albert Camus, *Resistance, Rebellion, and Death*, trans. Justin O'Brien (New York: Knopf, 1961), 212.
16. See *Conversations with Styron*, 232, 253–54. Fuentes, by the way, dedicated his latest novel, *The Old Gringo* (*El gringo viejo*): "To William Styron whose father included me in his dreams of the American Civil War."

a François Mitterrand or a John F. Kennedy—two enlightened political leaders with a fondness for writers and a trust in their instincts.[17] Styron's Marine Corps background would also make him sympathetic to Malraux's service in the Spanish Civil War and in the Resistance during World War II. In *This Quiet Dust*, Styron is unstinting in his praise of those "men who dedicate themselves to fighting our battles" (191). Finally, it can be said that Malraux's own work as a writer-critic may have offered Styron an irresistible model. *Sophie's Choice* seems to belong on the same shelf as such Malraux novels as *La Condition humaine*, *L'Espoir*, and *Les Noyers de l'Altenburg*; it has the same ambitious design and didactic instinct. *This Quiet Dust* has something of the same generous floor plan as those art books of Malraux, such as *Les Voix du silence* and *La Métamorphose des dieux*.

The other "father," André Gide, an older contemporary of Malraux, makes an interesting appearance in *Sophie's Choice*. Stingo makes fond reference to him on one occasion: "I had admired his journals inordinately, and had considered Gide's probity and relentless self-dissection to be part of one of the truly triumphant feats of the civilized twentieth-century mind" (172). And surely Gide's only novel, *Les Faux-Monnayeurs*, must have been one of a handful of experimental artist fictions that helped determine the contours of *Sophie's Choice*.[18]

Styron seems more at home in this French ambience—in the company of his "masters" and fondly appreciated by his contemporaries—than he is in his native America. *Delta*, a journal published at l'Université Paul Valéry at Montpellier by the Centre d'étude et de recherches sur les écrivains du Sud aux Etats-Unis, brought out number 23 in its series in January 1986, a collection on Styron. (Edgar Allan Poe, Flannery O'Connor, William Faulkner, Shelby Foote, Eudora Welty, Truman Capote, Walker Percy, Ralph Ellison, and John Barth are southern writers who have already been the subjects of special issues of this periodical.) A twelve-page bibliography, listing Styron's own works in French translation as well as French writing about him, points to the astounding fact that he has been interviewed in French magazines and newspapers more than twenty times.

Of the nine essays that precede the "Bibliographie française" in *Delta* No.23, four are written in French, five in English. The collection was brought together by André Bleikasten, the eminent French Faulknerian,

17. See Styron's "The Short, Classy Voyage of JFK," *Esquire* (Dec. 1983), 124–31.
18. Styron comments in his interview with Charles Monaghan: "Gide was very much in vogue then, and I think I read all of his *Journals*. Gide has sort of gone into eclipse, but I think he'll be resurrected. He's one of the archetypal French writers. . . . His whole approach to his own existence, the intensity of his living, the ability to filter all the details of life through this absolute self-absorption. He noticed so many details, yet his daily life was always in conflict with his existence. He's a remarkable writer" (*Conversations with Styron*, 112).

who has also written distinguished studies of other twentieth-century American writers. The result is very much a Franco-American occasion. The essays vary widely in their approaches, from a close look at aborted drafts of an early version of *Lie Down in Darkness* to feminist, Sartrean, Freudian, and Eriksonian readings of *Sophie's Choice*. *Sophie's Choice* is the central text in more than half of the contributions, as critics continue to pick away at its ample contours. One essayist, Georgiana M. M. Colville, whose persuasions are never in doubt, characterizes *Sophie's Choice* as "one of the worst male chauvinist novels 'ever penned by man or beast.'" She sees the narrator, Stingo, as embodying the classic "transference of erotic desire on to artistic creation." Styron himself does not emerge unscathed; the mildest epithet used about him is "misogynous."[19] A calmer, more reasoned essay by Marion Brugière sees *Sophie's Choice* as "un texte d'ontologie qui pose la question de l'absence de Dieu et de l'absence de l'homme." Brugière sees the novel as part of a "grande tradition littéraire" that includes Melville, Conrad, Joyce, Dreiser, and Faulkner, among others.[20] Richard W. Noland's reading of *Sophie's Choice* within a psychohistorical frame, in which Erik H. Erikson's theories are soundly applied, suggests a new category, "generational novel," for Styron's most recent fictional endeavor.[21]

The remaining essays make their way through other parts of the oeuvre, taking the criticism as well as the fiction into consideration. Three Americans who have written extensively and enthusiastically about Styron—James L. W. West III, John K. Crane, and Melvin J. Friedman— are on hand, as well as three French critics, Jacques Pothier, Rachel Price-Kreitz, and André Bleikasten. Pothier does interesting things with the themes of shame, exile, and guilt, with Sartre and Freud lurking in the background. Price-Kreitz goes over the embarrassingly familiar ground of the *Nat Turner* controversy; the sense of *déjà lu* is always painfully in evidence, especially in her final sentence: "La véritable histoire de Nat Turner reste sans doute à écrire."[22] There is a naïveté and lack of sophistication in this essay which is rarely in evidence in French Styron criticism. Bleikasten's essay, the last in the collection, offers the only serious, incisive, and convincing attack on Styron's work that I know of by a French critic. The ironical tone establishes Bleikasten's apparent discomfort with the pious elevation of a career he feels is indelibly marked by "vulgarité." While all of Styron's work comes in for some abuse, *Sophie's Choice* receives

19. Colville, "Killing the Dead Mother: Women in *Sophie's Choice*," *Delta* 23 (Jan. 1986), 113, 127, 132. All subsequent references will be to this issue.
20. "L'Imagination en pèlerinage ou la migration du récit dans *Sophie's Choice* de William Styron," *Delta*, 149, 138.
21. "Psychohistorical Themes in *Sophie's Choice*," *Delta*, 109.
22. Rachel Price-Kreitz, "William Styron, Nat Turner et les faits historiques," *Delta*, 86.

most of Bleikasten's attention. He is especially irritated by the attempts to compare this novel to those of Dostoevski and Faulkner, and he ends with the simple and devastating advice: "Oubliez Styron."[23] These final words of the final essay in the *Delta* collection leave their unmistakable sting. Yet the succession of French endorsements of Styron's work by writers and critics of the distinction of Michel Butor, Michel Mohrt, Roger Asselineau, Maurice-Edgar Coindreau, and Thérèse de Saint Phalle will partly blunt the effects of Bleikasten's attack.

The first conference devoted exclusively to Styron's work was held in April 1986 at Winthrop College, Rock Hill, South Carolina. Although the event took place in a characteristically southern setting, it took on a decisively French turn. The keynote address was given by the French novelist, Thérèse de Saint Phalle.[24] She brought to the occasion her own sense—echoing Roger Asselineau—that Styron's work is more French than American.

Bleikasten's view of Styron *vulgarisateur* notwithstanding, the French continue to be more welcoming of his talents than are the Americans.[25] Whether or not he is "un écrivain plus français qu'américain," one can surely say that his fiction and his criticism occupy an honored place in the domain of Franco-American literary exchange. I can think of not a single contemporary American author who enjoys quite the same privileged position.

23. André Bleikasten, "Un Romancier à façon," *Delta*, 165, 166, 170.
24. Thérèse de Saint Phalle, who interviewed Styron twice in *Le Figaro Littéraire* (July 1–7, 1965, and Oct. 28–Nov. 3, 1968), is the author of such novels as *La Mendigote*, *La Chandelle*, *Le Tournesol*, *Le Souverain*, *La Clairière*, and most recently, *Le Programme*—all under the Gallimard imprint. She has for many years been concerned with the American literary and artistic scene. She was on hand when François Mitterrand advanced James Baldwin and Leonard Bernstein "au grade de Commandeur de la Légion d'Honneur" in Paris on June 19, 1986. Styron had been decorated by the French government in 1984.
25. See Maurice-Edgar Coindreau's splendid collection of essays: *The Time of William Faulkner: A French View of Modern American Fiction*, edited and chiefly translated by George M. Reeves (Columbia: University of South Carolina Press, 1971).

[9]

Hybrid Blooms: The Emergent Poetry in English of Malaysia and Singapore

WOON-PING CHIN HOLADAY

One of the legacies of the two centuries or so of British colonial rule in Malaysia and Singapore is the English language. Though both countries, since gaining independence, have adopted Malay as their national language, English continues to be used, with different degrees of prominence and status in each country. In Singapore it is officially sanctioned as a second language in a policy aimed at encouraging bilingualism; in Malaysia it has been relegated to the rank of a foreign language and has been phased out as a medium of instruction in schools and universities.[1] The language, nevertheless, has retained its currency in the region in a wide variety of contexts and milieus, even functioning at times as a lingua franca; it has evolved over the years into local dialects with a continuum ranging from low to medium to high English (or what the linguists call basilect, mesolect, and acrolect), with the last comparable to standard international English. Most interesting to this discussion is the emergence in the region of a growing body of literature in English, including poetry, fiction, and drama, with poetry ranking as the most prolific and consistently achieved of the three.

For its vigor and scope, this poetry has received increasing recognition from critics, both local and foreign. It joins that larger body of world literatures in English from countries as diverse as India, Nigeria, Canada, South Africa, the West Indies and Papua New Guinea. Not only is this corpus of new literatures claiming its place beside the literature of Eng-

This essay is based on a paper delivered at the Congress of the International Comparative Literature Association, Paris, August 1985.

1. The National Language Bill of 1967 instituted Malay as the only official language in Malaysia.

land, it in fact seems to outweigh the latter in potential and sheer bulk and at the same time serves to enrich and revitalize the resources of the language itself. As John Gross put it, "No English critic today can remain unaware for very long how heavily the meteques outnumber the natives; nor of how much they have to offer the natives."[2]

My purpose is to examine the efforts of Malaysian and Singaporean poets to evolve indigenous forms and techniques and to define indigenous themes in their emergent poetry in English. I am particularly interested in their efforts to "domesticate" the English language, that is, to make it their own, to bend, tend, acculturate, or nativize it so as to render it suitable and workable as an instrument for forging an authentic image of themselves. Among the questions I would like to address are what special challenges and difficulties these poets face, what literary and cultural resources they have drawn upon, and what innovations have arisen from their efforts. A brief survey of the general landscape is followed by an analysis of the work of two leading poets, Muhammed Haji Salleh and Ee Tiang Hong, each representing a different ethnic group, poetic strategy, and political commitment.

The choice of writing in English is not a simple one. The Malaysian writer, for example, who chooses English rather than the national language, is open to the charge of being a reactionary, if not an antinational. The question arises, moreover, whether the use and knowledge of English results in an alienation from one's environment. Writing in English, as Norman Sims has suggested, has become a "socially specified" activity: it designates the writer in Singapore as a member of the rising elite and in Malaysia as a member of the fading one.[3] Furthermore, the existence of pluralistic cultures and languages, such as are to be found in both Malaysia and Singapore, confronts the writer with a number of difficulties and a bewildering set of alternatives. In such a situation, the choice of literary modes and linguistic options often becomes problematical.

Another issue is raised by Jean D'Costa, commenting on a situation in the Caribbean which bears some resemblance to that in Malaysia and Singapore:

Language usage is also the very medium in which the writer's imagination and consciousness thrive; expression demands not merely a simple authenticity of presentation, but it forces the writer to stretch the limits of style beyond that of the recorder so as to attain new levels of usage that evoke the essence of this unique

---

2. In the Epilogue to *The Rise and Fall of the Man of Letters* (London, 1969), cited by Lloyd Fernando in *English, Literature and Technology in South East Asia* (Kuala Lumpur: University of Malaya, 1970), ii.

3. "The Future of English as a Poetic Medium in Singapore and Malaysia," *CNL/Quarterly World Report*, 2, 4, 12.

world. Yet the writer also wishes to share this world with others outside its immediate confines, and in order to do so he or she must find a means of communicating that which by its very nature seems incommunicable.[4]

This related choice of "sharing this world with others outside" concerns, of course, the awareness of audience: whether to write for a local (and thus more knowing) one, which, by the nature of the pluralistic and divided communities mentioned, is essentially sectional and limited, or to attempt to reach a broader, international audience. Such a choice is naturally attendant upon one's choice of literary idiom. But for a few scattered efforts to use local dialect, most Malaysian and Singaporean poets have opted for international standard English.

Malaysian/Singaporean poetry in English can be said to have sprung up in the nationalist fervor of the late 1940s among students at the University of Malaya (then situated in Singapore). Its roots, therefore, are essentially academic and metropolitan, derived from an English education and influenced by British, Commonwealth, and later, American literature. As early as the 1950s, Wong Phui Nam, one of the major poets of this period, spoke of the poet's dilemma—whether, in his words, one "just wrote poetry, or a poetry identifiably Malayan." Wong believed that the language was at its best when the poet was attending to his or her response to the "sum total of conditions under which we as Malaysians live."[5] In the preface to his first and landmark volume of poems, *How the Hills Are Distant*, he attested that "these poems need to be written. They are of a time, of a place, of a people who find themselves having to live by institutions and folkways which are not of their heritage, having to absorb the manners of languages not their own."[6]

An initial and general literary response to such conditions was for poets to adapt the English language in ways that would permit them to "explore and meditate the permutations of [their own] culture and environment."[7] That is, they used the English language to reflect and, in a sense, to see their local landscapes for the first time. Not surprisingly, a great number of poems describe local flora, fauna, climate, and folkways. In place of daffodils and winter icicles, we have a landscape nativized and tropicalized. As Ellis Evans observes, "In a country of no seasons, a poet has to work out a nature symbolism very different from and perhaps almost in the teeth of the English system."[8] There are invocations to tembusu,

4. "Expression and Communication: Literary Challenges to the Caribbean Polydialectal Writers," *Journal of Commonwealth Literature* 19, 1 (1984), 126.

5. *New Cauldron*, 2d term (Nov. 1958), 2, cited by Edwin Thumboo, ed., *The Second Tongue* (Singapore: Heinemann, 1976), xx.

6. *How the Hills Are Distant* (Kuala Lumpur: University of Malaya, 1968), 1.

7. Edwin Thumboo, *The Second Tongue*, ix.

8. Preface to Edwin Thumboo's *Rib of the Earth* (Singapore: 1956).

Hybrid Blooms

bougainvillea, banyan tree, and cactus plant. Streets, villages, towns, and cities are named in an effort to evoke the spirit of the place in such poems as "Tranquerah, Malacca," "Heeren Street, Malacca," "Panchor," "Bukit Timah, Singapore," "Kuala Lumpur" and "A June Evening in Kuantan." There are attempts to define classic norms of beauty, as in Arthur Yap's poem:

> A beautiful kampong is one
> that has coconut trees, a sandy shore,
> atap huts, a water tap,
> leathery chicken, slow motion,
> smoke from cooking, children running,
> clothes-lines with clothes flapping in the breeze.[9]

Such places are evoked no longer as the exotic objects depicted in the early literature of English expatriates but with the intimate involvement and feeling of the native participant.

A discernible and prevailing theme, one common perhaps to emergent literatures, is that of "the enigma of identity."[10] Whether revealed in the introspective ruminations of Wong Phui Nam or the insistent questionings of Pretam Kaur, there is a general preoccupation with one's self, individual or collective. The writer must come to terms with the displacement of his roots due to such accidents of history as colonialism, the volitional changes attendant upon migrations, or the conscious coercion of new power or racial groups. Often the writer is aware of living in several worlds, is conscious of duality, of what Kamala Markandaya has described as "double vision"—double vision "not in the sense of a flawed vision, but a vision that is enlarged, like an over-active gland, and insists on perceiving two sides to every picture."[11] Muhammed Haji Salleh has described the sense of living in an "interworld, which is sometimes 'liveable,' at other times unintegrated, the setting for schizophrenia."[12]

Richard Ong's poem "Rhumba" captures the ambivalence that comes with the recognition of displaced roots:

> Multiplicity of cultures
> Intrigue

9. "A Beautiful Kampong," *The Second Tongue*, 93.

10. A phrase used by Syd Harrex in "Scalpel, Scar, Icon: Lee Kok Liang's *Flowers in the Sky*," in *The Writer's Sense of the Contemporary* ed. Bruce Bennett, Ee Tiang Hong, and Ron Shepherd (Nedlands: University of Western Australia, 1982), 35.

11. "One Pair of Eyes," in *Commonwealth Writers Overseas: Themes of Exile and Expatriation*, ed. Alistair Niven, (Liège: Revue des Langages Vivants, 1976), 27, cited by Anne Brewster, "Singaporean and Malaysian Women Poets," in *The Writer's Sense of the Contemporary*, 46.

12. Author's Foreword in *Time and Its People* (Kuala Lumpur: Heinemann, 1978), as cited by Ee Tiang Hong, "Creative Alternatives in Malaysia: Cecil Rajendra and Muhammed Haji Salleh," in *The Writer's Sense of the Contemporary*, 43.

Of cosmopolitan art—
Their fragments lie about the world,
Fallen pieces of pottery,
Discarded
Because the painter could not keep his vision whole.
Here and there a blossoming of vine,
Misplanted,
Gives flashes of delight.
This girl, once, in a Kwangtung village,
the classics of the sage intoned.
With hearty grasp of things
Her silver voice now breaks
Into this Latin subtlety and rhythm

.   .   .

Shades of Confucius, can you forgive her?
She makes your ancient language run like water.[13]

The enigma and ambiguity of identity is most succinctly captured in the Lee Tzu Pheng's "My Country and My People":

My country and my people
are neither here nor there, nor
in the comfort of my
preferences,
if I could even choose.
At any rate, to fancy is to cheat,
and, worse than being alien or
subversive without cause,
is being a patriot
of the will.[14]

Related to the theme of identity is the question of what can be called defamiliarization, a process resulting from the use of English in a basically non-English environment. Often, the application of the cool, singular rhetoric derived from the British poetic tradition to the multifarious, tropical Asian life of this region results in a transformation—a refraction or attenuation—of experience. Consider, for example, Lee Tzu Pheng's poem "September," which imposes upon the familiar local phenomenon of monsoon rain a distancing, indifferent, almost Eliotish sensibility and perception:

the cold suspends responses once
warming to reality

13. *The Second Tongue*, 175.
14. Ibid., 161.

Hybrid Blooms

how does one feel, knowing no sensation
except the numbing discomfort
of a thin life, unprepared
for the excesses of the seasons

the days grow quiet, nights longer
merging and emerging undefined
September isolates emotion
confines the mind in an awareness
of the coming darker end
the long rains inundate our uncompleted days
and seep into our lives[15]

If art (as the formalists claim) places experience at one remove by virtue of its "literariness," then what we have here is experience twice removed, from one plane, and one language, to another. It is a process that involves, as well, a yoking together or cross-fertilization of East and West, traditional and new, autochthonous and alien, resulting in what I have called in the title of this essay (for want of a more apt metaphor), hybrid blooms. Indeed, it can be argued that such a synthesis is but a reflection of the everyday reality of life in Malaysia and Singapore—particularly in the metropolitan areas—which, like other fast-developing Asian countries, tolerate the coexistence of thatched hut and skyscraper, gamelan music and Michael Jackson, and a myriad other such combinations in their cultural, social, and political life.

Where the existing English vocabulary proves inadequate or lacking in viable equivalents to encompass such a phenomenon as described, local poets have resorted to linguistic innovations such as code mixing and "collacational deviations."[16] Thus we have such compound words as "flood-time," "three-storeyed-gloom," "death-winds," "brick-dead-man-coddling-buildings"; such phrases as "the blukar of oppression" (*blukar* being a Malay word for undergrowth) and "On charpoy jaga fast asleep" (*charpoy* being an Indian word for a string bed and *jaga* a Malay term for a guard, though the English translation does not carry the same connotations); and such lines as "when you walk in the dusun, / the flying foxes gone, / mangosteens tightened up in knots / on shrivelled bough" (*dusun* is a Malay word for a fruit orchard and *mangosteen* is the name of a local fruit).

As to the question of the resources from which local poets may draw, it should be pointed out that there is as yet no established literary tradition of writing in English. Lacking this, and for other reasons, the main

15. Ibid., 10.
16. A term used by Ramesh Mohan, "Some Aspects of Style and Language in Indian English Fiction," in *Indian Writing in English*, ed. Mohan (New Delhi: Longman, 1978), 195.

impetus has been for these poets to tap the resources of their own ethnic and cultural traditions. Though Eliot and Yeats may figure largely in the general vocabularies, the chief inspiring and motivating force for each poet, with a few exceptions, is his or her own ethnic heritage. Many poetic themes are thus derived from the contemplation of one's own cultural tradition and mores. For example, Chandran Nair writes about a Hindu cremation ceremony, while Geraldine Heng celebrates the moon-cake festival and Sng Boh Khim invokes "Good Ching Ming Day." In Wong Phui Nam's "Nocturnes and Bagatelles"—a brooding existentialist meditation on time, death, and human fallibility—we have the insertion of translated passages from Tu Fu and Li Po. The central metaphor in Fadzillah Amin's poem "Dance," is derived from the Malay dance, the *ronggeng*.

At this point, I would like to focus my comments on two poets, beginning with the Malay writer Muhammed Haji Salleh, whose work may be regarded as one of the most thoroughgoing attempts to tap from one's own ethnic resources and to transfer into English the themes, nuances, and symbols of one's cultural ethos. The fundamental and operative aesthetic principle in Muhammed's poetry is the Malay concept of *rasa* (influenced by the Sanskrit, which traveled to this region as part of the historical expansion of Hinduism into Southeast Asia). Muhammed defines it thus:

Rasa essentially means "feeling" in its widest possible sense, including that of the heart, emotions, of the senses of touch and taste, and the important but not readily explainable insights that come from intuition. . . . It is an outlook on life where the emotional, intuitive, intellectual and aesthetic all come into play at once. No one faculty has predominance over all others. . . . It is a total response to an event or the world. It incorporates the external experience with the internal one and as a result creates a balanced and fuller response.[17]

A poem such as "keroncong" (based on the Malay musical form, which is itself a hybrid evolved from the mixture of native elements with European influences) succinctly exemplifies the principle of *rasa*:

> no, i shall never wade this river
> of music to the upper bank of dryness.
> the flute and heart-stringed ukelele
> soak a slow rhythm into me.
> the singer drowns by her own

17. *Tradition and Change in Contemporary Malay-Indonesian Poetry* (Kuala Lumpur: Universiti Kebangsaan Malaysia, 1977), 129–30.

Hybrid Blooms

> damp sadness floods me
> with two streams of being
> how can i ever dry myself
> from a keroncong,
> a sad song,
> for that is life.
> the music and the singer
> they continue
> with another
> keroncong.[18]

pantun
see Turco

In this poem, as the Singaporean poet and critic Edwin Thumboo has commented, "The whole matrix of his experience is concretised by a set of correlatives suggesting the sad flow of emotion," in which the tradition embodied "is a tradition of empathy, an interest in ancestral ways, literate but not literary, framed by bonds with padi fields, the tenor of season and immemorial ceremony."[19] The sensibility revealed in Muhammed's poetry can be described, in his own words, as a "*pantun* sensibility," namely, one characterized by a "quiet intelligence" and softness and refinement of emotion.[20]

Techniques derived from traditional Malay poetic forms abound in Muhammed's poetry. In "a star-petalled flower falls," for instance, the conventional bipartite division of the Malay *pantum*—into the *pembahyang* (preparatory lines) and the *maksud* (meaning)—is interestingly varied, with the meaning tersely stated, in *pantun* fashion, in the concluding line. And as in a *pantun*, a specific picture of nature is used to comment on human existence or perception:

> now when the small hours
> grow big with day
> when darkness keeps its perspective
> and the mist of the evening rain waits
> over bushes and streams
> a small star-petalled flower falls,
> propelling its single flight
> through the dawn-thick air
> folding softly on damp earth,
> its whiteness caught
> in the late window light.
> death is trivial.[21]

18. *Time and Its People*, 63.
19. *The Second Tongue*, xxiii.
20. *Tradition and Change*, 86.
21. *Time and Its People*, 51.

This is not to deny the Western influences on Muhammed's work, including Valéry, D. J. Enright, and Yeats. What is most significant, however, is his ability to subsume these influences to create a poetry that is distinctively Malay in theme, tone, and technique. Muhammed's symbols, for example, are directly translated from the Malay. In the poem "blood," he evokes *tanah tumpah darah*, the emotionally charged image of the earth as the womb of the Malays and as legitimization of their supposed cultural purity and antecedence over other groups. This image recurs in another poem, "seeds," in which the cycle of rice planting becomes a metaphor for the poet's own growth and development:

> these seeds in the hope-bowl of my palms
> i wet with the new water of the new season
> in my grip i feel their skins burst and slap my hands,
> their yellow shoots creeping into my bloodstream.
> now as i let them drop singly into the warm earth.
> they are already plants in me,
> growing and feeding on my blood and my sweat-salt.
>
> and as i patiently wait for them to emerge
> from the night of the earth-womb,
> i feel the youth of my blood return to my limbs
> and i re-live this seasonal love affair.
> the evenings and the mornings quench me,
> and i grow with them,
> inevitably aging, bearing fruit
> and jumping back into life,
> to repeat the life-cycle of my blood.[22]

Similarly, in "her children," the personification of padi shoots as a woman's children (translated from the Malay *anak*) is the central symbol of the poem and affirms, like the poem "blood," the poet's claim to the land:

> —where are you hurrying to, grandma
> walking so fast and not stopping at our hut?
> oh, i'm just goin' down to the fields to see the children.
>
> they always call their padi plants children,
> these wombs of seeds, human or vegetable,
> the sprouting nursery of love
> feeding awkward roots of new shoots
> that clutch hard at their breasts.[23]

22. Ibid., 56.
23. Ibid., 10.

Muhammed's poems are most successful in capturing the special flavor of life in the tropics, so that conventional connotations of English words, removed from their Anglo-Saxon, insular, temperate zone, take on new and startling significance. Take, for instance, the poem "night rain," (which also serves as an effective contrast to Lee Tzu Pheng's "September," quoted earlier):

> the night rain came
> as soft as low piano notes
> tingling the grass leaves
> along their veins
> wriggling down to the drying roots
> the rains always wake up
> some essential loneliness
> that lurks under the silence.
> drops fall between memories
> and cool them to life . . .[24]

Notice the odd phrase, "cool them to life," which paradoxically inverts the usual association of coolness with death and warmth with life. Anyone living in the tropics will know, surely, that it is in the cool hours when the blazing sun goes down that things (and people) come to life!

Other typically Malay characteristics—from the humble, self-effacing persona and infrequent use of the first-person pronoun to the use of the Malay oral tradition—place Muhammed's poetry at one end of the scale of poetic applications of the English language, namely, a complete immersion in and commitment to one's own ethnic and linguistic tradition. Low-keyed and self-effacing as Muhammed's poetic stance may be, however, it is essentially grounded in the cultural and political domination of his racial group and presupposes a secure ethnic identity, or at least an identity proud of its origins and resistant to the influence and claims of other groups. Muhammed's preoccupation with ancestral roots and cultural purity stems from his overriding concern with the preservation of traditional Malay customs. In an essay, "Cultural Justice," he defines the healthy society as one in which traditional values withstand, in his words, "the monstrous movement of universal urbanism."[25] Implicit in this statement is the identification of "traditional values" with Malay culture and "universal urbanism" with non-Malay influences. It is significant to note that Muhammed has recently announced he no longer writes poetry in English.[26]

24. Ibid., 62.
25. "Cultural Justice," in *Questioning Development in S.E. Asia*, ed. Nancy Chng (Singapore: Selected Books, 1977), 107.
26. Viva voce, at a conference titled "The Writer's Sense of the Past" at the National University of Singapore, October 1984.

In contrast to the traditionalist stance of Muhammed's poetry is that of the Straits-born Chinese poet, Ee Tiang Hong. Unlike Muhammed's, Ee's is a tentative voice representing the disenchanted and threatened position of the racial minorities in Malaysia, particularly the Chinese. As Muhammed has used the English language to reify Malay identity, history, and power, Ee uses it to express the displacement, frustration, and anxiety of the non-Malay. Both poets load the language with political meaning. In both, we find, collective social concerns predominate over those of the individual, and there is a conspicuous lack of absorption in the self, leading to what the Australian critic Bruce Bennett has described as a "subdued ego."[27]

In a political climate that prohibits the discussion of such "sensitive" issues as exclusive privileges for Malays and the use of the national language, most Malaysian writers are wary of touching on politics. Ee's engagement with exactly these matters can be considered courageous and even dangerous to his personal safety. Indeed, it should be noted that he now lives in exile in Australia. In an essay titled "Malaysian Poetry in English: Influence and Independence," Ee discusses the uncertain future of English as a literary medium in Malaysia. For him, the freedom to write in English is synonymous with political freedom. He regards the English language as a "living force that will ensure that a society may yet remain open, and so enable us to come to terms with the modern world in a diversity of ways." He thus defines his role as a poet in a political context. As he puts it, "to define oneself in context is to awake to one's possibilities and to stake one's freedom." This freedom, symbolized by the freedom to write in the language of one's choice, is, as Ee sees it, severely threatened: "Poet and nation do not always speak the same language. In that situation, nationalism is no more than the bawling of a perverse child demanding that it alone be heard, or it will mess up the whole place. On another note, it is a strident voice of one communal group, drowning and disparaging other voices, certifying them dead or insane as the case may be."[28]

Not surprisingly, among the poets of the region, Ee is one of the most self-conscious about his use of the English language. In "O to Be in England," he refers wryly to the patronizing comments of native speakers, drawing attention to his own uncertain status as the once-colonized:

> Sudden the crooked irony:
>
> "So you write poems—in English?
> You must teach us the language, you know,

27. "The Subdued Ego: Poetry for Malaysia and Singapore," *Meanjin* 37, 2 (July 1978), 240–46.

28. Ee Tiang Hong, "Malaysian Poetry in English: Influence and Independence," *Pacific Quarterly* (Moana) 4, 1 (1979), 69.

Hybrid Blooms

It's rather a reproach
On our incompetence at learning
French."[29]

Of the poets writing in Malaysia and Singapore, Ee has most consistently and successfully attempted to use local idioms and colloquialisms, beginning with his first volume, *I of the Many Faces*. Bruce Bennett has pointed out Ee's ability "to mix linguistic variants of his region, thus giving the sense not of kitsch, but of multi-cultural influences working towards synthesis. This combination of constraints and possibilities leads to a poetry of painful, though not humorless, accommodation to the hard facts of a changing situation."[30] It is a combination, I might add, that comes across in a characteristically restrained and quizzical voice that sounds British, reminiscent of such poets as W. H. Auden and Philip Larkin. The language Ee uses is drawn from the language of public schools, government offices (Ee has been a civil servant and a school-teacher), coffee shops and bazaars, and it comes closer than that of any of his peers to capturing a "Malaysian" sensibility. It is the sensibility, however, not of the ruling class but of the minority, conscious of its displaced position, dissatisfied with the political system, and mindful of the sanctions against open criticism and protest. In such an atmosphere, the poet must use the tools of the silenced and the oppressed, namely, indirection, ellipsis, irony, humor, innuendo, and allusion. In doing so, he transforms the English language into an instrument of "a developed sociological imagination" (using Bennett's phrase)[31] with pronounced Asian accents.

One of the best examples of Ee's use of local idiom is in "Mr. Tan Muses," which attempts to capture the rhythms and nuances of Malaysian-English dialect:

> How is it I'm always left behind?
> My friends all have some share
> In the country's prosperity, the increased
> Standard of living,
> My luck is still the same . . .
> Never have cash for shares—
> Industrials, rubber, tin—
> Or even unit trusts.
> Lotteries also I cannot touch.
> So many times I miss a prize
> By just one number . . .[32]

29. Ee Tiang Hong, *Myths for a Wilderness* (Singapore: Heinemann, 1976), 12.
30. "The Subdued Ego," 242.
31. Ibid.
32. *Myths for a Wilderness*, 10.

In this poem, the ironic use of the ingenue becomes an effective mode for criticizing the materialism and corruption of Ee's countrymen by allowing the reader to see the situation through innocent or naïve eyes. The use of typical Malaysian idioms such as "touching" lotteries; the placement of the words *also* and *all* after the noun, in keeping with Malaysian speech patterns; the use of the popular phrase "so many times"—all add humor and credibility to the portrait of someone who has been left out in the "new prosperity" engendered by the "new nationalism."

In most of the poems in his recent volume, *Myths for a Wilderness*, Ee plays the role of the *eiron*, concealing himself behind evasive and self-deprecating masks. Analogous to the Greek prototype who triumphs over the stupid and boastful *alazon*, it is the role of the weak but clever underdog. Ee makes use of all the classic weapons of irony, including litotes (understatement), antiphrasis (contrast), mycterism (the sneer), and mimesis (imitation, especially for the sake of ridicule). Together, they operate to create poems distinctively "Malaysian" in nature, dependent upon and presupposing a reader's emotional capital in certain Malaysian values and events. Of these, the most crucial and most frequently alluded to are those pertaining to that historical date, May 13, 1969, a day of racial riots which changed the balance of power in Malaysia and which Ee has called a "watershed."[33] In his poems, the day becomes the central symbol of betrayal and duplicity, the reason his "motherland" has turned into a "wilderness." Against those sanctions that prohibit discussion of this event, Ee can speak of it only by indirection and allusion. In "Retreat," "Reports on Experience," and "Letter to a Friend," he maintains his ironic stance by insinuating and understating the violence of that day:

> When we, ill-advised, chose
> To sit back, denying the catharsis
> In the shadowy acts against the backdrop
> Of sky, sea and hill, we had not reckoned
> On the backstage hands manipulating the scenes.
> The denouement has taken a twist,
> Villains are rewarded,
> The shades have become real.[34]

And in "Arrival," he alludes to the betrayal of loyal citizens:

> And this is the terminus of truth?
> Objective of the dream and all
> The speculations we saved up

33. See Ee Tiang Hong, "Creative Alternatives," 41.
34. "Letter to a Friend," *Myths for a Wilderness*, 47.

> A lifetime and paid for?
> This dust and this laterite?[35]

There is no mention of what "this" of the first line is, except its metaphorical embodiment as dust and laterite. The second geological term, laterite, has clear connotations to those familiar with the soil of Malaysia and Singapore, a red clay in which nothing but stubborn weeds will grow, the bane of all farmers and garderners—in short, a perfect image for sterility.

Whereas in Muhammed's poems, nature is richly personified to represent the assured values of his Malay tradition, it is an emblem in Ee's world of human callousness and treachery, as in "The Times, the Morals":

> And the thought sickens,
> The heart is shamed,
> That knowing all these,
> And hearing the hiss
> And the froth
> Of the sea's conspiracy
>
> I believe
> Neither you nor any one of us
> Possess the simple courage
> To leave the comfort of the times,
> Go forth into that eerie calm
> To stare
> Down the cold eye
> Of the snoring typhoon.[36]

In several other poems—"Daybreak," "Manifesto," "Justice," and "Epilogue," for example—nature is similarly burdened with social and political meaning; the landscape menaces and ensnares ("The air mutable with spores that irritate the imagination / Only beware of the taboos, planted among the flowers")[37] or inhabited by malignant creatures

> Who have withdrawn,
> Who have accepted the worst,
> Though they might have enriched,
> And have left the landscape
> To a conspiracy of frogs
> And snakes
> And crocodiles[38]

35. *Myths for a Wilderness*, 27.
36. Ibid., 42.
37. "Epilogue," 59.
38. "Justice," *Myths for a Wilderness*, 51.

The poem "For My Son" heightens irony by the use of antiphrasis, contrasting the Malaysian vegetation of swamp and undergrowth (typical metaphors in Ee's poetry for the oppressive and the base) with sun, sky, and cloud, universal symbols of idealism:

> One bright auspicious hour
> You will hear your elders speak
> Of Freedom soaring in the sky,
> And hovering on a cloud, and stirring
> In the leaves of sun-aspiring branches.
> Inspired, you will burn in your passion
> To hack through treacherous swamps
> And the darkly creeping *blukar* of oppression.

Whereas Muhammed identifies the rural and natural landscape with the most positive and enduring values of his culture, using the land, vegetation and sea as symbols of purity, fertility, and wholeness, Ee sees nature as a harsh wilderness to be confronted and tamed, as did his immigrant predecessors. No "prince of the soil" (a literal translation of the exclusive Malay term *bumiputra*) like Muhammed, assured of his place and priority, Ee nevertheless stakes his claim by reminding the reader, again in "For My Son," of the struggles of his pioneering ancestors to cultivate the wilderness. In the following lines, the burning of the jungle (a common practice of the early settlers still done today) becomes a metaphor for the conquest of adversity and trial:

> So it will go on and on,
> The flame, the smoulder and the ash,
> Clearing after patient clearing,
> As you cut and criss-cross
> Every hydra creeper of the mind
> Obscuring caves and corners
> Of an elusive wind.[39]

In that most poignant and denunciatory of his poems, "Patriotism," a similar sentiment is expressed with the same allusiveness and irony:

> Surely by the time one reaches
> The seventh generation,
> The seventh heaven,
> One is no longer subject
> To all these?
>
> The journey is over,
> The conflicts, the strains, the trials

---

39. *Myths for a Wilderness*, 49.

Resolved generations ago
In that choice, irrevocable,
To cross the seas.

And if there was gold
In the mines and in the jungles
There were also death, hunger and disease . . .[40]

As in Ee's other poems, much of the weight of meaning in the first stanza
falls on the allusive pronoun (these), which is neither elucidated nor
concretized but instead presupposes common understanding on the part
of the reader. Interestingly, a contradictory impulse against topical allusion can be seen in the last stanza quoted, in which Ee has transformed a
historical reference to the tin ore mined by Chinese immigrants into gold,
a more universal symbol of preciousness.

Ee's use of allusion and ellipsis can be seen, thus, as a tool for eliciting
political meaning in a context that forbids the expression of such meaning, appealing to the reader's familiarity with certain shared symbols,
adding the depth and authority of past experience to the present occasion
and providing an obvious way of avoiding scandal or prosecution.[41] In a
landscape charged with political meaning, even the most personal of Ee's
poems carries a slanted message, as in "Likes and Dislikes," which concludes a catalogue of his favorite and least liked things with "And ar-
rogant public men / Drive me to bedlam."[42] There is certainly a markedly
Asian quality in the way he suggests meanings and in the delicacy of his
tone, whereby that which is not said becomes as important as, or more
important than, that which is said. To "Malaysian Thanksgiving," the
speaker's restraint makes a sharp commentary on his environment:

Thank you, *Tuan*,
For all these little things in life—
Health, family, stable job,
A dream-house on an imaginary
Plot of land, and a redeeming conscience.

Given of your bounty
These I accept with open arms, and mind,
Mindful that as I did not know
When they would come, I may not
Choose the hour when they should go.[43]

40. Ibid., 52.
41. See James Liu's discussion of allusion in *The Art of Chinese Poetry* (Chicago: University
of Chicago Press, 1962), 131–45.
42. *Myths for a Wilderness*, 25.
43. Ibid., 39.

It is exactly this combination of restraint and outrage, understatement and hyperbole which imbues Ee's poetry with its ambiguity of tone and meaning and imparts to his poetic persona its self-conscious and enigmatic identity.

Ee's diffident persona shares with Muhammed's a similar quality of humility and self-effacement. Both, however, are poses—the one belying hidden rage and protest, the other a traditional attitude secured by a presumed collective cultural superiority. Such posing by both presupposes as well the primacy of that typically Malaysian (if not pan-Asian) value of courtesy. Says Ee in "O to Be in England," "Confucius through generations / Of my forefathers inhibiting / DO NOT BE RUDE"; for Muhammed, self-effacement is a given in Malay *adat*, or custom, with its many forms of the diminished personal pronoun.

As different as the themes may appear in Ee's and Muhammed's poetry, they essentially revolve around the crucial issues of cultural survival and political power. Both poets, in that sense, imbue the English language of their poems with sociological and political meaning. Both seem to seek, in their use of English, a wider forum and readership for the expression of their concerns than the immediate ethnic groups to which they belong, while they depend on common references of a local and often partisan nature. Of the two, Mohammed relies more heavily on his linguistic roots for the figurative embellishment of his English, whereas Ee draws freely from various traditions, peppering his poems with Malay, Indian, and Chinese words and symbols. And of the two, it is Ee who strains toward the ideal of Malaysian pluralism, whereas Muhammed seems to cling to what has been described by Frantz Fanon as a "will towards particularism."[44] Muhammed has responded to pluralism with the resolution, in Lloyd Fernando's words, "to go back to one's own heritage in the hope that homogeneity may be restored."[45] It is against the political expression of such urges that Ee's poems protest.

I have elsewhere addressed the problems inherent in the ethnic and linguistic sectionalism of Malaysia and Singapore in evolving a national literature, especially one in English.[46] While it is questionable at this time if such a national literature exists in both countries, there is no doubt that the poetic products that have emerged from this region thus far are rich, hybrid blooms deserving of attention and appreciation.

44. See Frantz Fanon, *The Wretched of the Earth*, trans. Constance Farrington (New York: Grove, 1963), 222–23.
45. Lloyd Fernando, "A Note towards the Re-Definition of Culture," in *Awakened Conscience*, ed. C. D. Narasimhaiah (New Delhi: Sterling, 1978), 329.
46. See Woon-Ping Chin Holaday, "Singing in a Second Tongue: Recent Malaysian and Singaporean Literature in English," *Journal of Commonwealth Literature* 18, 1 (1983), 26–41.

[1 0]

Comparative Literature as Cultural History: The Educational and Social Background of Renaissance Literature

I

I wish to submit that cultural history is a viable model of "comparative" study and can be taken as an example of what Comparative Literature can be and do. It is so specifically, I may suggest, when it relates the liberal arts, as learned in and out of school, to the creative writer's intellectual formation, as it must do when studying, say, the history of Renaissance humanism.

This view of one of several possible uses of Comparative Literature would now be classified as a form of interdisciplinary study, insofar as it integrates scholarly and critical activities that are also found separately under the headings of other disciplines, namely, history, education, and even sociology. This combination raises the question whether literary study is not distorted and diverted, rather than helped, by going outside literature and "literariness" proper—in other words, to use a terminology made canonical by René Wellek and Austin Warren, whether "extrinsic" rather than "intrinsic" approaches can be legitimate and fruitful in litera-ture. It is a question that has lost much of its dramatic impact in academia, since we have become accustomed to a host of pluralistic approaches envisaging a great deal of latitude for the nonliterary ingredients of literary evaluation, ranging from psychology/psychoanalysis to more or less Marxist economism and sociologism or, on a different level, the many, still proliferating denominations of linguistic sciences. On the other hand, even the notion (and discipline) of literary history, which is the necessary point of departure for the use of Comparative Literature I intend to illustrate, has become severely clouded by the theoretical de-

Aldo Scaglione

murrers heard in recent years from several quarters, and signally from
such hermeneuticists as H. R. Jauss, although a sort of revision of this
revisionism (more bark than bite, I suspect) has been in the making.[1]

In case one wondered whether the type of approach I have suggested
should not be more appropriately deferred to the domain of history,
chiefly as history of education, the answer could be, first, that education-
ists have not displayed a great eagerness to involve themselves in historical study or to develop the complex paraphernalia necessary for serious
competence in this field and, second, that so far, the best work in the
history of education has come from straight historians or "philologists,"
especially in the areas of medieval and Renaissance studies. Furthermore,
the focus changes when the same problems are approached by someone
whose primary concern is political or sociological (that is, "historians")
rather than by someone whose primary concern is the understanding of
literary activity. Within this latter possibility the literary comparatist can
step in and fulfill an inalienable and irreplaceable function.

Contemporary criticism has been widely conditioned by German phenomenology, especially through the Geneva school. Specifically, the
critics of this orientation have proposed that the poem be seen not as an
object but rather as the structured record of an individual consciousness.[2]
This might be regarded as biographical fallacy, departing from the idealistic (e.g., Crocean and New Critical) as well as the standard Aristotelian
postulates of the work of art as a separate objective whole. Nevertheless, it
reestablishes the necessary foundation for a holistic consideration of the
real historical circumstances and conditions of artistic creation. Literature
thus becomes an active intersubjective experience, with the work of art as
a sort of intermediary between the existential experience of the author
and the reader's reaction, these two events being the more central and
dynamic part of the life of literature. When literature is seen from such a
vantage point, the critic is called to discover, among other things, the
"mentality" behind the work, the author's cultural formation or *Bildung*.
But for a truly meaningful understanding of the author's mental predicament one has to add a broader dimension, which the Geneva school has
not seemed explicitly prepared to encompass, namely, the social dimension of the author's cultural background not, centrally, in an economic
and political sense but at least in the sense of reconstructing his or her
"education." The concentration on the individual that characterizes the
Geneva school must be integrated with those transindividual factors

1. See, e.g., Herbert Lindenberger, "Toward a New History in Literary Study," (MLA)
Professions 84 (1984), 16–23.
2. Cf. S. N. Lawall, "Geneva School," in *The Princeton Encyclopedia of Poetry and Poetics*, ed.
Alex Preminger et al., 2d ed. (Princeton: Princeton University Press, 1974), 933–35; and
Kevin Kerrane, "Phenomenology," ibid., 961–64.

through which society, by educating authors, makes them exactly what they are. The freedom of their imagination is exercised against a background of real personal and collective data without which we could have nothing but an empty and meaningless game played in an intellectual vacuum.

II

In previous studies on the development of the trivium arts I have focused on aspects of grammar and rhetoric, seen in themselves, in their interrelationship with each other and with the other arts, and in their relationship with literature (that is to say, their impact on literary theory and practice). I now propose to take up the entire trivium at a time—the sixteenth century—when its application to practical educational programs became particularly productive, since in that century formal education received an unprecedented stimulus with profound and durable consequences down to our own days.

The sixteenth century realized a far-reaching crystallization of criteria of practical education in which both Reformation and Counter-Reformation adapted to new ends the innovations brought about by fifteenth-century humanism. What is particularly interesting is the way the new programs (which in some cases remained continuously active well into the eighteenth and nineteenth centuries and are still in the background of much of contemporary Western practice) were conditioned by the new perceptions of the role and function of the traditional liberal arts and, more specifically, the arts of the trivium.

The "classics" are so called from their having been the texts regularly used in the "classes." It appears that it is precisely their enduring popularity in the medieval schools that preserved those portions of pagan literature which were saved.[3] The lists of textbooks in use in the schools of the High Middle Ages remained surprisingly constant through the centuries all over Europe, with only limited variations, and the canonical names were arranged according to the way they were used in the classroom curricula within the system of the liberal arts—the uniformity of curricula and basic textbooks extending beyond the Christian West well into the Greek Orthodox East and even the Arab world.[4] This dispersal encompassed not only the major poets and historians but also the theorists (e.g. of rhetoric, like Cicero) and the writers of model prose texts

3. See Pierre Riché, *Les Ecoles et l'enseignement dans l'occident chrétien de la fin du Ve siècle au milieu du XIe siècle* (Paris: Aubier Montaigne, 1979), 249–51.
4. Ibid., 215–16.

Aldo Scaglione

(typically, the collections of model letters, such as those of Sidonius Apollinaris, Avitus, Eginhardus, and Frotharius of Toul).[5]

The use of the classics after 1500 by all sorts of writers and intellectuals can be better understood if one has a clear picture of the change in educational attitudes and practices. We have read countless statements as to the general secularization brought about by the Renaissance, but as far as the writers are concerned, this secularization was most specifically a result of the new type of schooling they were receiving. According to Richard L. Kagan, "During the Middle Ages, Latin had predominantly been a specialized idiom, the language of scholarship [that is, "science"], diplomacy, and religion."[6] In the course of the sixteenth century the municipal schools became firmly established on a regular basis in direct competition with the traditional, ecclesiastically controlled episcopal and monastic schools. What this meant was that the Latin of the classics became the true staple of the new education, instead of being simply a prop for doctrinal formation and scriptural interpretation. The fact that the Church managed to bring this new system partially under control again, at least in the Catholic areas, by placing religious orders, especially the Jesuits, in charge of most colleges, did not much change the nature of the new teaching, which remained as classically oriented as it had become since 1500, and as it had not been before. Even the ecclesiastical control imposed by the Council of Trent on lay teachers in secular schools, in the form of official licensing by the local bishops, sanctioned by the civil authorities (a system that was accepted even by the proudly independent government of Venice), did not affect the programs, since the questions that were put to the teachers for their licensing were cautiously generic.[7]

When we try to understand the inherent ambiguities of late Renaissance and baroque literature, we face the problem of interpreting the ambivalence between classically oriented and humanistically grounded admiration for ancient moral standards and aesthetic forms, on the one hand, and, on the other hand, a Christian need to reject such attitudes as deceiving and corrupting. The true nature of some late Renaissance (or "manneristic") culture and much of baroque art lies in their being imbued with a need to counter and subvert the standard forms of classicism. This predicament acquires fuller meaning if we keep in mind that the same basic duality marked the programs of religious educators in these periods.

5. Ibid., 256.

6. *Students and Society in Early Modern Spain* (Baltimore: Johns Hopkins University Press, 1974), 36.

7. Cf. Vittorio Baldo, *Alunni, maestri e scuole in Venezia alla fine del XVI secolo* (Como: New Press, 1977), passim.

III

The Society of Jesus planned to operate on society chiefly through education and only secondarily by direct "political" means. The educational plan came about as a response to the Church's urgent desideratum to have the clergy trained in a systematic and efficacious way because of the challenge presented by the Reformation. The Catholic countries lacked the advantage Luther had given his followers, when, by listing among the formal duties of Christian parents that of providing for the instruction of their children to ensure that they would be able to read the Scriptures, he had created a powerful thrust toward literacy on the private level, even without public intervention. In provincial France the public attitude may have been partly motivated by Protestant influence.

The Jesuits' success in taking the education, first of the priests, then of the ruling classes, into their hands was due chiefly to their strong determination to be themselves well educated, by the prevailing standards of the day, and to pursue the vigorous application of the same standards by extending them to all their charges. Their program entailed the pursuit of all liberal arts, with a thorough grounding in Latin grammar and classical rhetoric and with scholastic dialectic as a logical link with the ultimate goal of a Christian humanism, i.e., orthodox theology. Because the headquarters from which the Jesuits' worldwide system was run was in Rome, Ignatius adopted the philosophy of culture that was inescapably suggested to him by the presence there of the likes of Marc-Antoine Muret and Paolo Manuzio.

The happy coincidence of having been exposed to the disciplined, tightly organized college methods of Paris and of starting their experiments in Italy made it possible for the Jesuits to establish colleges that offered a humanistically approved curriculum—a somewhat doubtful possibility in the Paris of the Sorbonne—with an efficient method, a mere desideratum in the somewhat chaotic environment of the Italian universities. Thus the Jesuits became the heirs of the best experiments of the Netherlands' Brethren on the secondary level, coupled with the high professionalism of the Sorbonne and the Sapienza (the Roman university) for the purpose of creating a vast network of colleges and college/universities where a unitary view could be offered of the whole spectrum, from elementary rudiments to doctoral and professional specialization.

It was natural that the public institutions would see the new college system as a direct competitor and that serious conflicts would arise, not only because students flowing into one system could be seen as lost for the other but, perhaps more important, because the secularism of the Renaissance had begun a process of emancipation from confessionalism which could only be guaranteed by increasing state control of education. The movement of state rights and of separation of church and state was on its inexorable way toward a decisive confrontation with the Jesuits as the champions of an identification of education with Christian formation.

The Jesuits shared with Protestant reformers a firm conviction in the *reductio artium ad Sacram Scripturam* (or *ad theologiam*, which was the same). The humanistic adventure of the Renaissance had seemed to sweep this philosophy out of the schools, more so in Italy than elsewhere, but the renewed religious fervor that caused the Reformation brought the medieval ideal back in full force—nowhere more firmly than in Calvin's Geneva, where pagan culture was not even allowed to cohabit with the Scriptures. Everywhere else the examples of Erasmus, Melanchthon, Sturm, and Loyola meant that the humanistic ideal could be not only saved but espoused in full strength, provided it could be allied with a renewed Christianity. The Jesuits were convinced that this espousal was desirable and possible.

From a sociological and political viewpoint, the Jesuits' intervention in the field of secondary education did not really change the nature of general education in Europe, but it confirmed the gradual evolution, or inversion, whereby, rather paradoxically, institutions (the "colleges") that had come into being in the sixteenth century as a means of providing all citizens' sons with an opportunity to improve their status by joining the higher bourgeoisie through the use of a classical culture that had been defined and made available by Renaissance humanism became, instead, in the course of the following centuries down to the beginning of our own, a means to produce an exclusive elite and to reinforce the existing separation of classes into the educated rulers and the uneducated populace. The outcome of this secular evolution might elicit some severe conclusions. George Huppert, for example, referring specifically to France, noted that the *collège*, starting out as a door to humanity and power, had become "a somber citadel for the defense of privilege," and that, "disguised as a modern institution purporting to offer careers open to talent, the *collège* had become a museum."[8]

It is important to bear in mind that, despite the only partly deserved charges of having bent the classical ideal of education to confessional purposes and emptied it of its true human (secular) substance, the Jesuits saved humanistic education from the politically, socially, and economically motivated attacks that endangered it on many levels. Toward the end of the sixteenth century the holders of social privileges—the nobility, old and new, and the higher bourgeoisie, largely with the help of the mercantile classes—started a determined campaign to denigrate the ad-

8. *Public Schools in Renaissance France* (Urbana: University of Illinois Press, 1984), 143.

Comparative Literature as Cultural History

vantages of teaching the liberal arts to the populace. The danger was seen in inculcating hopes and aspirations to higher social and intellectual destinies that would take the sons of the lower classes away from the humbler vocations that society needed. Huppert has eloquently illustrated these explicit antieducational policies of the French monarchy, but the same policies existed in other areas, signally in Spain, where the schools that taught Latin and the liberal arts drastically declined in numbers and enrollment between 1600 and 1750.[9] Even while the Jesuits took over many of the once-flourishing lay schools, they often kept them from going under altogether, and they went on running them with precisely those classically oriented programs that were being attacked from several quarters.

The success of the long series of worldwide experiments can be gauged by the demonstrable continuity between the Jesuit schools from 1548 to 1773 and the modern methods and programs, despite profound changes brought about by more recent ideas of progressive education. A fundamental issue that concerns us as much as it concerned our distant predecessors is the impact of education on social order and economic warfare, and here again the past can be illuminating. We are still wondering to what extent a liberal arts education—with literature playing a more or less central role—must be considered basic and formative and how it relates to the technical or professional preparation for life. At the same time, we wonder how much society must reasonably invest in general education for the masses. These are, in historically conditioned variant forms, the same basic questions that found most social groups at odds between 1500 and 1800 over the perceived "danger" of extending to the lower classes a classical education that would inculcate the desire to imitate the ancient heroes by becoming leaders and doers of better things, rather than going back to the farm or the humble trade of one's fathers. Medieval society was comparatively stable in that the *mentalités* of the different social groups persuaded them to accept their status as God-given and permanent. But Italy had possessed a more unstable and shifting society than most countries, and then the Renaissance, with the humanist proclamations of faith in unlimited human potentialities, imposed on the rest of Europe the cultural model of a practically open society in which nothing could bar personal talent and will from success in every direction. Latin and familiarity with antiquity became the irreplaceable symbolic keys to open any door in the upward social climbing that was expected of any able individual. Toward the end of the sixteenth century, however, the privileged classes began wondering aloud whether this new mobility was not more disruptive than constructive. They reacted

9. Cf. Kagan, *Students and Society*, 31–61.

by demanding outright, and often obtaining, the closing of all schools, especially the schools of Latin grammar and rhetoric, except where they catered to the higher bourgeoisie and the lower nobility (the grandees needed no schools, being generally satisfied with private tutoring at home). This situation is reflected in the literature of all regions in different but eloquent ways, and we see many a literary or even poetic work in a new and more significant light when we keep this concrete background in mind. The various phenomena of classicism at different times and in different regions were always in unstable states of balance when set against these social pressures.

IV

In Huppert's recent study, which is limited to France, the lay vantage point is clearly espoused with a wealth of archival documentation, while the Jesuits' interpretations are constantly challenged and at times appropriately corrected. France probably offered a considerably more elaborate and extensive system of secondary education than did other European lands, and this in the form of *collèges*, the very term chosen by the Jesuits for most of their schools. Yet the French situation was certainly neither unique nor essentially different from that of other regions, since, for example, even the much more conservative and orthodox realm of Hapsburg Spain under Castilian leadership showed very similar developments in the period 1500–1750 in the field of educational policies and practices.[10] We can assume that schools similar to the French type were available in other free communes and burgher towns, perhaps with great variations in their organization, which was not regulated by the model of Paris.

The format of the French college became established around 1530 and was quite general by the end of the century, although after 1560 the religious wars threw the system into a crisis from which it never recovered. It was designed to serve the needs of the middle class, although it was open to the sons of all residents, and hence the enrollments could be very large. It was entirely tuition-free except for nonresidents. It was usually housed in appositely designed new buildings and run by a lease-contract arranged directly between the town consuls and a principal, who was responsible for the hiring and supervision of the six or seven teachers (*régens*), all of them preferably from the Sorbonne with a good master of arts degree in hand. The programs were, after 1530, fairly uniform

10. Cf. ibid., esp. chap. 2.

throughout the country and consistently based on the classical curriculum of the liberal arts, while the modus operandi was explicitly *style de Paris*.

The typical curriculum of a French secular *collège* was eminently classical, and the classes were clearly divided and graduated, with one regent for each. (The division into graduated classes, which was to play such a major role in the Jesuit system, was considered part of the "Parisian style," even though it was not practiced in Paris.)

Public secondary schools existed in open opposition to the ecclesiastical diocesan schools normally run by the bishops' superintendent for education, called *écolâtre* in France. One reason for their rapid growth was precisely the need to provide the general, free education that the *écolâtre* was unwilling to consider, since diocesan schools were not financed with any church money except to the extent that they served to train men specifically for the priesthood. Even prospective priests had to bear most of the cost of their education, which was regarded as an investment soon to bear fruit. The standard policy of the *écolâtre* was to oppose any suggestion to extend the demographic scope of the schools as well as any requests for grants of tithe moneys toward the support of secular schools.

After 1530 Francis I began pressuring the bishops to turn over vacant benefices or tithe moneys to the secular colleges, to no avail. The bishops resisted, refused, or procrastinated. Rome often intervened and vetoed individual donations of ecclesiastical properties or revenues to the townships on behalf of their colleges. The Church also reacted to the secular pressures by using the weapon of censorship. The inquisitors investigated school boards and staffs and charged them with harboring heretical ideas, although burning good regents at the stake was a dangerous measure that could easily backfire. Indeed such penalties were enacted with great caution and later abandoned in favor of the new strategy of pressuring the town colleges to turn over their operations to religious orders in exchange for ecclesiastical subsidies. This practice was regularly resisted by the French towns but often accepted, however reluctantly, when the religious wars and widespread economic hardships left the towns in serious financial straits (the towns' strength reaching a nadir in the 1590s). In 1560 the estates general met at Blois in an atmosphere of virulent anticlericalism, and the deputies of the Third Estate proposed nationalization of the Church in its entirety. The resulting royal edict ordered every diocese to turn over to the town for the support of public education the first vacant prebend in a cathedral chapter. It was like a declaration of war, and the wounds would take long to heal. Even where the bishops prevailed over the town councils, they had to compromise on the methods and accept the Parisian style. The schools would then be jointly supervised by the consuls and the bishop.

A comparison with the French secular colleges of the provincial type is important in order to place in proper perspective the relative originality of the Jesuits' methods as well as their motivations. A number of features that seem so novel and so characteristic of the Jesuits turn out to have been quite standard in the secular colleges. Already in use were, first and foremost, the graduated distribution of classes and disciplines; then the thoroughly classical orientation of the curriculum, almost entirely based on the use of Latin (and some Greek) and the methodical reading of classical authors organized into the system of the seven liberal arts; the standardization of programs, curricula, textbooks, and schedules; and on a more technical level, the use of doormen for control and administration and the much-publicized and, at least in Italy, criticized use of the bell to signal the beginning of classes.

In 1603, the year after he decided to readmit the Jesuits into his realm, the French king Henri IV gave a generous endowment for the establishment of the first Jesuit college of nobles, the Collège de La Flèche in Anjou, attended, among others, by Descartes for eight years, 1604–1612.[11] The colleges of nobles were patterned after the academies for knights and riding schools that had first appeared in Italy, starting with the celebrated one established in 1532 by Federico Grisone in Naples. This kind of institution fitted well with Richelieu's ideas on education, and he followed suit by founding the exemplary Académie royale in Paris in 1636, one year after his Académie française.[12]

Richelieu's policy was the radical implementation of the new turn taken by the monarchy starting with Henri IV. After attempting to intervene directly in the running of the provincial collèges by appointing the regents and making grants available to the cities for teachers' salaries, Henri IV had set out on the subtler and more realistic policy of replacing the lay teachers with Jesuits (later flanked by the Oratorians and the Fathers of the Christian Doctrine—Pères de la Doctrine Chrétienne, or Doctrinaires), who would be sure to be loyal to the monarchy and whose revenues would include endowments from suppressed abbeys and episcopal funds.[13] Louis XIV and Mazarin wanted to go even farther, convinced as they were that the common people needed no more education than reading, writing, and counting and, indeed, that "writing should not be taught to those whom Providence caused to be born peasants; such children should learn only to read."[14] The absence of social discrimination in the admis-

11. Norbert Conrads, *Ritterakademien der frühen Neuzeit: Bildung als Standesprivileg im 16. und 17. Jahrhundert* (Göttingen: Vandenhoeck und Ruprecht, 1982), 79.
12. Ibid., 41, 75–81.
13. Huppert, *Public Schools*, xii and chap. 9.
14. Ibid.

sion policies of the *collèges* was seen as "a great disorder that is shocking to the principles of Christian moderation," since everyone should be taught to be content with his state and not aspire to rise beyond the rights acquired at birth.[15] As early as 1627 Richelieu had set his mind on closing down all provincial colleges except those of La Flèche, Pau, Rouen, Amiens, Troyes, Dieppe, Lyon, Toulouse, Bordeaux, Poitiers, and Rennes—all to be staffed by Jesuits or Oratorians.[16] As late as 1763 a French public official could still express the fear that the study of liberal arts would "turn children away from their fathers' occupations" and encourage "that spirit of idleness, of arrogance, and of irreligion which is so costly and dangerous to society."[17]

Bourgeois resistance to the Jesuits, on the other hand, was grounded in continuing loyalty to the well-tested secular *collèges*, which were often weakened when they were allowed to be turned over to the Jesuits, Oratorians, or Doctrinaires, more interested in fostering the cause of orthodoxy than in preserving the integrity of the humanistic programs. True enough, more than the competing religious orders, the Jesuits were justly renowned for efficiency, the maintenance of high scholastic standards according to the Parisian style, and improved discipline, which in the lay colleges seems to have suffered immeasurably from the disorders of the religious wars.[18] Yet the cities went on with their resistance, and even under Louis XIV it often took royal *lettres de cachet* to force them to sign with a religious order, as it happened at Laon, which accepted eight Jesuits in 1729.[19] French city councils agreed to accept the Jesuits in order to buy peace or to save their financially troubled schools, rather than out of a wish to change the educational programs, which generally remained as classically oriented and as Parisian in style as before, at least at the hands of the Jesuits.

Tensions also arose over the Jesuits' reluctance to continue with the lower, abecedarian classes. Whatever their initial reasons for this limitation, critics now saw this trend in its sociological perspective as excluding de facto the children of low condition from all education.[20] One way or the other, education through the seventeenth and eighteenth centuries became the clear prerogative of the ruling classes, and the religious orders contributed their share to this predicament. Even the French

15. Huppert, *Public Schools*, 117.
16. François de Dainville, S.J., *L'Education des Jésuites (XVIe–XVIIe siècles)*, ed. Marie-Madeleine Compère (Paris: Minuit, 1978), 129.
17. Quoted by Huppert, *Public Schools*, xii–xiii.
18. Ibid., 118.
19. Ibid., 124.
20. Ibid., 126.

Revolution did not change this state of affairs: French observers noted that fewer boys were attending college after 1800 than before 1789, and classical culture had suffered a significant retreat.[21]

The role of the bourgeoisie vis-à-vis the acceptance of both humanism and the Jesuits was not without contradictions. In Italy the mercantile bourgeoisie had once been the principal bearer of humanism, led by the chancery lawyers and such "moguls" among the high merchants as the Medici. And yet there was an inherent incompatibility between the interests of the lower merchants and those of the humanists. Boccaccio, as a symptomatic case in point, could not stomach the thought of a business career because of his passion for letters. Similarly, the French commercial communities might occasionally oppose the Jesuit colleges because they had no use for the humanities fostered by such colleges, which they believed would directly jeopardize the mercantile vocation of local youths. François de Dainville has assembled relevant historical documentation to show how, one after another, such purely commercial centers as Nantes, Bayonne, Saint-Malo, Le Havre, and Troyes rejected the Jesuit colleges from the very beginning through the seventeenth century, whereas they were welcome in towns of *parlements* and *magistrature*, like Rouen and Bordeaux, despite the Gallican distrust of the Jesuits (Gallicanism being particularly deep-seated in the *parlements*).[22] The records seem to show no religious objections from the merchants, who ostensibly rejected the Jesuits on the purely economic grounds of protecting their businesses.

Out of 664 students at the College of Bordeaux in 1644–1648, 300 (45.5 percent) were the sons of bourgeois functionaries but only 138 (21 percent) were sons of merchants, 54 (8.4 percent) were the sons of noblemen, and 38 (5.9 percent) were the sons of artisans or peasants. Similar documents show distrust of letters in Lille, Montpellier, even Lyon, after the "renaissance" of the earlier sixteenth century—at least when such curricula were offered by the Jesuits. When favorable opinions toward the colleges and schools of humanities, philosophy, or sciences were formally voiced in town councils, the arguments that were aired sounded curiously "mercantile." We must, however, bear in mind that resistance to classical education could often be less a result of bourgeois attitudes than of propaganda and hard pressure from the government, according to Richelieu's stated policy. Hence it is difficult to assess to what extent the good burghers were expressing their own convictions and interests and to what extent they were yielding to a propaganda that was very differently motivated. Moreover, one might wonder why a city like Nantes, for one,

21. Ibid., 142.
22. Dainville, *L'Education des Jésuites*, chap. 1.

would reject the college offered by the Jesuits when it had a college of its own as early as 1526, operating in 1557 with a staff of four, a budget of seven hundred livres, and Greek on the program—all facts not mentioned by Dainville—and even while the college was offered instead to the Jesuits' main rivals, the Oratorians, in 1626.[23] Dainville's exposé of this situation must, therefore, be used with caution, since it appears that, of the centers he mentions, not only Nantes but at least Bayonne and Troyes also had renowned colleges very early.

From the earliest time the classical education being offered in the secular schools was aimed at the development not of mercantile skills but of aptitudes for public office. As Huppert aptly summarizes it, "Although these [bourgeois classroom] texts promised worldly success, they did not praise the merchant's life. It was the officeholder's life that was presented as the eventual goal of the children's hard work. The officeholder's position in society was said to be endowed with a vaguely antique quality, as the only respectable position in the *République* in which wealth and virtue might easily be combined." He quotes Pierre Habert (*Le Miroir de la vertu*, [Paris, 1587]): "Apprendre faut la science d'escrire si sagement voulons la voye ensuyvre des gens de bien [that is, the higher bourgeoisie] qui vivent saintement."[24] This is the situation the Jesuits had to face when they took over such schools or opened their own new ones, and this is what the public demanded and expected.

The magistrates and high burghers of the French townships found in Plato the confirmation of their will to control the educational processes. The preamble to the 1574 *règlement* for the College of Valence eloquently pointed out that "Platon fourmant l'idée d'une république ferme et stable veult et ordonne que les magistrats et gouverneurs d'icelle soient tenus et ayent la charge de l'éducation," and the preface to the principal Baduel's 1548 *Traité de la dignité du mariage* spoke of Socrates as "le terrestre oracle de l'humaine sapience."[25]

Indeed, the heritage of Renaissance humanism, with its vivid examples of the virtues and wisdom of the ancient heroes, fitted into these burghers' ideal of education much better than did the models of the monk, the priest, the aristocratic gentleman, or the wealthy merchant, which the burghers wanted their sons to be able to transcend.[26] Hence they found it natural to distrust the ecclesiastical schools and, within their own, any teacher who came from a religious order. The monks were notorious for their deficiencies in formal education, and the priests for their greater interest in benefices than in the work of education. Only the Paris masters

23. Huppert, *Public Schools*, xiv n.
24. Ibid., 85.
25. Ibid., 86.
26. Ibid.

of arts were regarded as culturally "sufficient" (*suffisants*), and the Jesuits, in particular, usually lacked such degrees, since they had studied in their own institutions.

The parents tended to take their children out of the Jesuit schools before they entered the philosophy class, as if this were less useful, yet this was precisely the grade where, in the Jesuit scheme of things, the teaching of *res* would reach its fruition. Families that were intellectually more aware might have been concerned over the confessionally slanted orientation imparted at that stage, but more frequently the reasoning was less lofty, since the students also often missed the class of physics, judged equally useless and unworthy of a gentleman, like geometry, astronomy, and music—that is, the quadrivium.[27]

During the eighteenth century bourgeois attendance increased, as the lower middle class sought a liberal education to gain access to public offices, military careers, the priesthood, and the liberal professions. Dainville sees in this a cause for the weakening of the classical *humanitas* and for increasing pressures toward more "useful" and "practical" subjects, including the applied sciences and modern languages, while Latin and literature faded into the background as social ornaments without crucial interest.

V

A conclusive remark may be in order to close the circle, as it were, with which we started. If, as I began by saying, intrinsic "literariness" as exclusive of nonliterary considerations is no longer, or so it seems, a central concern today, it is, I presume, in part because we have been moving in the direction of "total" history and holistic criticism. This approach has enabled us to emphasize the rich and challenging interrelationship of all human activities, and it is part of the growing realization that, even though a scientific definition of fields of research must abstract specific human endeavors from attendant circumstances, a comprehensive understanding of any phenomenon cannot prescind from all its multiple dimensions.

Such a predicament characterizes not only every scientific field but even the question of science as a whole, as shown by the ongoing arguments concerning the correct way to analyze, understand, and explain the history of science itself. I am referring to the question of whether scientific activity is essentially the cumulative result of discoveries of the objective nature of the real or, rather, the progressive sequence of responses to

27. Dainville, *L'Education des Jésuites*, 207.

ideological paradigms, imposed on the scientist by extrascientific acts of
human will—religious, moral, political, and so on, that is, broadly cultural
and social. To perceive the full extent of this current polemic it suffices to
refer to the authoritative works of Karl Popper, T. S. Kuhn, or I. Bernard
Cohen.[28] A now classic example is that of Louis Pasteur, who is alleged to
have sought to disprove the principle of spontaneous generation not on
the basis of sufficient experimental evidence but in response to the then-
governing paradigm of positivistic materialism and anticreationism. As
far as I am concerned, the answer lies not in accepting either of these
opposing postulates unilaterally but in keeping in mind the relative validity of each discovery even while one remains aware that they may come
about as a response to an external stimulus which is not necessarily and
exclusively "scientific." Similarly, the understanding of the literary act is
enhanced and made more concrete by the discovery of the most complex
and real historical circumstances—once again ideological, social, economic, and broadly cultural—even while one must keep in mind that
literature, like, say, music or science, has its own peculiar inner rules and
thrusts. Far from diluting or losing sight of these peculiar qualities, the
study of the full set of historical circumstances of the work of art enhances
our understanding of it.

28. See Cohen's *Revolution in Science* (Cambridge: Harvard University Press, 1985).

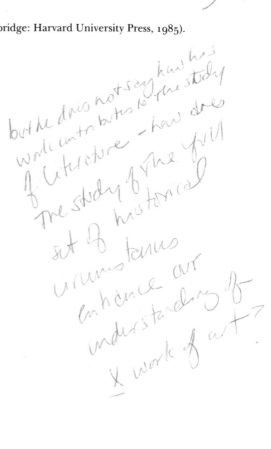

[11]

Alienation Effects: Comparative Literature and the Chinese Tradition

PAULINE YU

I

For someone attempting to study Chinese literature from a comparative perspective, the disincentives can be powerful. Many scholars of Western literatures may briefly lend an interested ear to someone discussing an Asian literature but then lapse quickly from a rather patronizing tolerance to an all-too-visible impatience to get back to what really matters. The excuse, and it is a good one, is that the linguistic and cultural differences are so profound as to render futile or meaningless any attempts at serious comparative study. From the other side, the resistance has entrenched itself equally stubbornly. Hard-core sinologists often refuse to gainsay what they consider the unique difficulty of their own enterprise and cast a suspicious, if not outrightly contemptuous, eye on those who claim to know about China *and* something else as well. Audible sniffs, for example, convey a widespread skepticism, and even hostility, toward those presumptuous scholars not content to remain within the safe confines of a single dynasty, genre, or botanical species.

As frustrating as such mutual parochialism may be, there are unfortunately a number of good reasons for its dogged persistence. Comparative Literature itself is of course a relatively youthful discipline and has only recently ventured beyond the European cultural sphere to incorporate non-Western literatures within its scope. In the case of China, the influence studies upon which the discipline cut its teeth can, to be sure, be pursued with some success by those working with twentieth-century materials, on both sides, and there are certain earlier, isolated, and well-known instances of interest on the part of European thinkers in things Chinese. For scholars focusing on Chinese literature before 1900, however, the *rapports de fait* demanded by old-school comparatists simply do

[162]

not exist. The alternative search for rapprochements has been undertaken, but all too often within a kind of methodological and contextual vacuum. Some of us have seized with delight upon apparent affinities in theme or practice between otherwise unrelated authors or works, explored the parallelisms, and been content to conclude that the exercise was a fruitful one if only because it was "mutually illuminating." Others have moved from the demonstration of such similarities to posit the existence of certain literary "universals." Still others have rejected the mechanics of one-to-one comparison and chosen instead to cross cultural boundaries by attempting to apply various Western critical methodologies to Chinese texts.[1]

theory + method us universal

Needless to say, the results have been mixed. Individual comparisons of authors, works, or even literary movements are usually conducted without attention, for example, to cultural assumptions and institutions and concrete extraliterary conditions and are therefore so inconclusive as to seem pointless. Most Western approaches, from New Criticism onward, find no counterparts in the Chinese critical tradition, are based on very different sets of philosophical and literary presuppositions, and can therefore be castigated as irrelevant at best, culturally imperialist at worst. Similarly, literary "universals" on close examination almost invariably turn out to be Western ones, requiring, for instance, great expenditures of energy on arguments to show why China lacks tragedy or epic or, conversely, that they did develop after all, albeit in disguise. Significant differences over time and space evaporate in the hypostasis of forms and genres: all Chinese poetry is presented as concrete, mystical, personal, impersonal, static, cinematic, or whatever. And finally, entire richly varied traditions become unqualified monoliths in the face-off of "East-West" Comparative Literature.

As an admitted perpetrator of many of the embarrassments catalogued above, I am nonetheless reluctant to throw up my hands in despair and dismiss the integration of non-Western cultures into the purview of Comparative Literature as a hopelessly flawed enterprise. In the case of China, at least, it seems to me that both sides lose when a major tradition either is consigned to the margins of serious critical and theoretical study or chooses to retreat behind the inviolable walls of esoterica. Resemblances certainly can be found, but though the value of their discovery is all too often vitiated by unsystematic examination and a general inattention to context, such problems are not necessarily insuperable. There is much to learn, I should think, from a more critical examination of the situation of

1. For a more lengthy recent survey of the field and its problems, see Heh-hsiang Yuan, "East-West Comparative Literature: An Inquiry into Possibilities," in *Chinese-Western Comparative Literature: Theory and Strategy*, ed. John J. Deeney (Hong Kong: Chinese University Press, 1980), 1–24. The volume itself contains several essays illustrating different approaches to the study of Chinese-Western Comparative Literature.

Pauline Yu

literature in premodern China that might take inspiration from the recent surge of interest in the West in comparative studies of discourse and
society, literary history and literary institutions. The integral relationship
between letters and the sociopolitical order has long been taken for
granted in China; so such an approach could not be accused of cultural
appropriation. It would simply subject sanctified dicta on such issues as
the place and function of literature or the nature of canon formation to
question, with the answers thrown into sharper relief by comparison with
other cultures. Another possible route lies in a somewhat different direction—the exploration of difference, a cautionary consideration, made
possible by the crossing of major cultural boundaries, of the wisdom of
assuming the universality and therefore transportability of certain concepts and terms.

Few scholars of Chinese literature, if Western-trained, can avoid em-
ploying a terminology that has developed out of the study of European
literatures. One must, after all, start out with some kind of vocabulary.
Only in the past few years, however, has awareness grown of the culture-
bound nature of even the most apparently neutral of terms. James J. Y.
Liu, for example, warned against the wholesale application of methods
and standards of Western criticism to Chinese literature, and I myself
have attempted to show how what have been called metaphor and allegory in Chinese poetry are actually grounded in a set of philosophical
presumptions fundamentally different from those out of which the terms
arose in the European tradition.[2] In what follows I shall briefly turn my
attention to questions about the lyric which illustrate similar problems in
transferring generic or critical conventions across cultures, for although
the Chinese short poem (*shi*) and Western lyric appear analogous in
nature, their different roots have given rise to rather different sets of
critical concerns.[3] For the sweeping generalizations to which I am still
susceptible, I beg the reader's indulgence.

II

One hardly needs reminding that, despite Plato's and Aristotle's differing evaluations of it, mimesis undeniably lies at the core of Greek poetics
and its legacy. There seems to be no question that the concept owed its

---

2. James J. Y. Liu, *Chinese Theories of Literature* (Chicago: University of Chicago Press,
1975), 5; Pauline Yu, "Metaphor and Chinese Poetry," *Chinese Literature: Essays, Articles,
Reviews* 3 (July 1981), 205–24; Yu, "Allegory, Allegoresis, and the *Classic of Poetry*," *Harvard
Journal of Asiatic Studies* 43 (Dec. 1983), 377–412.

3. I am indebted to Earl Miner for his consideration, from a comparative perspective, of
the important implications for the development of genre and critical theory in general, of
the focus of ancient Greek poetics on the drama, and of Japanese and Chinese on poetry.
See, for example, "On the Genesis and Development of Literary Systems," *Critical Inquiry*
(Winter 1978–Spring 1979), 339–53, 553–68.

mimesis
imitation
representation

importance to the position of drama within Greek culture.⁴ I would
suggest that certain philosophical concepts might also have motivated the
development of the notion and the focus on its most obvious generic
embodiment. Mimesis is, after all, predicated on a fundamental ontological dualism—the assumption that there is a truer reality transcendent to
the concrete historical realm in which we live and that the relationship
between the two is replicated in the creative act and artifact. Earl Miner
notes that the focus on dramatic mimesis may have prevented the Greek
theorists from developing the tripartite division of genres that was not to
emerge full-blown until the sixteenth century: "Taking imitation as the
norm, they were unable to distinguish lyric from narrative."⁵ Both Plato
and Aristotle are noticeably reticent about treating the lyric, but perhaps
as much for lack of interest as for inability. Anything other than dramatic
poetry was of less concern to Plato because it was less egregious in its
mimesis of characters other than the poet, and Aristotle may have given
the lyric short shrift because it did not provide as extended an imitation of
human action as did drama and epic. Moreover, it was the form in which
poets speak in their own voices, something not to the critic's taste because
less clearly mimetic.⁶

Whatever the reasons behind their disinclination to examine the lyric in
any systematic way, Plato and Aristotle did establish the framework within
which later discussions of the genre in the West were to evolve. The
assumption that poetry involves mimesis has survived virtually intact to
the present day, enshrined, for example, in the following dictionary
definition: "In its modern meaning, a lyric is a type of poetry which is
mechanically *representational* of a musical architecture, and which is the-
matically *representational* of the poet's sensibility as evidenced in a fusion of
conception and image. In its older and more confined sense, a l[yric] was
simply a poem written to be sung."⁷ Restricting ourselves to this "older

4. Ibid., 350.
5. Ibid.
6. Of epic poets, for example, he writes: "The poet should say very little *in propria
persona*, as he is no imitator when doing that. Whereas the other poets are perpetually
coming forward in person, and say but little, and that only here and there as imitators,
Homer after a brief preface brings in forthwith a man, a woman, or some other character—
no one of them characterless, but each with distinctive characteristics." Aristotle, *Poetics*,
trans. Ingram Bywater (New York: Modern Library, 1954), 258 (line 1460a). In other
words, he at least implicitly distinguishes between first- and third-person narration, which
later became one way of distinguishing lyric from epic. Plato, of course, is more explicit,
observing that "poetry and fiction fall into three classes. First, that which employs representation only, tragedy and comedy. . . . Secondly, that in which the poet speaks in his own
person; the best example is lyric poetry. Thirdly, that which employs both methods, epic and
various other kinds of poetry." *The Republic*, trans. H. D. P. Lee (Baltimore: Penguin, 1955),
131.
7. James William Johnson, "Lyric," in *The Princeton Encyclopedia of Poetry and Poetics*, ed.
Alex Preminger et al., enlarged ed. (Princeton: Princeton University Press, 1965), 462, my
emphasis.

sense" might allow us to arrive at a definition of the lyric that transcended cultural boundaries, but it would also not take us very far. What interests me are the more important distinctions in formulation that one finds. And because Western attempts to characterize the lyric have typically been based on this presupposition of mimesis, certain critical questions recur, chief among which is that of truth value or historicity.

Whatever their vantage points, critics have by and large accepted the implicit link in Aristotle's *Poetics* between representation and fabrication. Poets are makers precisely because they imitate. "*Mimesis* is *poiesis*, and *poiesis* is *mimesis*," as Paul Ricoeur puts it.[8] Cleanth Brooks claims that "the poem, if it be a true poem is a simulacrum of reality—in this sense, at least, it is an 'imitation'—by *being* an experience rather than any mere statement about experience or any mere abstraction from experience."[9] Susanne K. Langer writes, "The poet uses discourse to create an illusion, a pure appearance, which is a non-discursive symbolic form. . . . The poet's business is to create the appearance of 'experiences,' the semblance of events lived and felt, and to organize them so they constitute a purely and completely experienced reality, a piece of *virtual* life."[10] And according to Barbara Hernnstein Smith, "We may conceive of a poem as the imitation or representation of an utterance. This is not to say that a poem is a false or merely 'emotive' form of speech. It is an imitation in the same sense that a play is the imitation or representation of an action."[11] Whereas here she notes that by "poetry" she means both verse and prose, in her later essay, "Poetry as Fiction," she develops the argument with specific reference to poetry alone.[12] Käte Hamburger, who tries to distinguish lyric poetry as a "reality-utterance" (*Wirklichkeitsaussage*) from the mimesis of reality in fiction, appears to voice a conspicuous, lone dissent: "Precisely this differentiates the lyrical experience from that of a novel or drama, that we do *not* experience the utterances of a lyrical poem as appearance, fiction, illusion. . . . For we always confront it without mediation, just as we confront the utterance of a true 'other,' a Thou speaking to Me."[13] Yet even she takes care to point out that she is talking about how one apprehends a poem. She rejects the popular distinction between a "lyrical"

8. *The Rule of Metaphor: Multi-disciplinary Studies of the Creation of Meaning in Language*, trans. Robert Czerny et al. (Toronto: University of Toronto Press, 1977), 39. Cf. also Käte Hamburger, *Die Logik der Dichtung*, 2d rev. ed. (Stuttgart: Ernst Klett, 1968), 18–20.

9. "The Heresy of Paraphrase," *The Well Wrought Urn* (New York: Harcourt, Brace, and World, 1947), 213.

10. Susanne K. Langer, *Feeling and Form* (New York: Charles Scribner's Sons, 1953), 211–12.

11. *Poetic Closure: A Study of How Poems End* (Chicago: University of Chicago Press, 1968), 15.

12. Barbara Hernnstein Smith, *On the Margins of Discourse: The Relation of Literature to Language* (Chicago: University of Chicago Press, 1978), 14–40.

13. *Die Logik der Dichtung*, 19. All translations in this essay are my own.

and an "empirical" self.[14] She also notes, however, that the "logical identity" between the subject of the poetic utterance and the actual poet does
not mean "that every utterance of a poem, or even the whole poem, must
coincide with a real experience of the poetizing subject," nor, furthermore, does the lyrical utterance claim to have a *"function in any connection
with objects or reality."*[15]

In addition to the generally held presumption of fictiveness, other
recurrent themes in Western discourse on the lyric follow from the classical view of poetry as mimesis. One common, though not undisputed
distinction is that made by both Plato and Aristotle—though more explicitly by the former—between lyric poets, who speak in the first person,
and epic poets, who do not; the concern with the speaker of a literary
work was a natural one, given the focus on drama. Hence we find M. H.
Abrams defining the lyric as "any fairly short, non-narrative poem presenting a single speaker who expresses a state of mind or a process of
thought and feeling. . . . Although the lyric is uttered in the first person,
we should be wary about identifying the 'I' in the poem with the poet
himself."[16] From this attention to the speaker of the poem arise a recurring debate over personality and impersonality, further support for the
disjuncture between lyrical and empirical selves, as well as disagreements
regarding the rhetorical function of the speaker, that is, whether the
poem is meant to be heard or, in John Stuart Mill's formulation, "overheard."

Yet another prevalent concern is with the temporality of the poem: if
lyric and narrative both imitate actions, perhaps they can be distinguished
by their use of time. Whereas critics have generally agreed with Gerald
Prince that "any narrative is the representation of real or fictive situations
and events in a time sequence,"[17] writers from Longinus to Poe have
emphasized the intensity and hence necessary brevity of the lyric poem.
Rather than the past tenses of narrative, moreover, which build a continuity rooted in time, the lyric also characteristically uses the present and
may, according to Langer, suspend the sense of time altogether:

The semblance most frequently created in a lyric is that of a very limited event, a
concentrated bit of history—the thinking of an emotional thought, a feeling

14. As Hamburger explains it, there is no formal basis for making this distinction: "We
have neither the possibility and thereby the right to claim that the poet meant the utterance
of the poem—no matter whether or not it follows the first-person form—to be about his
own experience, nor to claim that he did not mean 'himself.' We can no more decide this
than with any other nonpoetic utterance. The form of the poem is that of an utterance, and
this means that we experience it as the field of experience of the subject of the utterance—
which is precisely what enables us to experience it as reality-utterance" (Ibid., 219).

15. Ibid., 220, 213, Hamburger's emphasis.

16. *A Glossary of Literary Terms*, 3d ed. (New York: Holt, Rinehart and Winston, 1971), 89.

17. "Narrative Analysis and Narratology," *New Literary History* 13 (Winter 1982), 179.

about someone or something. The framework is one of occurring ideas, not external happenings; contemplation is the substance of the lyric, which motivates and even contains the emotion presented. And the natural tense of contemplation is the present. Ideas are timeless; in a lyric they are not said to have occurred, but are virtually occurring; the relations that hold them together are timeless, too. The whole creation in a lyric is an awareness of a subjective experience; and *the tense of subjectivity is the "timeless" present*. This kind of poetry has the "closed" character of the mnemonic mode without the historical fixity that outward events bestow on all memories; it is in the "historical projection" without chronology. Lyric writing is a specialized technique that constructs an impression or an idea as something experienced, in a sort of eternal present; in this way, instead of offering abstract propositions into which time and causation simply do not enter, the lyric poet creates a sense of concrete reality from which the time element has been canceled out, leaving a Platonic sense of "eternity."[18]

The continuity of a lyric poem, then, is not that of time, context, or actual experience but of speaker, emotion, or metaphor.

While I am clearly oversimplifying a long and diverse tradition and have selected these statements from but a narrow band in the critical spectrum, certain issues have persisted in Western discourse on the lyric that derive from essentially unquestioned assumptions: first, that—like all literature—it is mimetic and hence fictive and, second, that it must therefore be distinguished from other kinds of literary forms on the basis of the kind or subject matter of its mimesis. Similarly, the Chinese tradition is hardly monolithic, and yet it has asked a somewhat different set of questions of a poem than those taken for granted in the West. Here I shall also start with the earliest writing of any length on poetry, a passage from the Great Preface (*Da xu*) to the first anthology of poetry, the *Shi jing*, or *Classic of Poetry*. The collection of 305 poems itself, in existence by the sixth century B.C., predates this critical preface by some six centuries:

Poetry is where the intent of the heart/mind goes. What in the heart is intent is poetry when emitted in words. An emotion moves within and takes form in words. If words do not suffice, then one sighs, if sighing does not suffice, then one prolongs it [the emotion] in song; if prolonging through song does not suffice, then one unconsciously dances it with hands and feet.

Emotions are emitted in sounds, and when sounds form a pattern, they are called tones. The tones of an orderly world are peaceful and lead to joy, its government harmonious; the tones of a chaotic world are resentful and lead to anger, its government perverse; the tones of a doomed state are mournful to induce longing, its people in difficulty. Thus in regulating success and failure,

18. Langer, *Feeling and Form*, 268. For a development of these ideas through exhaustive examination of specific examples, see George T. Wright, "The Lyric Present: Simple Present Verbs in English Poems," *PMLA* 89 (May 1974), 563–79.

moving heaven and earth, and touching spirits and gods, nothing comes closer than poetry.[19]

What we have here is a classical statement of the expressive-affective concept of poetry prevalent in Chinese literary theory. While certain assumptions resemble those in the European tradition—the importance of song, emotion, and formal patterning for poetry—the world view on which these are based is significantly different. Indigenous Chinese philosophical traditions agree on a fundamentally monistic view of the universe; the cosmic principle, or Tao, may transcend any individual phenomenon, but it is totally immanent in this world, and there is no suprasensory realm that lies beyond, is superior to, or is different in kind from the level of physical beings. True reality is not supernal but in the here and now, and this is a world, furthermore, in which fundamental correspondences exist between and among cosmic patterns (*wen*) and processes and those of human culture.[20] Thus the Great Preface can assume that what is internal (emotion) will naturally find some externally correlative form or action and that poetry can spontaneously reflect, affect, and effect political and cosmic order. Because of the seamless connection between the individual and the world, the poem can at once reveal feelings, provide a gauge of political stability, and serve as a practical didactic tool.

The assumption implicit in this statement that the poetic emotion is provoked by contact with the world was made explicit in slightly later critical texts. Lu Ji's (261–303) *Exposition on Literature* (*Wen fu*), for example, begins with the assertion that the writer "stands at the center of the universe":

> He moves with the four seasons, to sigh at transience,
> And looks at the myriad objects, contemplating their complexity.

19. This preface has been traditionally attributed to Wei Hong (ca. first century A.D.). Although frequently printed separately as the Great Preface to the entire collection, it also appears as part of the preface to the first poem in the anthology, in, for example, *Mao shi zheng yi*, ed. Kong Yingda (574–648), 6 vols. (rpt. Hong Kong: Zhonghua shuju, 1964), 37–41 (1A/3a–5a), the edition I use throughout this essay. This passage has also been translated, in whole or in part, by several other scholars, including Liu, *Chinese Theories of Literature*, 69, 63.

20. For an exposition of the view that Chinese thought conceives of the universe as a spontaneously self-generating organism in which all phenomena exist in orderly, mutually implicating, correlative harmonies, see Joseph Needham and Wang Ling, *History of Scientific Thought*, vol. 2 of their *Science and Civilisation in China* (Cambridge: Cambridge University Press, 1951), 279–344; Frederick R. Mote, *Intellectual Foundations of China* (New York: Alfred A. Knopf, 1971); and Mote, "The Cosmological Gulf between China and the West," in *Transition and Permanence: Chinese History and Culture*, ed. David Buxbaum and Fritz Mote (Hong Kong: Cathay Press, 1972), 3–21.

He laments the falling leaves during autumn's vigor,
And delights in the tender branches of fragrant spring.[21]

Lyric poetry "originates in emotion," he writes somewhat later, and this emotion is engendered by the response of the poet to the external world. Similar statements suggesting a stimulus-response model of writing also appear throughout Liu Xie's (ca. 465–523) more comprehensive work, *The Literary Mind: Dragon-Carvings* (*Wen xin diao long*). The chapter "Elucidating Poetry," for instance, explains that "man is endowed with seven emotions, which are moved in response to objects. When moved by objects one sings of one's intent totally spontaneously." Somewhat later he echoes the preface to the *Classic of Poetry*: "Emotions are moved and take form in words; reason emerges and literature appears; for in following the hidden to reach the manifest, one matches the external to the internal." Throughout the work he develops this correlative thinking by providing specific examples of how, "when things move, the heart/mind is also stirred." Emotions vary according to seasonal and atmospheric changes, since all phenomena are mutually resonant: "Things all call to one another—how can a person remain at rest?"[22] Instead of the mimetic view that poetry is the imitation of an action, it is seen here as a *literal reaction* of the poet to the external world of which he or she is an integral part. There are no disjunctures between true reality and concrete reality or between concrete reality and literary work, gaps that may have provoked censure in some Western quarters but that also establish the possibility of poiesis, fictionality, and the poet's duplication of the "heavenly Maker's" creative act.[23] For the reader of Chinese poetry, not only is there no heavenly maker but—and this despite the fact that only rarely does a first-person pronoun appear—the lyrical and empirical selves are one and the same.[24]

The implications of these views become obvious upon examination of

21. Included in the *Wei Jin Nan Bei Chao wenxue shi cankao ziliao* (1962, rpt. Hong Kong: Hongzhi, n.d.), 254. These lines have also been translated by Achilles Fang, "Rhymeprose on Literature," *Harvard Journal of Asiatic Studies* 14 (1951), rpt. in *Studies in Chinese Literature*, ed. John L. Bishop (Cambridge: Harvard University Press, 1965), 531; Chen Shih-hsiang, "Essay on Literature," in *Anthology of Chinese Literature*, ed. Cyril Birch, 2 vols. (New York: Grove Press, 1965), 1:205; and Liu, *Chinese Theories of Literature*, 72.

22. Fan Wenlan, ed., *Wen xin diao long zhu* (rpt. Taipei: Daming, 1965), 2/65, 6/505, 10/693. Cf. the translation by Vincent Yu-chung Shih in *The Literary Mind and the Carving of Dragons*, bilingual ed. (Taipei: Chung Hwa, 1975), 43, 222, 348.

23. From Sir Philip Sidney's *Apology for Poetry*, included in *Criticism: The Major Texts*, ed. Walter Jackson Bate, enlarged ed. (New York: Harcourt Brace Jovanovich, 1970), 86.

24. While a few subgenres, like the literati's imitations of folk ballads (*yuefu*), do allow poets to speak in personas not their own, the power of the assumptions I have just outlined can be seen in the fact that traditional interpretations of those poems invariably assume that the poets were only using those forms to comment on contemporary political conditions in an indirect and therefore perhaps less dangerous way.

almost any selection of poems and sample commentaries on them.[25] Consider, for example, the following poem from the *Classic of Poetry*, one of twelve Airs of Tang supposedly collected from the feudal state of Jin in north China (present-day Shanxi province). The poem, like the others in the anthology, is known simply by the first two words in the first line.

> Tightly bound is the firewood.
> Three stars are in the sky.
> What evening is this?
> I see this fine person.
> Ah thee! Ah thee!
> Wherefore such a fine person?
>
> Tightly bound is the hay.
> Three stars are in the corner.
> What evening is this?
> Ah thee! Ah thee!
> Wherefore such a happy meeting?
>
> Tightly bound is the thornwood.
> Three stars are at the door.
> What evening is this?
> I see this beautiful person.
> Ah thee! Ah thee!
> Wherefore such a beautiful person?[26]

As is the case throughout most of the collection, an early commentary known as the Little Preface (*Xiao xu*) interprets this poem as a critique of the sociopolitical situation in its state of origin. The Airs of Tang as a group are said to trace a rough chronology—the first supposedly being directed against Duke Xu, who reigned from 839–822 B.C., and the last criticizing Duke Xian (r. 675–650 B.C.); various other rulers are mentioned along the way. "Tightly bound," unlike many, is viewed as addressing itself more generally to contemporary mores; according to the Little Preface, it "is a criticism of the chaos in Jin. The state was in chaos, thus marriages did not take place at the proper time."[27]

Commentators over the centuries elaborate on this reading by focusing on the poem's succession of images; their interpretations, however, are

25. See, for example, my "Allegory, Allegoresis, and the *Classic of Poetry*," and my *The Reading of Imagery in the Chinese Poetic Tradition* (Princeton: Princeton University Press, 1987).

26. *Mao shi zheng yi*, 2: 539–42 (6B/1a–2b); cf. translation by Bernhard Karlgren, *The Book of Odes* (Stockholm: Museum of Far Eastern Antiquities, 1974), 76.

27. *Mao shi zheng yi*, 2: 539 (6B/1a); cf. trans. by James Legge, *The She King*, vol. 4 of *The Chinese Classics* (Oxford: Clarendon, 1871), 55.

Pauline Yu

far from harmonious. The Han dynasty Mao annotation explains to the reader that the poem presents positive images of couples waiting until proper ritual times for marriage, "like firewood and hay awaiting human action to be bound." The "three stars" are placed in the constellation Shen (Orion), which is said to be "just appearing in the eastern quadrant" of the sky, in the tenth lunar month,[28] marking a permissible time to marry.[29] The early Tang dynasty scholar Kong Yingda argues, however, that this image is meant to signal the *absence* of such proper observances in the state of Jin; he also assumes that Mao takes the speaker throughout the poem to be a man, an assumption warranted by the fact that Mao glosses the word for "beautiful person" (*can zhe*) in stanza 3 (lines 4 and 6) as "a great minister's wife and two concubines."[30] In opposition to Mao, the late Han scholiast Zheng Xuan (127–200) proposes that the three stars refer to the constellation Xin (Scorpio), which is not seen in the eastern sky until the end of the third lunar month or beginning of the fourth; hence the poem is chronicling the *failure* to be married at the proper time. In other words, his reading, like Kong's, confirms more directly than Mao's the preface writer's opinion, although Zheng and Kong employ contradictory philological evidence.[31] The Song scholar Zhu Xi (1130–1200) accepts Zheng Xuan's identification of the three stars as part of Scorpio but believes that the thrust of the poem is to celebrate a marriage that has occurred, however late, rather than to criticize a breach of propriety.[32] We should note that whatever their disagreements the traditional commentators all read the three stars as a specific, literal, temporal reference for the song; it would not occur to them to assume with a twentieth-century European scholar that the constellation "of course symbolizes the three beautiful girls."[33]

As these examples from the Chinese exegetical tradition suggest, a poem is generally read as a literal comment on an actual historical situation, and the task of the commentator is to explain what particular stimulus produced that response—to reconstruct the context of the poem. Some scholars are less inclined than others to view poems in the *Classic of Poetry* as actual chronicles of the state of their origin, but even so, their interpretations never shake off their conviction of historicity. No doubt the belief that the poems in the *Classic* had been collected to gauge the sentiments of the people and the canonical status of the anthology guided

28. According to Legge, 180.
29. *Mao shi zheng yi*, 2: 539 (6B/1a).
30. Ibid., 2: 540 (6B/1b), 542 (6B/2b).
31. Ibid., 2: (6B/1a).
32. Zhu Xi, *Shi ji zhuan*, included in *Shi jing zhuan shuo hui zuan*, ed. Wang Hongxu (compiled by imperial authority in 1727; rpt. Taipei: Dingwenhua, 1967), 191 (7/9a–10a).
33. Karlgren, 76.

Alienation Effects

Confucian commentators to produce such moralizing, topically allusive readings, but their legacy also shaped the "secular" poetic tradition, which would continue to regard a poem not as a work of fiction but as what Barbara Smith has called a "natural utterance." Such an utterance "not only occurs *in* a particular set of circumstances—what is often referred to as its *context*—but is also understood as being a response *to* those circumstances. In other words, the historical 'context' of an utterance does not merely surround it but *occasions* it, brings it into existence." This occasion *is* the meaning of a poem, ascertained from asking "*why* it occurred: the situation and motives that produced it, the set of conditions, 'external' and 'internal,' physical and physiological, that caused the speaker to utter that statement at that time in that form—in other words, what we are calling here its *context*."[34] Such an approach can only be dismissed as "shallow," reductive, or "literal-minded"[35] by critics working within a different set of norms, but it was perhaps the most logical course for a tradition based on a stimulus-response model of poetic production rather than a mimetic one.[36] In the traditional Chinese view, poetry chronicles the life of an individual as naturally as it does the fate of a feudal state, and the reading process becomes one of contextualization rather than the attribution of some referential otherness.

This conviction of historicity leads to a curious vacillation in critical discourse on the status of a poem's natural imagery. On the one hand, the strongest impulse is to locate the image within some putative original, stimulative context. For example, commentators find it so difficult not to assume that an image is part of some empirically observed and recorded scene that they fail to note the suspicious recurrence of images from poem to poem in the *Classic of Poetry*. Yet, on the other hand, they also seem to recognize the stereotypical quality of such images, for they assume that they conveniently correspond in some meaningful way to the human situation with which the poem is primarily concerned. They do not, however, construe such correspondences between two objects or between an object and an idea as artificial or contrived in any way, the ingenious creation of the poet as maker. Rather, in a system of correlative thinking that can be traced back to commentaries on the *Yi jing* or *Classic of Changes*, links between things are always already there, grounded by a shared membership in an unarticulated yet a priori category (*lei*) antece-

34. Smith, *On the Margins of Discourse*, 16, 22.
35. Ibid., 34.
36. For a discussion of how presumptions of nonfictionality might affect the readings of Tang dynasty poetry, see Stephen Owen, "Transparencies: Reading the T'ang Lyric," *Harvard Journal of Asiatic Studies* 34 (Dec. 1979), 231–51. His *Traditional Chinese Poetry and Poetics: Omen of the World* (Madison: University of Wisconsin Press, 1985), also discusses many of the same issues I have been considering here.

dent to any individual artifice. The important point remains, however, that the critics do not attribute any fictional, novel, or creative qualities to those images: the oscillation of critical opinion restricts itself to the two possibilities of convention and experience. Furthermore, that the images in the *Classic of Poetry*, for instance, could have been selected for no semantic reason at all, but only for purposes of rhythm and rhyme—a reasonable conclusion given the nonincremental nature of many of the repetitions in the poems—was not even proposed until the twelfth century and was not really taken seriously until the twentieth. Notions fundamental to the Confucian world view dominate the commentaries: that politics is simply ethics writ large, and that it is impossible for any individual, speaking of him- or herself, not to implicate a larger context as well. These holistic assumptions came to underlie, in some form, readings of noncanonical texts as well and, in fact, later poetic theory.

III

Thus, although the Western lyric and the Chinese *shi* share an important original integral connection with song, the underlying assumptions of these two forms have diverged in crucial ways. Originally defined over against other genres, the Greek lyric was conceived within a framework suggested specifically by the drama. The concept of mimesis, itself predicated on the notion of a fundamental disjunction between two spheres of reality, encouraged a view of the poem as a fictive artifact which, while always able to be considered in relation to poet or world, nevertheless retained a presumption of its self-sufficiency. Chinese conceptions of the *shi*, however, focused on the poem as response rather than fabrication, shaped and patterned, of course, yet never considered apart from its context and effect. There was no "other" reality that it was attempting to replicate or evoke. And not only was no presumption of fictionality made, but other issues taken for granted in the West never arose either. The Chinese *shi* developed its early critical tradition without competition from either drama or narrative, so it was not compelled to distinguish itself on the basis of, for instance, speaker or temporality. (Such distinctions would at any rate have been difficult to make, given a classical language uninflected for person, number, case, or tense, and a tendency to omit subjective pronouns.) Moreover not only were drama and the novel to integrate the lyric into their structure, but their critical tradition, as a rule, shared its conviction of historicity as well.

What I have been discussing, of course, are traditional Chinese notions of the origins and function of a poem and some possible reasons behind them; what this has to do with the "real" ontological status of the work is another question. It is a question, moreover, that one might be better off withholding, for it is precisely there that one runs the risk of reading a poem with inappropriate expectations. To assume, as one often does from reading Western lyrics and criticism, that lyrical and empirical selves are divorced or that imagery owes its provenance to individual, meta-phorical fabrication is to ignore the broad context within which the classi-cal Chinese poem was written. Valid comparisons involving any literature must begin with an adequate knowledge of the norms, conventions, and rules within which it was produced. Terms like lyric, metaphor, and allegory will no doubt continue to be applied to Chinese poetry, with all the murkiness and contradictions in their definitions further exacerbated by the transfer. I would hardly wish to encourage the notion that no meaningful discourse across cultures is possible or desirable. Nor am I proposing that Chinese theories of literature be granted exclusive author-ity over our readings of texts in the tradition, thereby rendering them immune from questions about the ideological and institutional frame-works that undergird them. But at the least, one would hope that an awareness of literary traditions other than those of Western Europe might alert one to the problems of taking basic terms and concepts for granted, without consideration for the contexts in which they have arisen and to which they are being applied.

extrinsic approaches

Literary Criticism
and Other Disciplines

W. WOLFGANG HOLDHEIM *philosophy*
ROBERT MAGLIOLA *religion/religious art/money*
SUSAN RUBIN SULEIMAN *psychoanalysis*
RICHARD WEISBERG *law*
ULRICH WEISSTEIN *painting*

[12]

The *Cogito* in
Sartre's *La Nausée*

W. Wolfgang Holdheim

This is the culminating point of Antoine Roquentin's Cartesian interior monologue in Sartre's novel *La Nausée*: "Je suis, j'existe, je pense donc je suis: je suis parce que je pense, pourquoi est-ce que je pense? je ne veux plus penser, je suis parce que je ne veux pas être."[1] This lengthy episode (117–22, E98–103), which highlights the protagonist's first major *crise de conscience* after a series of progressively exacerbated minicrises, occurs a little more than halfway through the book. But although it is by now a classic, it has (to my knowledge) never received the critical attention it should command. One can only speculate about the reasons. It may be confusing to see so eminently reflective a preoccupation in an almost aggressively narrativized form. Are we in fact dealing with literature or philosophy? In an early commentary, Claude-Edmonde Magny contended that *La Nausée* lacks unity of form and inspiration, being part metaphysical meditation and part narrative.[2] And indeed, later criticism has usually emphasized one of those aspects at the expense of the other. The "narrativists" may have tended to view the *cogito* section as an unassimilated piece of ratiocination, but why have the "philosophers" as well given short shrift to the episode? Perhaps because there is little energy left for Descartes when one's mind is firmly set on incursions of unadulter-

1. Jean-Paul Sartre, *La Nausée*, in *Oeuvres romanesques*, Pléiade ed. (Paris: Gallimard, 1981), 120. In English, *Nausea*, trans. Lloyd Alexander (New York: New Directions, 1964), 100: "I am, I exist, I think, therefore I am. I am because I think, why do I think? I don't want to think any more, I am because I think that I don't want to be." The English translation will be used in the text for shorter passages when possible, but a close reading demands basic reference to the French original. Future page references to these two editions will appear as follows: 120, E100.
2. "Sartre; ou, La Duplicité de l'être: Ascèse et mythomanie," in his *Les Sandales d'Empédocle: Essai sur les limites de la littérature* (Neuchâtel: Baconnière, 1945), esp. 167–68.

ated objects and nauseating encounters with chestnut trees. Only Georges Poulet seems to have devoted a full-length essay (although a characteristically impressionistic one) to that important passage. He had an inkling of its possible significance, writing that Sartre "has conceived his novel [note: his entire novel!] as a parody of the *Discours de la Méthode*."[3] But it was to remain no more than an inkling: for all its burlesque components, Sartre's work surely cannot be dismissed as merely parodistic, and it is really a little facile to conclude that "the *cogito* can no longer be pronounced otherwise than derisively."[4]

If such concerns were derisory, then the young Sartre must truly have been consumed with self-contempt, for the *cogito* was probably the central philosophical problem with which he grappled during the 1930s. His preoccupation with it was refracted through the reading of Husserl, whose *Cartesianische Meditationen* appeared in French as early as 1931 in the translation of Gabrielle Pfeiffer and Emmanuel Levinas, published in Paris by Armand Collin. Sartre took it up in the early study *La Transcendance de l'égo* (1936) and finally in his first major philosophical work *L'Etre et le néant* (1943). The dates overlap with those of the elaboration of *La Nausée*, the evolution of which is well documented.[5] Already in its original conception it was both ideational and literary: a concern with contingency was to find expression in a "factum" (a loosely conceived polemical meditation), which, under the influence of Rilke's *Aufzeichnungen des Malte Laurids Brigge*, was to be diaristic in form. Over the years, it became progressively more narrative. At some point, the crucial Cartesian problem was caught up in the narrativization of the treatise on contingency—a process that one should not mistake for the superimposition of an extraneous philosophical idea, since the *cogito* reflection (just like the "factum") deals with the question of being. In fact, it takes that question back to the foundation of modern thought.

For that matter, Descartes's *Discours de la méthode* (1637) already could be considered dual in form and inspiration. It not only initiates modern philosophy but is also a link in the old literary tradition of the philosopher's autobiography. There is Plato's *Seventh Letter*, Saint Augustine, Peter Abelard and, in the East, Michael Psellos, Avicenna, al-Ghazali; and as a kind of universal model, there is the Platonic Socrates of the *Phaedo*, who already progresses from the *pragmata* to the *logoi*, from things to thought. The Cartesian treatise was never meant to be a pure exercise in ratiocination. Written in French rather than Latin, it addresses a broader

3. Georges Poulet, "*La Nausée* de Sartre," in his *Le Point de départ* (Paris: Plon, 1964), 227, translation mine.
4 Ibid., 228.
5. There is a detailed account of it in the Pléiade edition of Sartre's *Oeuvres romanesques* (1657–78) by Michel Contat and Michel Rybalka, the editors of that edition.

public of *honnêtes gens*.[6] Biographical and historical circumstances move perceptibly to the fore whenever a withdrawal into abstract thought is reported, as if to emphasize the narrative and existential essence of the work.[7] In fact, Descartes stresses that his enterprise is narrative and individual, a tableau of his life, *une histoire* or perhaps *une fable*. *Fable* does not imply that the account is fictional, but merely that its lessons do not necessarily have universal validity. Magny's contention that *La Nausée* leaves us pending between such validity and a personal experience would therefore apply to the *Discours* as well and ultimately to all knowledge whatsoever. And indeed the question was raised immediately after the appearance of Descartes's treatise. Some critics claimed that the *cogito ergo sum* cannot pretend to primacy because it is based upon the hidden proposition that "he who thinks exists." Descartes countered that universal propositions are not primary but are founded upon particular prehensions that precede the chain of reasoning.[8] The founding *cogito*, then, is not a syllogism but a direct and unitary existential insight, anterior to all ratiocinative deductions. It shares in the narrative substance of Descartes's *histoire* or *fable*, which challenges the reader to choose or reject— in short, to interpret: "Among the examples one can imitate, one will perhaps also find some others which one will be justified in not following."[9] Reading the *Discours* is not comparable to following a mathematical demonstration; it is a hermeneutic enterprise.

One should therefore not exaggerate the distance between a Cartesian "discourse" that is essentially a story and a Sartrean diaristic novel that tends toward discursivity. "Je voudrais voir clair en moi avant qu'il ne soit trop tard," writes Roquentin, in the manner of other diarists before him— but also very much like the autobiographer of 1637, who wanted to distinguish truth from falsehood "pour voir clair en mes actions."[10] Descartes (after traveling widely and learning what the world could teach him) retreated into self-reflection, although without producing a diary, which was not yet the accepted literary vehicle for such purposes. His

6. The same thing is true of a later, unfinished text by Descartes, "La Recherche de la vérité," written in the form of a Platonic dialogue.

7. There are two such passages: first the retreat into the well-known *poêle* in Germany, after a military campaign and the crowning of the emperor; later the withdrawal impelled by public pressure due to Descartes's growing reputation, eight years before the writing, into a country (Holland) whose favorable atmosphere is described at some length. See René Descartes, *Discours de la méthode*, ed. Etienne Gilson (Paris: Vrin, 1930), 11, 30–31.

8. See Gilson's commentary in *Discours*, 293.

9. "Parmi les exemples qu'on peut imiter, on en trouvera peut-être aussi plusieurs autres qu'on aura raison de ne pas suivre." *Discours*, 4, translation mine.

10. E6: "I would like to see the truth clearly before it is too late." The translation fails to render the Cartesian emphasis on subjectivity, which is essential: Roquentin wants to see *clearly in himself*. Descartes' statement is in *Discours*, 10: "to see clearly in my actions" (translation mine).

solitude was to be rich in consequences, since it installed the principle of subjectivity at the core of modern sensibility and thought—in literature and philosophy alike. For whatever the differences between the Cartesian and (for example) the romantic subject, it was finally Descartes's withdrawal that set the stage for the romantic and postromantic outsider, including introspective diarists from René and Adolphe via Amiel to Dostoevski's man from underground, in whom that increasingly unhappy consciousness developed into a paralyzing solipsistic intellectuality. Roquentin, the first of Sartre's cerebrating protagonists, is distinctly a member of that lineage. The quintessence of the "impossible" intellectual hero, he is the latecomer in whom the tradition seems to come full circle: as an uneasy philosopher who lives in almost total loneliness after having traveled widely, he enacts (more clearly than any of the intervening links) a veritable return to the Cartesian sources of his heritage.[11] A return with a difference, no doubt, for the intervening links have left their traces. Descartes's progression to contemplation was active, consistent, guided by deliberate volition; Roquentin, a thinker *malgré lui*, seems a playball of events and of incomprehensible impulsions. He is the weak protagonist, the ruminatory antihero of a more modern literary era. If he ends up by abandoning his globe-trotting, it is for reasons he never fully understands. As for his supreme *retour aux sources*, the *cogito* crisis, it pounces upon him when his projected biography of the marquis de Rollebon collapses. The monologue of the self is precipitated by a breakdown of hermeneutic dialogue.

The nature and position of doubt underscores the difference between the narrators of the *Discours* and *La Nausée*. The original *cogito* is preceded by a development in which the thinker, questioning all his certainties, finally realizes that his very act of questioning is umimpugnably an act of thought. That development is a purely argumentative preparation that does not partake in the narrative substance of the *Discours*; indeed it is prefaced by a downright apology for indulging in so uncommon and metaphysical a meditation.[12] It is a purely methodical doubt, which does not affect the existential primacy of the *cogito ergo sum*. Another distinguished philosophical autobiographer, Kierkegaard's alter ego Johannes Climacus, has in fact directed the barbs of his irony against those thinkers who pretend to have doubted but have remained totally unaffected by their alleged *epoché*.[13] He could not have faulted Roquentin on

11. The Sartrean intellectual antihero has been brilliantly discussed by Victor Brombert in *The Intellectual Hero: Studies in the French Novel, 1880–1955* (Philadelphia: Lippincott, 1960), 181–203.
12. See *Discours*, 31–32.
13. See Søren Kierkegaard, *Johannes Climacus; or, De Omnibus Dubitandum Est and a Sermon*, trans. T. H. Croxall (London: Adam and Charles Black, 1958), 143–45. The work, whose

that score. His doubt is a matter of life and not of method, not theoretical but experienced, a general existential uncertainty that can no longer be contained within the limits of epistemology. Indeed, it is no longer confined to any one particular passage: the whole book is the story of its evolution. Accordingly, the distribution of narrative masses in the two works differs significantly. The *cogito* in the *Discours* can be analyzed into the three components of thought, consciousness of self, and existence[14]— but only through an ex post facto logical operation that does not affect the integrality of the experience. There is no such integrality in *La Nausée*. The episode at hand, in fact, is entirely devoted to the construction of the *cogito*. It presents itself as the result of a painfully protracted process of gestation in which the discrete components emerge, overlap, and intertwine, until they are finally assembled in the completed formula after three long pages—after which the episode peters out in another two.

Structurally at least, however, this distribution creates an odd parallel to the *Méditations* (1641), Descartes's other major treatise on doubt and its transcendence. There, as well, the *cogito* is gradually built up from its component parts; in fact the formula *cogito ergo sum* never appears in its completed form. That construction, however, is totally ratiocinatory in nature. Could it be that the Sartrean *cogito* section, which stands in the overall generic framework of the *Discours*, should be viewed with reference to the *Méditations* in its actual execution? Keeping this question in mind, let us turn to the critical examination of the episode, for clarity's sake dividing it into five consecutive parts.

The Primacy of the *J'existe* (117, E98)

Here are Roquentin's first reactions when he is thrown back upon himself after discontinuing the biography of Rollebon:

Surtout ne pas bouger, *ne pas bouger* . . . Ah!
Ce mouvement d'épaules, je n'ai pas pu le retenir . . .
La Chose, qui attendait, s'est alertée, elle a fondu sur moi, elle se coule en moi, j'en suis plein.—Ce n'est rien: la Chose, c'est moi. L'existence, libérée, dégagée, reflue sur moi. J'existe.[15]

---

title is taken from Descartes's *Principia*, is unfinished. While Kierkegaard is primarily attacking the epigones of the Hegelian system, the master who set the *dubitandum est* at the beginning of modern philosophy is by no means immune from his existential reproach.

14. As clearly appears in Etienne de Courcelles's Latin translation of the formula: "*ego cogito, ergo sum, sive existo*" (see *Discours*, Gilson's commentary, 292).

15. "Above all, not move, *not move* . . . Ah! I could not prevent this movement of the shoulders. . . . The thing which was waiting was on the alert, it has pounced on me, it flows through me, I am filled with it. It's nothing: I am the Thing. Existence, liberated, detached, floods over me [*sic*]. I exist."

W. Wolfgang Holdheim

A cursory reading might leave the following impression: some external object, an unnameable *Chose*, lies in wait for the narrator and (like a wild animal) pounces upon him when he moves. After it invades him, he recognizes that it is really himself. The earmark of this reading is that objectality and otherness are somehow primary, so that selfhood must be identified thereafter.

Such a view will evidently not resist a careful examination of the text. There is no gradual identification but a sudden recognition of something already familiar: "Ce n'est rien: la Chose, c'est moi." Above all, the process does not involve the integration of an alien substance but the restoration of a natural and preexisting condition. "L'existence . . . *re*flue sur moi": existence is not an invading foreign body; it flows *back* to its point of origin. "J'existe": existence and consciousness of self, always together, *re*emerge as an originary evidence, presupposing that they have been temporarily alienated, and there lies the significance of the (seemingly preceding) *Chose*. Note that *la Chose* itself is actually preceded by the subject's movement, which in its turn is preceded by an effort to avoid all movement. What else are movement and mental effort than the very quintessence of a dynamic consciousness, which is at all times also consciousness of self? The straining for immobility betrays the mind's effort to escape from its inherent dynamism. *La Chose*, far from being the original datum, is therefore the derivative result of an attempt at defamiliarization and reification. It is consciousness hopelessly projecting itself into otherness and thingness. The attempt collapses because movement is unavoidable, because existence qua consciousness cannot escape from itself.

"La Chose, c'est moi": the phrase has a Cartesian flavor, although the subject is not yet "une chose qui pense." But note that Sartre's text shares this trait with Descartes's *Méditations*, which likewise begin by establishing the *ego existo* and then proceed to thought as a later determination. In a sense, Roquentin is more Cartesian than Descartes, who had to go to considerable trouble to drive home the primacy of consciousness. Both the First and the Second Meditations end with veritable ascetic exercises, designed to overcome a natural attitude that would accord cognitive precedence to corporeal being. But for the intellectual heir to three centuries of Cartesianism, the natural attitude seems to be an orientation toward disembodied consciousness (the *rien* of "ce n'est rien"). After a spasmodic initial attempt at self-alienation, existence comes into its own as self-existence, "libérée, dégagée" from the burden of objectality.[16]

16. Geneviève Idt is therefore totally wrong when she writes that Roquentin's statement "la Chose, c'est moi" means that he is reduced to the consciousness of his corporality (in *La Nausée: Sartre* [Paris: Hatier, 1971], 46). *La Chose*, first of all, is a kind of abstract and nondescript objectality, not at all identifiable as his body. When his body does impose itself a

The *Cogito* in *La Nausée*

The Discovery of Corporality (next two paragraphs, 117–18, E98–99)

The next paragraph, a meditation on the theme "j'existe," begins with the joys of weightless spirituality. Existence is sweet (the word *doux* occurs four times), floats lightly in the air, stirs ("ça remue") in gently melting and evaporating touches: movement is no longer to be shunned. The protagonist is now in his natural element. Yet there are indications that he cannot maintain himself in that precarious airiness. Insensibly, more material aspects of himself come to the fore. Sweetness, not just a mental impression but a sensory attribute, becomes identified with his saliva, which first appears in the unobtrusive form of a "pool of whitish water." Even water, however light, is a physical substance. Grazing his tongue, running through his throat, it marks a progression toward the heavier solidity of bodily organs, until Roquentin must recognize with some surprise that "this pool is still me. And the tongue. And the throat is me."[17]

Surprise presently turns into horrified fascination. "I see my hand spread out on the table. It lives—it is me."[18] The quintessence of corporality, that organ is unmistakably a reminiscence of an earlier hand that kept recurring in the First Cartesian Meditation. "How could I deny that these hands and this body are mine?" Descartes' question is purely rhetorical. "I stretch out this hand, and I feel it, with purpose and deliberation," and no dream could be so clear and voluntary. The self-evident familiarity of the hand is such that the philosopher must take pains to remind himself "that perhaps our hands, nor indeed our whole bodies, are not such as we see them."[19] But Roquentin's hand is on the contrary the apogee of strangeness; it might as well be a crab or a fish, with its surrealistically grotesque movements; it must be painfully integrated into the primary evidence of the *ego sum*.[20] Only by experimenting can Ro-

---

little later, the point will be precisely that Roquentin proves unable to reduce himself to corporality. Brian T. Fitch offers a similar misreading (in *Le Sentiment d'étrangeté chez Malraux, Sartre, Camus et S. de Beauvoir* [Paris: Minard, 1964], 111). These are instances of an interpretation that seems to have become more or less a stereotype and is no longer even investigated.

17. "Cette mare, c'est encore moi. Et la langue. Et la gorge, c'est moi."
18. "Je vois ma main, qui s'épanouit sur la table. Elle vit—c'est moi."
19. "Comment est-ce que je pourrais nier que ces mains et ce corps-ci soient à moi?" "C'est avec dessein et de propos délibéré que j'étends cette main, et que je la sens." "Peut-être nos mains, ni tout notre corps, ne sont pas tels que nous les voyons." René Descartes, *Méditations touchant la première philosophie*, in *Oeuvres philosophiques* (Paris: Garnier, 1967), 2: 405–7, translations mine.
20. Idt (*La Nausée: Sartre*) writes that the organs of Roquentin's body tend to acquire a disquieting independence (45). In this context, however, the impact goes in the opposite direction: Roquentin the quintessential Cartesian discovers that they are part of himself and tries to come to terms with the fact.

quentin persuade himself that it really obeys the dictates of his will. His efforts at appropriation are not entirely useless. "I feel my hand": from "I see" to "I feel," we have a progression in proximity. "I feel its weight on the table which is not me."[21] It is not the same, after all, as a non-ego-related object. But finally the weight proves intolerable to one who is committed to the weightlessness of the inner self. Whatever he does, he cannot suppress the material substantiality of that interloping *res extensa*. It resists all efforts at reduction and cannot be dissolved in consciousness. Roquentin, a tormented Cartesian, truly lives the problem of the pineal gland!

At the end, nevertheless, bodily weight and disincarnate lightness merge in an uncomfortable zone of semisolidity. The bizarre animality of the body has been reduced to a teeming vegetality, its materiality has been diluted into a sweaty "graisse chaude qui tourne paresseusement, comme si on la remuait à la cuiller." It is anything but an improvement, a far cry from the original "pool of whitish water." The delicate grazings of a disembodied ego have deteriorated into sensations "qui végètent douce-ment, du matin jusqu'au soir, dans leur coin habituel."[22] The ambiguous term *doucement* now suggests the kind of gentle sweetness that spells nausea. Roquentin's unhappy consciousness reflects the ambiguity of incarnation—a state of messy intermediacy that is experienced as insipid-ity ("fadeur").

The Primacy of Thought (next two paragraphs, 118–19, E99–100)

"Je me lève en sursaut: si seulement je pouvais m'arrêter de penser, ça irait déjà mieux."[23] The ego suddenly emerges as a *thinking* ego. More precisely, Roquentin realizes that all his previous activities (seeing, feel-ing, sensing, even his original striving for passive insensibility) were in fact exercises of thought. Even Descartes had provisionally described the *res cogitans* as one "qui doute, qui conçoit, qui affirme, qui nie, qui veut, qui ne veut pas, qui imagine aussi, et qui sent,"[24] though the *intellectus* did end up by acquiring primacy. Do we now have a reversal of that intellec-tualism, so that "thought" is expanded to embrace all modes of intention-ality? We may be tempted to think so in light of a study on Husserl written

21. "Je sens ma main." "Je sens son poids sur la table qui n'est pas moi."
22. The translation speaks of "this warm obesity which turns lazily, as if someone were stirring it with a spoon" (the French says "fat" or even "grease," not "obesity"). The sensa-tions are "quietly vegetating from morning to night, in their usual corner."
23. "I jump up: it would be much better if I could only stop thinking."
24. The *res cogitans* is one "that doubts, that conceives, that affirms, that denies, that wants, that does not want, that also imagines, and that feels." *Méditations*, 421. Later repeated in an even more expanded form on 430.

The *Cogito* in *La Nausée*

by Sartre at that period, where he contends that fearing, hating, and loving (for example) should not yield second place to cogitation in furnishing knowledge about the world.[25] But our passage, quite on the contrary, contracts all mental life into an exacerbated cogitation. Thinking goes on and on, "s'étire à n'en plus finir." It is "ce qu'il y a de plus fade. Plus fade encore que la chair." And it becomes increasingly self-enclosed and autotelic—a thinking about thought ad infinitum: "Je ne veux pas penser . . . Je pense que je ne veux pas penser. Il ne faut pas que je pense que je ne veux pas penser. Parce que c'est encore une pensée." The Cartesian primacy of the intellect, far from being overcome, has been carried ad absurdum. What is peculiar to Roquentin is his revulsion from the process. Does not his diatribe look like a desperate effort to escape from his own constitutional Cartesianism? He disgustedly experiences the dynamics of the thinking ego as a case of active complicity: "cette espèce de rumination douloureuse: *j'existe*, c'est moi qui l'entretiens."[26]

There are reasons for this self-creating, self-sustaining activity of the thinking ego. "Ma pensée, c'est *moi*": the statement is not quite the same as the Cartesian "je suis une chose qui pense."[27] There is no *chose* in the Sartrean version, while the *pensée* seems to take a certain precedence over the *moi*. This shift in emphasis is underlined by another revealing formulation: "J'existe par ce que [not 'parce que'!] je pense."[28] The ego is no longer a substance that can be apprehended in a unitary act of self-certainty: it is sheer dynamics, bottomless and outer-directed. We here touch upon the crucial post-Cartesian aspect of Roquentin's experience, which reflects a peculiarly Sartrean emphasis on the Husserlian notion of intentionality. Consciousness is always consciousness *of* something; Roquentin cannot desist from cogitating because the ego has no firm foundation but is a continual activity of positing; Descartes's self-certainty must therefore turn into an incessant positing of self, even in the very process of rejecting it. If Roquentin's existence is thought, he clearly cannot think himself out of existence.

25. See Sartre, "Une Idée fondamentale de la phénoménologie de Husserl: L'Intentionnalité," in *Situations*, (Paris: Gallimard, 1947), 1: 34.

26. Thoughts "stretch out and there's no end to them." They are "the dullest things. Duller than flesh" (note that the crucial term *fade* is here translated as "dull," which is only one of its various implications). "I don't want to think . . . I think I don't want to think. I mustn't think that I don't want to think. Because that's still a thought." "This sort of painful rumination: *I exist*, I am the one who keeps it up."

27. Sartre: "my thought is *me*." Descartes: "I am a thing that thinks" (for example in *Méditations*, 430).

28. The translation says, however, "I exist because I think," based on the reading "parce que," which indeed does appear in the Pléiade edition. Other recent editions say "par ce que," and the "Notes et variantes" in the Pléiade edition point to this and declare it to be wrong (1775). But is it? Meaning "I exist by virtue of what I think," it expresses the state of affairs so precisely that I am inclined to take it for a correction rather than an error.

Is there an alternative? Earlier, Roquentin had noted a difference in the mode of being of the body: "Le corps, ça vit tout seul, une fois que ça a commencé. Mais la pensée, c'est *moi* qui la continue, qui la déroule."[29] Could one perchance stop the rumination by fusing the thinking ego actively and more intimately with the body, that half stranger in the domain of selfhood? Such a quest for substantiality might be more promising than a paradoxically passive hypostatization of the ego into the total otherness of *la Chose*.

Peripeteia: Return to the Body (next paragraph, 119, E100)

"Ma salive est sucrée, mon corps est tiède; je me sens fade": attention reverts to the sugary insipidity that marks the ego's ambiguous psychophysical condition. How to break the domination of *fadeur*? Roquentin focuses on the body, on the hand. Taking a penknife from the table, he stabs his left hand, like a new Julien Sorel. It is a Gidean "gratuitous act," for he has not much of an explanation to offer: "Pourquoi pas? De toute façon, ça changerait un peu."[30] No doubt he is acting under the dual impulsion of testing yet penetrating the solidity of the organ, of wishing to lose himself in the firmness of his body, yet, at the same time, of making it entirely his own.

On second thought, his seemingly futile explanation does touch upon an essential aspect by introducing the theme of sudden change. *Fadeur*, that gustatory expression for a state of mind reflecting a certain existential condition, has a temporal side. It represents dullness, sheer ruminatory succession, a nauseatingly monotonous flux of time.[31] This is the very opposite of the time of adventure—an irreversible structure of closely and meaningfully concatenated moments with a beginning, a middle, and an end. Thus it is also the contrary of dramatic time. And Roquentin's violent bid for an appropriation by and of his body, coming in the fourth act of his hopelessly undramatic Cartesian drama, is an aborted peripeteia, an ineffective incursion of dramatic temporality. It fails to bring change, to explode the universe of *fadeur*. True, the "little

29. 119, E99: "The body lives by itself once it has begun. But thought—*I* am the one who continues it, unrolls it."
30. "My saliva is sugary, my body warm: I feel neutral" (now *fade* is translated as "neutral"—not very incisively). "Why not? It would be a change in any case."
31. The kind of flux which various critics have associated with Flaubert's *L'Education sentimentale*. Dominick LaCapra, in *A Preface to Sartre* (Ithaca: Cornell University Press, 1978), rightly points to many Flaubertian echoes in *La Nausée*, though not to this particular one (109–10). Among others, he relates the satirical Sunday walk of the Bouville bourgeoisie, with its reified ceremonies, to the fiacre scene in *Madame Bovary*. Actually it is even more reminiscent of various party scenes in *L'Education sentimentale*.

pool of whitish water" has now been replaced by a "tiny pool of blood which has at last stopped being me."[32] In Descartes's First Meditation, the seemingly indubitable evidence of the hand was reinforced by the writing paper held by it.[33] Now, in a typically Sartrean arabesque, the protagonist's blood is drying on the sheet of paper that already bears the final lines of the discontinued biography; the ejected substance of the body mingles with the writing (the typographically alienated discourse) of the abandoned project. Soon this reification of art and life dries out into "un beau souvenir." The blood flows on monotonously, then coagulates: "Sous la peau, il ne reste qu'une petite sensation pareille aux autres, peut-être encore plus fade."[34] The peripeteia has evaporated; *fadeur* prevails again, and its mode of duration will regain ascendancy: the fifth and final act of the drama will go on and on, endlessly and undramatically; it will need to be terminated by a deus ex machina.

The Hapless Triumph of the *Cogito* (119–22, E100–3)

Roquentin is thrown back upon his "j'existe" rumination, which after half a page (precisely in the passage that I cited at the outset) finds its accepted Cartesian formulation. Concurrently, the hero seems to have reached the end of his solitary meditation. "C'est la demie de cinq heures qui sonne," as a reminder of the outside world.[35] The lonely thinker heeds the call and leaves his Cartesian *poêle*, where he has no good reason to stay and is obliged to face his own existence. The purchase of a newspaper, a symbol of collectivity, underscores his escape into the public sphere. But the paper merely prolongs and intensifies his previous preoccupations, at the same time turning into an aggravated version of the Rollebon sheet. The estranged discourse of the writing is materialized into smelly print, while the bloodstain escalates into a journalistic story of rape and murder. The obsession with corporality is now reawakened in the form of a young girl's abused corpse—a reminiscence of Baudelaire's poem "Une Charogne." Roquentin's erotic fantasies about that lifeless body of another will poignantly reenact the contradictory impulses of penetration and repulsion which his own flesh had evoked. The girl no longer exists; her body does; so do the houses and the sidewalk—and just then, right before the crucial passage, both world and syntax (*significatum* and *significans*) show distinct symptoms of dissolution: "Le pavé sous mes

32. A "petite mare de sang qui a cessé enfin d'être moi."
33. *Méditations*, 405.
34. "Under the skin, the only thing left is a small sensation exactly like the others, perhaps even more insipid."
35. "Half-past five strikes."

pieds existe, les maisons se referment sur moi, comme l'eau se referme sur moi sur le papier en montagne de cygne, je suis."[36]

It is profoundly ironic that the insight "je pense donc je suis" (once the foundation of cognitive certainty) should emerge at the very moment when language and reality disintegrate. Indeed the formula sets off an arabesquelike interior monologue, in which important themes of the novel intermingle in a veritable orgy of distortedness and in which the *cogito* itself seems to be perversely unhinged and deconstructed: "L'existence est molle et roule et ballotte, je ballotte entre les maisons, je suis, j'existe, je pense donc je ballotte."[37] The very evidence that, for Descartes, resisted every suspicion of being a mere dream[38] is here appropriated by an oneiric play of free associations; Cartesian logic degenerates into a nightmarish logorrhea. Roquentin's experience now really looks like "a kind of tragic caricature of the *cogito* of Descartes."[39] And this parodistic reversal of Descartes is ironically underlined by the many structural and thematic echoes of the *Méditations*, which (unlike the more literary *Discours*) were written in Latin for professional philosophers, in a strictly ratiocinative mode. Cartesian reason has obviously been turned inside out.

There is, however, more than caricature in this reversal, and parody and irony are many-sided and should not be taken in a dismissive sense. The ruminatory ego remains focal and never ceases to preside over this exercise in modernistic narrative. Upon close examination, it is not really the *cogito* as such that is unhinged and deconstructed. For all its oddity, the association "je pense donc je ballotte" still cannot help identifying the *moi* as the principle of movement. The world and language may disintegrate, but the thinking and narrating ego, however reluctantly, presents itself as the (itself indissoluble) fulcrum of dissolution, the centripetal locus of all centrifugality. Far from abolishing the *cogito*, Sartre's reversal of Descartes extends it over the totality of discourse and reality. Everything is drawn into the maelstrom of the cogitating ego, which becomes the principle of all existence; even the *res extensae* (one's own body or external objects) are now mere cogitations endowed with varying modes and degrees of "otherness." The logorrhea is a pointed narrative demonstration that existents are nothing else than restless phenomena in a dynamic and inalienable consciousness. Only a deus ex machina can put a

36. 119, E100: "The pavement under my feet exists, the houses close around me, as the water closes over me, on the paper the shape of a swan. I am." It seems that the translation tries to make some sense of the end of this quotation. If so, the purpose is laudable but misguided.

37. 120–21, E101: "Existence is soft, and rolls and tosses, I toss between the houses, I am, I exist, I think therefore I toss."

38. See, e.g., *Discours*, 33.

39. Poulet, "*La Nausée* de Sartre," 227, translation mine.

temporary stop to this universal cogitative flux. Relief comes through a song that dispels Roquentin's ruminations and restores his syntax: "Par-delà toute cette douceur, inaccessible, toute proche, si loin hélas, jeune, impitoyable et sereine, il y a cette . . . cette rigueur"[40]—the rigor of adventure, a firmly structured time, of a domain of ideality beyond "exis-tence." Salvation through art, as a kind of Schopenhauerian nirvana that frees us from existence—the theme has long been a familiar one. It recurs throughout *La Nausée* and will culminate in Roquentin's literary project at the end. Is it perhaps a trifle *too* familiar? And could there be some irony in the fact that this solution is usually suggested by a popular song hit played on a record in a cheap cafe?

A close reading of the Sartrean *cogito* section has clarified the position of Roquentin, that late link in a chain of philosophical autobiographers, and the nature of his *retour aux sources*. He is the Western intellectual who is condemned to live with his Cartesian heritage and cannot get away from the principle of subjectivity, however he may try. The question remains to what degree this section is representative of *La Nausée* as a whole. It could, after all, be a mere stage in Roquentin's development—a temporary relapse into a Cartesian subjectivism that he will ultimately overcome. According to a widespread tradition in Sartre studies, the novel largely deals with the pressure, incursion, and triumph of *les choses*. This view has been rather curiously related to the phenomenological interests of the Sartre of that period: some critics have tended to apply the epithet "phenomenological" to a sheer description of objects, contending that *La Nausée* is an exemplification of that method. In reality, of course, phe-nomenology is (in Husserl's word) an "egology," and is entirely concerned with the phenomena, processes, and nuances of consciousness. Indeed the most recognizably "phenomenological" section of *La Nausée* is the parodistic Cartesianism at the end of the *cogito* episode, whose incessant stream of cogitations is (no doubt deliberately) suggestive of Husserl's modification and continuation of Descartes.

Yet Sartre's philosophical writings of the period do supply evidence for a possible antisubjective view of *La Nausée*. Thus, in his brief essay on Husserlian intentionality, Sartre (interpreting "intentional" conscious-ness as a veritable flight into alterity) triumphantly exclaims that Husserl's notion frees us in one stroke from Proust and "inner life."[41] Despite its polemical nature, that study still reflects a peculiar radicalization of Hus-serl that is more fully expounded in the treatise *La Transcendance de l'égo* (1936). Husserl had criticized Descartes for short-circuiting his own proj-

40. 122, E103: "Beyond all this sweetness, inaccessible, near and so far, young, merciless and serene, there is this . . . this rigour."
41. See Sartre, "Une Idée fondamentale," 34.

ect of a transcendental *epoché* when he insensibly replaced the ego (the transcendental pole of all mental activities) by *mens sive animus*, an empirical thinking *substance*, thus laying the foundation for the subsequent rampant psychologism in Western thought.[42] Sartre argues that Husserl's assumption of a putatively transcendental" ego in fact perpetuates the Cartesian error, what is originarily given in merely an anonymous stream of cogitations. Consciousness is not egological; there is no ego in the transcendental field.[43]

One can see how this thesis must have furthered theories about the dissolution of the subject which have by now attained the status of cliches. I, for one, am unconvinced by Sartre's critique. I think that even in his purely philosophical writings, he cannot rid the transcendental field of a self-generating ego that continually constitutes itself as identical substrate of perceptions and cogitations.[44] The "I" is not (as he contends) a derivative creation of reflectivity, it is implicitly cogiven on the prereflective level—like the first-person vowel ending of the Latin word *cogito*. But Sartre's philosophical arguments are not at issue here. It is quite possible that the author of *La Transcendance* intended to project his conclusions programmatically into his novel, but I am not about to revive the intentional fallacy. My only interest is how his concerns are actually reflected in the text of *La Nausée*.

Geneviève Idt is perhaps the most systematic spokesperson for the "programmatic" philosophical perspective on Roquentin's subjectivity. She points to the dry abstractness of a "self" that is supposedly devoid of temporal dimensions: "Without either a past or affectivity, Roquentin evades every analysis, every psychology of passions."[45] Let us note in passing that this judgment is not at all antiegological in its impact: analyses of passions are the very essence of the empirical psychologism Husserl has attacked. More cogently, Idt points to the protagonist's last walk before his departure from Bouville. Feeling that the town has already left him, he literally loses his self: "A présent, quand je dis 'je,' ça me semble creux." Accordingly, the first-person pronoun is replaced by the neutral "il y a" ("there is"), expelling the ego from consciousness: "Il y a . . .

---

42. See Edmund Husserl, *Cartesian Meditations: An Introduction to Phenomenology*, trans. Dorion Cairns (The Hague: Nijhoff, 1960), esp. 24. The demonstration will be taken up at greater length in Husserl's posthumous book *The Crisis of European Sciences and Transcendental Phenomenology: An Introduction to Phenomenological Philosophy*, trans. David Carr (Evanston, Ill.: Northwestern University Press, 1970), esp. 78–81.

43. See Jean-Paul Sartre, *La Transcendance de l'égo: Esquisse d'une description phénoménologique* (Paris: Vrin, 1966). The investigations of that early study culminate in the sections on the prereflective (and nonegological) *cogito* in *L'Etre et le néant* (reproduced in the Appendix of *La Transcendance*, 114–21).

44. See Husserl, *Cartesian Meditations*, 67.

45. Idt, *La Nausée: Sartre*, 61.

conscience d'un visage" and "il y a connaissance de la conscience."[46] Idt concludes that *La Nausée* is in fact an application of the antiegological theses of *La Transcendance* and is a stylistic experimentation designed to demonstrate "the anonymity of consciousness, which is usually masked by the grammatical use of the first-person pronoun."[47]

Idt's thesis about the sheer grammaticality of the pronoun is as doubtful as it is fashionable.[48] Her point about Roquentin's waning sense of identity in those pages is to be taken more seriously. But I must emphasize: *in those pages*, for we are merely dealing with one particular episode.[49] It is pointedly terminated when the anonymous voice recaptures its identity with a vengeance, underscoring that the experiment is over: "Voilà le 'Rendez-Vous des Cheminots' et le Moi jaillit dans la conscience, c'est moi, Antoine Roquentin. . . ."[50] It is really not permitted to ignore so aggressive a resurgence of the ego! And similarly, in the final pages of the novel, the "I" (and with it the sense of existence) revives with such force that it needs to be exorcised by another replaying of the record. Roquentin, as he is listening, plans an ideal work of art: "Alors peut-être je pourrais, à travers lui, me rappeler ma vie sans répugnance." *Me rappeler ma vie*: are those the words of one devoid of selfhood, stripped of pastness and temporal horizons? Rather, they seem the words of a man who feels a need to transfigure an inescapable *moi* that stretches back in time: "Et j'arriverais—au passé, rien qu'au passé—à m'accepter."[51]

As we close the pages of *La Nausée*, the hero still has not escaped from the *ego existo*. Far from being a passing stage, the *cogito* episode sets the rhythm for the entire book. And we can now measure the intimacy of the relationship between philosophy and literature in Sartre's novel and its significance for both fields alike. Philosophically, *La Nausée* is nothing less than an existential-narrative modification and correction of its author's speculations of that time. On the literary side, a rereading of the novel is in order, along with a redetermination of its place in modern literature. Its putative *chosisme*, the triumph of chestnut trees and other objects,

---

46. 200, E170: "Now when I say 'I,' it seems hollow to me"; 201, E170: "There is . . . consciousness of a face"; 202, E171: "There is knowledge of the consciousness."

47. Idt, *La Nausée: Sartre*, 62.

48. Idt, *La Nausée: Sartre*, 61, contends that the "I" employed by Descartes and Husserl is a purely grammatical subject. This is totally unphenomenological. Nor would Sartre ever have contended it. Indeed, in *La Transcendance de l'égo* he explicitly writes that the "I" is not a simple syntactical form but an empty concept—like the concept of a chair, which can be conceived apart from any particular chair (71).

49. Already Jean Wahl, in his "Note sur *La Nausée*," had pointed to that passage. See his *Poésie, Pensée, Perception* (Paris: Calmann-Lévy, 1948), 103.

50. 202, E171: "There is the 'Railwaymen's Rendez-vous', and the *I* surges into the consciousness, it is *I*, Antoine Roquentin . . ."

51. 210, E178: "Then, perhaps, because of it, I could remember my life without repugnance." "And I might succeed—in the past, nothing but the past—in accepting myself."

needs to be analyzed from new perspectives and with greater nuance. And we should perhaps qualify the view that we are dealing with "the first novel where the character is dissolving and where the status of the subject becomes highly problematical."[52] Even at best, this is an overstatement: surely the subject became problematical much earlier; the ego underwent a radical process of dissolution, for example, in André Gide's *Les Nourritures terrestres* (1897).[53] Could Roquentin's nauseating receptivity be, among others, an inversion of Gide's ecstatic sensualism, which was still very much in the air in 1938? And what light could be cast, by a more suspicious reading of *La Nausée*, on the currently widespread disintegration of selfhood, which (for all its "postmodernity") had already found its critic in the Kierkegaard of *The Sickness unto Death*? The informed analysis of a sophisticated text like *La Nausée*, with its unsuccessfully disintegrating hero, may do much to expose postmodernism's modalities and inner motivations. If literary criticism can merge with philosophy, why should it not contribute to cultural critique?

52. Michel Contat and Michel Rybalka's "Notice" in the Pléiade edition of Sartre's *Oeuvres romanesques*, 1675, translation mine. The observation is ascribed to Lucien Goldmann.

53. I have discussed this aspect of *Les Nourritures terrestres* in some detail in: W. Wolfgang Holdheim, *Theory and Practice of the Novel: A Study on André Gide* (Geneva: Droz, 1968), 20–27.

[1 3]

Sexual Rogations, Mystical Abrogations: Some Données of Buddhist Tantra and the Catholic Renaissance

ROBERT MAGLIOLA

Among possible titles for this essay, the one I have chosen may seem pretentious. Apropos content, however, and style aside, the title serves my subject matter, an earnestly intended subject matter. The imagery of female and male consorts characterizes not only the tantric tradition (in Tibet, eighth century to the present) but the Catholic Renaissance (Europe, circa A.D. 1200–1550), and it is only post-Renaissance puritanism, be it Catholic or Protestant, that chooses to deemphasize the fact. As orthodox movements, the tantras and Renaissance Catholicism both deconstruct the dominant philosophy or theology (respectively) which historically precedes them and which, alas, surrounds and then comes after them, even in postreligious societies, up to this very day.[1] And whether the consorts be yogin and Prajnâ or God and Mary-as-spouse, they constitute their mystical liaison by that special sort of deconstructive work I call mutual abrogation:[2] a mutual abrogation that has much to teach the

1. Tantric Buddhism, or the *Vajrayana*, lays claim to Buddhist orthodoxy and can be said to deconstruct the nontantric Buddhism that dominates in all Buddhist countries except the Tibetan/Nepalese region. Catholic Christianity distinguishes between the teaching authority of the Church, which is official, and speculative theology, which is constructed by Catholic theologians and often dominates the thought of a given historical period.

2. For the purposes of this essay, it suffices to know that "mutual abrogation" is neither destruction nor construction. The two consorts do not simply annul each other (logocentric voidism), nor do they merge into one (logocentric *plenum*). Nor is a sponsoring source from the outside or a shared essence or a synthesis involved. Mutual abrogation is "deconstructive," that is, it constitutes the unity of the consorts by way of pure negative reference. The consorts absolutely negate each other, but each remains intact, and their unity is not identity proper but rather that sameness which is not identity. Mutual abrogation is explained in technical detail and at length in my recent book, *Derrida on the Mend* (West Lafayette, Ind.: Purdue University Press, 1984), where it belongs to the treatments of *effacement* and pure negative reference. This present essay hopes, instead, to demonstrate the abrogating maneuver by way of praxis.

world, especially today's world, about the glory of real sexual equality and
of a really religious bliss, a mutual abrogation that generates a literature
and generates an art truly beautiful to experience, beautiful to talk about.
So let us wend our way.

> Vergine sola al mondo, senza esempio,
> Che'l ciel di tue bellezze innamorasti,

> Only virgin in the world, without compare,
> That heaven fell in love with your beauty!

Thus sings Petrarch in "To the Virgin," the hymn Macaulay called the
finest in the world.[3] "Per te il tuo Figlio e quel del sommo Padre,"
"Through you, your Son and That of [Son of] the supreme Father," came
to save us. "Tre dolci e cari nomi ha' in te raccolti, / Madre, figliuola e
sposa, / Vergine, gloriosa, / Donna del Re," "Three sweet and dear names
have been harvested in you, / Mother, daughter, and spouse, / Glorious
virgin, / Lady of the King." The figure of triple oxymoron used by
Petrarch here, and he is—of course—echoing many illustrious predecessors, gives us our fascinating problem. As a creature, Mary is the daughter
of God. According to medieval Catholic theology, all of God's acts "outside" of himself are performed by his Divine Unity, so in the technical
sense one can properly call Mary the daughter of the holistic God here.
But the theology also permitted attribution to one person (either Father,
Son, or Holy Spirit) of the work really done by the Divine Unity, when
that work reflects what is, in God's immanent trinitarian life, the work
most proper to that person. Thus Mary is often specifically called, by way
of this attribution, daughter of the Father, the First Person of the Trinity.
Two other theological principles, the circumcession and the homeostatic
union, go on to complicate the rhetoric further. Christ is said to have two
natures, the human and the divine. Mary is literally the mother of the
Christ's human nature, but because his human nature is homeostatically
united with his divine nature she is the mother as well of the Second
Person of the Trinity. And because, by way of the circumcession, each of
the trinitarian persons is "in" the others, Mary is the mother of the whole
God.

Mary has yet a third role. She is called the spouse of the Holy Spirit
because the conception of the Christ in her womb, though the work of the
Divine Unity, is attributed to the Holy Spirit. Mary is, moreover, a spouse
in two figurative senses. She is the allegorical sign (or "type") representing
the graced human soul, whose spiritual union with God is analogous to

---

3. Italian text from *The Limits of Art*, ed. Huntington Cairns, (Princeton: Princeton
University Press, 1948; Bollingen paperback, 1969), 1:401 (canzone 366).

connubial union. And she is the allegorical sign representing the Church, the body of believers, which—according to Scripture—Christ takes as his bride. Leo Steinberg, in his pioneering work *The Sexuality of Christ*, points out very correctly that this theology had its beginnings in the early patristic age, so that already in the fourth century Saint Augustine is invoking a convention when he talks of Christ's "appearance as an Infant Spouse, from the bridal chamber, that is, from the womb of a virgin" (Augustine, sermon 9).[4] The verbal formulas are easily expressible, but their depiction in the visual arts presents more of a problem. How does one depict an infant as a spouse?

The solution the Catholic artist discovers during the trecento, and continues well past the mid–sixteenth century, is to deploy a very physical sexuality as emblematic of the triple paradox—Mary as mother, daughter, and spouse of God. This "solution," even if it were technically possible, could not have been used before, of course, because it is not until the trecento that Christians have enough faith to really affirm what their religion has been teaching them all along: both that Christ's Incarnation had blessed the "matter" of the world, the "flesh" of humanity, and that especially in him, the Christ, was the flesh blessed, because in his flesh there was no sin or inordinance.[5] Thus Renaissance religious art sets about doing exactly the opposite of what later art critics, distanced from the Renaissance by culture and theological assumption, will understand them to be doing.[6] Renaissance art, psychologically comfortable in the presence of the human body, sets about the task of elaborating a new sign system—a system wherein sexuality is the sign for Christ's redemptive sacrifice, for Christ's perfect humanity, for his saving power and, as in the case we are discussing, his relation to the Virgin Mary. But later centuries will grossly misread this very art and will take the portrayed flesh to be not a signifier of spiritual signifieds but rather the signified itself—so the spirit becomes according to their reading the hypocritical signifier whereby the flesh is (perhaps unconsciously) gratified.

Paintings of the Madonna and Child by Simone Martini, for example,

4. Leo Steinberg, *The Sexuality of Christ in Renaissance Art and in Modern Oblivion* (New York: Pantheon, 1983), 4.

5. Convincing documentation that this new appreciation of the Incarnation characterized the Renaissance is set forth in John W. O'Malley, S.J., *Praise and Blame in Renaissance Rome* (Durham: Duke University Press, 1979).

6. Steinberg's *Sexuality of Christ* discusses what surely has always been noticed: that pictorial emphasis in Renaissance religious art is very often upon the primary sex characteristics of the Christ. He argues, with much supporting evidence, that the intention is theological and the style emblematic. Deconstructionists should enjoy the precision with which he debunks readings inspired by either naturalism or Freudianism—the first because of its clumsy attempts to cover up the obvious, the second because of its own repressed puritanical assumptions.

Robert Magliola

or by Marco Zoppo,[7] far from being exercises in verisimilitude, are post-modern *maquettes* of sorts: Mary's role as mother, represented by her protective hands, and her role as consort, represented by the child's erotic gesture, flaunt themselves precisely by way of their mutual abrogation. That the Christ Child in much of Renaissance art is bestowing on his mother what Steinberg calls the "chin-chuck," that is, a pat or squeeze under the chin, is not meant as a naturalistic display of the child's tenderness. The chin-chuck, rather, was a long fixed secular convention for sexual union, and the religious artist's appropriation of it clearly signals that Mary is a bride, and Christ her bridegroom. That Mary's two roles mutually abrogate themselves in this art marks the pictorial text with a kind of internal deconstruction. This is to say, Mary's role as mother and her role as consort (and in some of these paintings, her role as daughter too) do not relate to each other by way of any traditional law of similarity/dissimilarity.[8] The two (and sometimes three) roles neither "share" an essence-in-common said to "ground" their relationship, nor do they depend per se on an originating "source" that "justifies" their comparison and is *hors de scène*, nor, finally, do they generate a "synthesis" claiming to "hold together" their similarity/dissimilarity. Instead, the Marian roles mutually abrogate, or "deconstruct," each other (the mark of "pure negative reference"),[9] and this action is at this point so very important for us precisely because it unconceals the equality of Mary and Christ *qua* spouses. If Mary as daughter "depends on" the Christ, and as mother is "depended upon," her espousals by pure negative reference are cut clean from these other two roles and she can be *as* consort his equal.[10] And in fact, as consort she *is* his equal, and the Renaissance art establishes this in many ways.

For a modern viewer, both the equality of Christ and consort and, for that matter, the use of sexuality as a sign for spiritual concerns are perhaps more obvious when displayed by means of a second motif—the erotically empassioned face. In Jan van Hemessen's *Madonna and Child*,

7. Steinberg, *Sexuality of Christ*, plates 9 and 10 respectively.

8. To consult how I deploy Derrida's refutation of (classical) "similarity/dissimilarity," see my *Derrida on the Mend*, 22, 23, 32–34.

9. "Pure negative reference," though itself *sous rature*, is an alternative way of accounting for "relationship": the entities in question are absolutely different from each other ("pure *is-not*"), yet related by that "movement of signification" which "at one stroke" constitutes/negates. See Magliola, *Derrida*, 35–37.

10. If an orthodox theologian were to express shock at this claim, it would be because he misunderstands pure negative reference. Since the latter accounts for relationship between Mary's roles as daughter and spouse in a way that requires no common ground between the two roles, that she is Christ's equal as spouse does not at all affect her creaturehood (part of her role as daughter). The same provision applies in the relationship between Mary and the Divine Persons, as long as one recalls we are operating here in the domain of attribution. For detailed theological applications of pure negative reference, see my *Derrida*, chap. 4.

for example, the Child gives Mary the ritualized chin-chuck and accompanies it with a fervent glance of such "mature masculine admiration" that—in Steinberg's words—"all his upper body bespeaks the warmth of the Heavenly Bridegroom"; Mary, in turn, "sits on the ground . . . , demure in her mystic character as the bride of her Son."[11] The motif of the enamored face, though most often reserved for the relationship between Christ and Mary, can by rights emblematize (you will recall) the spiritual bond between Christ and any graced soul: thus the ravished face of Saint Teresa in ecstasy, so often misread as a species of Freudian displacement and—in one of my favorite examples—the sensual swoon on the dead Savior's face, cradled in Saint Mary Magdalene's arms in Botticelli's most famous *Pietà*.[12] No doubt, however, the enamored face, and the chin-chuck too, appear most often in portrayals of the Child and Mother, and I would argue this is so because such a format annuls any misgiving, for the Renaissance viewer, that sexual union is the signified. (Mutatis mutandis, the same can be said of Botticelli's dead Christ, of course; the point is that eroticism is almost never used in depictions of an adult, commanding Christ.) Nonetheless, the equalizing function of this eroticism is what should speak loudest to moderns, it seems to me. A look at Barent van Orley's "*Madonna and Child with Angels*," for instance, establishes at once that the exchange of amorous glances depicted there does not permit domination or exploitation.[13] And because the amorous exchange is again a signifier of mystical union, the extrapolation to the mystical level must be made: to wit, even as authentic sexual nuptials equalize the partners, so too do the spiritual espousals of Christ and bride bring about parity. Perhaps, indeed, it is this very equality, proffered by the Child Savior by means of chin-chuck and fervent glance, that so astounds the two cherubs in the same painting. They stand in the background to the Virgin's right, their mouths agape—their expectations (of how Divinity should interact) deconstructed[14] on the spot. And in another *Madonna and Child* featuring chin-chuck and enamored glance, an anonymous Dutch painting contemporary to Barent van Orley's, not even the instruments of Christ's torture and crucifixion (presented proleptically by two angels) can dim his bliss, or Mary's.[15] Great Bliss, this!

The sexual parity of Mary and Christ her groom, we should remind

---

11. *Sexuality of Christ*, plate 49 and accompanying text, 39.

12. See *Religious Painting: Christ's Passion and Crucifixion*, ed. Stephanie Brown (New York: Mayflower, 1979), figure on 68 (top), and illustration on title page. For a brief but rich comparison of such female Christian mystics as Saint Teresa with the Buddhist yogini, see Alex Wayman, *The Buddhist Tantras: Light on Indo-Tibetan Esotericism* (New York: S. Weiser, 1973), 183.

13. Steinberg, *Sexuality of Christ*, plate 11.

14. Not added to or subtracted from but given an awe-ful twist.

15. Steinberg, *Sexuality of Christ*, plate 12.

ourselves again, is intended in Renaissance art to be a sign of their spiritual parity—a parity that maintains itself insofar as they are spiritual beloved and lover. Given the intimate connection of art and literature, however, I think already at this point the following question demands a hearing: What is the relationship of sexual image and religious meaning in, say, the written texts of the Italian trecento, the century when the shift to "sex as signifier" was just beginning in the Italian visual arts? Even a small acquaintance with Italian texts—theological and literary both, and written in Latin—reveals at once that the emblematic use of sex to represent religious relationship is already well established by the trecento. It seems that the visual arts, their sexual imagery unmediated by the *graphe*, or written sign, had to await the exuberant ease of the Italian Renaissance, whereas the written texts did not. Apropos my question, I would argue that what is new in the written texts is to be found in Petrarch's sonnets, and in only a few of them at that. "Sex as signifier of (orthodox) religious relationship" (the Fathers; medieval writers—Saint Bernard, etc.) and "sex as adversary of (orthodox) religious relationship" (also the Fathers; many devotional and homiletic tracts)—these two seem to be, throughout the Christian era, the most commonly found formulations, though they transmute into many variant forms.[16] In the sixteenth and seventeenth centuries, for example, John of the Cross, Teresa of Avila, and Richard Crashaw opt for "sex as signifier" while Racine is more often at the work of denigrating it; John Donne, at least in his more famous sonnets, often experiences sex and spirit as adversarial but implies their contention through double entendre so the "dark" sexual side of each pun reaches up to exacerbate the "light" side in a sort of Bakhtinian revel; Boccaccio during the Italian Renaissance and Rabelais during the French one also set sex and religion in contention but are clearly arrayed "on the other side" in this battle. They purge out orthodox religion with lusty laughter, and if sex signify spirit at all in their work, the spirit is humanist and protodeist.

I argue that some sonnets of Petrarch show a third formulation and help the most to introduce a rare variant of it. The formulation is "sex as concomitant with (orthodox) religious relationship."[17] The English-language literary tradition is most familiar with the twentieth-century nonorthodox (for Christianity) version of it supplied by D. H. Lawrence, but the most common orthodox version—"legitimate" sex and specifically religious activity as two performances that celebrate, each in its own right, the human life sanctified by God—seems not to generate the tension so

16. In these terms, "sex as signifier of religious relationship," the formulation characterizing much of Renaissance painting, finds its converse in Freudianism, where "religious relationship" is signifier of a "sexual signified."

17. *Concomitant* here means "in tandem with, functioning jointly with."

important for Western literature. The case is quite otherwise when the orthodox version coordinates not satisfactory sex and religious fulfillment but romantic pain and religious suffering. And I argue that it is precisely this variant which Petrarch broaches in the trecento, setting off an infrequent but still-recurrent theme that meanders through to the twentieth century and Paul Claudel. Petrarch's famous sonnet 62, usually taken to be an expression of pain over sex and spirit "at odds," really works—I argue—in quite the opposite way and is, indeed, perhaps the best instance he offers us of pain over sex and spirit "in tandem." I grant, of course, that in the majority of the poems about Laura, Petrarch is either protesting his love or repenting it or—and here sex and spirit become adversarial—protesting and repenting at once. Let us remember, however, that Petrarch remains very devout, very Italian, and—like just about all Italians of the trecento—very Franciscan, that is to say, very influenced by the mysticism of "coredemptive passion"; and surely this combination puts him at a far remove from most of his modern-day readers. Franciscan spirituality particularly emphasized Saint Paul's dictum, "In my own flesh I fill up what is lacking in the suffering of Christ, for the sake of His body the Church" (Col. 1:24–26). The Christian was to become an *alter Christus*, an "other Christ"—was to empathize with Christ's Passion, link personal pain with Christ's Passion—and this for three reasons: to sanctify the individual's own pain, to console Christ in pain, and to help to redeem others (*com-passio*).[18]

According to this mode of thinking, that Petrarch's romantic love for Laura includes (and perhaps even is grounded in) bodily and psychological attraction in no way invalidates it—because Christ's Incarnation consecrated the natural world and its impulses. What Petrarch is obliged to do is to imbue his romantic love with Christian nobility. That is, he must orient it toward true loving service to Laura, thus thwarting selfish use (for selfishness, and certainly *not* sexuality, is the ongoing residue of humankind's "original sin").[19] That Petrarch's love is unrequited and that, even if Laura were favorably disposed, Church law would forbid physical consummation—these also do not invalidate it. Petrarch can *affirm* his love (*not* repent it) and, indeed, consider it sent by God (*not* by evil), even though he must accept as well its nonfulfillment (Laura is

18. It was widely believed (and still is) that the historical Christ could, because of his divine nature, see ahead in time. In the midst of his Passion, then, he could be consoled right then and there by those Christians who, even centuries after his historical life, were to offer him their loving compassion. Apropos coredemption, it was thought (and still is) that while Christ's infinite merit, only and alone, suffices to save humankind, that Christ out of his generosity gives Christians the privilege to throw their lot in with him, i.e., to participate in the redeeming act. Their cooperation is technically superfluous but enables them to be *alteri Christi*. The scriptural basis of this teaching is the aforementioned Col. 1:24–26.

19. The sin of lust, then, is not sexual appetite but selfish use.

Robert Magliola

married to another). In such wise, Petrarch can link his *passio* with Christ's *Passio*, as he does in that lovely sonnet so often misunderstood, sonnet 62. I present herewith the Italian text, accompanied by a prose translation by Susan Noakes:

> Padre del ciel, dopo i perduti giorni,
> dopo le notti vaneggiando spese
> con quel fero desio ch'al cor s'accese,
> mirando gli atti per mio mal sì adorni,
>
> piacciati omai, col tuo lume, ch'io torni
> ad altra vita et a più belle imprese,
> sì ch'avendo le reti indarno tese,
> il mio duro adversario se ne scorni.
>
> Or volge, Signor mio, l'undecimo anno
> ch'i' fui sommesso al dispietato giogo
> che sopra i più soggetti è più feroce:
>
> miserere del mio non degno affanno:
> reduci i pensier vaghi a miglior luogo:
> rammenta lor come oggi fusti in croce.

> Father of heaven, after the days lost,
> after the nights spent raving,
> with that fierce desire whose flames consumed my heart,
> while gazing at the movements which, alas for me, are so graceful,
>
> may it henceforth please you that, with the aid of your light, I might turn
> to another type of life and to more worthy undertakings,
> so that, his nets stretched in vain,
> my brutal Adversary might be put to shame.
>
> Now it is, my Lord, the eleventh year
> since I was subjected to the pitiless yoke
> which presses with greatest harshness on the backs of those who are most
>   submissive.
>
> Have mercy on my unworthy anguish;
> lead my erring thoughts back to a better place;
> remind them how today you were crucified.[20]

---

20. Italian text from Francesco Petrarca, *Canzoniere*, ed. Aldo Garzanti, Introduction and notes by Piero Cudini (Garzanti, 1974). The English translation by Susan Noakes was done especially for this essay.

The tradition as read this clever sonnet in at least two ways: as a poem wherein Petrarch, addressing God the Father and Son consecutively, repents his romantic passion for Laura; or as a poem wherein Petrarch, while addressing God overtly, is covertly (and perhaps unconsciously) addressing Laura and still begging her to relent. My own reading sees the poem as working in quite a different way, so that it intentionally addresses God and Laura at the same time in order to link *Passio* and *passio*. When we interpret the first quatrain as addressed to God the "Padre del Ciel," the "perduti giorni" can be days "lost" or wasted because Petrarch had not known at first to consecrate his *passio* as a sacrificial offering to the Father (one thinks of Saint Paul's exhortation, "I make my body a living sacrifice, a burnt offering"). When we interpret the first quatrain as simultaneously addressed to Laura—and on this level it is very possible to take the "Padre del ciel" and the "Signor mio" of the first tercet, as pious Italian expletives—the days are lost because Laura refuses to Petrarch the holy pity that a Beatrice gave a Dante. Indeed, from this point of view, it is Laura and not Petrarch who is impious. The last two lines of the same quatrain, long a subject of critical debate, when addressed to Laura, refer to her sensuous charms and, when to Christ, refer—as Piero Cudini puts it—to His "suave and attractive" saving deeds.[21] This latter usage for *adorni*, a word more often than not reserved for feminine *appât*, makes the rhetoric deconstructive of the *stil dolce* tradition.

The proper referents for "col tuo lume" ("with the aid of your light") and "mio duro adversario" ("my brutal adversary") have generated the critical disputes over the second stanza. In recent times the standard commentaries, with an insistence so redundant, so strident, that I can only describe it as already suspicious on that count, have tried to limit the referents to "grace" and "Satan" respectively.[22] I agree that these readings are correct on their level, but when Laura rather than God is the addressee, the "light" belongs to Laura (as it often did to Beatrice for Dante), and the "brutal adversary" can be unredeemed *passio*, a sort of Albigensian Eros that resists transformation into the "altra vita," the "another type of life," of coredemptive Passion. This same Eros appears as the "dispietato giogo" or "pitiless yoke" in the first tercet, the easiest of the stanzas because its key meanings remain the same in both discourses: whether God or Laura is addressee, the "eleventh year" is dated from Petrarch's original encounter with Laura, and the "pitiless yoke' is that Eros which, ironically, weighs most fiercely on those who are naturally meek. The last

21. Cudini's note: "adorni—gentili ed attraenti" (87).
22. Cudini's notes: "lume—grazia"; "duro avversario: il diavolo" (87). Bernard Bergonzi's notes: "light—the light of grace"; "bitter foe—the Devil, not Love as some commentators have thought" (*World Masterpieces*, rev. ed., gen. ed. Maynard Mack [New York: Norton, 1965], 1: 1187).

tercet, in contrast, is the most complicated, with Petrarch skillfully generating two very distinct discourses and referential tracks from one and the same syntactic chain, and then, in a marvelous tour de force, combining them into the "two-and-one" of the last image, "in croce" ("on the cross").

Petrarch asks of Christ that the Savior have mercy on his "affano," or "anguish," which has been thus far "non degno," or "not worthwhile," since he has failed to place it "in tandem" with the Crucifixion. "Lead back wandering thoughts to a better place," begs Petrarch. That is, may Christ gather his liegeman's squandered sentiments and fix them in the "luogo," or "place," where he, the Savior, was crucified, thus valorizing them once and for all. By way of precisely the same words Petrarch is in the last tercet asking of Laura that she too have mercy on his sorrow. Because Laura is Petrarch's unrequiting lady, I would in this discourse take "non degno" in its other sense, to mean "unworthy." Petrarch's sorrow is unworthy because—according to the troubadour convention—the lover is always unworthy of his exalted lady, but more important, in this unique poem it is unworthy because it has been only secular, not secular-and-spiritual. The penultimate line of the tercet I read as wholly involving Laura, so that Petrarch implores her to lead back *her* thoughts, straying from any concern, any compassion for him, to the "better place" which is the cross. And finally, she must recall to them that today she was on the cross, by virtue of the fact that Petrarch chose to be there—to be there where Christ was.

Though I have argued that some contemporaries read Petrarch's code of *passio et Passio* as adversarial and others read it correctly as concomitant, most readers at least recognized the relevant imagery as simultaneously sexual and religious. They were able to do so because signifiers of this kind were supported by a well-known convention. Petrarch's "Hymn to the Virgin," cited earlier, gives us common examples when it calls Mary the window, temple, and cloister[23]—nonsexual signifiers (architectural, here) representing sexual signifieds (vagina and womb) signifying in turn both the physical (Mary's biological maternity) and the spiritual (Mary as Christ's spouse and mother of humankind). Much more consequential for our immediate concerns, however, is a version of this same semiological code that—especially in its paintings—the Renaissance seems to have recognized only tacitly. I refer to those images that unite male and female sexual traits into one figure, thus producing an androgynous signifier. More specifically, I refer to various techniques whereby the spiritual nuptials of Mary and Jesus are signified, this time not by an erotic relation of their two figures but rather by the absorption of either one into the other, depending on the case. It has already been convincingly argued elsewhere that the "effeminate" Christs of a Raphael or the "virile" Marys

23. See stanzas 3, 5, 6, *Limits of Art*, 1:401.

Sexual Rogations, Mystical Abrogations

of a Michelangelo are not homosexual representations, as recent "naturalistic" critiques insist, but rather emblems of prelapsarian innocence.[24] I would add that the quality of these figures is specifically androgynous and that adrogyny is, if anything, a better alternative than is erotic pairing when the purpose is to signify the *unity* and *equality* effected by spiritual nuptials. To say that in the Renaissance there is little or no theological commentary on the androgynous figure is not to deny, of course, that the theme is implied. It was already implied most clearly in Scripture, where Christ constitutes himself the "head" and all his communicants, female and male, the "body" united to this head. And elsewhere in the same scripture this body appears specifically as *feminine*, as the Church attached to Christ's virile head in one singular and glorious formation. I do not think it farfetched to claim that the ongoing development during the Renaissance of this doctrine of the Mystical Body (as it came to be called) served to condition the androgynous imagination.

With our definitions in place, it becomes a fairly simple matter to recognize various single formations as androgynous. Most commonly, the androgynous effect is achieved by a religious sign that internally marks the figure with a sexual value the opposite of that figure's biological gender: thus the representation of a very masculine Christ holding to his chest the womb-shaped chalice, and the Eucharist or round sacramental bread. Here the chalice and bread, by dint of convention and force of archetype, function at least on one level as emblems of Mary, for convention, and archetype too, present Mary as the everlasting chalice who mothers the body of Christ, the Eucharist. In turn, that Eucharist carries her inescapable trace; it is "flesh of her flesh." And more precisely in terms of our interest, it is archetype at least which presents Mary as the everlasting chalice, or vessel of intercourse, receiving Christ's spiritual body as groom. The converse of this formation likewise appears often in the Renaissance: the representation of a very feminine Mary holding a rosary to her bosom, its cross prominent and phallic; the lily, one might add, is an even more intriguing case, conventionally symbolizing virginity and archetypally symbolizing both phallus and floral maidenhead, it marks its bearer, be that Mary or Christ, with the "opposite" gender. These emblems, though very characteristic of the Renaissance, had their origins in the medieval period. The Renaissance per se seems to have contributed more indirect formations of androgyny, and I turn to one of these now because of its relative sophistication. Anyone looking without inhibition at Rogier van der Weyden's *Madonna and Child*[25] (which I

24. See Steinberg, *Sexuality of Christ*, 23 and passim.
25. Ibid., plate 22. For continuation into the baroque period, see as a good example El Greco's *The Holy Family* in Charles Wentinck, *El Greco* (New York: Barnes and Noble, 1964), 55.

choose as our example) should notice that Mary's hand is poised just above the Christ Child's loins and assumes ithyphallic form. What we have here is a fine case of "substitution," so that the theological meanings of the Christ Child's *membrum virile* are configured into Mary's own body. The theological meanings for Christ's virility were several,[26] but it suffices to acknowledge the most important—Christ's spiritual power. Having structurally assimilated Christ's virility, the portrayal of Mary becomes androgynous—and so represents the unity of Christ and Spouse. That a similar version of ithyphallic substitution recurs in portrayals of the saints (see, for example, Crivelli's *St. Mary Magdalene*)[27] shows that *ut multo potest* any Christian can qualify for these nuptials.

In the art of tantric Buddhism, far on the other side of the world from Europe, we also find the configurations of masculine and feminine consorts and of androgyny, and in both cases the mysteries of equality and identity and of mutual abrogation are very much involved. And again, the literature in question both supports and diverges from the iconography. If we look first at the standard yab-yum icon, we find the yum, or goddess, seated astride the yab, or Buddha/bodhisattva, so that the two figures are in sexual embrace.[28] Most scholars consider the yab-yum icon a Buddhist adaptation of tantric Hindu iconography, but—as is to be expected in the case of religions so contrary—the differences between the Hindu prototype and the Buddhist sequel are striking indeed. In standard Hindu tantrism Siva is of course a real god, and the Sakti a real goddess, and the union of the two symbolizes the nexus of male and female forces constituting the cosmos. Buddhism interprets the yum and yab, the female and male figures, as symbols for "wisdom" (*prajnâ*) and "skillful means" (*upâya*) respectively. There is much intriguing complication at work here—both in the iconography proper and in the history of influence and counterinfluence. While the Hindu tantra, written and iconic, regards the female as active and the male as passive, the Buddhist tantra manages to "have it both ways." Reversing the Hindu arrangement, the Buddhist written texts—so weighty in volume and authority—present the male ("skillful means," also "compassion") as active and the female ("wisdom") as passive, and they do so with a fervor that seems well-nigh polemical. But from the sidelines the Buddhist iconography marks the aforesaid written canon with a silent and subversive but nonetheless absolute difference. In Agehananda Bharati's words, "The yab-yum icon behaves in direct contradiction to the doctrine—the yum sits astride of the yab, the latter sits in *padmâsana* (lotus posture) or *vajrâsana* (*vajra*-posture); in

26. See Steinberg, *Sexuality of Christ*, 78–104.
27. See plate in Paul Stirton, *Renaissance Painting* (New York: Mayflower, 1979), 42, right.
28. For good examples, see plates 5, 6, 9, 10, in Tarthang Tulku, *Sacred Art of Tibet* (Berkeley: Dharma, 1974).

these postures, no movement is possible—whereas the posture of the yum suggests intensive motion to even the most casual observer."[29] Simply put, mutual and pure abrogation—the deconstructive maneuver that, you will recall, defined the roles of Mary and constituted relations between Mary and Jesus—operates again here. In this scenario, icon and written sign absolutely obvert each other in order to release the one Buddha-nature, that "sameness which is not identity."[30]

Two other points bear mentioning at once. The first involves the use of sexuality as a code. It can be said that in Hindu icons the sexual embrace operates both as signifier and signified.[31] Sexual embrace is signifier of the transcendent religious polarity, the male and female principles; and sexual embrace is the signified immanent to itself—that is, the actual sexual union of bodies is sacred (this latter formula is akin to the Christian sacrament of matrimony, which is concretely authenticated by Christ's Incarnation). In tantric Buddhist icons, however, sexuality functions much as we found it in the Renaissance madonna and child paintings— that is, exclusively as signifier of spiritual relation. Such is the case because Buddhism regards all entitative attachment (be it to "thing" or even to human and divine "beings") as "short of the goal," that is, short of the "enlightenment" that is advaya (blissful nonsubstantiality). Thus Buddhism, though it reinstates the validity of phenomena by way of the "two truths,"[32] is if anything much less "incarnational" (to resort quite unfairly to the Christian concept) than Christianity, and even the left-handed tantric rites, which leave so many occidentals dismayed, are in fact designed to bring about precisely the opposite of indulgence, viz., the cessation of desire.[33]

The second point we must register immediately is that the consorts "Wisdom" and "Skillful Means" (or sometimes "Devoidness" and "Compassion") are qualitatively equal in tantric Buddhism, and in this respect they echo the nuptial equality of Mary and the Christ. This parity of the static and dynamic will emerge most clearly if we trace the historical development of a second female-male configuration, that of the "female dancing on the male." For what we shall find is that in terms of this iconic

29. Agehananda Bharati, The Tantric Tradition, rev. pbk. ed. (New York: S. Weiser, 1975), 216.

30. For a very fine treatment of Derridean "sameness which is not identity," see Christopher Norris, Deconstruction: Theory and Practice (London: Methuen, 1982), chap. 2, esp. 33–37, and the short discussion of iterability on 110. For the Buddhist version of this sameness, see Magliola, Derrida, chap. 3.

31. A typical Hindu icon of this kind can be found in Heinrich Zimmer, Philosophies of India (Princeton: Princeton University Press, 1951), plate 11.

32. If, while recognizing its gross inadequacy, we limit our definition to the concepts already introduced in this essay, we can say the doctrine of the two truths is that phenomena and nonentitativeness are one-and-the-same (but not self-same).

33. See Bharati, Tantric Tradition, 294–99.

development it is as if the religious histories of India and Tibet conspire, as it were, to purge out sexual inequality. In the early Hindu version, the female (Sakti) dances on her spouse (Siva) because Indian erotic sentiment ascribed the active role in lovemaking to the woman. When mainstream nontantric Buddhism assimilates such iconography, it initiates what becomes an important deconstructive moment. While the *configuration* of female and male remains much the same (thus the "deconstruction" proper, since neither a "new entity" nor a "synthesis" is introduced), the *gloss* reverses values. Sakti becomes Aparâjitâ or some other Buddhist female deity, and she is trampling on a Hindu god (war of religion!). As for historically transitional icons such as the Buddhist Ganapatihrdayâ, they operate *in between* the active, dancing attitude of a Hindu Sakti and the passive, static attitude of a Tibetanized Buddhist Tara.[34] The motif of love's arrow also wends a tortuous way, settling, finally, into an equitable balance of the female and male. In early and divergent Hindu versions, the Saivitic saint alternately wards off (negative) and welcomes (affirmative) the arrows of Kâma (the Hindu god of love).[35] In non-tantric Buddhism it is Mâra's (the Tempter's) evil daughter who personifies lust, aversion, and craving.[36] Not until the advent of Tibet's tantric Buddhism does the feminine come into its own: the story of the wisdom *dakini* (intuitive wisdom personified) whose arrow saves the Buddhist monk Saraha[37] is so important because it restores the feminine to parity. In a grand sweep of cosmic irony, the *dakini* restores sexual balance by destabilizing the male and deconstructing his rational formulas. In the words of Trungpa Rimpoche, "The playful maiden is all-present. She loves you. She hates you. Without her your life would be continual boredom. But she continually plays tricks on you. When you want to get rid of her, she clings. To get rid of her is to get rid of your own body—she is that close. In Tantric literature she is referred to as the dakini principle. The dakini is playful. She gambles with your life."[38]

We proceed now to androgynous formations in Buddhism, a religion that affirms what can be called a "moment of dispersal" as one of its two truths, so that such a moment disperses all distinctions in the "sameness which is not identity." Thus even more than in Christianity, where the unity of Christ and Mother Church retains differentiation and is never perfectly "one and the same," Buddhism finds in androgyny a very apt

34. Ibid., 203.
35. See Wayman, *Buddhist Tantras*, 207; Zimmer, *Philosophies of India*, 38.
36. Consult Diana Y. Paul, *Women in Buddhism: Images of the Feminine in Mahayana Tradition* (Berkeley: Asian Humanities Press, 1979), 303.
37. See Tsultrim Allione, *Women of Wisdom* (London: Routledge and Kegan Paul, 1984), 39.
38. Cited ibid., 38, from Chögyam Trungpa, *Maitreya IV*, 25.

emblem for "sameness."[39] That is, *from this point of view*, the androgynous form is a more competent signifier than the two-figured form of the consort icons. If, for example, one looks at Tibetan icons of Avalokitesvara, the bodhisattva, or holy manifestation, who emanates from Amitabha Buddha, the epicenic traits are often very obvious and intentional.[40] Here androgyny not only signifies the spiritual fusion of "Wisdom" and "Skillful Means," but also the potentiality to materialize—for the sake of one's disciples—as either female or male (depending on what the occasion demands). Indeed, whole chapters of the Lotus Sutra, more popularly known in China as the Kuan-Yin Sutra, emphasize the many male and female embodiments of Kuan-Yin.[41] The sutra speaks of synchronic embodiments, but historians like to trace the evolution of the Kuan-Yin motif itself, since it plays out its own sort of diachronic androgyny: in short, the Indian Avalokitesvara—though he can, like all bodhisattvas, appear as female and male—has a privileged male form (in what is called, technically, the *Sambhoghakâya* body); but when, centuries after his provenance in Indian thought, news of him reaches China, the Chinese choose to depict a female form as privileged, the slim white-clad "Mother of Mercy," Kuan-Yin.[42]

It is Tibetan Buddhism, the *Vajrayana*, that often rescues femininity from Buddhism's more patriarchal variants.[43] And it is also *Vajrayana* that reinstates the full value of the "other" of the two truths. If there is a "moment of dispersal" (*paramârtha, nirvâna*), there is also a "moment of entitative gathering" (*samvrti, samsâra*), though of course the two moments are "one and the same" (*samvrti* is *paramârtha, samsâra* is *nirvâna*).[44] When Buddhism marks a Buddha or male bodhisattva with the conventional implement of the feminine sex or marks the female bodhisattva with a male emblem, the resulting formation is not epicenic (as was the Avalokitesvara icon). Rather, in this respect the artist's intention is to signify the still phenomenal (though spiritual) nexus of female and male power, of "Wisdom" and "Compassion," say. Cross-sexual marking can achieve this intention effectively because the female and male constitu-

39. In traditional Buddhist terms, this "sameness which is not identity" is *sûnyatâ*, "devoidness."

40. Inspect, for example, plate 1 in Tulku, *Sacred Art of Tibet*; in plate 25 one finds an epicenic Milarepa.

41. See Paul, *Women in Buddhism*, 253.

42. For good examples of Kuan-Yin iconography, see plates 1–16 in John Blofield, *Compassion Yoga: The Mystical Cult of Kuan-Yin* (London: George Allen and Unwin, 1977).

43. Consult Paul's discussion, *Women in Buddhism*, 285, 286; Allione, Introduction to *Women of Wisdom*, and passim.

44. For an excellent general introduction to the doctrine of the two truths, see Frederick Streng, *Emptiness* (Nashville: Abingdon Press, 1967), 94, 95, and circa; for the Tibetan version of this doctrine, see Wayman, *Buddhist Tantras*, 69, 70; for my comparison of the two truths and deconstructive thought, see my *Derrida*, 119–24.

Robert Magliola

ents, though united in one formation, are still very distinct (body marked by artificial implement) whereas in the epicene they are not. The epicenic is asexual, and though it carries the potentiality for female and male embodiment, it tends itself to signify the "moment of dispersal." Cross-sexual marking, instead, tends to represent the "moment of gathering" wherein the "sameness" of two contrary forces is generated by "mutual abrogation," not indifference. We noted earlier that Catholic Christianity represents gender, at least on the subliminal level, by way of such clearly archetypal signs as the crucifix, cross, chalice, rosary, lily, and so on. Buddhism has its own well-developed emblems, though it does not hesitate to profess that their role as sexual signifier is important (important, please note, as signifier of the nonsexual): thus the diamond thunderbolt is male, the bowl and conch shell female, the lotus bivalent (much like the lily of Catholicism), and so on. A look at female *vajra-yoginî* holding the masculine thunderbolt staff or the male sâkyamuni holding the feminine bowl[45] reveals at once that cross-gender marking by way of emblem can resort specifically to mutual abrogation (that is, each figure retains its own sex, and very clearly so, but is androgynous because of the artificial cross-gender mark). It is interesting also, I think, to note that in depicting androgyny Buddhist art even uses the bodily ithyphallic substitution we found in the European Renaissance. Most often the *dakini* is in stylized dancing posture, with the right leg bent at the knee and the foot raised all the way to the groin, where it assumes ithyphallic form.[46] Sometimes the female bodhisattva is sedent in what is called the bodhisattva pose, the pose of first emergence from meditation, with the legs unlocked and the left foot, clearly ithyphallic in form, positioned precisely between abdomen and thigh.[47] Just as the male member is configured via substitution into the very body of the feminine bodhisattva, Buddhist art also assimilates the vagina into the body of the male Buddha, or celestial holy one. In this case the male figure, sedent in full lotus position, places the hands below the navel in the *hokkai-join mudra* (gesture): the left hand with palm up and fingers together rests on the palm of the right hand; and the inner sides of the tips of both thumbs touch in mutual contact, forming an elliptical circle.[48]

In tantric Buddhism, androgynous form is inscribed into the language system, phonic and graphic. The tantric Nagarjuna[49] asserts that "Wis-

---

45. See Allione, *Women of Wisdom*, plate 10; Tulku, *Sacred Art of Tibet*, plate 31.
46. For example, ibid., plate 21.
47. Ibid., plate 2.
48. Plate 8, ibid., provides an example, but this *mudra* so abounds in Buddist art that it can easily be found everywhere.
49. Not to be confused with the Nagarjuna who founds Madhyamika, a much earlier school of Buddhism.

dom" is inscribed into vowels, "Action" inscribed into consonants, and "Wisdom/Action" into the semivowels, and he goes on to explain that these three classes of signs "are the nature of female, male, and androgyne. Hence *Ah*, which condenses the vowels, is the intrinsic nature of *prajnâ*. *Hûm*, which condenses the consonants, is the intrinsic nature of *upâya*. *Om*, which condenses *ya, ra, la, va*, is the intrinsic nature of the androgyne."[50] If we search about, however, for a more suitable (that is, less susceptible to a gloss that reads it as "synthetic") display of "sameness" precisely by way of abrogation, we find it in the fascinating "twilight language" (*sandhâbhâsâ*) of the tantras, called sometimes the language of the *dakinis*.[51] The semantic of the twilight language is split into two senses, afferent and efferent. A word that names an entitative object but intends a mystical concept is afferent, as when *sihlaka* ("frankincense") intends *svayambhu* ("self-originated," "the absolute"). Conversely, a word naming a mystical concept but intending an entitative object is efferent, as when *bala* (Buddhist "power," "discipline of mind") intends *mâmsa* ("meat"). The likeness in Buddhism to the usage we found dominant in European Renaissance painting is that twilight language (and its associated practice) also deploys sexuality only as signifier of the nonsexual.[52] This is the case not only with afferent terms, when, for example, *samarasa* ("sexual congress") intends "cessation of logical thought." It is the case with efferent terms too, when—for example—*bodhicitta* ("enlightened mind") intends "male seed," but the latter, in the wider sign system, symbolizes nonsexual experience (that is, the metasignified is nonsexual). The situation is very different in tantric Hinduism, where the parallel is much better drawn to Petrarch and what we called sex as concomitant with religious relation.[53] Nonetheless, though their goal remains resolutely nonsexual throughout, the Buddhist tantrics, rather than the Hindu ones, better approximate what in the West is now called Derridean doubling.[54] That is, perhaps remembering the provenance of the metaphor "twilight"[55] to designate *dakini* language, the Buddhists keep—in their changing glosses of any given text—the linguistic boundary between efferent and afferent forever shifting, situational, unnamed.

Sexual re/torts inevitable are, but mystical re/sorts do well and more

50. As cited in Wayman, *Buddhist Tantras*, 178.
51. All the following examples, and the definitions of *afferent* and *efferent*, derive from Bharati, *Tantric Tradition*, chap. 6.
52. See Wayman, *Buddhist Tantras*, 41, 130; Bharati, *Tantric Tradition*, 297 and passim.
53. See Bharati, *Tantric Tradition*, 266.
54. The doubling that cannot be reduced to a dyad and involves instead a forever altering reinscription. Text is ever turning against itself and breaking, yet it discontinuously "repeats" itself and "staggers on."
55. Twilight as the unnameable interval constituting the "between" of day and sunset: temporally unfixed, it changes with each diurnal cycle.

than well, and do better. Sixteenth-century Europe knew this, and the tantras do. Listen to a text from the *Hevajra Tantra*, long considered a literary jewel, proclaiming the moments of gathering and dispersal which are "sameness":

> The yogin is Means and Compassion, and the yogini
> Wisdom and Voidness for she is deprived of causation.
> The thought of enlightenment is the undivided unity
> of Compassion and Voidness.
>
> There is no recitation of mantras, no austerities,
> no oblations, no mandala, and none of its components.
>
> This is the recitatation of mantras, the austerities,
> and oblations, this is the mandala and its components.[56]

56. See the excerpt from the *Hevajra Tantra* in *World of the Buddha: A Reader—from the "Three Baskets" to Modern Zen*, edited with an introduction by Lucien Stryk (New York: Doubleday Anchor, 1969), 311, 312.

[14]

Mastery and Transference:
The Significance of *Dora*

Susan Rubin Suleiman

The contemporary critical imagination has been captivated by certain literary texts. "Les Chats," "The Purloined Letter," *The Turn of the Screw*, *Frankenstein*—these are among the works, none of them "central" in the traditional sense ascribed to that term by literary history (the way, say, *The Iliad* and *King Lear* and *Ulysses* are central works in constant need of commentary), that have elicited readings, rereadings, and concurrently rewritings from literary critics and theorists, as well as, occasionally, philosophers and psychoanalysts, in the United States and Europe, over the past twenty years. Taken as a whole, this body of commentary points us as much, if not more, toward the controversial issues and the evolution of recent critical thinking about literature as it does toward the literary texts in question. Poe's short story may recede from view as we follow the complicated, much longer stories and counterstories—about truth and interpretation, about the status of readers and texts—that it gave rise to; and Mary Shelley's "hideous progeny" may appear small in comparison to the body of speculations—about female authorship and autobiography, about motherhood and the romantic imagination—to which it has given birth.[1]

1. On "The Purloined Letter," see, for example, Jacques Lacan, "Le Séminaire sur 'La Lettre volée,'" in his *Ecrits* (Paris: Seuil, 1966); Jacques Derrida, "The Purveyor of Truth," *Yale French Studies* 52 (1975), 31–114; Barbara Johnson, "The Frame of Reference: Poe, Lacan, Derrida," *Yale French Studies* 55/56 (1977), 457–505; and Norman Holland, "Recovering 'The Purloined Letter': Reading as a Personal Transaction," in *The Reader in the Text: Essays on Audience and Interpretation*, ed. S. Suleiman and I. Crosman (Princeton: Princeton University Press, 1980). All of these essays after the first engage in self-conscious dialogue with one or more of the others, as well as with Poe's text. On *Frankenstein*, see, among many others, Sandra Gilbert and Susan Gubar, "Horror's Twin: Mary Shelley's Monstrous Eve," in *The Madwoman in the Attic* (New Haven: Yale University Press, 1979);

Susan Rubin Suleiman

It is probably not accidental, however, that such crucial critical dialogues and revisionary reflections should have been provoked by these texts, not others. There must be something about them that peculiarly resonates with modern critical preoccupations. Their significance may lie precisely in their capacity to generate a multitude of other texts, to act as the focal point for an expanding intertextual space of contemporary debate and commentary.

Freud's "Fragment of an Analysis of a Case of Hysteria," more commonly known as *Dora*, possesses a similar capacity. Written in 1901, first published in 1905, published again with additional footnotes in 1923, *Dora* not only occupies a privileged place in Freud's oeuvre and in the history of psychoanalysis (it was the first of Freud's five major case histories and the first work in which he dealt explicitly with the question of transference) but has increasingly come to preoccupy literary critics and theorists. As a recently published anthology of essays "on" this work makes clear, *Dora* fascinates.[2] Why? Why has this text not only provoked a seemingly endless outpouring of "readings" but given rise to rewritings in other media—a play, a film? What is it, about *Dora*, that touches us?

I will not try to answer these questions directly. Why invoke the recent rise of feminist criticism (Dora was a young woman much sinned against) or the peculiarly modern fascination with madness (Dora was a hysteric), incompletion (*Dora* is a "fragment"), failure (*Dora* is a broken-off case)? Instead, I shall run the risk of adding one more commentary to the crowd around the woman and the text—a commentary spinning out some implications of the relationship between the couple in my title, mastery and transference.

It was Shoshana Felman, I believe, who first developed the idea that the analytic experience of transference can also serve to define the experience of literature.[3] More recently, Peter Brooks has proposed a "transferential model" of reading in which the relationship between narrator and narratee, and between author and reader, is analogous to the relationship between analysand and analyst. Between Felman and Brooks, however, there is a difference. Brooks's model is classically Freudian: for him,

Mary Poovey, " 'My Hideous Progeny': Mary Shelley and the Feminization of Romanticism," *PMLA* 96, 1 (1981), 332–47; Barbara Johnson, "My Monster/My Self," *Diacritics* 12, 2 (1982), 2–10; as well as the anthology edited by G. Levine and U. C. Knoepflmacher, *The Endurance of Frankenstein* (Berkeley: University of California Press, 1979).

2. See Charles Bernheimer and Claire Kahane, eds., *In Dora's Case: Freud—Hysteria—Feminism* (New York: Columbia University Press, 1985). The play, *Portrait de Dora* (1976), is by Hélène Cixous (English translation by Anita Barrows, "Portrait of Dora," in *Diacritics* [Spring 1983], 2–32); the film *Sigmund Freud's Dora* (1979), is by Tyndall, McCall, Pajaczkowska, and Weinstein.

3. In "Turning the Screw of Interpretation," *Yale French Studies* 55/56 (1977), 94–207.

narrator   narratee
author   reader
analysand   analyst

how we are affected by the myth is an important part of it + [handwritten marginalia]

transference is the effect of the *patient*'s desire, to be "read" by the analyst; Felman's model is Lacanian: for her, transference is also the effect of the *analyst*'s desire. For Brooks, the "task of the analyst is to recompose the narrative in order to represent better the story of the patient . . . , to account better for its dominant themes and to capture better the force of [the patient's] desire." Correlatively, the task of the reader is "not only to recapture [*ressaisir*] the . . . story, but to judge its relation to the narrative and to make himself the critic of the narrative in relation to the story, seeking not only to understand what the narrative says but also what it wants to say."[4] For Felman, this one-way relationship, in which the reader/analyst is in a position of judgment, of mastery over the other's desire, is impossible. Interpretation, whether analytic or literary, is an *interpretation is mutual* [handwritten marginalia] enterprise of mutual seduction and displacement. Felman can thus read Freudian interpretation itself through and with Lacan, seeing its blind spot: "To his great astonishment [this is Lacan talking about Freud, quoted by Felman], he noticed that he could not avoid participating in what the hysteric was telling him, and that he felt affected by it. Naturally, everything in the resulting rules through which he established the practice of psychoanalysis is designed to counteract this consequence, to conduct things in such a way as to avoid being affected."[5]

What Freud was blind to, contemporary Freudians have said, was the unavoidable necessity and presence of countertransference, "the effects of the analyst's own unconscious needs and conflicts on his understanding or technique."[6] Donald Spence, for example, argues that far from being a "possible source of error, something to be 'analyzed away' so as not to contaminate the therapeutic conversation . . . , countertransference may be a necessary part of active listening," so that "unless the analyst is continually supplying his own private associations, he can never hope to understand the clinical encounter."[7] This, however, is still not the same as the Lacanian view, which sees transference itself as the entanglement of two desires. "Transference," Lacan said in one of his many pronouncements on this subject, "is a phenomenon in which the subject and the analyst are included together. To divide it in terms of transference and countertransference, no matter how bold and daring the propositions one allows oneself to make on that theme, is never anything but a way of eluding what is involved."[8] What is involved, I would suggest, is not only

4. Peter Brooks, "Constructions psychanalytiques et narratives," *Poétique* 61 (1985), 65, 72, my translation.

5. Felman, "Turning the Screw," 118.

6. Reich, quoted in Donald P. Spence, *Narrative Truth and Historical Truth: Meaning and Interpretation in Psychoanalysis* (New York: W. W. Norton, 1982), 188.

7. Spence, *Narrative Truth*, 284, hereafter cited parenthetically in the text.

8. Jacques Lacan, *Le Séminaire, XI: Les Quatre concepts fondamentaux de la psychanalyse* (Paris: Seuil, 1973), 210, my translation.

who desires what and whose desire "comes first" but also, more important, the aim of the clinical encounter itself.

The aim of the encounter is the cure, Freud would say—Freud did say,
in *Dora* among other places. And in what does the cure consist? In the
removal of symptoms and in the construction, or reconstruction, of an
"intelligible, consistent, unbroken" story:

> It is only toward the end of the treatment that we have before us an intelligible,
> consistent, and unbroken case history. Whereas the practical aim of the treatment
> is to remove all possible symptoms and to replace them by conscious thoughts, we
> may regard it as a second and theoretical aim to repair all the damages to the
> patient's memory. These two aims are coincident. When one is reached, so is the
> other; and the same path leads to them both.[9]

If the sign of true neurotics is their "inability to give an ordered history of
their life" (31), then the analyst's task is to help them achieve that capacity.
As Steven Marcus has remarked, in his pathbreaking essay on *Dora*, "No
larger tribute has ever been paid to a culture . . . which had produced as
one of its chief climaxes the bourgeois novels of the 19th century" than
this faith of Freud's in the healing capacity of coherent storytelling.[10]
Donald Spence's influential recent book, *Narrative Truth, Historical Truth*,
criticizes Freud's notion that the story thus reconstructed corresponds to
historical truth; yet Spence remains totally faithful to the notion that the
analytic cure consists in the production of narrative coherence: "Gaps
must be filled; explanations must be supplied; puzzles must be clarified.
What we are after, it seems, is a narrative account that provides a coherent
picture of the events in question" (180). Spence's thesis that this narrative
does not necessarily have to correspond to "historical truth," that it can be
effective by virtue of its aesthetic unity and pleasingness alone, is a revision of Freud. More exactly, Spence carries to its logical conclusion what
Freud himself saw but was loath to admit, as his defense of the "story" he
constructed for the wolf-man makes clear.[11] Spence's thesis does not,

9. Sigmund Freud, *Dora: An Analysis of a Case of Hysteria* (New York: Collier Books, 1963),
32. All subsequent page references will be to this edition and will be given in the text. In *The
Standard Edition of the Complete Psychological Works*, ed. James Strachey et al., 24 vols.
(London: Hogarth Press, 1953–74), the Dora case appears in vol. 7 under the title "Fragment of an Analysis of a Case of Hysteria."

10. Steven Marcus, "Freud and Dora: Story, History, Case History," in his *Representations:
Essays on Literature and Society* (New York: Random House, 1975), 278. A shortened version
of this essay is reprinted in *In Dora's Case*.

11. See Sigmund Freud, "The Case of the Wolf-Man: From the History of an Infantile
Neurosis," in *The Wolf-Man by the Wolf-Man*, ed. Muriel Gardiner (New York: Basic Books,
1971), esp. 191–203. For an excellent discussion, see Peter Brooks, "Fictions of the Wolf-
Man: Freud and Narrative Understanding," in his *Reading for the Plot: Design and Intention in
Narrative* (New York: Alfred A. Knopf, 1984), 264–85.

What other goals are there? more instruction

however, change or put into question the fundamental premise that the aim of analysis is interpretation, and that interpretation consists in the construction by the analyst of a unified, aesthetically pleasing, plausible story for, about, and ideally with the collaboration of the patient.

This is precisely where Lacan's notion of transference complicates and entangles things. For it is not at all clear, reading Lacan, that the aim of analysis, or of analytic discourse, is to construct a coherent—that is to say plausible, finished—story. I would go so far as to say that this is precisely *not* the aim of analytic discourse, according to Lacan.

But I am getting ahead of myself, rushing from Vienna to Paris. My subject is *Dora*, and I realize that my apparent reluctance to stick to it, my desire to rush beyond her, manifests anxiety of a particularly transferential kind. In order to reach Dora, will I have to displace all the other texts around her? Or will I have to settle for writing commentaries on the commentaries? But what kind of text will that produce? Perhaps it will be hysterical.

At the end of his 1912 paper "The Dynamics of Transference," Freud speaks about "the struggle between physician and patient, between intellect and instinct. . . . This is the ground on which the victory must be won, the final expression of which is lasting recovery from the neurosis."[12] And in the postscript to *Dora*, he says it was because he did not "succeed in mastering the transference in good time" that he lost the struggle. As many commentators, starting with Lacan, have pointed out, however, Freud's real error lay not in failing to master the transference but in trying too hard to master Dora and her story.[13] Indeed, Freud tried to ram down Dora's throat the story of her love for Herr K.: "'So you see that your love for Herr K. did not come to an end with the scene, but that (as I maintained) it has persisted down to the present day—though it is true that you are unconscious of it.'—And Dora disputed the fact no longer" (125).[14]

Dora did not dispute the "fact," but she opened the next sitting by informing Freud that it was her last. Whereupon he continued the love story by supplying (via the governess that Dora told him about that day)

12. Sigmund Freud, "The Dynamics of Transference," in *Therapy and Technique*, ed. Philip Rieff (New York: Collier, 1963), 114.

13. Jacques Lacan, "Intervention on Transference," trans. Jacqueline Rose, in *In Dora's Case*, 92–104.

14. Herr K., much older than Dora, was the husband of Dora's father's mistress. In the "scene by the lake," which occurred when Dora was sixteen, he openly propositioned her, and she slapped him. He, his wife, and Dora's father all denied the truthfulness of her account of the scene by the lake. Dora's anger stemmed partly from her sense that she was being used as a pawn by the three adults. Although Freud refused to cooperate with Dora's father, who asked him to "bring her to reason," his insistence that she loved Herr K. could have been interpreted by Dora in that light.

motives of jealousy and revenge for her slapping Herr K. in the crucial
"scene by the lake," as well as for her subsequently telling her parents
about his attempted seduction: "You waited for [a fortnight] so as to see
whether he would repeat his proposals; if he had, you would have con-
cluded that he was in earnest, and did not mean to play with you as he had
done with the governess" (129). Finally, Freud even began to envisage an
alternative "happy ending" to the story, in which Dora would have married Herr K., whom his wife would have been only too happy to divorce,
given her relations with Dora's father! Dora did not dispute this either,
but "she said goodbye . . . and came no more" (130). Marcus's comment
seems more apt: "Dora refused to be a character in the story that Freud
was composing for her."[15]

The most common explanation for why Freud was so intent on forcing
this unsavory story on Dora is that he himself identified too much with
Herr K., a man "still quite young and of prepossessing appearance," as he
put it in a footnote (44). Here, then, would be an example of unrecog-
nized countertransference (or, more simply, transference) on the part of
the analyst. I would suggest, however, that Freud's love story for Dora was
inspired by his putting himself not only in Herr K.'s place but in the place
of an omniscient narrator who, having a limited number of "characters"
to work with, must find the most plausible and psychologically motivated
solution to their entanglements. In other words, it was the desire for
narrative coherence *as such* (based on the only model Freud appreciated,
that of the nineteenth-century realist novel, whose privileged subject, as
Tony Tanner has shown, was adultery) that may have been a central
driving force. Freud's own transference, then, was not only to Herr K.,
but to Balzac—by which I mean not that Freud desired to write fiction (he
vigorously defended himself against that idea, which he considered an
accusation) but that, to the extent that he had to construct stories, he
desired to possess the authority of a Balzacian narrator. It is extraordinary, in fact, how tenaciously and single-mindedly Freud pursued the
construction of the love story for—and to—Dora, from the first kiss in
Herr K.'s place of business when Dora was fourteen right through the
interpretation of the second dream and after. He didn't miss a single
occasion to draw connections that would reinforce the tale, providing
ever more subtle motivations, establishing ever tighter links between
events.

At the same time, even as he was hammering home his tale of heterosexual jealousy and passion, Freud set in motion a major counterstory,
that of Dora's homosexual love for Frau K., *but it was not a story he told to
Dora herself.* This story is elaborated in digressions—first in a four-page

15. Marcus, "Freud and Dora," 307.

digression in the text just before the analysis of Dora's first dream(77–81), then in three long footnotes, which were all already in the 1905 text (126, 133, 142). Whereas the heterosexual love story is addressed to Dora, who is both narratee and recalcitrant protagonist (this is most clear in the bit of second-person narration I quoted earlier—"You waited . . . so as to see"—where Dora is supplied with both action and motives, in the best nineteenth-century tradition), the alternative, homosexual love story is communicated, as a "complication" (77), only to the reader.

What links, if any, can we establish between Freud's desire for narrative mastery (what I have called, somewhat facetiously, his transference to Balzac) and his splitting of Dora's story into two versions? The simplest answer would be this: the desire for narrative mastery is part of Freud's therapeutic desire for the cure (his mistake being that he was too impatient, forcing the story on Dora before she was ready to accept it), and the splitting is the result of the delay between the treatment and its writing up into the case history. In other words, Freud was not aware, during the treatment itself, of the "other story," that is why he made no use of it in his interpretations to Dora.[16] He himself suggests as much, in a note toward the end of the text: "The longer the interval of time that separates me from the end of this analysis, the more probable it seems to me that the fault in my technique lay in this omission: I failed to discover in time and to inform the patient that her homosexual (gynaecophilic) love for Frau K. was the strongest unconscious current in her mental life" (142). As one group of commentators has pointed out, this remark appears surprisingly disingenuous on Freud's part, since "he had long since abandoned the notion that it was sufficient for the analyst to inform the patient of the contents of her unconscious to effect a cure." In order to make Dora realize her homosexual love for Frau K., the authors argue, he would have had to "fight it out in the sphere of transference," which means that he would have had to be willing to accept identification with Frau K. This, however, he was unable to do, not only because Frau K. was a woman but because she was a "woman that is the object of a love that is homosexual."[17]

This explanation—which does not suggest that Freud was lying, only that he was "blind"—seems to have some validity, especially if we com-

16. An even simpler, although not altogether implausible explanation would be that Freud was aware all along of the "other story" but consciously chose not to pursue it with Dora, either because of a cultural prejudice against lesbianism (he didn't want to give her ideas) or for aesthetic reasons (he didn't want to confuse things by offering her alternative stories that might, in addition, delay the cure). The problem with this explanation is that Freud would then have to have been less than honest in his encounters with Dora, a conclusion I do not wish to draw.

17. Jerre Collins et al., "Questioning the Unconscious: The Dora Archive," *Diacritics* 13, 1 (1983), 40, rpt. in *In Dora's Case*, 248.

Susan Rubin Suleiman

pare Freud's footnote (which implies that it took him some time to realize the fact that he "had failed to discover in time" Dora's love for Frau K.) with a remark he made to Wilhelm Fliess in a letter dated January 30, 1901, less than a month after Dora's last visit. In the letter Freud describes his already finished manuscript, "Dreams and Hysteria" (the original title of the case history, which he finished on January 24):

The main thing in it is again psychology, the utilization of dreams, and a few peculiarities of unconscious thought processes. There are only glimpses of the organic, that is, the erotogenic zones and bisexuality. *But bisexuality is mentioned and specifically recognized once and for all*, and the ground is prepared for detailed treatment of it on another occasion. It is a hysteria with tussis nervosa and aphonia, . . . and *the principal issue in the conflicting thought processes is the contrast between an inclination toward men and an inclination toward women*.[18]

Could it be that Freud discovered "the principal issue in the conflicting thought processes" only in the course of writing up the case history, that is, in the three weeks following termination of the treatment? Even if that is so, we may wonder why he insists in his footnote (added later, perhaps, but certainly by 1905) that it took him a long time to realize Dora's love for Frau K.? And why does he return to the question again so emphatically at the end of the footnote? "Before I had learnt the importance of the homosexual current of feeling in psychoneurotics, I was often brought to a standstill in the treatment of my cases" (142). This remark seems curiously at odds with the much earlier digression *in the text*, in which Freud was at pains to establish that even in normal people, adolescence is a period when there exists "an affection for people of their own sex" (77); all the more so will one find such affection in neurotics, *"for I have never yet come through a single psychoanalysis of a man or a woman without having to take into account a very considerable current of homosexuality"* (78, my emphasis). If this digression in the text is a revision added after the first writing in 1901, perhaps around the time Freud was writing the *Three Essays*, that only heightens the contradiction, for the footnote seems also to have been written quite a while after the end of the treatment. Whatever its date of writing, the note's purpose was evidently to emphasize Freud's "ignorance of the homosexual current" in this particular case at the time of the treatment. But textually, the digression occurs fifty pages *before* the note, so that textually both the reader and Freud "knew" long before the note what he now claims he didn't know until much later. And besides, there is

18. *The Complete Letters of Sigmund Freud to Wilhelm Fliess, 1887–1904*, ed. and trans. Jeffrey Moussaieff Masson (Cambridge: Harvard University Press, 1985), 434 (my emphasis). Freud mentions finishing the manuscript "yesterday" in his letter of Jan. 25, 1901 (433).

the letter to Fliess, which insists that "bisexuality is mentioned and specifically recognized once and for all" already in the very first draft.

Curiouser and curiouser, Alice would say. So curious, in fact, that a stronger explanation is needed than the one founded on Freud's inability to let himself be placed in the position of Frau K., or even of Dora's mother. Such a strong explanation has been offered by Neil Hertz. According to Hertz, the real problem involved Freud's possible or impossible identification not with transference objects but with Dora herself. Freud had, above all, to defend himself against the possibility of being confused with Dora, not so much because he feared feminization (although that was surely a factor) but because *this* feminization would lead to an "epistemological promiscuity, in which the lines would blur between what Dora knew and what Freud knew and, consequently, in which the status of Freud's knowledge, and of his professional discourse, would be impugned."[19] In other words, Freud did not want his own discourse and knowledge to be contaminated with the discourse and knowledge of the hysteric.

This, it seems to me, is the most interesting entanglement of Freud in Dora's case. The desire for narrative mastery would then turn out to be not only a therapeutic desire for the cure but also a personal and intellectual defense against the contamination of psychoanalysis and of the psychoanalyst's discourse by its object. A year before he began the treatment of Dora, Freud had already expressed anxiety about mastery in talking about the style of his "dream book," which he had just finished. He wrote to Fliess: "Somewhere inside me there is a feeling for form, an appreciation of beauty as a kind of perfection; and the tortuous sentences of my dream book, with their parading of indirect phrases and squinting at ideas, deeply offended one of my ideals. Nor am I far wrong in regarding this lack of form as an indication of insufficient mastery of the material."[20] The "material" in this case was chiefly his own dreams. In Dora's case, the material was Dora's dreams, Dora's history, and Dora's desire. Freud could not "sufficiently master" these either, no matter how hard he tried. The splitting of Dora's love story can be read as one indication (symptom?) of how the case history itself becomes "hysterical," caught up in the "conflicting thought processes . . . between an inclination toward men and an inclination toward women."

But perhaps even more interesting, from my point of view, is a single moment in the case history where it is not Freud's *narrative* that is contaminated by hysteria but Freud's own unconscious that seems to become

19. Neil Hertz, "Dora's Secrets, Freud's Techniques," *Diacritics* 13, 1 (1983), 72, rpt. in *In Dora's Case*, 234.
20. *Complete Letters*, 374.

Susan Rubin Suleiman

indistinguishable from Dora's. Neil Hertz notices this moment but fails to notice what is, I think, most significant about it. It occurs during the interpretation of Dora's second dream, the one in which a thick wood (*Wald*), a train station (*Bahnhof*), and a cemetery (*Friedhof*) figure prominently. Associating to this dream, Dora produces yet another memory of the scene by the lake ("The wood in the dream had been just like the wood by the shore of the lake" [119]) and then recalls that she saw a similar wood the day before in a picture at an exhibition. "In the background of the picture were nymphs." Following this is a paragraph Hertz quotes in its entirety:

At this point a certain suspicion of mine became a certainty. The use of *Bahnhof* and *Friedhof* to represent the female genitals was striking enough in itself, but it also served to direct my sharpened curiosity to the similarly formed *Vorhof*—an anatomical term for a particular region of the female genitals. This might have been no more than a witty error. But now, with the addition of "nymphs" visible in the background of a "thick wood," no further doubts could be entertained. Here was a symbolic geography of sex! "Nymphae," as is known to physicians though not to laymen (and even by the former the term is not very commonly used), is the name given to the labia minora, which lie in the background of the "thick wood" of the pubic hair. But any one who used such technical names as *Vorhof* and "nymphae" must have derived his knowledge from books, and not from popular ones either, but from anatomical text-books or from an encyclopaedia—the common refuge of youth when it is devoured by sexual curiosity. If this interpretation were correct, therefore, there lay concealed behind the first situation in the dream a phantasy of defloration, of how a man seeks to force an entrance into the female genitals. (119–20; I have modified the translation somewhat to conform more closely to the original German.)

What strikes Hertz as most curious are the last three sentences and the logic by which Freud arrives at the very last sentence. Hertz asks: "Is the shift to the masculine pronoun ['any one who used such technical names . . . must have derived *his* knowledge'] a way of suggesting that such reading habits, though indulged in by women, are essentially masculine, and hence coordinate with male fantasies of defloration?" He concludes that the shift to the masculine pronoun would be in line with Freud's "persistence in characterizing Dora's love for Frau K. as 'masculine'" but that it is above all a sign of Freud's anxiety "to preserve certain clarities in his thinking about the transfer of psychoanalytic knowledge. It required a vigilant effort, it would seem, to draw the line between the operations in the hysteric which produce the text of her illness, and those in the analyst which seek to interpret and dissolve that text."[21]

21. Hertz, "Dora's Secrets," 73 (*In Dora's Case*, 236).

[223]
Mastery and Transference

I agree with Hertz's conclusion but am surprised that he did not notice the astonishing way in which the beginning of Freud's paragraph fails, precisely, to "draw the line" between operations in the hysteric and those in the analyst. For the really curious slip in this text is not the use of the masculine qualifier, which in the German construction of the sentence is grammatically required ("*Wer* aber solche technische Namen . . . gebrauchte, *der* musste seine Kenntnis aus Büchern geschöpft haben"—the "Wer . . . der" construction is obligatory).[22] The really curious slip is the way Freud, not Dora, produces the word *Vorhof* in association with *Bahnhof* and *Friedhof* and *then* proceeds to say that "anyone who used such technical names as *Vorhof*, and 'nymphae' must have derived his knowledge from books."[23] At this point, we can no longer be certain whose associations are being interpreted, since Freud has merged his own *Vorhof* with Dora's "nymphae" to produce the "fantasy of defloration." Whose rape fantasy, exactly, is this? And is the position of the subject of the fantasy masculine or feminine? (Dora fantasizes being raped, Dora fantasizes raping; Freud fantasizes that Dora fantasizes she is being raped, Freud fantasizes Dora raping; Freud fantasizes being raped, Freud fantasizes raping . . .)

Psychoanalysis, we have known for a long time, is about the unconscious and about human sexuality. It is also, as Marcus, Brooks, and others have reminded us and as any reading of Freud confirms, about the possibilities and limits of narrative. One great virtue of the Dora case—which may explain its apparently endless capacity to generate commentaries and rewritings—is that it dramatizes, as perhaps no other of Freud's writings does, how the desire of the narrating and of the interpreting subject is caught up, entangled with, contaminated by its object. Freud's multiple entanglements with Dora—on the levels of discourse, of desire, and of sexuality—can be read as an allegory of the failure of psychoanalysis, which is at the same time, in a modern perspective, its greatest success: the failure to achieve complete "mastery of the material." Such a reading is, of course, itself necessarily caught up in a process of displacement, the reader/writer, I, contaminated by other texts, other "sexts" (Hélène Cixous's portmanteau word). Interpreters beware: desire is contagious.[24]

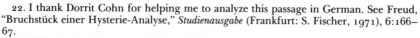

22. I thank Dorrit Cohn for helping me to analyze this passage in German. See Freud, "Bruchstück einer Hysterie-Analyse," *Studienausgabe* (Frankfurt: S. Fischer, 1971), 6:166–67.

23. This slip has been noted, in a different context of argumentation, by Madelon Sprengnether. See Sprengnether, "Enforcing Oedipus: Freud and Dora," in *In Dora's Case*, 66.

24. The bulk of this essay forms part of a much longer piece entitled "Nadja, Dora, Lol V. Stein: Women, Madness, and Narrative," in *Discourse in Literature and Psychoanalysis*, ed. Shlomith Rimmon-Kenan (London: Methuen, 1987). For the present volume I have reframed and expanded the section on *Dora*.

[15]

Law in and as Literature:
Self-Generated Meaning in
the "Procedural Novel"

RICHARD WEISBERG

Lawyers and literary scholars are talking to each other from both sides of the cultural divide. In every year save two since 1976, major panels on law and literature have taken place at the annual conventions either of the Modern Language Association or its equivalent in the law school community, the American Association of Law Schools. As at these panels, so in the literary journals and the law reviews, prominent scholars have broken through the unidisciplinary restraints that had characterized law and literature for many decades.[1] Three books integrating the two have recently appeared,[2] and several major universities—the University of Michigan and Duke University, among them—have set the precedent of joint appointments in law and literature. With the German romantics, we may be rediscovering the untimely fact that all narrative-centered knowledge is one.

The principal lines of discourse connecting the two fields are beginning to emerge. As to the place of law in literary criticism and theory, we find (quite naturally) that most work so far has been in the domain of textual criticism and history. There is so much law in the traditional canon that

This essay was first delivered as a paper at the MLA conference titled Law as Literature: Minimal or Seminal Significance, December 1984.

1. See Richard Weisberg and Jean-Pierre Barricelli, "Literature and Law," in *Interrelations of Literature*, ed. Barricelli and Joseph Gibaldi (New York: Modern Language Association, 1982), 150.

2. James Boyd White, *When Words Lose Their Meaning: Constitutions and Reconstitutions of Language, Character, and Community* (Chicago: University of Chicago Press, 1984); Robert A. Ferguson, *Law and Letters in American Culture* (Cambridge: Harvard University Press, 1984); Richard H. Weisberg, *The Failure of the Word: The Protagonist as Lawyer in Modern Fiction* (New Haven: Yale University Press, 1984).

Law in and as Literature

one could spend a lifetime on such individual authors as Balzac, Scott, Dickens, Dostoevski, Tolstoi, Twain, Trollope, and Melville, and even this most apparent generic outpouring of the law in literature—the nineteenth-century novel—barely overtakes such predecessors as Elizabethan and Jacobean theater, medieval poetry, the Icelandic family sagas, and fifth-century Greek tragedy, to mention only literary genres and periods whose proclivity to law has already been worked through in the scholarship. Our own century, of course, has not lagged behind its predecessor, and the names Kafka, Camus, Solzhenitsyn, and Böll, as well as Barth, Doctorow, Mailer, and Malamud in the United States, come quickly to mind.

But if their move toward literature may ultimately lure lawyers away from theory[3] to the fictional text itself,[4] so in literary studies the next phase of law-related inquiry may move us from text to theory.[5] And to round out the phenomenology, the effect of law may be to move literary theory back in the direction of textual primacy just as the effect of literature in the law schools has been to *question* that primacy.

This constant tilt in the hermeneutic balance lends further validity to the interdisciplinary impulse. For if legal theory may need some correction from the idea of so-called plain meanings and universal principles of textual interpretation, so recent literary theory arguably has pitched excessively in the opposite direction.[6] The legal structure, as integrated into modern fiction, ultimately implies a shifting back toward the primacy of

3. See, e.g., Stanley Fish, "Working on the Chain Gang: Interpretation in the Law and Literary Criticism," in *The Politics of Interpretation*, ed. W. J. T. Mitchell (Chicago: University of Chicago Press, 1983), 271–86; Fish, "Fish v. Fiss," *Stanford Law Review* 36 (1984), 1325–48, in dialogue, respectively, with Ronald Dworkin, "Law as Interpretation," *Critical Inquiry* 9 (1982), 179, and with Owen Fiss, "Objectivity and Interpretation," *Stanford Law Review* 34 (1982), 739. The theoretical debate, which inquires into the availability of "disciplining rules" for the legal interpreter, is hardly new, but it has been reenergized. See also W. B. Michaels, "Against Formalism: The Autonomous Text in Legal and Literary Interpretation," *Poetics Today* 1 (1979), 23–34; S. Mailloux and S. Levinson, *Constitutional Hermeneutics* (Evanston: Northwestern University Press, forthcoming).

4. See for instance James B. White, *Heracles' Bow* (Madison: University of Wisconsin Press, 1985); and Richard Posner, review essay, "*Billy Budd* to Buchenwald," *Yale Law Journal* 96 (April, 1987).

5. I say this with full knowledge of thinkers such as Stanley Fish who predict (at this writing) that "theory's day is dying." See, e.g., Fish, "Pragmatism and Literary Theory," *Critical Inquiry*, 2 (1985), 455. This prediction is, in my view, knowingly premature, designed perhaps to deflect the onslaught of revisionist or reformist theories opposed to Fish's own. At least in the field of law and literature, the "marketplace conditions in the humanities" (to quote Fish himself) which have brought literary theory to the law are merely part of a background virtually ensuring an expanding theoretical dialogue between lawyers and critics over the next decade. And every new utterance of Attorney General Edwin Meese on constitutional hermeneutics makes clear that that dialogue should go on.

6. See Tzvetan Todorov, "American Literary Criticism," *Times Literary Supplement* (Oct. 4, 1985); but also Richard Weisberg, reply to Todorov, "Nietzsche and Modern Literary Criticism," *Times Literary Supplement* (Nov. 8, 1985).

the text and toward a notion of textual meaning apart from the subjectivity of any given interpreter or audience. This trend is especially prevalent in the great novelistic texts, generated at a time of increasing skepticism and even nihilism during the mid–nineteenth through the mid–twentieth centuries. We must grapple with the paradox, revealed in law-related masterpieces, that one of fiction's most iconoclastic and questioning epochs produced a repetitive structural pattern that endorses the notion of a verifiable reality anterior and preferable to that of subjective interpreters or their audience.

The years 1860–1960 form one of several periods in Western literature in which there is a striking fascination with law, lawyers, trial scenes, and detailed legal investigations. The lawyers who populate these modern novels in disproportionate numbers are presented (particularly after Balzac and Dickens) not for purposes of mere caricature or even social satire. Rather, with their gift of articulateness and their inclination to reorder reality narratively, they best metaphorize the literary artist's own enterprise, and when these lawyers' personal values fall under the sign of an internal psychic malaise (*ressentiment*), they serve as vehicles for authorial *self*-criticism.[7] The lawyers in Flaubert, Dostoevski, Melville, Kafka, Faulkner, and Camus, or for that matter in Barth, Malamud, and Doctorow[8]—our contemporaries—influence us to be skeptical *of the word*, precisely of the word as most effectively employed, by clever, articulate beings in positions of institutional and cultural power.

Paradoxically, the legal *procedures* in many of these novels influence us to safeguard a nonskeptical notion of the availability of truth, either within a single text or regarding the larger text: a person or historical event. In those novels presenting a full-scale legal investigation—procedural narratives, as I will call them—a structure is created that endorses a verifiable comprehension of anterior events at the same time as it questions a merely subjective, highly articulate, interpretation of those events.[9]

Now, as Camus's greatest proceduralist, the lawyer Jean-Baptiste Clamence, suggests to us in *La Chute*, truth is oppressive—"La vérité est

7. Weisberg, *The Failure of the Word*, 6.
8. See Barth, *The Floating Opera*; Malamud, *The Fixer*; Doctorow, *The Book of Daniel*. Most recently, see Scott Turow, *Presumed Innocent*.
9. A list of "true" procedural narratives in modern fiction should include: Camus, *L'Etranger*; Dostoevski, *Crime and Punishment* and *The Brothers Karamazov*; Faulkner, *Sanctuary* and "The Spotted Horses Incident"; Malamud, *The Fixer*; Melville, *Billy Budd, Sailor*; Wassermann, *Der Fall Maurizius*; and Wright, *Native Son*. A list of "modified" procedural narratives (imperfect variations on the structural norm) might include: Barth, *The Floating Opera*; Camus, *La Chute*; Conrad, *Lord Jim*; Doctorow, *The Book of Daniel*; Dürrenmatt, "Die Panne"; Faulkner, *Intruder in the Dust*; Forster, *A Passage to India*; Kafka, *Der Prozess*; Lee, *To Kill a Mockingbird*; Melville, "Benito Cereno"; and Twain, *Pudd'n head Wilson*.

assommante." Recognition of the structural effect of legal ratiocination in procedural narratives takes patience. Much like a juror in a complicated trial, the reader is asked to focus upon detail, sometimes at the expense of grandiose statements or human dramatics. Unlike the trial scene in theatre or popular culture, the narrative form of investigation does not produce drama or even resolution; rather it produces narrative, often reams of narrative. Not only is the reader symbolically a juror, weighing evidence as to textual meaning; in procedural narratives, the reader is overtly asked to play that role, and his or her response to the data presented—the care of or disregard for textual detail—in fact tests the very theory that the structure is uniquely producing.

Many readers have failed in their role as jurors. Incapable of or uninterested in resisting the seduction of clever language, such readers all too often swallow whole the perspective of the articulate lawyer or lawyer-figure.[10] Resistance, while textually mandated, requires great care and even a willingness to retard the natural Aristotelian progress through the fictional text in order to make sure that the various interpretations of the earlier narrative event are accurate. So it is not surprising that few of us recall, much less relish, the procedural sections of long novels like *The Brothers Karamazov*, even though these sections are structurally central and quantitatively unavoidable. Even in shorter narratives like *L'Etranger*, which (as Wolfgang Holdheim first observed)[11] mimics Dostoevski's legalistic structure, the web of detail is rarely remarked. And only recently have we seized upon the inquiry overtly thrust upon us by the narrator of *Billy Budd, Sailor*—to judge with precision the legal arguments mounted by the articulate Captain Vere in his rush to condemn the "angel of God."[12]

These three works, and other procedural narratives like them, create a dyadic or tripartite structure to recount the central action of the story. This action is frequently a crime (as in *Crime and Punishment*, Faulkner's *Sanctuary*, or Malamud's *The Fixer*), but it can also be a noncriminal event (the alleged gift in Faulkner's "Spotted Horses" and various other commercial episodes in his Snopes Trilogy, Faulkner being a kind of twentieth-century Dickens and Twain in his love of everyday legal transactions).[13] The first part of the structure is the narration of the event itself; next there is a kind of preliminary inquiry conducted by a lawyer or

10. The predilection of novel readers toward acceptance of almost anything a verbally gifted hero says is most compellingly tested in the procedural novel. This observation, to be elaborated in another forum, strikes me as a legitimate outgrowth of true "reader-response" criticism.

11. W. W. Holdheim, *Der Justizirrtum als literarische Problematik* (Berlin: de Gruyter, 1969).

12. See Weisberg, *The Failure of The Word*, chaps. 8 and 9.

13. See symposium, "The Law and Southern Literature," *Mississippi College Law Review*, 4:2 and 5:1 (1984).

lawyer-figure, culminating in a new narrative version of the event; and usually—though this is not structurally required—there is then a trial that produces yet another narrative rendition of the event and an institutionally condoned resolution of any legal conflict it has produced.

Amazingly and somewhat counterintuitively, the depiction of an actual trial is not required. In *Crime and Punishment*, for example, the trial takes up a few short paragraphs in the aesthetically displeasing "Epilogue," whereas the investigation absorbs three full chapters and is structurally vital; *The Fixer* ends just as the trial, so long awaited by protagonist and reader alike, is about to begin! The procedural narrative (unlike the theatrical trial scene) is less interested in conflict resolution than in the production of successive narrative versions of verifiable anterior events. The structure is not that of a "whodunit" but that of a "who said what"; the spotlight is on the interpreter—the lawyer and the lawyer's narrative techniques—as much as or more than it is on the parties to the litigation. Thus the lawyer stands ready to take the narration of the matter to any possible venue, from the traditional forum of a pretrial hearing room to the less conventional domain of the salon, the tavern, the brickyard, or even the boudoir.[14] Adversarial pyrotechnics in the courtroom are quite unnecessary to the procedural novelist's purposes.

With great care, modern novelists portray the subtle distancing of the authoritative interpretation from the original account of the event in the narrative. This original account—the first part of the structure—I call the anterior position. Accessibility throughout the procedural narrative to the anterior position superficially distinguishes the literary phenomenon from a real-life investigation into a past event. Six people witness a traffic accident. Ten minutes later, we have six different versions of the event. What really happened? In a novel, that "what really happened," however obliquely recounted, is available to the reader simply by thumbing back through the pages of the text to find the anterior position. Thus the procedural narrative posits an identifiable anterior reality against which the legal investigation and its outcome must be tested. The anterior position, while rarely lacking in ambiguity, structurally occupies a privileged place and, for the reader, rises (as we shall see) to the level of truth.

Thus if the lawyer in part 2 of *L'Etranger* manages to elicit testimony to the effect that Meursault did not want to view his mother's body at the time of her funeral, we as readers have the capacity to find in part 1 of the text narrative data proving the precise opposite. A similar check is avail-

14. Examples include Porfiry Petrovich in *Crime and Punishment*; Nikolai Nelyudov and Ippolit Kirillovich in *The Brothers Karamazov* and Camus's Clamence (whose procedural narrative, disguised as a "confession," originates in Amsterdam's Mexico City Bar); Grubeshov in *The Fixer*; and the examining magistrate in *Der Prozess*.

able to verify the number of rubles allegedly spent by Mitya Karamazov at Mokroe or the relevance to the charge against that nonmutineer Billy Budd of Captain Vere's repetitious "mutiny" argument.[15] We need patience, indeed sobriety, to retard our temporal progress through the narrative, but then we have been invited to be careful by the writer, who has lovingly interwoven all this detail into the plot for no other discernible reason.

Gradually our care pays off. The reader inevitably notices that the lawyer or lawyer-figure conducting the investigation, despite or because of his verbal facility, loses almost all sight of the anterior position. Distortions, first minor, then catastrophic, filter into the lawyer's analysis, always artfully conveyed, usually in the form of prolix narrative statements that become metaphors for the writer's own enterprise. Error is not inevitable. But in modern fiction, the cleverer and more articulate the interpretation, the more likely the error.

Analysis, in terms of reader-response, shifts from the defendant, or even the law, to the lawyer and the lawyer's interpretive techniques. Caught up in a self-serving system of narrative and form, even the ostensibly neutral lawyer or judge in literature may violate the anteriorism he or she is charged with uncovering. More often, a subjective bias or even deep-rooted psychological problems are subtly revealed. The rational outer forms of the law are shown to mask professional ambition, envy of the criminal, *ressentiment*, or powerlessness. This comment, self-consciously made by literary artists, may be less about law than about narrative endeavors generally. Thus lawyer-figures often are created late in the novelist's oeuvre and are derivative of earlier priestly, philosophical, and intellectual characters sharing, more privately, the same resentments and distorting narrative proclivities. Articulate misinterpretations of various sorts take on the aura, more glaring than that of the alleged criminal act itself, of transgression.[16]

Since *Hamlet*, literature has perceived the risk that eloquent language would be employed as a substitute for the inner strength to face reality as it is. Words tend to deflect, rather than to reflect, the trained intuition (if it exists at all) of the articulate being. But in the procedural novel, readers are specifically asked to challenge their own ingrained (professional) proclivity by becoming skeptical of the word. Readers, acting as

15. For discussion of these three instances, see Weisberg, *The Failure of The Word*, 115–23, 54–64, 154–57.

16. Indeed, modern fiction often confounds law and crime—views law *as* crime and the criminal as hero. An early but quite subtle example is in Dickens's *Great Expectations*. There the seminal lawyer-figure, Jaggers, is introduced through a narrative description by Pip strongly evocative of his earlier encounter on the marsh with the criminal, Magwitch. As both figures, originally inspiring Pip's terror, gain a more lasting influence over him, the interchangeability of lawyer and criminal becomes increasingly provocative.

jurors, must suspend their belief in the articulate lawyer-figure; noticing instead the workings of a distorted intelligence, readers correctly come to emphasize the veracity of the anterior position. At the least, a verbalizer's interest in words for their own sake is cast, given the legal context, in an odd light. If a pyschologically unbalanced interpreter is described in the act of misconstruing earlier events or texts, the anterior position is seen as all the more privileged. The reader's intuition, despite a verbal pre-dilection, perceives the primacy of the anterior narration ("O my pro-phetic soul!").[17] We finally reject Hamlet's fatal urge first to repress anteriorism and then to move to more aesthetically pleasing but less accurate renditions of reality.

Readers capable of finishing, much less reflecting upon, such texts as these, will find themselves strongly inclined to respect and believe the lawyer-figure's verbally adroit rendition of reality. We admire the lawyer, who shares our own uncommon interest in language. Thus the tripartite structure of the procedural narrative may preliminarily yield a sense of playfulness or even charm about the interpreter's deviation. Anything— even historical, legal or textual error—is more amusing than the recon-stitution of reality apart from our own love of words. The tragic pseu-donihilist Clamence fulfills a destiny spotted with laughter. But it is the isolated, double laugh of the condemned man.

Procedural narratives, by lifting the verbalizer's milieu out of the un-derground and into the light of the communal courtroom, challenge the perspective of nihilistic good fun. These books almost always end unhap-pily, not merely in the banal sense of lost love or even lost life. Two more serious structural negations also occur: a communally condoned but er-roneous institutional evaluation of a person or an event and the upsetting of the aesthetic balance of the novel as a whole just as it ends.

Regarding this first negation, the law-interested novelist with a fascina-tion for legalistic detail must intend special audience awareness of the legal procedure and its outcome. Law may be satirized for many other reasons (avarice, cruelty, injustice, the idiosyncrasies of its practitioners), but the erroneous outcome of a fully painted legal procedure brings the satire around to author and reader alike: words in the service of a ver-balizer unmindful of any constraining reality wreak havoc on a culture unless either the verbalizer or the audience comes to recognize not only the extreme tension between unconstrained interpretation and integral anterior textuality but the heavy burden on the interpreter to validate a purely subjectivist methodology. No wonder the auditor of Jean-Baptiste Clamence's long confessional monologue is deemed at the very end of that narrative also to be a lawyer.

17. *Hamlet*, 1.5.40.

The second structural negation points to a theoretical as much as a thematic revaluation of the movement from anterior to authoritative rearticulation. It urges us to look beyond the erroneous linguistic formulation produced by the text's admittedly brilliant and creative lawyers and toward the posttrial conclusion of the novel itself. The latter, too, has developed from the anterior position, stressing more and more a series of prolix summations that tug its reader toward self-flattering mendacity. As the procedural novel ends, its creator (almost perversely) tempts us to negate the primacy of the less wordy anterior position, a primacy that the author has (ironically) posited.

The ending of the procedural novel, usually shortly after the conclusion of the legal procedure, often portrays a previously nonverbal and nonlegalistic protagonist, lost in prolixity for the first time. The logocentric reader often mistakes this development for growth, thus fallaciously reasserting the primacy of the word, which has been denied by the rest of the text. For example, many readers assume that Meursault has somehow "matured" only when, at narrative's end, he becomes verbose. That the jarring reversal is in fact intended to be *negative* is indicated by the association of these virginal outpourings with death. Meursault becomes articulate just before the execution of his sentence; Alyosha Karamazov achieves prolixity at the innocent Ilyusha's graveside; Billy Budd's utterance (or that of his fellow sailors in "Billy in the Darbies") at his death negates his essence as a spontaneous being unbound to any verbal formalism. But since this indication is subtle, and since the novelistic ending is at least as privileged as its beginning, most readers tend to see increased articulation as a good. Subjective distortions through language lead, therefore, both to judicial error and to novelistic falsehood.[18]

The structure of the procedural novel thus covertly reverses its overt admiration of the verbal mode. The text as a whole counsels us to avoid a self-gratifying dependence on language for its own sake, particularly in the vitally important task of interpreting anterior realities extrinsic to ourselves. We can avoid figurative transgression only through the most caring and careful attention to persons, texts, and events, which have a right to be indifferent to our idiosyncrasies.[19] These novels commend themselves to our scrupulous attention. Readers must come to the text prepared to submerge themselves in its intuitively plain and structurally mandated meanings, not to sacrifice them upon the altar of a legalistic philocentrism. In Hans Gadamer's words,

18. The precisely opposite conclusion to that drawn by René Girard in *Deceit, Desire, and the Novel*, trans. Y. Freccero (Baltimore: Johns Hopkins University Press, 1965), chap. 12.
19. Derrida (himself): "Le texte se passe de nous," faculty seminar, Cornell University, Nov. 1975.

Richard Weisberg

All correct interpretation must be on guard against arbitrary fancies and the limitations imposed by imperceptible habits of thought and direct its gaze "on the things themselves" (which, in the case of the literary critic, are meaningful texts, which themselves are concerned with objects), it is clear that to let the object take over this way is not a matter for the interpreter of a single decision, but is "the first, last and constant task." For it is necessary to keep one's gaze fixed on the thing throughout all the distractions that the interpretor will constantly experience in the process and which originate in himself.[20]

The task of verifying anterior realities is difficult in life, art, and perhaps especially in literary criticism itself. It may be important, however, as a matter of theory, to value it and place it again in the realm of the desirable. This revaluation may in time be recognized as the most salient contribution of the law to literary studies.

20. H. G. Gadamer, *Truth and Method* (New York: Seabury, 1975), 236.

[16]

Was noch kein Auge je gesehn:
A Spurious Cranach in Georg Kaiser's
Von Morgens bis Mitternachts

ULRICH WEISSTEIN

I

In the last two decades or so, Comparative Literature, which in its initial stages limited itself to the study of purely literary works, has branched out to embrace studies devoted to the relations between literature and the other arts. The Comparative Arts, as the new subdiscipline has come to be known in academic circles, still lacks a sound theoretical and methodological basis. As regards the scholarly endeavor focusing on the interplay between literature and the visual arts, I have offered some guidelines in a paper delivered at the Innsbruck Congress of the International Comparative Literature Association and in my subsequent contribution to the Modern Language Association–sponsored volume *Interrelations of Literature*.[1] But much remains to be done, and one eagerly awaits the appearance of a complement to Calvin S. Brown's exemplary *Music and Literature* and to Steven P. Scher's *Literatur und Musik*.[2]

1. "Comparing Literature and Art: Current Trends and Prospects in Critical Theory and Methodology," in *Literature and the Other Arts*, ed. Steven P. Scher and Ulrich Weisstein, vol. 3 of the Proceedings of the Ninth Congress of the International Comparative Literature Association (Innsbruck: Institut für Sprachwissenschaft der Universität, 1981), 19–30; "Literature and the Visual Arts," in *Interrelations of Literature*, ed. Jean-Pierre Barricelli and Joseph Gibaldi (New York: Modern Language Association of America, 1982), 251–77.

2. *Music and Literature: A Comparison of the Arts* (Athens: University of Georgia Press, 1948). Long out of print, the book, with a new preface by the author, has recently been published in a paperback edition (Hanover: University Press of New England, 1987). *Literatur und Musik: Ein Handbuch zur Theorie und Praxis eines komparatistischen Grenzgebietes*, ed. Steven P. Scher (Berlin: Erich Schmidt, 1984). I am preparing a companion piece to this volume, *Literatur und Bildende Kunst*, to appear under the same imprint.

Ulrich Weisstein

In surveying the evidence, one quickly realizes that while there exists a large body of lyric poetry concerned with painting and exemplified by the plethora of *Bildgedichte* surveyed and classified by Gisbert Kranz,[3] the pragmatic genres offer considerably less food for thought. In narrative prose we have the *Künstlerroman* (subdivision *Malerroman*) as well as an amazingly large number of novels featuring paintings or, as in the case of Thomas Mann's *Doktor Faustus*, an engraving.[4] *Künstlerdramen*, while not necessarily rarer than *Künstlerromane*, tend to have writers or, in the operatic context (for example, in Hans Pfitzner's *Palestrina*), composers as protagonists. Plays and operas which feature specific paintings, on the other hand, are hard to find.[5] The case of Georg Kaiser's *Von Morgens bis Mitternachts* is rarer still, for its dramatis personae include an art historian as well. And this is where my story begins.

In this characteristically Expressionist play, a lady from Florence has accompanied her son to Germany to provide moral and financial support in his search for unknown works by Lucas Cranach the Elder (1472–1553). In the second scene the young man shows his mother the canvas he has accidentally discovered in a wine merchant's shop. The unveiling of the picture, which depicts the biblical Fall, takes place in the Hotel zum Elephanten in Weimar, where both have taken lodging while the lady is waiting for her check to clear. The following dialogue, turning into a scholarly lecture, ensues:

Son (*laughs*): How do you like it?
Lady: I find it—very naïve.
Son: Splendid, isn't it? Marvelous, for a Cranach.
Lady: Do you think of it that highly as a picture?
Son: As a picture, of course. But notice also the strange conception, strange for Cranach and for the treatment of the subject in general. Is there anything like it in the Pitti, the Uffizi, the Vatican galleries? There is nothing of the kind in the Louvre. This is surely the first and only erotic presentation of Adam and Eve. The apple is still lying in the grass, and the snake peeps out of the ineffable foliage. The event, then, takes place in Paradise itself, and not after the expulsion. This is the true Fall. A rarity. Cranach has painted a dozen Adams and Eves, stiff, a branch between them and setting them apart. It says there: they knew each other. Here, for the first time, is the blissful gospel of humanity: they loved each other. Here a German master shows himself to be an erotic painter of the most southerly passion. (*Close to the picture.*) And this control despite the ecstasy. This line of the male arm intersecting the female hip. The horizontal

---

3. *Das Bildgedicht:Theorie, Lexikon, Bibliographie*, 2 vols. (Cologne: Böhlau, 1982).
4. Thirteen examples are treated in Jeffrey Meyers's *Painting and the Novel* (Manchester: Manchester University Press, 1975).
5. In act 2, scene 1, of Wagner's *Meistersinger*, Eva mentions a spurious Dürer painting depicting David and Goliath.

formed by one pair of thighs, and the vertical by the other. The observer's eye is never strained. The painting radiates love. The flesh tone, naturally, enhances this effect. Don't you feel the same way?
Lady: You are, like your picture, naïve.[6]

This art-historical description-cum-analysis of the work, subjectively colored by the speaker's emotional *engagement*, focuses first on its content and then on its formal properties; it is primarily thematic and iconographical[7] and only secondarily stylistic. In order to gauge its full significance, we must place it in its dramatic context and judge it in the light of subsequent events, which can be summarized as follows:

For the son, who is working on a monograph devoted to Cranach, the sensational discovery means additional work: "At home it will affect me

6. Sohn (*lacht*): Wie findest Du es?
Dame: Ich finde es—sehr naiv.
Sohn: Köstlich, nicht wahr? Für einen Cranach fabelhaft.
Dame: Willst Du es als Bild so hochschätzen?
Sohn: Als Bild selbstverständlich. Aber daneben das Merkwürdige der Darstellung. Für Cranach—und für die Behandlung des Gegenstandes in der gesamten Kunst überhaupt. Wo findest Du das? Pitti- Uffizien- die Vatikanischen? Der Louvre ist ja ganz schwach darin. Wir haben hier zweifellos die erste und einzige erotische Figuration des ersten Menschenpaares. Hier liegt noch der Apfel im Gras—aus dem unsäglichen Laubgrün lugt die Schlange—der Vorgang spielt sich also im Paradies selbst ab und nicht nach der Verstossung. Das ist der wirkliche Sündenfall! Ein Unikum! Cranach hat ja Dutzend Adam und Eva gemalt steif—mit dem Zweige in der Mitte—und vor allem die zwei getrennt. Es heisst da: sie erkannten sich. Hier jubelt zum erstenmal die selige Menschheitsverkündung auf: sie liebten sich! Hier zeigt sich ein deutscher Meister als Erotiker von südlichster, allersüdlichster Emphatik! (*Vor dem Bild*) Dabei die Beherrschtheit noch in der Ekstase. Diese Linie des männlichen Armes, die die weibliche Hüfte überschneidet. Die Horizontale der unten gelagerten Schenkel und die Schräge des anderen Schenkelpaares. Das ermüdet das Auge keinen Moment. Das erzeugt Liebe im Hinsehen—der Fleischton leistet natürlich die wertvollste Hilfe. Geht es Dir nicht ebenso?
Dame: Du bist wie Dein Bild naiv.
Georg Kaiser, *Von Morgens bis Mitternachts: Ein Stück in zwei Teilen*, ed. Walther Huder (Stuttgart: Reclam, 1964), 17. Translations throughout this essay are my own. See *From Morn to Midnight*, trans. Ulrich Weisstein, in *Plays for the Theatre: An Anthology of World Drama*, ed. Oscar G. and Lenyth Brockett (New York: Holt, Rinehart and Winston, 1967).
7. According to Erwin Panofsky, iconography "is that branch of the history of art which concerns itself with the subject matter or meaning of works of art, as opposed to their form." In his view, iconographers are primarily concerned with images and combinations of images. Unfortunately, Panofsky's terminology is somewhat confusing insofar as *meaning*, in his usage, is limited to literal meaning on the story level, whereas according to him the "intrinsic meaning constituting the world of 'symbolical' values" is the proper domain of "iconological interpretation" rather than "iconographical analysis." Panofsky, "Iconography and Iconology: An Introduction to the Study of Renaissance Art," in *Meaning in the Visual Arts: Papers in and on Art History* (Garden City, N.Y.: Doubleday Anchor, 1955), 26–54. This version of the essay should be compared with the earlier ones reproduced in *Bildende Kunst als Zeichensystem*, vol. 1 of *Ikonographie und Ikonologie: Theorien, Entwicklung, Probleme*, ed. Ekkehard Kaemmerling (Cologne: Du Mont Schauberg, 1979).

Ulrich Weisstein

Plate 1. Titian. By permission of the Museo del Prado, Madrid.

even more strongly. Florence and this Cranach! The completion of my book will have to be delayed. I shall have to digest the experience. It has to enter the bloodstream, or the art historian commits sacrilege."[8] The mother, unable to fathom the depth of his feeling, responds rather coolly and matter-of-factly. Her son, having had his *Aufbruch*, leaves the scene and vanishes from the play, presumably in order to absorb the profound aesthetico-moral shock. Not so the bank teller (*Kassierer*), the protagonist

8. "Zu Hause wird es ja erst mächtig auf mich wirken. Florenz und dieser Cranach. Der Abschluss meines Buches wird natürlich weit hinausgeschoben. Das muss verarbeitet sein. Das muss aus eigenem Fleisch und Blut zurückströmen, sonst versündigt sich der Kunsthistoriker" (17).

Was noch kein Auge je gesehn

of Kaiser's *Stück in zwei Teilen*, who has been aroused from his sleep of the senses by the bank director's verbal portrait of the lady as a tramp, thief, embezzler, and creature of the *va banque* atmosphere of Monte Carlo. He has taken sixty thousand marks from the bank that employed him and, with all the verve of the New Man, as which he now sees himself, has rushed to the hotel to persuade her to elope with him.

Confronted with the painting, which the son, in departing to rejoin the wine merchant in the hotel lobby, has left uncovered, he reacts, plausibly enough, not like a specialist or connoisseur—he and his family possess little *Bildung*, as their meaningless chatter about Wagner and Boieldieu in the caricaturistic fourth scene demonstrates—but like one for whom everything is at stake. Mistaking fiction for fact, he proceeds to project himself and the lady into the picture:

Teller (*his coat still hung over his arm, enters*)
Lady (*points to an easy chair and sits down on the couch*)
Teller (*sits down, still holding his coat*)
Lady: The bank has . . .
Teller (*sees the picture*)
Lady: The picture is closely connected with my visit to the bank.
Teller: You?
Lady: You notice a resemblance?
Teller (*smiling*): At the wrist?
Lady: Are you an expert?
Teller: I wish to acquire more expertise.
Lady: You like these pictures?
Teller: I am in (on) the picture.[9]

No doubt, the teller sees himself as the New Adam and the lady from Florence as the New Eve, his companion in a secular paradise ruled by Eros. But his euphoria is short-lived, for the lady, thoroughly respectable and in no way conforming to the slanderous image conveyed by the bank director, who may have (as it turns out, successfully) tried to pull his

9. Kassierer (*noch den Mantel überm Arm—tritt ein*)
Dame (*zeigt nach einem Sessel und setzt sich ins Sofa*)
Kassierer (*den Mantel bei sich, auf dem Sessel*)
Dame: Bei der Bank ist—
Kassierer (*sieht das Bild*)
Dame: Das Bild steht in enger Beziehung zu meinem Besuch auf der Bank.
Kassierer: Sie?
Dame: Entdecken Sie Ähnlichkeiten?
Kassierer (*lächelnd*): Am Handgelenk?
Dame: Sind Sie Kenner?
Kassierer: Ich wünsche—mehr kennenzulernen.
Dame: Interessieren Sie diese Bilder?
Kassierer: Ich bin im Bilde. [19]

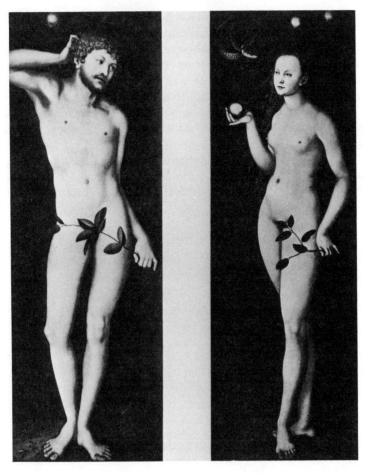

Plate 2. Cranach. By permission of the Galleria degli Uffizi, Florence.

subordinate's leg, quickly undeceives him by suggesting that he return to office and home, pleading "temporary insanity." This is the first of many shocks administered to the protagonist on the various Stations of his secularized Cross. Repulsed but full of energy and resolution, he rushes off to his encounter with death in the scene "Verschneites Feld mit Baum mit tiefreichender Astwirrnis. Blauschattende Sonne" ("A snow-covered field with a tree whose branches hang down in great profusion. The sun casts bluish shadows").

Despite the successive blows he receives in scene 5 ("Sportpalast"—Sports arena), 6 ("Ballhaus. Sonderzimmer"—Dancehall. A private room), and 7 ("Lokal der Heilsarmee"—Salvation Army hall), the teller preserves, if only subconsciously, the utopian ideal of an Edenic life here on earth. Thus when the greedy crowd has, literally, rolled out of the Salvation Army Hall and he is left with the lass who has doggedly pursued him with her battle cry (*Kriegsruf*), he envisions a postlapsarian, postdiluvial scene which visually and conceptually relates to "Cranach's" painting:

Teller (*looks smilingly at the girl*): You are at my side. You are always at my side. (*He notices the abandoned drums and picks up two sticks*) Onward. (*Brief drum roll*) From station to station. (*Individual drum beats corresponding to the units of meaning*) Crowds back there. Mass dispersed. Void all over. Space created. Space. Space. (*Drum roll*) A girl stands there. As the waters recede. Upright. Waiting. (*Drum roll*) Woman and man. Primeval gardens unlocked. Cloudless sky. A voice from the silent treetops. Peace on earth. (*Drum roll*) Woman and man. Forever loyal. Woman and man. Promise fulfilled. Woman and man. Seed and fruit. Woman and man. Sense, goal, and aim. (*Repeated drum beats ending in a continuous drum roll*).[10]

That blissful image, too, is promptly shattered, for like her fellow soldiers, the lass betrays him for filthy lucre, and the teller, his vision destroyed, kills himself in an act that takes the visual form of an autocrucifixion: "*With outstretched arms, the Kassierer has fallen against the cross sewn onto the curtain. His sighs hack Ecce, his breath hums Homo.*"[11]

Clearly, the thematic and structural pattern sustained in the two visual phenomena—a portrait of Adam and Eve, allegedly Cranach's work, and a vision of paradise incarnate—is too important to be overlooked in any analysis of *Von Morgens bis Mitternachts* that seeks to do justice to this masterpiece of dramaturgical engineering. In fact, what must be considered de rigueur is a two-step analysis consisting of, first, a detailed comparison of relevant passages with the corresponding biblical ones and, second, an inquiry into the stylistic and thematic properties of the pseudo-Cranach as measured against the authentic canon. Such a study has

10. Kassierer (*sieht lächelnd das Mädchen an*): Du stehst bei mir—du stehst immer bei mir. (*Er bemerkt die verlassenen Pauken, nimmt zwei Schlägel*) Weiter. (*Kurzer Wirbel*) Von Station zu Station. (*Einzelne Paukenschläge nach Satzgruppen*) Menschenscharen dahinten. Gewimmel verronnen. Ausgebreitete Leere. Raum geschaffen. Raum. Raum. (*Wirbel*) Ein Mädchen steht da, Aus verlaufenen Fluten aufrecht—verharrend, (*Wirbel*) Mädchen und Mann. Uralte Gärten aufgeschlossen. Entwölkter Himmel. Stimme aus Baumwipfelstille. Wohlgefallen. (*Wirbel*) Mädchen und Mann—ewige Beständigkeit. Mädchen und Mann—Fülle im Leeren. Mädchen und Mann—vollendeter Anfang. Mädchen und Mann—Keim und Krone. Mädchen und Mann—Sinn und Ziel und Zweck. (*Paukenschlag nach Paukenschlag. Nun beschliesst ein endloser Wirbel*). [64]

11. "*Kassierer ist mit ausgebreiteten Armen gegen das aufgenähte Kreuz des Vorhangs gesunken. Sein Ächzen hüstelt wie ein Ecce—sein Hauchen surrt wie ein Homo*" (65).

Plate 3. Cranach. By permission of the Gemäldegalerie Berlin-Dahlem, Stiftung Preussischer Kulturbesitz.

never been undertaken, which is hardly surprising given the few close readings of Kaiser's plays.

Most of the essays and book chapters that deal with *Von Morgens bis Mitternachts* mention the *Adam and Eve*, with or without reference to its complementary vision, but few manage to rise to the occasion. Thus Wilfried Adling, applying Marxist standards of critical judgment, castigates Kaiser for his failure to denounce capitalism:

Such a critique, to be sure, does not penetrate to the depth of the social problems prevalent in those years; and Kaiser is no exception in this regard. His play is mainly directed against the reification of human relations. [. . .] The actual cause of these phenomena—the social order of capitalism within which human beings are exploited, degraded to the status of goods, and forced to fight with each other for a livelihood—he fails to expose. His criticism does not touch the basic social, political and economic laws; it gets bogged down in moral issues.[12]

And in the chapter "The Strategy of Exchange: Georg Kaiser's *Von Morgens bis Mitternachts*" of his book *The Playwright and Historical Change*, Leroy R. Shaw, without offering any supporting evidence, claims that the playwright's "burden" was "primarily personal and conditioned by historical circumstances [. . .] but ultimately distinct and independent" and that the strategy Kaiser devised was intended to release him from that onus "symbolically without exposing its nature to others." The autobiographical fallacy to which Shaw succumbs leads this otherwise perceptive critic to conclude: "It seems obvious that Kassierer's original situation stands for the artist's alienated predicament in a rationalized money-oriented society where he is merely used and does not 'count' for anything. Similarly, the various stages of Kassierer's search correspond to the playwright's abortive attempts to assert an identity by forcing the world to accept him on his own terms."[13]

This is hardly the place to review the divergent trends in Kaiser scholarship at length or to unmask the reductionism inherent in most critics' obsessive focus on the New Man. The remarks just quoted were merely aimed at showing that even the few extended readings of *Von Morgens bis Mitternachts* which have been offered suffer from biases which keep their authors from discerning and adequately assessing decisive structural and symbolic configurations in that text. As concerns the "Cranach" painting, which constitutes the central focus of my essay, most critics fall into that category. Let us briefly review the evidence.

In his lengthy disquisition, Adling devotes a single sentence ("But it turns out that she is a lady of high social standing who is in Germany in order to assist her son in the gathering of material for his art-historical

---

12. "Allerdings dringt eine solche Kritik nicht ganz bis zur Tiefe der gesellschaftlichen Problematik jener Jahre vor, und Kaiser bildet dabei keine Ausnahme. Sein Stück wendet sich vor allem gegen die Versachlichung der menschlichen Beziehungen. [. . .] Die eigentliche Ursache für diese Erscheinungen dagegen kann Kaiser nicht blosslegen: die Gesellschaftsordnung des Kapitalismus, in der Menschen ausgebeutet, zum Konkurrenzkampf gezwungen und zur Ware herabgewürdigt werden. Kaisers Kritik dringt nicht bis zu den sozialen, politischen und ökonomischen Grundgesetzen vor; sie bleibt im Moralischen stecken." Wilfried Adling, "Georg Kaisers Drama *Von Morgens bis Mitternachts* und die Zersetzung des dramatischen Stils," *Weimarer Beiträge* 5 (1959), 369–86, quotation 378.

13. Leroy R. Shaw, *The Playwright and Historical Change: Dramatic Strategies in Brecht, Hauptmann, Kaiser, Wedekind* (Madison: University of Wisconsin Press, 1970), 74, 89.

studies")[14] to the issue and totally ignores the art-historical implications. For his part, Ernst Schürer, author of the most comprehensive survey of Kaiser's oeuvre undertaken so far, treats the play at some length in the section "The *Stationendrama*" of a chapter titled "The Vision of a New Man: The Expressionist Plays." In his plot summary, he covers scene 2 in one paragraph, which merely hints at the painting's subject matter: "A disappointment awaits [the teller], for [the lady] is a respectable mother traveling with her son, an art historian who has just discovered an old painting he wants to buy and for which he needs money. His description of the content of the picture, an idyllic, peaceful scene in paradise, is a stark contrast to the mad rush of the Cashier when he bursts into the lady's room."[15] These are slim pickings, indeed, for the phrase "an idyllic, peaceful scene in paradise" hardly conveys the intended meaning of "Cranach's" unorthodox version of the Fall and seems more appropriate for the transcendent pastoral vision at the play's end.

More to the point, but still problematic, is Manfred Durzak's interpretation in his highly eclectic study *Das expressionistische Drama: Carl Sternheim, Georg Kaiser*. Durzak fails to realize that "Cranach's" depiction of the event differs from the account given in Genesis, for before quoting the key sentence of the son's description ("The event takes place in Paradise itself, and not after the expulsion. That is the true Fall."), he states ingenuously: "The painting portrays the Fall,"[16] which is most emphatically not the case.

Durzak also fails to perceive or to enunciate the highly significant fact that the interpretation is offered not by the protagonist himself but by an expert whose iconographic knowledge immediately permits him to pinpoint the uniqueness of "Cranach's" conception. In short, while the art historian in the play is fully conversant with the discrepancy between the restrictive moral code that is embedded in the biblical story and the healthy amoralism which, in Nietzsche's wake, propels the New Man into hitherto unheard-of spheres of activity, the teller, acting on impulse, ignores the dichotomy. What, at this point in the action, Kaiser illuminates from two angles are the positive aspects of this double breakthrough and not, as Durzak will have it, its delusionary side: "In the description of that biblical motif in the Cranach painting, the same possibility is raised as a contrast to the *Kassierer*'s fiction; for what applies to him is not the biblical 'they knew each other' but its very opposite. His fictive image of

---

14. "Es stellt sich indessen heraus, dass er es mit einer vornehmen Frau zu tun hat, die in Deutschland weilt, um ihren Sohn bei der Materialsammlung für kunsthistorische Forschungen zu unterstützen" (Adling, "Kaisers Drama," 372).

15. Ernst Schürer, *Georg Kaiser* (New York: Twayne, 1971), 82–88, quotation 83.

16. Manfred Durzak, *Das Expressionistische Drama: Carl Sternheim, Georg Kaiser* (Munich: Nymphenburger, 1978), 121–38, quotation 129.

Plate 4. Cranach. By permission of the Westfälisches Landesmuseum für Kunst und Kulturgeschichte, Münster.

the Italian lady rests on a total misapprehension regarding her character."[17]

Actually, in *Von Morgens bis Mitternachts*, the fatal disillusionment is

17. "In der Beschreibung jenes biblischen Motivs auf dem Cranach-Gemälde wird die gleiche Möglichkeit als Kontrast zu der Fiktion des Kassierers angedeutet, denn nicht das biblische 'sie erkannten sich' gilt für den Kassierer, sondern genau das Gegenteil trifft auf ihn zu: seine Fiktion von der Italienerin ist auf einer völligen Verkennung ihrer Person aufgebaut" (ibid., 129).

postponed to a much later stage along the trajectory, and in spite of its lethal effect on the protagonist, it is, surely, less significant, dramaturgically speaking, than the impulse responsible for the original *Aufbruch*.

The most extended discussion of the passage is found in the central portion of Shaw's essay, which also stresses the ambiguity inherent in the son's interpretation of *Adam and Eve*. Shaw aptly observes: "Paradise, then, is depicted as a state in which male and female are already together, knowing and being known to each other, their union an anticipation of the human community and of mankind's future blessedness." He then proceeds, however, to link the painting with what he takes, erroneously in my view, to be the basic thrust of Kaiser's play, namely the indictment of modern life exemplified by a symptomatic paradox:

> The most striking thing about this painting, apart from Kaiser's devoting so much attention to it, is its ambivalence. On the one hand it appears to offer a counterideal to the historical anarchic situation and a reminder of what constitutes ideal creativity. [. . .] At the same time, however, the painting offers an interpretation of the "real Fall of Man", which, according to the art historian (obviously [*sic!*] speaking for the playwright), consists in the attempt to juxtapose incompatibles; an act inappropriate to the place, Adam and Eve enjoying the fruits of their knowledge at the very scene of their disobedience. [. . .] It is a graphic way of picturing man's blasphemously acting as if there were no difference between creativity and sin.

Shaw, wrongly accusing the teller of being preoccupied with sex "throughout the various stages of his search," is the only critic to have noticed the conceptual bracketing of the spurious Cranach and the protagonist's final vision, but he misunderstands Kaiser's basic intention.[18]

II

Before turning to the visual evidence provided by Cranach's paintings and those of some of his contemporaries and determining, in its light, the true nature and function of the fictitious painting in Kaiser's play, we must dwell in passing on the verbal record constituted by the biblical narrative, viewed in relation to the son's idiosyncratic paraphrase. Here is a standard English version of the text, Genesis 2:23 to 3:7:

> And Adam said: this is now bone of my bone, and flesh of my flesh. She shall be called woman because she was taken out of man. Therefore shall a man leave his father and his mother, and shall cleave unto his wife; and they shall be one flesh. And they were both naked [. . .] and were not ashamed.

18. Shaw, *Playwright and Historical Change*, 83–93, quotations 90, 92, 93.

Was noch kein Auge je gesehn

Plate 5. Albrecht Dürer. By permission of the Graphische Sammlung Albertina, Vienna.

Now the serpent was more subtle than any beast of the field which the Lord God had made. And he said unto the woman: hath God said "Ye shall not eat of every tree of the garden?" And the woman said unto the serpent: We may eat of the fruit of the trees of the garden, but of the tree which is in the midst of the garden God has said: "Ye shall not eat of it, neither shall ye touch it, lest ye die." And the serpent said unto the woman: "Ye shall surely not die. For God doth know that in the day ye shall eat thereof your eyes shall be opened and ye shall both be as gods, knowing good and evil." And when the woman saw that the tree was good for food and [. . .] pleasant to the eyes, and a tree to be desired to make one wise, she took of the fruit thereof and did eat, and gave also unto her husband with her; and he did eat. And the eyes of them both were opened, and they knew that they were naked; and they sewed fig leaves together and made themselves aprons.

I have already quoted the equivalent passage from Kaiser's drama: "Hier liegt noch der Apfel im Gras—aus dem unsäglichen Laubgrün lugt die Schlange—der Vorgang spielt sich also im Paradies selbst ab und nicht nach der Verstossung. [. . .] Es heisst da: sie erkannten sich. Hier jubelt zum erstenmal die selige Menschheitsverkündung auf: sie liebten sich!" It must be compared with its biblical model, which, at first glance, it would seem to parody. The son's paraphrase of the account is striking in many ways, not least in that the only verbal reference to the Luther Bible, unquestionably the playwright's source, consists in the phrase "sie erkannten sich," which echoes that standard German version "Und Adam erkannte sein Weib Eva," an assertion which, relating to the postlapsarian state, identifies sexual intercourse as part of the life-death cycle imposed by the Creator as punishment for original sin.[19]

What Kaiser is saying, then, through his persona, is that in "Cranach's" revolutionary work intercourse takes place not after and as a result of the Fall but long before it—perhaps shortly after Eve's creation—and that this is clearly implied by Genesis 2:25 ("They were both naked [. . .] and were not ashamed"), on which more attention should, therefore, be lavished.

How can this hermeneutic dilemma be resolved? And is it possible to say with any degree of conviction what the redactors of the biblical text intended in this particular instance and whether, accordingly, Georg Kaiser worked with or against the grain of biblical scholarship? This is, to say the least, a knotty problem, especially in view of the vague chronology in Genesis 2:25; for in saying "Therefore *shall* a man leave his father and mother, and *shall* cleave unto his wife; and they *shall* be one flesh," the narrator seems to make a general observation or to point to an as yet unspecified moment in the near or distant future. Though, at first glance, Kaiser's view seems to be highly unorthodox and truly blasphemous, it is by no means unique. Thus, a learned reader offers the following exegesis of the passage:

According to some commentaries, this means that sexual desire had not yet been aroused in them, but there is no foundation for such an interpretation in the verse before us. It is preferable to explain it as follows: since they did not yet know good or evil, nor had they yet learned that sexual desire could also be directed toward evil ends, they had no cause to be ashamed at the fact that they were naked; the

19. The major consequence of the eating from the Tree of Knowledge (of good and evil) is the barring of access to the Tree of Life. In other words, immortality was taken for granted in the prelapsarian state. One should note that both in German and in English, as in the original Hebrew, the sexual connotation of *knowing* is a metaphorical extension of its psychological and epistemological meaning. In Hebrew, no words were explicitly reserved for the sexual sphere; and in the two modern languages, the sexual implications of *knowing* and *erkennen* were translators' neologisms—in England as early as 1300, according to the *OED*—which are now considered archaic.

Plate 6. Jan Gossaert. Hampton Court Palace. Copyright reserved to Her Majesty Queen Elizabeth II.

feeling of shame in regard to anything is born only of the consciousness of the evil
that may exist in a thing.[20]

Putting it in psychological and, ultimately, moral terms, consciousness is
bound to produce self-consciousness which, in turn, engenders conscience.

20. Umberto Cassuto, *A Commentary on the Book of Genesis*, trans. Israel Abrahams
(Jerusalem: Magnes Press of Hebrew University, 1961), 137.

Ulrich Weisstein

Clearly, both for Kaiser's persona and for the biblical scholar I have invoked the difference between "they were both naked [. . .] and were not ashamed" and "they knew that they were naked" is essential for a correct reading of the biblical passage in question. What complicates matters in the case of pictorial representations of the event is the question, implicitly raised in *Von Morgens bis Mitternachts*, as to whether the two figures in "Cranach's" painting are nudes or whether they are covering their pudenda, as artistic convention decrees.[21] By noting that the work he has unexpectedly come across is iconographically anomalous ("ein Unikum"), at any rate, Kaiser's art historian seems to hint that they are depicted "in the altogether."[22]

III

After these necessary preliminaries, I have now reached the point of transition, or qualitative leap, from one art (literature) and its concomitant discipline (*Literaturwissenschaft*) to another art (painting) and the branch of learning (art history) that is concerned with it. This marks a crucial stage in all interdisciplinary endeavors since, as James P. Merriman has keenly observed, the gap separating two media can be bridged only if one remains fully aware of the dangers inherent in the indiscriminate metaphorical use of technical terms derived from one of them.[23] Not surprisingly, the method best suited for such a double-pronged enterprise has been evolved by an art historian. Speaking only of representational art, into whose exegesis purely formal values do not enter, Erwin Panofsky, the scholar in question, discerns three levels, or stages, of inquiry, to wit: (1) "pre-iconographical description (and pseudo-formal analysis),"[24] which occupies itself with "primary or natural subject matter," either factual or expressive, and in its totality constitutes "the world of artistic motifs"; (2) "iconographical analysis," that is, the study of "secondary or conventional subject matter, constituting the world of images, stories, and allegories"; and (3) "iconological interpretation," which

21. In a painting from the catacomb of Saints Pietro and Marcellino reproduced in the *Lexikon der christlichen Ikonographie*, ed. Engelbert Kirschbaum, S.J. (Rome: Herder, 1965), vol. 1, col. 46, they cover their genitalia with their hands.

22. In exceptional cases, Cranach himself depicts them in that fashion. See the painting, now in a private Swiss collection, that is reproduced as no. 114 in Max J. Friedländer and Jakob Rosenberg, *The Paintings of Lucas Cranach*, 2d enl. ed. (Ithaca: Cornell University Press, 1978), subsequently referred to as F/R.

23. "The Parallel of the Arts: Some Misgivings and a Faint Affirmation," *Journal of Aesthetics and Art Criticism* 31 (1972–73), 154–64, 309–21.

24. "Pseudo-formal" supposedly because on that level of scholarly discourse form and content are inextricably linked.

is engaged in the recovery of "intrinsic meaning or content, constituting a world of 'symbolical' values."[25]

Taking into account, without detailing them, the terminological difficulties that arise partly from Panofsky's perplexing usage and partly from the incompatibility of the literary and art-historical discourses,[26] we might sum up the argument by positing a progression from *Gestalt* (form, structure) by way of *Inhalt* (content or subject matter) to *Gehalt* (meaning), the Goethean triad.[27] According to Panofsky, who is wary of the pitfalls of *Geistesgeschichte* crudely undertaken, the "intrinsic meaning or content" with which iconology is preoccupied "is apprehended by ascertaining those underlying principles which reveal the basic attitude of a nation, a period, a class, a religious or philosophical persuasion—qualified by one personality and condensed into one work." Exorcizing the demon of generalization, he goes on: "Needless to say, these principles are manifested by, and therefore throw light on, both 'compositional methods' and 'iconographic significance.'"[28]

If we wish to apply the iconographic/iconological method to the problem at hand, we must remember, from the outset, that our case is more complex than those typically discussed by art historians; for while, in studying the pictorial embodiments (viz. illustrations of a verbal narrative), the *Kunsthistoriker* works with two primary texts, the written account and its visual complement, the literary critic in analogous circumstances has to cope with three such documents: the narrative, the painting based on it, and the re-creation/interpretation of one or both by an author and/or his creatures. In *Von Morgens bis Mitternachts*, a work intended for the stage, the difficulty is compounded by the fact that the dramatis personae may or may not be the author's mouthpiece.[29]

Let us open the discussion of the "Cranach" in Kaiser's drama by listing, pre-iconographically, the objects or props which are needed for a beholder to be able to identify the subject matter of the painting as the Fall. Insofar as pictorial representations of this event are usually synoptic, encompassing, as it were, part or all of the Temptation (Genesis 3:1–5), the Fall proper (Genesis 3:6), and its dire consequences (Genesis 3:7),

---

25. Panofsky, "Iconography and Iconology," 40 (snyoptic table).

26. Thus, in the quotation *motif* is used in a specifically art-historical rather than in the general thematic sense that prevails in literary discourse, and *meaning* and *content* are interchangeable.

27. Goethe draws these distinctions in his "Noten und Abhandlungen zum *West-Östlichen Divan*." The triad is discussed in Elisabeth Frenzel's *Stoff-, Motiv- und Symbolforschung* (Stuttgart: Metzler, 1965), esp. 21.

28. Panofsky, "Iconography and Iconology," 30.

29. While it cannot be denied that, in some essential ways, the art historian speaks for the author and the teller does not, the kind of identification of the creature with its creator proposed by Shaw is rather questionable.

Plate 7. Jan Gossaert. Schloss Charlottenburg, Berlin. By permission of the Verwaltung der Staatlichen Schlösser und
Gärten.

there is room for variation. In melded versions of Genesis 3:1–7, the
repertory would have to include a male nude; a female nude; a tree; a
fruit taken, or about to be taken, from that tree; and a snake.

Art-historically, the number of variants, introduced for ideological or
aesthetic reasons, is rather substantial in this instance. Thus Eve—and
occasionally her helpmate—may be literally nude (in accordance either

with classical doctrine or with a Christian view as reflected in Titian's allegory of earthly and heavenly love in the Galleria Borghese at Rome),[30] or emulating Cranach's own Venuses and Lucretias, she may wear a transparent loincloth. Both may wear an apron made of a fig leaf, fig leaves (as in the biblical story, which draws on ancient Near Eastern flora), or an apple bough, or the pudenda may simply be covered by the offending couple's hands, as is the case in the third-century mural mentioned earlier. Furthermore, the fruit itself may be a fig (as in early Christian and Byzantine representations of the event) or an apple (love symbol in the Song of Songs and homonymically—*malum* = apple and *malum* = evil—predestined as the tool of temptation.[31] Or there may be several apples, apart from those still hanging on the tree, as in certain paintings by Cranach himself, perhaps implying that the guilt should be equally shared by both.[32]

In addition, the snake may have a woman's head and thus represent Lilith, the archtemptress, or, as in Titian's erotically charged version of 1658 (Plate 1), now in the Prado in Madrid, which would have appealed to Kaiser's art historian, it may be a putto serving the God of Love.[33] And in a striking instance, Albrecht Dürer's engraving of 1504, which Cranach repeatedly "cited" in his paintings, Adam and Eve may be surrounded by a foursome of animals, for which there is no biblical precedent and which, in Panofsky's words, was to remind the beholder "of a widespread scholastic doctrine which connects the Fall of Man with the theory of the 'four humors' or temperaments."[34]

To these motivic and thematic norms and deviations from the norm we must add those features of the depiction of the Fall which one might call spatial configurations, including the relative positioning of figures—their gestures, poses, and physical postures, which may be expressive of mental attitudes and human relationships, that is, what Panofsky would include under expressional subject matter. Thus Adam ordinarily stands to the

30. The painting dates from ca. 1515. For a general discussion of nakedness as a Christian virtue see the entry "Nacktheit" in the *Lexikon christlicher Kunst: Themen, Gestalten, Symbole*, ed. Jutta Seibert (Freiburg: Herder, 1980), 213d.

31. See the entry "Apfel," ibid., 26–27.

32. This is the solution offered by Cranach in paintings owned by the museums in Braunschweig and Dresden. See plates 40–43 in Heinrich Lilienfein's monograph *Lukas Cranach und seine Zeit* (Bielefeld: Velhagen and Klasing, 1942).

33. This painting, reproduced in color in *Kindlers Malerei-Lexikon*, ed. Rolf Linnenkamp, 6 vols. (Zurich: Kindler, 1968), 5:527, also meets some of the formal requirements suggested in Kaiser's drama. The *Encyclopedia Britannica* characterizes Lilith (= night monster) as a female demon in Jewish folklore equivalent to the English vampire. In rabbinical literature, she appears as Adam's first wife who left him to become a demon.

34. See Erwin Panofsky, *The Life and Art of Albrecht Dürer* (Princeton: Princeton University Press, 1955), 85. The engraving is reproduced in plate 117. All or some of these animals are also found in certain Cranach versions of *Adam and Eve*. It is clear that, on the whole, Cranach was deeply indebted to Dürer.

Ulrich Weisstein

left (from the viewer's perspective), Eve to the right. Both tend to face the onlooker (frontal view) instead of each other (profile). And they either appear on different panels or are separated by a tree (Kaiser's "vor allem die zwei getrennt") without touching each other. It is easy to see that while, in this formal respect as well, there exists a stereotypical formula, there is so much leeway in the portrayal of major and minor details as to permit a host of eccentric or even esoteric approaches.

In order to exemplify the commonplace solution of the compositional problem which Kaiser's expert contrasts with the extraordinary depiction of the scene he has found in the provincial German town, I adduce a panel—one of roughly thirty versions of the Fall by Cranach and his circle[35]—which dates from 1528 (Plate 2) and is now in the Uffizi, one of the two Florentine museums referred to in the passage from *Von Morgens bis Mitternachts* that is my central point of reference.[36] Closely matched by several other versions of the scene, this one is a diptych composed of two panels of roughly equal height (170 cm) and width (60 cm).[37]

Here Adam and Eve are manifestly apart, and the tree which is wedged between them is split in half in such a way as to demonstrate *their* split. Both figures face the viewer but are placed at a slight angle and strike a pose that is rather mannered, especially in the case of Eve, who puts one leg before and at a right angle to the other and whose thighs intersect with one another. Both cover their nakedness with leaves, which are different in shape and size. Eve holds an apple—surely the one she has picked at the snake's suggestion—in her right hand, while Adam seems to scratch the back of his head with his raised right arm. And the snake, coiled around a branch, its head pointed toward Eve's right ear in a parody of divine inspiration, is seen in its traditional position.

Such then, judged by the historical evidence as surveyed by the scholar from Florence, is Lucas Cranach, intrepid painter of Adams and Eves, at his least original. At his level best, and transcending the limitations of his chastely Gothic style, he is, in the spurious work which its lucky finder apostrophizes as "die erste und einzige Figuration des ersten Menschenpaares" conceived and executed by a Northern master, metamorphosed into an "Erotiker von südlichster, allersüdlichster Emphatik." What a distance there is between the ends of this spectrum, and nothing would be more natural than for art-historically informed readers of Kaiser's play to ask themselves whether, in fact, the German playwright had a specific

35. F/R catalogues thirty versions of the Fall and reproduces many of them.
36. Plates 72 and 73 in Hans Posse, *Lucas Cranach d.Ä.*, 2d ed. (Vienna: Schroll, 1943); and F/R, plate 194. There are no Cranachs in the Pitti Palace. The Louvre has six Cranachs but no *Adam and Eve*, and the Vatican owns only one Cranach, a portrait.
37. The Dresden version (plates 40 and 41 in Lilienfein, *Lukas Cranach*) is of roughly the same ilk.

Plate 8. Jan Gossaert. By permission of the Staatliche Museen, Berlin.

model for the idealized version in mind or whether he simply invented the extraordinary canvas. As I shall try to demonstrate in the concluding portion of the essay, the hunt for such a prototype may not be altogether quixotic, although, given the lack of documentation, its outcome is decidedly speculative.

Kaiser himself was, of course, no trained art historian and perhaps not even a connoisseur *sensu stricto*, but being of upper middle-class origin, he undoubtedly possessed a modicum of *Allgemeinbildung*, even though his formal education ended at age seventeen with the so-called *Einjährige*. There is no evidence to show that he was a frequenter of museums or a reader of specialized monographs. Yet, living in Weimar from 1911 to 1918 (*Von Morgens bis Mitternachts* was probably written in 1913 although it was not premiered until five years later) he had relatively easy access to nearby collections containing works by Cranach, who, from 1505 until his death in 1553, had lived and worked in neighboring Wittenberg.[38] His own, by no means negligible interest seems to have focused on the modern period. Thus a self-portrait by Van Gogh plays a prominent role in *Vincent verkauft ein Bild* (1938);[39] *Die Bürger von Calais*, first performed in 1914 and Kaiser's most famous play, is based on Rodin's sculpture by that name and may actually have been inspired by Rilke's description in his book on the French master; and *Das Floss der Medusa* (1942), a *Kindertragödie*, owes its title and its principal motif, a shipwreck, to Théodore Géricault's acknowledged masterpiece of 1819. Judging by his correspondence, visual art did not figure significantly in his life. Only a handful of artists are mentioned, usually in passing, and the sole reference to the art of the Renaissance is not to Cranach or Dürer but to the head of the so-called Danube school, Albrecht Altdorfer.[40]

For an art historian bent on sniffing out a model for Kaiser's "Cranach," it would be sensible to look for so startling a treatment of the subject first among that painter's authentic works and, that search failing, among the works of his German contemporaries. Barring success, one would look next at pertinent works by Flemish masters and, as a final resort, at works produced south of the Alps, which the Northern master did not cross. For, as the phrase "südlichste, allersüdlichste Emphatik" seems to indicate, the panel under scrutiny must be thought of as distinctly Italianate. Actually, the Fall, being, as it were, a characteristically Protestant subject, cannot be regarded as a popular theme in Italian painting and has rarely been depicted south of the Alps, except in murals such as the Masolino/Masaccio frescoes in the Brancacci Chapel in Florence.[41] Not surprisingly, then, the present search will lead us to a Northern artist imbued with *Italien-Sehnsucht*.

To begin with Cranach: my iconographic survey will have to limit itself, for reasons of economy, to the chief variants among that painter's depiction of the Fall in a typological sequence calculated to propel us, step by step, from conventional to experimental treatments, along a path that

38. The cities in question are, in addition to Weimar itself, Gotha, Dessau, Apolda, Veste Coburg, and the Wartburg near Eisenach.

39. See Schürer's *Georg Kaiser*, 184–86.

40. Altdorfer is mentioned, in connection with Kaiser's novel *Villa Aurea*, in a letter dated October 10, 1939. See Georg Kaiser, *Briefe*, ed. Gesa M. Valk (Frankfurt: Ullstein, 1980), esp. the *Personenverzeichnis*. Some of Cranach's early paintings actually betray Altdorfer's influence.

41. It is startling to see how few representations of the Fall are listed in Bernhard Berenson's *Italian Painters of the Renaissance* (London: Phaidon, 1954) and his *Italian Pictures of the Renaissance: Venetian School*, 2 vols. (London: Phaidon, 1957). One of the few pertinent illustrations in the latter set is Palma Vecchio's *Adam and Eve* (plate 916, at Braunschweig), a cool and, in its detachment, eminently Northern painting.

leads toward increasing intimacy between Adam and Eve and thus, pictorially speaking, to greater unity of their physical configuration. A first step in that direction, that of depicting the pair in one panel, was taken in a fairly early canvas, formerly in the Breslau museum, in which Adam and Eve are separated by an exceptionally sturdy oak tree! In another panel, still divided by a trunk, which is now pushed to the rear and is exceedingly thin, our common ancestors, Gothically elongated—especially Eve, who could have stepped right out of a Hans Memling panel—stand, right arms bent and right hands closing around the fruit which the woman is offering to the man.[42] This work, owned by the Courtauld Institute in London, marks the midpoint of the compositional spectrum.

Greater intimacy by far is achieved in a panel from Berlin (Plate 3), where Adam and Eve are seen still closer to each other, each surrounded by a halo of shrubbery, but with no tree dividing them. In this version, in fact, the Tree of Knowledge, with the snake wound around its trunk, has been pushed to the extreme right and is partly cut off by the frame. Here, where their physical proximity is so great, the painter has managed to place their bent arms, Adam's left and Eve's right, so close together as to create a perfect parallel which is contiguous down to the elbows. But the most daring treatment which the subject has received in the hands of the Wittenberg master is found in a picture at the Landesmuseum in Münster (Westphalia) (Plate 4), in which, backgrounded by a tree whose trunk is nearly obliterated by the pair, Adam is shown embracing Eve by putting his left arm around her shoulder in an outright gesture of endearment, while the woman, seen in semiprofile, daintily lifts the lower portion of her left leg in such a way as nearly to touch Adam's left leg.

That is as far, compositionally speaking, as Cranach goes—not nearly as far, that is to say, as Dürer does in a drawing at the Albertina in Vienna (Plate 5) which shows the naked and stunningly muscular couple in profile (Eve) and semiprofile (Adam), locked in a tight embrace (Adam's left arm holding Eve by her midriff) and moving in the direction of the gnarled oak tree around which a dragonlike snake is coiled. Among the German works treating this subject, this one appears closest to meeting at least one formal criterion ("Diese Linie des männlichen Armes, der die weibliche Hüfte überschneidet") adduced by Kaiser's art historian. What is more, the couple's legs are intertwined—Adam's left lower extremity being wedged between Eve's thighs—and arranged in planes that overlap precariously, as if Dürer had, for once, decided to emulate the wild experiments in foreshortening conducted by the Florentine painter Paolo Uccello, known for his depiction of equestrian battles. Yet, admittedly, we

---

42. The first is reproduced in F/R, plate 44, as well as in Lilienfein, *Lukas Cranach*, plate 39. It is now in the Warsaw National Museum. The second is reproduced in F/R, plate 191.

Plate 9. Jan Gossaert.

do not encounter here "die Horizontale der unten gelagerten Schenkel und die Schräge des anderen Schenkelpaares" on which the specialist in *Von Morgens bis Mitternachts* insists in his reading of the spurious Cranach. In fact, the positions he describes presuppose a sitting, crouching, or even reclining posture such as is best accommodated in an oblong format.

Throughout the history of art it is in the graphic media, notably in pen or pencil drawings, that artists have displayed the greatest versatility and the greatest daring, simply because here, in sketches and five-finger exercises, they could "let themselves go" as they could not in major works of larger format intended for public viewing. It is, therefore, not surprising to find that in works of this kind we come closest to the solution of our problem, which is to identify pictorial representations of the Fall that

Was noch kein Auge je gesehn

match the description of the pseudo-Cranach in Kaiser's expressionist drama.

Having exhausted my search for exemplars within the ambience of Cranach, I began to explore the art of Flanders and the Low Countries, in the hope that it would yield some clues. More by accident than by design I checked out a monograph on the well-known and slightly eccentric Jan Gossaert known as Mabuse, who, as it turned out, fits the bill in many particulars. An almost exact coeval of Cranach—he was born around 1478 and died fairly young in the 1530s—he studied and worked in the Netherlands but, unlike his German compeer, embarked on an Italian journey, probably in 1508. The evidence I was looking for was neatly assembled in the pictorial appendix to Ernst Weisz's study.[43] It consists of three unsigned paintings, executed around 1520 (?), and two drawings.

The first two members of this quincunx are less relevant than the remainder; yet they, too, are highly idiosyncratic and boast of some unique iconographic features. Thus Plate 6 (Royal Castle, Hampton Court, England) shows Adam and Eve in a frontal view, framed by two trees—the Tree of Life (?) on the left and the Tree of Knowledge on the right—and putting their hands, the left and the right respectively, around each other's shoulders in what strikes one as a double gesture of mutual affection.[44] Strangely enough, Adam puts the fingers of his right hand into his mouth.

Plate 7 (Berlin) shows Eve in hot pursuit of her mate, who is walking away from her, the index finger of his left hand raised as if in a warning signal. As Weisz demonstrates, Mabuse, in executing this work, was compositionally inspired by Raphael's fresco in the papal apartments of the Vatican.[45] Plate 8 (also in Berlin) is truly remarkable, given my bias and the manifest drift of my argument, for here Adam is seen sitting, legs spread semicircularly, and embracing the half-reclining Eve, whose right arm lifts the apple to his mouth while the left, clasping an apple that lies on the ground, supports her torso.[46] Together, their bodies form a circle neatly inscribed in the rectangular panel.

43. *Jan Gossart, gen. Mabuse: Ein monographischer Versuch und Beitrag zur Geschichte der vlämischen Malerei in der ersten Hälfte des XVI. Jahrhunderts* (Parchim: Freise, 1913).

44. The dimensions of this painting, of which there are copies in Berlin and Brussels, are given as "fast lebensgross" (almost life-size).

45. The dimensions are given as 170 cm by 114 cm. Raphael's fresco, dating from ca. 1510, is reproduced in Kenneth Clark's *The Nude: A Study in Ideal Form* (New York: Pantheon, 1956), 108, together with an engraving, after Raphael, by Marcantonio Raimondi, which is remarkable in that Adam offers two apples on a dish to his helpmate.

46. The dimensions given for this painting are 78 cm by 64.5 cm. The fact that the apple clasped by Eve lies on the ground should not be construed as meaning that this was the work Kaiser's art historian had in mind. Perhaps that persona's observation "Hier liegt noch der Apfel im Gras" is meant to convey the impression that Eve picked up an apple that had already fallen, rather than plucking it from a bough on the tree. Her action, then, could be seen as a venial sin.

Plate 10. Jan Gossaert.

Even more to the point, and more manifestly erotic, is Plate 9, a pen drawing in which the snake, still present in Plates 6–8, is conspicuously absent. Here both perpetrators are seated—Adam facing the beholder, his legs spread out as in Plate 8, and Eve in profile—and hold the apple in their joined hands, lips pursed and seemingly on the verge of kissing.[47] The two pairs of legs intersect and overlap vertically, as in Dürer's drawing. Structurally, the climax is reached in Plate 10, another pen drawing, but this time executed in an horizontal format. Adam, as always on the left, reclines on the ground, his torso slightly raised and supported by his right arm, while Eve, touching his tousled hair with her right hand, bends over him from a kneeling position.[48] Both clasp the apple, as in Plate 9. Here the interplay of horizontals, verticals (Eve's right arm) and diagonals is especially prominent; and one could argue that, up to a point, this drawing actually meets the formal criteria for the spurious Cranach: "Diese Linie des männlichen Armes, die die weibliche Hüfte überschneidet. Die Horizontale der unten gelagerten Schenkel und die Schräge des andern Schenkelpaares."

47. The dimensions of this drawing from the Albertina (Vienna) are given as 26 cm by 21 cm.
48. The dimensions of this drawing from the Staedelsches Museum (Frankfurt) are given as 27 cm by 38 cm.

Was noch kein Auge je gesehn

This brings me to the end of a critical journey which was triggered by the legitimate desire to investigate the contextual meaning of the "Cranach" painting in Georg Kaiser's drama *Von Morgens bis Mitternachts* and which, after that meaning had been fixed, turned into an art-historical search for a possible model of this most unusual representation of the Fall. Since the expert in the play who unearths this sensational panel identifies it as unique in the Cranach canon, curiosity drove me to explore this question. After the persona's assertion had been corroborated, I decided to follow a line of inquiry that was to lead, beyond Cranach and his German contemporaries, first to Italian art and subsequently to the Flemish painter and draftsman Jan Gossaert known as Mabuse, several of whose works evidenced a striking formal likeness to Kaiser's spurious Cranach, which, by offering such a close description, the playwright virtually forces us to visualize. Thus, even though no documentary proof of actual *rapports de fait* could be provided, my search was methodologically enlightening insofar as it demonstrated that in cases such as this the visual evidence may be effectively used to bolster the verbal evidence marshaled in the service of close reading.

PART FOUR

Comparative Perspectives
on Current Critical Issues

STANLEY CORNGOLD

JONATHAN CULLER

CLAYTON KOELB

JULIET FLOWER MACCANNELL

SUSAN NOAKES

MICHAEL RIFFATERRE

[17]

The Curtain Half Drawn:
Prereading in Flaubert and Kafka

STANLEY CORNGOLD

I

Finding is nothing. The difficulty is in acquiring what has been found.

Paul Valéry, *The Evening with Monsieur Teste*

As readers, we are haunted by the ghost of what we have already read. We do not enter even once into the same river of signs, and sometimes a book grows turbulent from the confluence of ghosts. We could get lost in the disturbance when memories of what we have read usurp what we want to read for the first time.

This phenomenon, which I call prereading, heightens the flux of spectral associations accompanying every sentence which seems to offer only itself to be read. In prereading, we are so taken up with remembering passages newly invoked that the result may be a single impression—the sense that we never read for a first time. Such an experience of possession could make us despair of reading, but despair is only optional. The phenomenon of prereading also creates a place for the new as what has already happened without our knowing till now that it has happened. Indeed this could be a particular aim of the *novel*: to alert us explicitly and for the first time to the truth of prereading, displacing but not destroying the acquisition of knowledge from the future into an eternal present perfect: Become, as readers, what you have already read.

It can seem the goal of novelists to plot prereading in ever more refined and telling ways. Flaubert and Kafka are two who manipulate the time of reading with cunning and design. What they finally require is the understanding, "You will not be able to read this novel for a first time." But

[263]

Stanley Corngold

prereading, for them, is also an opportunity for laying traps, for delaying the goal of acquisition. They introduce into the turbulence of memories another turbulence—an anxious impression of something forgotten—so that, before we can say, "I already know what this is about," they make us say, "I have forgotten what."[1] In their novels Flaubert and Kafka so arrange the process of acquiring the preread that only a special vigilance will reveal the way it works. But in thus revealing by concealing prereading, they only make us marvel, after we have discovered it, at its universal operation.

To illustrate the way Flaubert deploys prereading, I shall focus on the penultimate scene of *L'Education sentimentale*—the visit of Madame Arnoux to Frédéric's room, their last encounter.

He was alone in his study when a woman came in. [. . .] In the twilight he could see nothing but her eyes under the black lace veil which masked her face.

After placing *a little red velvet wallet* on the edge of the mantelpiece, she sat down. The two of them sat there, unable to speak.[2]

I shall be concentrating on this little red velvet wallet—on its past and also its projections into the future of this scene.

Frédéric breaks the silence by asking Madame Arnoux about her husband; Marie Arnoux's answer is immediately to speak about money. After leaving Paris she and her husband had settled in the depths of Brittany, where they could live cheaply and pay off their debts. Frédéric recalls the financial disaster which had overtaken them, and this reminds her of the reason for her visit: "Pointing to the little red wallet, which was covered with golden palms, she said: 'I embroidered that specially for you. It contains the money for which the land at Belleville was supposed to be the security.'"[3] Thereupon Madame Arnoux, after describing the house where she lives,

1. Or, before we can say, "I already possess what is essential to make this scene work," they make us say, "I cannot find it." Valéry wrote, "A work of art should always teach us that we had not seen what we see": "Introduction to the Method of Leonardo da Vinci," in *Paul Valéry: An Anthology*, ed. James Lawler (Princeton: Princeton University Press, 1977), 50. Flaubert and Kafka play with this point and then reverse it. They teach us that we never see for a first time.

2. Gustave Flaubert, *The Sentimental Education*, trans. Robert Baldick (Middlesex, Eng.: Penguin, 1964), 412, my italics, hereafter cited as E with page number. The French text used in the notes is *L'Education sentimentale* (Paris: Garnier, 1958), cited hereafter by page number. This passage reads:

Il était seul dans son cabinet, une femme entra. [. . .]

Dans la pénombre du crépuscle, il n'apercevait que ses yeux sous la violette de dentelle noir qui masquait sa figure.

Quand elle eut déposé au bord de la cheminée un petit portefeuille de velours grenat, elle s'assit. Tous deux restèrent sans pouvoir parler (419).

3. E413, 420: Et désignant le petit portefeuille grenat couvert de palmes d'or: "Je l'ai brodé à votre intention, tout exprès. Il contient cette somme, dont les terrains de Belleville devaient répondre." The land at Belleville refers to a farm that Frédéric had sold for a sum he had then lent to M. Arnoux in an attempt to bail him out of trouble.

started looking with greedy eyes at the furniture, the ornaments, and the pictures, in order to fix them in her memory. The portrait of the Marshal was half hidden by a curtain. But the golds and whites, standing out in the midst of the shadows, attracted her attention.

"I know that woman, don't I?"

"No, you can't!" said Frédéric. "It's an old Italian painting."[4]

This moment is broken off by the narrator, who speaks for Madame Arnoux in indirect discourse the sentence which Kafka treasured among all the sentences of Flaubert he knew: "Elle avoua qu'elle désirait faire un tour à son bras, dans les rues" (420) ("She confessed that she would like to go for a stroll through the streets on his arm" [E413]).[5]

I call attention to the repetition and also to the intensification of the red velvet wallet as "the little red wallet, which was covered with golden palms." The "golden" palms might by themselves point ahead to the figure of the Marshal, who can be bought for gold, whose name conjures a uniform with gold trim, and who in at least one striking scene has been linked with gold, especially by contrast with Madame Arnoux. During the wild night at the Alhambra, dancing in a whirl, the Marshal has "nearly caught Frédéric with the tip of her golden spurs." Thereafter, in bed, Frédéric hallucinates "two big dark eyes" before dreaming that "he was harnessed side by side with Arnoux in the shafts of a cab, and the Marshal, sitting astride him, was tearing his belly open with her golden spurs."[6] The connection is made explicit when Madame Arnoux's big, dark eyes catch sight of the Marshal's portrait half hidden by a curtain. "The golds and the whites" attract her attention and lead her to believe that she has recognized the subject. Frederic fobs her off, but his denial (*Verneinung*)—that "it is an old Italian painting"—only confirms its identity. The reader remembers that Pellerin, the painter of the portrait, had chosen to paint Rosanette in the style of "a Titian, which would be set off with touches in the style of Veronese."[7]

In two places in this passage Madame Arnoux herself prereads. Her plain purpose is to fix things in memory as if there were no previous

4. E413, 420: se mit à regarder les meubles, les bibelots, les cadres, avidement, pour les emporter dans sa mémoire. Le portrait de la Maréchale était à demi caché par un rideau. Mais les ors et les blancs, qui se détachaient au millieu des ténèbres, l'attirèrent.
—"Je connais cette femme, il me semble?"
—"Impossible!" dit Frédéric. "C'est une vieille peinture italienne."

5. "What a sentence!" wrote Kafka to his fiancée, Felice Bauer, "What a construction!" *Letters to Felice*, trans. James Stern and Elizabeth Duckworth (New York: Schocken, 1973), 157.

6. E127, 120: "du bout de ses éperons d'or, elle manquait d'attraper Frédéric"; E134, 127: "deux grands yeux noirs"; E134, 128: "il lui semblait qu'il était attelé près d'Arnoux, au timon d'un fiacre, et que la Maréchale, a califourchon sur lui, l'éventrait avec ses éperons d'or."

7. E154, 150: "un Titien, lequel serait rehaussé d'ornements à la Véronèse."

memories of them, to make of this moment of reading the pure occasion of personal experience. But while meaning to fix the new for future remembering,[8] she is quickly arrested by an object already dimly remembered. A scene projected as the birth of the new becomes crucially a scene awakening ghosts of the past.

At this moment Madame Arnoux incorporates the figure of the reader of this novel. Flaubert stages the experience of prereading through her as the reader's alter ego, one who here only surmises that she has previously seen the painting. The reader, on the other hand, remembers exactly which painting she fails to see. His or her consciousness of prereading is heightened, as if for the feat of recollection that she or he will now be required to perform, for there is more historical irony in motion here than meets the eye put off from penetrating the scene by a half drawn curtain. The curtain half conceals more than Pellerin's painting of Rosanette; it veils a prehistory of scrupulously incised signs, masking a revelation unspeakably—unseeably—harmful to Madame Arnoux, to Frédéric, and perhaps to the reader. Frédéric's impulse to draw the curtain is prompted by horror.

The scene represents a virtual but uncompleted junction between Madame Arnoux and the Marshal, whose portrait she is in danger of seeing. Throughout the novel Madame Arnoux and the Marshal continually approach one another in the imagination of the characters: they cohabit in the experience of Monsieur Arnoux, Frédéric, and, of course, each other. On two brief occasions they see each other face to face, and Frédéric sees them see each other—once in Arnoux's shop, toward the close of the novel, and once or possibly several times on the Champ de Mars. Frédéric has taken Rosanette to the races. "A hundred yards away, a lady appeared in a victoria. She leant out of the window, then drew back quickly; this happened several times, but Frédéric could not make out her face. A suspicion took hold of him: it seemed to him that it was Madame Arnoux. But that was impossible! Why should she have come?"[9] And then, a little later, out of nowhere,

8. The temporality of this mental impulse informs the entire conversation between Frédéric and Madame Arnoux that follows. The verbal tense equivalent of this movement is the future perfect, which at one point surfaces explicitly and with particular force. After Frédéric has praised her for what she had made him feel in the past, Madame Arnoux says, "We shall have been well loved" (mistranslated in E413 as "We have loved each other well" ["Nous nous serons bien aimés" (421)]). With this she gives away her hand, the "hand" of a type of perception that intends to become memory as swiftly as it can. It is the signature of their entire meeting, and here we see it signed at the outset.

9. E206, 205: A cent pas de lui, dans un cabriolet milord, une dame parut. Elle se penchait en dehors de la portière, puis se renfonçait vivement; cela recommença plusieurs fois. Frédéric ne pouvait distinguer sa figure. Un soupçon le saisit, il lui sembla que c'était Mme Arnoux. Impossible, cependant! Pourquoi serait-elle venue?

the victoria reappeared; it was Madame Arnoux. She turned extraordinarily pale.
"Give me some champagne!" said Rosanette.
And, raising her glass [. . .], she shouted:
"Hi there! Here's a health to decent women, and my protector's wife!"
There were roars of laughter all round her; the victoria disappeared.[10]

In the first scene discussed, Frédéric's dismay is plain in the irritated defensiveness of his language. In the second, in which the full reality of the horror is at hand, a muteness or emptiness, an effacement of Frédéric as receptor, or second narrator, enacts his aversion. This mode of aversion again overwhelms the report of the second and final meeting of the two women. Frédéric and Madame Arnoux have met after their broken rendezvous, and Frédéric says,

"What torments I have suffered! Don't you understand?" [. . .]
A passionate sob shook her body. Her arms opened; and, standing up, they clasped each other in a long kiss.
The floor creaked. A woman was beside them, Rosanette. Madame Arnoux had recognized her, and gazed at her with staring eyes, full of surprise and indignation. At last Rosanette said: [. . .] "So you're here, are you, darling?"
This familiarity, in her presence, made Madame Arnoux blush, like a slap in the face. [. . .] Then the Marshal, who was looking idly round the room, said calmly:
"Shall we go home? I've a cab outside."
He pretended not to hear.
"Come along, let's go!"
"Why, yes!" said Madame Arnoux. "Now's your chance! Go! Go!"
They went out. She leant over the banisters to have a last look at them; and a shrill, piercing laugh came down to them from the top of the staircase. Frédéric pushed Rosanette into the cab, sat down opposite her, and did not utter a single word all the way home.[11]

10. E208–9, 207: le milord reparut, c'était Mme Arnoux. Elle pâlit extraordinairement.
—"Donne-moi du champagne!" dit Rosanette.
Et, levant le plus possible son verre rempli, elle s'écria:
—"Ohé là-bas! les femmes honnêtes, l'épouse de mon protecteur, ohé!"
Des rires éclatèrent autour d'elle, le milord disparut.
11. E353–55, 358–59: "Quel supplice! Vous ne comprenez pas?" [. . .] Un sanglot de tendresse l'avait soulevée. Ses bras s'écartèrent; et ils s'étreignirent debout, dans un long baiser.
Un craquement se fit sur le parquet. Une femme était près d'eux, Rosanette. Mme Arnoux l'avait reconnue; ses yeux, ouverts démesurément, l'examinaient, tout pleins de surprise et d'indignation. Enfin Rosanette lui dit: [. . .] "Te voilà ici, toi?"
Ce tutoiement, donné devant elle, fit rougir Mme Arnoux, comme un soufflet en pleine visage. [. . .] Alors, la Maréchale, qui regardait çà et là, dit tranquillement:
—"Rentrons-nous? J'ai un fiacre en bas."
Il faisait semblant de ne pas entendre.
—"Allons, viens!"
—"Ah! oui! c'est une occasion! Partez! partez!" dit Mme Arnoux.
Ils sortirent. Elle se pencha sur la rampe pour les voir encore; et une rire aigu, déchirant,

Stanley Corngold

These scenes are charged with a kind of horror for Frédéric, because in his imagination Madame Arnoux and Rosanette are rivals. But the horror is not intense; it is mitigated into a form of embarrassment since, while these scenes jeopardize Frédéric's possession of the women, they do not jeopardize his consciousness of their rank. Madame Arnoux's difference from and superiority to Rosanette survive: in the code of character, her delicacy and intensity of feeling contrast with Rosanette's shallow brashness through such signs as her veiled presence in the victoria, her blush at Rosanette's familiarity, and the force of her "shrill, piercing laugh," which registers in advance Frédéric's "humiliation and regret for a happiness he would [now] never know."[12]

Throughout the greatest part of the novel, up until the end, Frédéric's sense of self is defined by a position which at each moment may be occupied by one or the other woman but not both. To substitute the one woman for the legitimate occupant of that position is to commit a kind of sacrilege, and this is what Frédéric does by inviting Rosanette on the first day of the Revolution of 1848 to sleep in the bedroom he has rented for Madame Arnoux. Rosanette duly sees Frédéric punished, "sobbing with his head buried in his pillow."[13] The same point is made indirectly after Frédéric's brief fling, during which time both women are simultaneously present to him—one in actuality and one in memory—without their causing him the most obvious pain:

The company of these two women made as it were two melodies in his life: the one playful, wild, amusing; the other grave and almost religious. And the two melodies, sounding at the same time, swelled continually and gradually intermingled; for, if Madame Arnoux, merely brushed him with her finger, his desire immediately conjured up the image of the other woman, since in her case his hopes were less remote; while if, in Rosanette's company, his heart happened to be stirred, he promptly remembered his great love.[14]

---

tomba sur eux, du haut de l'escalier. Frédéric poussa Rosanette dans le fiacre, se mit en face d'elle, et, pendant toute la route, ne prononça pas une mot.

12. E355, 359: "une humiliation écrasante et le regret de sa félicité."

13. E283, 285: "sanglotait, la tête enfoncée dans l'oreiller." This point is not of course a new one, but it is essential to review it. It was made extremely well by Victor Brombert in *The Novels of Flaubert: A Study of Themes and Techniques* (Princeton: Princeton University Press, 1965), 127–40. My discussion of the "substantial" content of the concealed revelation in the half-hid painting is in many places indebted to Brombert's chapter on *L'Education sentimentale*.

14. E149, 145: La fréquentation de ces deux femmes faisait dans sa vie comme deux musiques: l'une folâtre, emportée, divertissante, l'autre grave et presque religieuse; et, vibrant à la fois, elles augmentaient toujours, et peu à peu se mêlaient;—car si Mme Arnoux venait à l'effleurer du doigt seulement, l'image de l'autre, tout de suite, se présentait à son désir, parce qu'il avait, de ce côté-là, une chance moins lointaine;—et, dans la compagnie de Rosanette, quand il lui arrivait d'avoir le coeur ému, il se rappelait immédiatement son grand amour.

Is this mingling painful? The account in the passage covers up Frédéric's pain by producing a "beautiful" musical simile for the joining. But
it does not rule out a suspicion of its horror—a horror which becomes
plain at the beginning of the next paragraph when the melodic mingling
is reduced to a "confusion brought about by the similarity between the
two establishments." The musicalizing of the two strains is furthermore
cast in the *style indirect libre*, which allows us to hear Frédéric's own voice as
dominant ("his heart happened to be stirred," "his great love"). It is he,
then, who supplies the optimistic analogue, and it is the more nearly
authoritative narrator who thereafter steps outside Frédéric's perspective
to define it as a confusion.[15] A genuine principle is affirmed through its
violation: if the one woman is present, the other must be remote, so that
the knowledge that the inferior is infringing on the place of the other can
be denied. To hold them both present in the same position is insupportable; to see them both as chosen and to have to decide between them is
horrible.

But even more horrible for Frédéric, it seems, would be to admit to
knowing that no such tension exists, to be conscious of the fact that as
between these women, the sacred and the profane lover, there might be
no distinction, that it has not and would not matter who was chosen, that
the tension, the excitement, between them was never more than a wish-
dream or a frantic surmise. Frédéric weeps with sorrow that it is the
Marshal and not Madame Arnoux who lies in his arms: he weeps for their
difference. Afterward, in order to feel the passion he is simulating for
Madame Dambreuse, he has to "summon up the image of Rosanette or
Madame Arnoux."[16] There is no question but that the reader is supposed
to feel what Frédéric fails to—namely, the horror he represses when
without qualms he substitutes Madame Dambreuse for Madame Arnoux
and Rosanette for Madame Arnoux—and furthermore to feel that this

15. After writing these lines I read Peter Brooks's discussion of this passage in his essay on
l'Education sentimentale, "Retrospective Lust; or, Flaubert's Perversities," in his *Reading for the
Plot: Design and Intention in Narrative* (New York: Vintage, 1985), 190: "There is a kind of
anti-principle of form at work in the novel: the principle of interference. Its theory is first
explicitly offered when Frédéric finds himself dividing his life between sacred and profane
love, as it were, paying court to both Mme Arnoux and Rosanette. [. . .] By couching the
passage in terms of music, pre-eminently the artistic medium of passion and the apex of the
Romantic hierarchy of the arts, Flaubert appears to promise some superior harmonic
resolution of Frédéric's passional conundrum. But the start of the next paragraph characterizes the blending of the two melodies as 'this confusion,' and such clearly is the result."
This conclusion is like my own. I shall be disagreeing with Brooks, however, by identifying
the logic of this and related passsages not as an "anti-principle" but as a principle whose
violation this passage recounts, a principle whose violation must not occur, except at
immense personal cost, and one which goes a long way toward establishing the meaning of
the novel, where Brooks finds none.
16. E369, 374: "il lui fallait évoquer l'image de Rosanette ou de Mme Arnoux."

leveling of the key difference which has sprung his life risks stultifying him irreparably.

It is coherent within this account that Frédéric's simultaneous affair with Madame Dambreuse and Rosanette can be giddy and energizing when for a time it proceeds without an effective consciousness of Madame Arnoux. Frédéric's life here becomes a kind of loop-the-loop whose configuration resembles the fundamental figure of his life—the tension of the sacred and profane lover—but is like a harmless, masterful fiction or replica of it. It is organized around a pair of lovers who never come close to being (horribly) substituted for one another, because the difference between them is trivial from the start—trivial in the sense that it can be consciously articulated and mastered without pain. This triangle imitates the triangle organized by a "sacred" mediator, but it is in fact vacuous. Flaubert makes the point plain: "The more [Frédéric] deceived one of his mistresses, the more she loved him, as if the two women's passions stimulated one another and each woman, out of a sort of rivalry, were trying to make him forget the other."[17] In the same passage Flaubert makes equally clear the condition of the lucky delirium of an empty rivalry: the extinction from consciousness, through the motivation of the alibi, of the Third. "Soon his lies began to amuse him; he repeated to one the vow he had just made to the other; he sent them two similar bouquets, wrote to them both at the same time, then made comparisons between them; but there was a third woman who was always in his thoughts. The impossibility of possessing her served as a justification for his deceitful behavior, which sharpened his pleasure by providing constant variety."[18]

This situation is in principle unstable for the man whose vitality is a function of the difference between the women he cares for. And indeed the relation with Madame Dambreuse founders on a return to consciousness of the effaced figure of Madame Arnoux. For if it is true that the alibi of the "impossibility of possessing her" has extinguished practical consciousness of her, then it follows that an awareness of her can be awakened only by a penetrating impingement of a sign from the outside. That impingement indeed comes, in the form of a "little casket with silver . . . clasps," which "Madame Dambreuse playfully describe[s] as an old tin

---

17. E383, 388: "et plus il avait trompé n'importe laquelle des deux, plus elle l'aimait, comme si leurs amours se fussent échauffés réciproquement et que, dans une sorte d'émulation, chacune eût voulu lui faire oublier l'autre."

18. E383, 388: Bientôt ces mensonges le divertirent; il répétait à l'une le serment qu'il venait de faire à l'autre, leur envoyait deux bouquets semblables, leur écrivait en même temps, puis établissait entres elles des comparaisons;—il y en avait une troisième toujours présente à sa pensée. L'impossibilité de l'avoir le justifiait de ses perfidies, qui avivaient le plaisir, en y mettant de l'alternance.

can." It is one of Madame Arnoux's personal effects displayed for bidding at the auction which Frédéric and Madame Dambreuse attend—

the casket [Frédéric] had seen at the first dinner-party in the Rue de Choiseul; afterwards it had passed to Rosanette before coming back to Madame Arnoux; his gaze had often fallen on it during their conversations; it was linked with his dearest memories, and his heart was melting with emotion when all of a sudden Madame Dambreuse said:
"You know, I think I'll buy that."[19]

Frédéric fights off the moment in which Madame Dambreuse will usurp Madame Arnoux by absorbing into her the metonymical figure of her casket: " 'There's nothing remarkable about it,' he says. On the contrary, she thought it very pretty; and the crier was praising its delicate workmanship: 'A jewel of the Renaissance! Eight hundred francs, gentlemen!' "[20] The scene has the pathos, for Frédéric, the one tender onlooker, of, let us say, "The Roman Slave Market" of Jean Leon Gérôme.[21]

The monstrous conjunction of "a jewel of the Renaissance" and the sum of money for which it is being prostituted now prereads the scene of Madame Arnoux's return to Frédéric, with her bag of money and his glimpse of an old "Italian" portrait. Between these two moments run all the futility and inanition of the years in the middle of Frédéric's life— years in which he did indeed have "other loves, but the ever-present memory of the first made them insipid."[22]

At the end of the novel Frédéric is briefly restored to life by the reappearance of Madame Arnoux. But this reunion is threatened by Madame Arnoux's glance at the half-curtained Renaissance painting. Why? What horror is at stake in the revelation? That horror is, as it were, contained in the prehistory of the little silver box, with which, right from the start, Monsieur Arnoux has entangled the two women—his wife and his mistress. We can review its progress.

Frédéric catches sight of "a little box with silver clasps" on the occasion

---

19. E407, 414: le même qu'il avait vu au premier dîner dans la rue de Choiseul, qui ensuite avait été chez Rosanette, était revenu chez Mme Arnoux; souvent, pendant leurs conversations, ses yeux le rencontraient; il était lié à ses souvenirs les plus chers, et son âme se fondait d'attendrissement, quand Mme Dambreuse dit tout à coup:
—"Tiens! je vais l'acheter."

20. E408, 414: " 'Mais ce n'est pas curieux,' reprit-il. Elle le trouvait, au contraire, fort joli; et le crieur en prônait la délicatesse:—'Un bijou de la renaissance! Huit cents francs, Messieurs!' "

21. See the analysis of this painting in Anne, Margaret, and Patrice Higonnet, "Façades: Walter Benjamin's Paris," *Critical Inquiry* 10 (March 1984), 406–7.

22. E411, 419: "d'autres amours encore. Mais le souvenir continuel du premier les lui rendait insipides."

of his very first visit to Madame Arnoux's quarters. He sees it among various "homely objects [. . .] lying about: a doll in the middle of the sofa, a fichu against the back of a chair, and on the worktable some knitting from which two ivory needles were hanging with their points downwards." The narrator comments, "It was altogether a peaceful room, with an intimate yet innocent atmosphere." The conjunction of the box with an innocent and sanctioned sexuality is strengthened when Marie Arnoux goes "into her boudoir to fetch the little box with the silver clasps which [Frédéric] had noticed on the mantelpiece. It was a present from her husband, a piece of work of the Renaissance. Arnoux's friends complimented him, and his wife thanked him; he was touched, and suddenly kissed her in front of all the guests."[23]

When the box reappears, it is in a sharply changed scene of domestic laceration. Madame Arnoux and her husband have been quarreling about his having bought a cashmere shawl for his mistress—for Rosanette. Monsieur Arnoux denies the charge. " 'In short, I tell you that you're wrong. Do you want me to give you my word of honor?' [. . .] She looked him straight in the eyes, without saying anything; then she stretched out her hand, took the silver casket which was on the mantelpiece, and held out an open bill to him."[24]

Frédéric, who watches the scene and sees Arnoux flush with guilt, is implicated in his guilt, for it is he who urged Arnoux to buy the present for Rosanette; he had taken Rosanette's side in order to ingratiate himself with her. And so when Frédéric, to console Madame Arnoux, says, "You know that I don't share,"[25] he is simply lying. Rosanette is precisely the being whom he wishes to share with Monsieur Arnoux, if only by an eccentric path of desire to his wife, one that will bring him into intimacy with her by way of her conjunction with Rosanette in the life of Arnoux. This tangled connection, meanwhile, of their sacred and profane desires, is imaged by the beautiful Renaissance casket prostituted to a trade in prostitutes. In this scene, too, the casket is preread by the earlier scene displaying Rosanette posing as a "lady" of Venice, according to a Renaissance conception of Pellerin's which Frédéric is buying.

23. E56, 46: "un coffret à fermoirs d'argent." E59, 48: "Çà et là, des choses intimes traînaient: une poupée au milieu de la causeuse, un fichu contre le dossier d'une chaise, et, sur la table à ouvrage, un tricot de laine d'où pendaient en dehors deux aiguilles d'ivoire, la pointe en bas. C'était un endroit paisible, honnête et familier tout ensemble." E59, 48: "Elle alla chercher dans son boudoir le coffret à fermoirs d'argent qu'il avait remarqué sur la cheminée. C'était un cadeau de son mari, un ouvrage de la Renaissance. Les amis d'Arnoux le complimentèrent, sa femme le remerciait; il fut pris d'attendrissement, et lui donna devant le monde un baiser."
24. E170, 166: " 'Enfin, j'affirme que tu te trompes! Veux-tu que je t'en jure ma parole?' [. . .] Elle le regarda en face, sans rien dire; puis allongea la main, prit le coffret d'argent sur la cheminée, et lui tendit une facture grande ouverte."
25. E171, 168: "Vous ne doutez pas que je ne partage . . . ?"

The Curtain Half Drawn

On the carpeted balustrade there would be a silver dish [. . .] and a casket of old, yellowish ivory, overflowing with gold sequins; some of these sequins would have fallen on the floor and lie scattered in a series of shining drops, so as to lead the eye towards the tip of her foot. [. . .] Taking a stool to do duty as the balustrade, [Pellerin] laid on it, by way of accessories, [. . .] a tin of sardines [. . .]; and after scattering a dozen ten-centime pieces in front of Rosanette, he made her take up her pose.[26]

The next time the silver casket appears it is fully depraved—in Rosanette's house; it has become the tin (of sardines, the "tin can," in Madame Dambreuse's phrase). On his way out, after a futile exchange, Frédéric spies "on the table, between a bowl full of visiting-cards and an inkstand, [. . .] a chased silver casket. It was Madame Arnoux's! He felt deeply moved, and at the same time horrified, as if by sacrilege. He longed to touch it, to open it; but he was afraid of being seen, and he went away."[27] Whom is he afraid of being seen by? Evidently by Rosanette, who would here witness the symbolic penetration; moreover, by touching the box Frédéric would identify, in the language of desire, the literal body of Madame Arnoux. It is intolerable that both women should occupy the same position.

Afterward, when Arnoux is again straitened and no longer possesses Rosanette, the box finds its way home again, stripped of its glamour. Hence it resurfaces at the auction, where it is bought by Madame Dambreuse as a thing "perhaps [good] for keeping love letters."[28]

What I have chiefly wanted to stress is the cross-linkage between the two chains of images: the first is anchored in the little silver box, which sometimes has the aura of "the Renaissance" and of a licit (married) sexuality but also contains bills having the modern aura of illicit sexuality; finally it acquires a sarcastic reminiscence of its sacred function as a container of love letters. This is the one chain; the other is anchored in the portrait of Rosanette. In its original conception it also frames a little box charged with the aura of "the Renaissance," spilling out its quantity of gold sequins represented by a dozen ten-centime pieces. A little like the famous plates in *Madame Bovary* depicting the glories of Mademoiselle de

26. E155, 151: Sur le balustre couvert d'un tapis, il y aurait [. . .] un plat d'argent [. . .] et un coffret de vieil ivoire un peu jaune dégorgeant des sequins d'or; quelques-uns même, tombés par terre çà et là, formeraient une suite d'éclaboussures brillantes, de manière à conduire l'oeil vers la pointe de son pied [. . .]; puis il disposa comme accessoires, sur un tabouret en guise de balustrade, [. . .] une boîte de sardines [. . .] et, quand il eut jeté devant Rosanette une douzaine de gros sous, il lui fit prendre sa pose.
27. E259, 260: "Il y avait sur la table, entre un vase plein de cartes de visite et une écritoire, un coffret d'argent ciselé. C'était celui de Mme Arnoux! Alors, il éprouva un attendrissement, et en même temps comme le scandale d'une profanation. Il avait envie d'y porter les mains, de l'ouvrir. Il eut peur d'être aperçu, et s'en alla."
28. E408, 415: "y mettre des lettres d'amour, peut-être!"

la Vallière, a mistress of Louis XIV—plates adored by the young Emma
but into which the points of meat knives have scratched a different legend
of greed—so these art objects of the Renaissance, in *L'Education sentimentale*, are scratched with the script of a cruder purpose. In their history they
exhibit a steady decline from the values of the Renaissance, the work of
art, and precious metal to anonymous modernity, careless sexuality, and
coin. The little silver box, with its chain of predicates, passes from Madame Arnoux to Rosanette and then back to Madame Arnoux; by means
of it Madame Arnoux is degraded, so that her difference from Rosanette
is compromised. Consider now Rosanette's portrait and the ivory casket it
is supposed to frame. Does the painting also threaten Madame Arnoux—
and hence Frédéric's sanity? Can it be linked with her? In the closing
scene Madame Arnoux stands in danger of seeing it, but what exactly
would she see if she did see Rosanette rigged out as a lady of Venice?

It is precisely here that we are required to perform our feat of prereading: for the "original" of Pellerin's conception has changed—changed in a
way that once startled Frédéric, too. One day following his successful duel
with Monsieur Cisy,

[Frédéric,] coming out of the reading-room, [. . .] caught sight of some people in
front of a picture-dealer's shop. They were looking at the portrait of a woman with
these words beneath in black letters:

"Mademoiselle Rose-Annette Bron, the property of Monsieur Frédéric Moreau
of Nogent."

It was her all right, or something like her, with her breasts bare, her hair down,
and holding a *red velvet purse* in her hands, while a peacock poked its beak over her
shoulder from behind, covering the wall with its great fan-like feathers.[29]

This painting of the Marshal clutching a "red velvet purse" amid
plumes—all in white and gold—is what Marie Arnoux, bringing Frédéric
a "red velvet wallet" embroidered with golden palms, would see if he
lifted the curtain: an intolerable semblance of herself. What is kept from
Madame Arnoux, what is half kept from Frédéric, is not kept from the
reader, who discovers in this moment of prereading the horrible suggestion that inculpates all storied objects both inside and outside Flaubert's
text: they are subject to a universal destiny of erosion, degradation, and

29. E236–37 (my italics), 235: En sortant du cabinet de lecture, [. . . Frédéric] aperçut du
monde devant la boutique d'un marchand de tableaux. On regardait un portrait de femme,
avec cette ligne écrite au bas en lettres noires: "Mlle Rose-Annette Bron, appartenant à
M. Frédéric Moreau, de Nogent."

C'était bien elle,—ou à peu près,—vue de face, les seins découverts, les cheveux dénoués,
et tenant dans ses mains une bourse de velours rouge, tandis que, par derrière, un paon
avançait son bec sur son épaule, en couvrant la muraille de ses grandes plumes en éventail.

disgrace. As the story of Mademoiselle de la Vallière (in *Madame Bovary*), painted on plates to Emma's delight, glorifies "religion, the tendernesses of the heart, and the pomps of court," thus leveling and mingling spirit, authority, and sexuality, so that its legend of glory propped up by need already contains the legend of appetite in the "scratching of knives,"[30] so too it is the fate of art, power, and eroticism in *L'Education sentimentale* to contain its own degradation. Frédéric's half consciousness of Madame Arnoux's degradation can be grasped thus: the romantic object, Frédéric's polestar, upon her appearance is already "scratched" by his awareness of its potential contamination by the half-curtained portrait. Like the auratic, the storied silver box stuffed with a bill, like her velvet purse stuffed with coin, the substance of Madame Arnoux is itself virtually corrupt. Such figures of corruption are grotesque, derisory, *kitschig*: their beauty is only specious, their contents are objects of need and are fungible. One expects of the storied object that it will be valued and kept in the possession of its owner, that it will have the aura of its creator and confer something of this aura on its possessor. *L'Education sentimentale* horrifies by presenting storied objects as objects of exchange and as already containing the marks of their abuse. This is the insight from which Frédéric means to shelter Madame Arnoux at a moment of greatest "meaning," shelter himself and any reader who does not at all points preread the novel. It is a moment that cannot, however, even be bypassed except as an avoidance of prereading.

The figure of the half curtain protects Rosanette's portrait from being read by Madame Arnoux; reading is half-curtained in Flaubert. That is to say, the force and promise of what one has already read in the novel, preparing one's way into later scenes, is made only half-plain. This veiling movement is in Flaubert's case part of a system which includes as its dominant syntactical feature "veiled discourse."[31] We could recall now, for example, how deliberately inexplicit is the hint at the beginning of the novel which makes intelligible the crucial scene concluding it—the evocation of the brothel at Nogent: "Venus, queen of the skies, your servant! But Poverty is the mother of Continence, and heaven knows we've been

30. Gustave Flaubert, *Madame Bovary*, ed. Paul de Man (New York: Norton, 1965), 25. "Les explications légendaires, coupées çà et là par l'égratignure des couteaux, glorifiaient toutes la religion, les délicatesses de coeur et les pompes de la Cour" (Gustave Flaubert, *Madame Bovary* [Paris: Aux Quais de Paris, n.d.], 43).
31. "Veiled discourse" is a translation of Hugo Friedrich's phrase "*verschleierte Rede*," with which, in his study of the French novel, *Die Klassiker des französischen Romans* (Leipzig: Bibliographisches Institut, 1939), he characterizes Flaubert's distinctive narrative technique as one of theatrical impersonation. The source of the characters' gestures is concealed. (I was alerted to this expression by Victor Brombert's treatment of the *style indirect libre* in *The Novels of Flaubert*, 169–73.)

slandered enough about that!"[32] And, similarly, there is the veiling of the narrator's judgment of the lovers throughout their final reunion.

Flaubert wishes to half hide the knowledge that were Madame Arnoux to see Rosanette's portrait she would see her double. Frédéric would see these women, and we too would see them, for the last time, at the end of Frédéric's life—face to face, identical. This is too dangerous: it is the novel's principle that these women must not be seen beside each other, *inside* each other, and equivalent. And Flaubert, it seems, must himself shelter from the too vaunting and visible yoking of the sacred and the profane. That we know this (or think we know this) is tribute to his art of evoking the consequences of what we have once read.

But we are not to forget that as Madame Arnoux's double, the reader, for all the superiority of his or her memory, is nonetheless implicated in her degradation. For just as the romantic figure, on entering the scene, is already "scratched" by the corrupt semblances of her which her past throws up, so too each reader, in prereading, shares her fate: each has already read the present text, each is its ghost. The reader cannot become the word which offers itself to be read as an original word; prereading, he or she lags behind its freshness. The reader judges it, hence is judged by it, and hence is condemned as a semblance.

We shall now see the connection between Flaubert and Kafka.

II

And for the sake of greater discretion they even referred to [. . .] Frédéric as K.

Flaubert, *The Sentimental Education*

The reader's act of bringing prereading to light, which is chiefly inductive and implicit in Flaubert, is explicit in Kafka. Flaubert's reader could value his discovery of prereading mainly as the reward of diligent memory work. In Kafka the phenomenon is written into the novel with blindingly clear evidence, for *Der Prozeß* (*The Trial*) *begins* with a moment of prereading. That it does so, however, can come to light fully only for the

---

32. E30, 18: "Vénus, reine des cieux, serviteur! Mais la Pénurie est la mère de la Sagesse. Nous a-t-on assez calomniés pour ça, miséricorde!" In the memory of the brothel at Nogent the positive possibilities of sacred and profane love are mingled. The alibi of this "happy memory" is the sanctification of a first state of sexual indifference before love and sensuality, before the Madame Arnoux and Rosanette possibilities of experience have become separate. Frédéric conjures a utopia of leveled difference which in empirical fact amounted to the "confusion" of his mature project. The brothel is an economic utopia, generating from the complete fungibility of its objects an aura of the sacred untouchable individual; there Buridan's ass is ennobled as a knight of resignation.

reader who has afterward been alerted to it, who has read on, prereading in turn a later scene. I refer to chapter 9, the scene of Joseph K.'s discussion with the prison chaplain, which contains K.'s defense of "personal experiences."

The opening exchange in the cathedral between the chaplain and K. turns on K.'s behavior during the year of his trial. The chaplain tells K. that he fears his case "will end badly" and asks him what step he proposes to take in the matter.[33]

"I'm going to get more help," said K., looking up again to see how the priest took his statement. [. . .] "You cast about too much for outside help," said the priest disapprovingly, "especially from women." [. . .] The priest leaned over the balustrade, apparently feeling for the first time the oppressiveness of the canopy over his head. What fearful weather there must be outside! There was no longer even a murky daylight; black night had set in. All the stained glass in the great cathedral could not illumine the darkness of the wall with one solitary glimmer of light. [. . .] "Are you very angry with me?" asked K. of the priest. "It may be that you don't know the nature of the Court you are serving." He got no answer. "*These are only my personal experiences*," said K. There was still no answer from above. "I wasn't trying to insult you," said K. And at that the priest shrieked from the pulpit; "Can't you see one pace before you?" It was an angry cry, but at the same time sounded like the unwary shriek of one who sees another fall and is startled out of his senses."[34]

The chaplain makes a key distinction between the light produced by "personal experiences" and the light that would be necessary to illuminate at least one step of K.'s way. For him, in the words of a great aesthetician, "personal experience is a most vicious and limited circle,"[35] despite the fact that it is exactly what "all guilty men" invoke.[36] But how

33. Franz Kafka, *The Trial*, trans. Willa and Edwin Muir (New York: Modern Library, 1956), 264, hereafter cited as T with page number. The German text used in the notes is *Die Romane: Amerika, Der Prozeß, Das Schloß* (Frankfurt a.M.: S. Fischer, 1972). This quoted phrase reads: "es wird schlecht enden" (430).

34. T265–66 (my italics), 431: "Ich will noch Hilfe suchen," sagte K. und hob den Kopf, um zu sehen, wie der Geistliche es beurteile. [. . .] "Du suchst zuviel fremde Hilfe," sagte der Geistliche mißbilligend, "und besonders bei Frauen." [. . .] Der Geistliche neigte den Kopf zur Brüstung, jetzt erst schien die Überdachung der Kanzel ihn niederzudrücken. Was für ein Unwetter mochte draußen sein? Das war kein trüber Tag mehr, das war schon tiefe Nacht. Keine Glasmalerei der großen Fenster war imstande, die dunkle Wand auch nur mit einem Schimmer zu unterbrechen. [. . .] "Bist du mir böse?" fragte K. den Geistlichen. "Du weißt vielleicht nicht, was für ein Gericht du dienst." Er bekam keine Antwort. "Es sind noch meine Erfahrungen," sagte K. Oben blieb es noch still. "Ich wollte dich nicht beleidigen," sagte K. Da schrie der Geistliche zu K. hinunter: "Siehst du denn nicht zwei Schritte weit?" Es war im Zorn geschrien, aber gleichzeitig wie von einem, der jemanden fallen sieht und, weil er selbst erschrocken ist, unvorsichtig, ohne Willen schreit.

35. Oscar Wilde, "The Decay of Lying," in *Oscar Wilde: Selected Writings* (London: Oxford University Press, 1961), 26.

36. T264, 431: "So pflegen die Schuldigen zu reden."

Stanley Corngold

reliable is any such distinction produced by an official of the court? It does seem very reliable in this scene, where the imagery of darkness and blindness evokes a low point in K.'s mastery of his situation.[37] The balance of authority between K. and the court here shifts decisively in favor of the court: nothing about the chaplain's response suggests that he is vicious or benighted, and the weight of the accusation of ignorance falls on K.'s appeal to his personal experiences, just as if the narrator had insisted on making the point directly. And indeed the chaplain's accusation has a good deal of plausibility.

For from the beginning K. has determined on conducting his case in the light—for him the unaccustomed light—of personal experiences. The decision is actually made for him with the rarely invoked authority of a directly intervening narrator. This occurs early in the novel, during the scene of K.'s arrest. In a flash of clarity, K. poses the essential questions pertaining to his arrest: "Who could these men be? What were they talking about? What authority could they represent?" And then the narrator begins to involve him in his situation in a way that destroys his own critical distance, saying directly of K.: "He had always been inclined to take things easily, to believe in the worst only when the worst happened, to take no care for the morrow even when the outlook was threatening."[38] The text resumes in its more dominant mode of *erlebte Rede*, of "veiled discourse," except for a second decisive interpolation on the part of the narrator, which I italicize:

But that struck him as not being the right policy here. [. . .] There was a slight risk that later on his friends might possibly say he could not take a joke, but he had in mind—*though it was not usual with him to learn from experience*—several occasions [. . .], when against all his friends' advice he had behaved with deliberate recklessness and without the slightest regard for possible consequences, and had had in the end to pay dearly for it. That must not happen, at least not this time; if this was a comedy he would insist on playing it to the end.[39]

37. See my "The Trial of Law/The Trial of Writing," in *Twentieth Century Interpretations of "The Trial,"* ed. James Rolleston (Englewood Cliffs, N.J.: Prentice-Hall, 1976), 100–101. In a recent essay on *The Trial*, Walter Sokel also assigns plain authority to the prison chaplain on the basis of what seems his superior understanding of the parable of "The Man from the Country." Walter Sokel, "The Trial," in *Deutsche Romane des 20. Jahrhunderts: Neue Interpretationen,* ed. Michael Lützeler (Königstein: Athenäeum, 1983), 112.

38. T7, 261: "Was waren denn das für Menschen? Wovon sprachen sie? Welcher Behörde gehörten sie an?" T7, 261: "Er neigte stets dazu, alles möglichst leicht zu nehmen, das Schlimmste erst beim Eintritt des Schlimmsten zu glauben, keine Sorge für die Zukunft zu treffen, selbst wenn alles drohte."

39. T7–8, 261–62: Hier schien ihm das aber nicht richtig [. . .] . Darin, daß man später sagen würde, er habe keinen Spaß verstanden, sah K. eine ganz geringe Gefahr, wohl aber erinnerte er sich—ohne das es sonst seine Gewohnheit gewesen wäre, aus Erfahrungen zu lernen—an einige, an sich unbedeutende Fälle, in denen er zum Unterschied von seinen Freunden mit Bewußtsein, ohne das geringste Gefühl für die möglichen Folgen, sich

The Curtain Half Drawn

K. is determined to approach his predicament with the wisdom drawn from personal experience—one that tells him, namely, that even if this is a legal comedy, he will play his part in it. Indeed, he never steps out of his role, and his comedic vision survives until the moment before his death. Observing the warders of the court who have come to stab him, he asks: " 'So you are meant for me?" The gentlemen bowed, each indicating the other with the hand that held the top hat. [. . .] 'Tenth-rate old actors they send for me,' said K. to himself."⁴⁰

The interpretive decision which K. makes on the strength of personal experiences proves fatal. He is led to read his situation as a "case," as a trial by civil authority, to which he brings conventional expectations: that in being apprehended he will have been arrested and in being arrested he will be detained; that his arrest is based on a specific charge and that the charge, being plausible, constitutes grounds for arrest; that the verdict will conform with the sense of the charge, and so forth. For in a state governed by law—as personal experience attests—what other than a comedic fiction is a trial in which none of these conventions holds?

Once, however, K. begins to reason this way, he is lost. The project of maintaining and demanding from a court confirmation of innocence of a charge which is never specified is a manifest impossibility; grasped as a court case, his *Prozeß* is bound to fail. In adapting his predicament to personal experience, he only confirms the chaplain's point: in a case in which "the proceedings gradually merge into the verdict," the manner in which the accused conducts his case determines its outcome.⁴¹

Another way of putting K.'s situation is to say that he is determined to read his *Prozeß*—a word which means "trial" but also means a "process" of whatever sort—through the common metaphor of a civil trial. This is what personal experience drives him to, though this model of understanding will destroy him.

What then is the alternative? How could K. conduct his case otherwise? The alternative lies in his overcoming this dominant, persuasive metaphor furnished by personal experience; the liberating perspective lies, like the reader's own hope for enlightenment, in interpreting his process with the seized freshness of a literal reading, one faithful to the details conveyed by the narrator. But then of course there would have to be such a thing as a state of affairs different from K.'s own prejudgment of it.

---

unvorsichtig benommen hatte und dafür durch das Ergebnis gestraft worden war. Es sollte nicht wieder geschehen, zumindest nicht diesmal; war es eine Komödie, so wollte er mitspielen.

40. T280, 440: "Er stand gleich auf und sah die Herren neugierig an. 'Sie sind also für mich bestimmt?' fragte er. Die Herren nickten, einer zeigte mit dem Zylinderhut in der Hand auf den anderen. [. . .] 'Alte, untergeordnete Schauspieler schickt man um mich,' sagte sich K."

41. T264, 431: "Das Verfahren geht allmählich ins Urteil über."

Stanley Corngold

Events would have to stand out for a moment and assume the character of an objectlike text existing apart from the expectations of the interpreter. How could K. or the reader see the object steadily and see it whole? The object would have to have a beginning, would have to be unfolded for at least an instant as what it truly is. There would have to be a beginning to K.'s ordeal, a moment when it is his alone and before it has become the "personal" but in fact vulgar and anonymous vehicle of conventional understanding, namely, a case, which, even as an infelicitous case, falls under the jurisdiction of civil law. His ordeal would have to have a beginning before it has been preread.

But this is precisely what the novel is determined to prevent. Consider the famous opening sentence of *Der Prozeß* "Someone must have traduced Joseph K., for without having done anything wrong he was arrested one fine morning."[42] The narrative begins not with the first event of the plot but with a first interpretation of the event; the interpretation of the arrest as part of a conventional trial provoked by K.'s denunciation *is* the beginning. The novel is ahead of its own plot in the radical sense that Joseph K.'s manner of continually prereading the events of his trial is itself preread by the narrator. And even if, thereafter, Kafka at times breaks up the one perspective in which reader, narrator, and Joseph K. appear to be immersed, creating by these breaks the illusion that K.'s is a potentially corrigible, only one-sided, and merely particular or personal perspective, we see that from the outset, in the crucial matter of the kind of process that this is, there is to be no other perspective.

K.'s own interpretation has been preread by the narrator. It is forced on him, as it is forced on the reader, before the process begins, as an inescapably self-evident mode of understanding. Impersonating the incontrovertible voice of personal, of worldly experience, the narrator erects legal thinking as the only legitimate type of interpretation. He connects an arrest with a charge, as its condition, and defines an arrest in the absence of a charge, according to the logic of civil law, as a comedy parasitic on the norm, which, as a result, like himself, has been "traduced." He utters all this in a matter-of-fact tone impossible to resist, because it is at the beginning and we are disarmed. And yet it would have to be resisted, it seems, for life depends on not being so disarmed and on thinking this beginning event differently. K. has grounds enough to approach or leave his case differently, since his arrest is basically peculiar and hence not an arrest. To seize these grounds would be to liberate the perspective of a literalism unconstrained by previous personal experiences of law and legal metaphor. But by *defining* the arrest as only the

---

42. "Jemand mußte Josef K. verleumdet haben, denn ohne daß er etwas Böses getan hätte, wurde er eines Morgens verhaftet" (259).

miscarriage of a civil arrest, the narrator defeats this liberation in advance.

The structure of prereading in *The Trial* differs from what we have seen in Flaubert in its degree of evidentness. In Kafka the circle of signifying moments, which turns on K.'s "personal experiences," is not only realized explicitly by the detective reader, is not only realized implicitly by the actors in the text—like Madame Arnoux in *L'Education sentimentale*—but is also *identified* by the actors in the text. They act out their knowledge of it, indeed immediately after the opening, in the exchange between K. and the warder in the traveler's suit, who is called Franz!

K.: "Who are you?"
Franz: "Did you ring?"
K.: "Anna is to bring me my breakfast."
Franz: "He says Anna is to bring him his breakfast."[43]

In the perspective of Joseph K., the narrator then remarks: "The strange man could not have learned anything from [this sentence] that he did not already know" [for "have learned," Kafka writes, literally, "have experienced" (*erfahren*)].[44] The effect of this comment is to undermine from the start the value of experience, which is here said to have the cognitive authority only of what is already known—indeed, to have cognitive authority at all only as the repetition of a previous moment, only insofar as it is preknown. Quite consistently, when the warders (Franz included) speak of the dwindling value of the personal property of the accused deposited at the depot as a truth "confirmed by experience" (*erfahrungsgemäß*), "K. paid hardly any attention to this advice."[45] Thereafter, quite *inconsistently*, K. resolves to learn *from experience* to play along with the arrest. He will be reproved for this by the chaplain, and both he and the reader will have reason by the end to doubt the promise made early by the deluded warder Willem, that K. will learn from "experience [*erfahren*] everything" pertaining to the proceedings.[46]

Prereading, as a term demystifying "experience," is vivid all throughout *The Trial*, in the passages I have quoted and thereafter in the prejudgments made by K. on his own arrest and trial. It is performed essen-

---

43. T4. I have abstracted this little stage scene from the novel. The German reads: "'Wer sind Sie?' fragte K. [. . .] 'Sie haben geläutet?' 'Anna soll mir das Frühstück bringen,' sagte K. [. . .] Aber dieser [der Mann . . .] wandte sich zur Tür [. . .] um jemandem [. . .] zu sagen: 'Er will, daß Anna ihm das Frühstück bringt'" (259).

44. T4, 259: "Der fremde Mann [konnte] dadurch nichts erfahren haben [. . .], was er nicht schon früher gewußt hätte."

45. T7, 261: "'und weiter verringern sich solche Erlöse erfahrungsgemäß [. . .].' K. achtete auf diese Reden kaum."

46. T6, 260: "Sie werden alles [. . .] erfahren."

Stanley Corngold

tially by the plot, which is prejudgment itself, in the sense that "the world [of experience] in Kafka's text is seen as the result of the thought process peculiar to the perspectival figure, the hero Joseph K."[47] More radically, as we have seen, it structures the narration, being incorporated directly in the narrator's prejudicial surmise which precedes the *mise en scène*. These are the senses in which prereading in *Der Prozeß* is explicit— though it is fully explicit only for readers who know that what they are looking for is what they have already read, and that, therefore, in the spirit of Kafka's aphorism, they are, in a certain sense, already "found." For "he who seeks does not find, but he who does not seek will be found."[48]

The ways in which novels of Flaubert and Kafka elaborate prereading together illustrate a growing tendency of the modern philosophical novel. The plot of *L'Education sentimentale* is anticipated by moments of prereading that invite excavation and exposure; by virtue of this obligatory salvaging work, the plot becomes implicitly and in part the struggle of reading for the half-curtained plot.[49] The reader is charged with the task of constituting the novel's design. In Kafka the function of the preread is more overt, though it is not necessarily easier to grasp. Here the novel's plot is not in question: the plot is itself the repetition and proved ubiquity of prereading. On lines found between Flaubert and Kafka showing the increased explicitness of prereading, especially as it enters the narrative

47. Theo Elm, "Der Prozess," in *Das Werk und seine Wirkung*, vol. 2 of *Kafka-Handbuch*, ed. Hartmut Binder (Stuttgart: Alfred Kröner, 1979), 435. In "Kafka's Rhetorical Moment," *PMLA* 98, 1 (1983), Clayton Koelb shows how a similar temporal structure informs the very language of K.'s arrest. What effectively justifies the arrest for K., for the complicit narrator, and for the unwary reader is an appeal to an anonymous personal experience, which endows the moment with anterior reference. Koelb writes: "The first K. hears of [his arrest] is from one of the 'warders' who appear in his room: 'Sie dürfen nicht weggehen, Sie sind ja verhaftet.'" (38). The "ja" is very odd and in fact dysfunctional if it is supposed to strengthen the performative effect of the utterance. In fact it appeals to and ascertains a prior state of affairs. Thereafter the inspector appears in turn to appeal to the warder's statement in saying, "You're under arrest, that's correct, that's all I know." Koelb adds: "It would seem therefore that the Inspector is assuming that K. is already under arrest. But that, of course, is what the warder also apparently assumed. Who has arrested K.?" (39). The answer, of course, is that K. (and the narrator) have. K. (and the narrator) have bought into K.'s arrest on the strength of personal experience, and Kafka the narrator does everything at once to reveal and conceal this truth.

48. Franz Kafka, *Dearest Father*, trans. Ernst Kaiser and Eithne Wilkins (New York: Schocken, 1954), 80. "Wer sucht, findet nicht, aber wer nicht sucht, wird gefunden." *Hochzeitsvorbereitungen auf dem Lande und andere Prosa aus dem Nachlaß*, ed. Max Brod (Frankfurt a.M.: Fischer, 1953), 94.

49. In *Reading for the Plot* Peter Brooks is concerned to stress that *L'Education sentimentale* is without plot, and that the reading it defines is of a new type that must endure the absence of plot, albeit with the residual consciousness (left over from Balzac) of what the missing plot must be. While Brooks's argument is cogent, I am more concerned to stress the equally important promise of a particular meaning adumbrated in this novel, namely, the threat to meaning of a leveling of difference between sacred and profane lovers.

mechanism itself, one could begin to redescribe the consciousness shaping modern philosophical novels such as Rilke's *The Notebooks of Malte Laurids Brigge*, Gide's *The Counterfeiters*, and Faulkner's *Absalom, Absalom!* Each arises as a model type within the development of prereading, whose counterpart in the human sciences is the elaboration of the hermeneutic circle of interpretation.

[18]

The Modern Lyric: Generic
Continuity and Critical Practice

Jonathan Culler

Having learned that "comparaison n'est pas raison," practitioners of Comparative Literature have frequently found it difficult to give anything but a negative definition of their practice: Comparative Literature is literary study that does not respect national frontiers or assume that a national literature is the proper focus of literary study. Perhaps one may feel less embarrassed by such negative definitions if one recalls that, according to Ferdinand de Saussure, the identity of a linguistic fact is purely negative and differential: "Its most precise characteristic is to be what the others are not." Whether this analogy heightens or diminishes one's confidence in "the comparative perspective," as our editors call it, the comparatist, like the linguist, has no object of study given in advance. "C'est le point de vue qui crée l'objet," Saussure declares.[1]

Two points of view that clearly belong to the comparative perspective are the focus on a genre (its instantiations in different languages and periods) and the study of an international literary movement. These seem the closest thing to natural objects of inquiry for comparative literature— objects, shall we say, that inescapably come into view when one tries to adopt the comparative perspective. But incontrovertible genres, such as the novel or tragedy, are so few and so massive that they cannot easily be studied without further delimitation, and well-defined international literary movements, such as surrealism, are relatively rare, so that these two sorts of objects do not in fact solve the comparatist's methodological problem. The literary phenomena that most imperiously or intriguingly demand attention often prove more slippery—difficult to characterize either as genre or as historical movement.

1. *Cours de linguistique générale* (Paris: Payot, 1967), 162, 23.

The Modern Lyric

The "modern lyric" is an instance of this sort of object: of particular interest to the comparatist but not quite a genre or an international literary movement. Though hard to define, it seems a necessary concept. When reading or working on nineteenth- and twentieth-century poetry in any European language, one implicitly draws upon some notion of modern poetry or the modern lyric. Specialists in a single national literature might well expect comparatists to provide them with a general model of the modern lyric that they can use in analyzing the particular achievements of the poets they study. On the other hand, critical writings on important poets, such as Baudelaire, for example, who is frequently presented as a key figure in the development of modern poetry, reveal that one of the stakes in discussions of his poetry is a conception of modern poetry, its projects and achievements. The comparatist's task in this case would be to pursue critical analyses of the model of the lyric implicit in interpretations of individual poets and to assess that model in the larger comparative perspective.

This essay explores the notion of the "modern lyric" in two ways: as a conception that emerges from recent readings of Baudelaire and as an implicit generic model that guides the reading of poetry. The relationships between historical claims and structural models are not easy to sort out, since the effect of successful claims about modern poetry is to establish a general model of what poetry does or can do. Such problems structure a domain defined by the comparative perspective and illustrate the importance of working out appropriate notions of genre. The question is not just "What is the lyric?" but, above all, "What does such a question ask?" What are generic concepts supposed to do?

Although the distinction between lyric, dramatic, and epic has proved historically resilient, emerging in one form or another as the basis of most accounts of genres in the past two hundred years, there has been considerable disagreement about what lyric or the lyric is or should be. Is it a genre, a mode, a style, an attitude toward experience, a conception of the world, a spirit? Theories have taken each of these lines. Suffice it to say that the most common move, the association of lyric with subjectivity, may depend on the similarity of the noun *lyric* and the adjective *lyric*. When the distinction is made, as it is by Emil Staiger, who distinguishes between *die Lyrik* and *das Lyrische*, critics incline to prefer the latter, as a style, key (*Tonart*), or mode that can be found in plays, novels, epics, as well as in short poems.[2] In *Beyond Genre*, an ambitious survey of approaches to genre, Paul Hernadi seems to despair of finding in the tradition of genre theory a pertinent account of the lyric: "As for lyric poetry, I am not aware

---

2. Emil Staiger, *Grundbegriffe der Poetik*, 6th ed. (Zurich: Atlantis, 1963), 7–10, 223–39.

of any widely shared concept of its generic structure. While deep insights have been attained with regard to certain kinds of non-dramatic, non-narrative writing, critics do not seem to have succeeded in providing a unified conceptual map of this 'no man's land.' Perhaps they ought to quit trying; this at least is what René Wellek suggests."[3]

Wellek, in an article titled "Genre Theory, the Lyric, and *Erlebnis*," concludes that

lyrical theory—at least with the terms which we have discussed, *Erlebnis*, subjective, presence, *Stimmung*—seems to have arrived at a complete impasse. These terms cannot take care of the enormous variety, in history and in different literatures, of lyrical forms and constantly lead into an insoluble psychological cul de sac: the supposed intensity, inwardness, immediacy of an experience which can never be demonstrated as certain and can never be shown to be relevant to the quality of art.

"The way out is obvious," he continues. "One must abandon attempts to define the general nature of the lyric or the lyrical. Nothing beyond generalities of the tritest kind can result from it. It seems much more profitable to turn to a study of the variety of poetry and to the history and thus the description of genres which can be grasped in their concrete conventions and traditions."[4]

Though I agree with Wellek that psychological and existential categories do not generally advance the study of poetry or poetic forms, his critique here both begs the question of what accounts of the lyric should try to do and uses an unabashedly biographical and psychologistic concept of the lyric as the excuse to dismiss the project of defining the general nature of the lyric. He proposes a shift of attention, from the lyric to more narrowly defined lyric genres, such as the elegy, the ode, and the song. These are certainly valid subjects for comparative investigation, but if one is interested in modern poetry, these generic models scarcely seem a first priority. The elegy, the ode, and the song are special cases—sorts of poems which writers might compose and which critics might discuss, asking, for example, how a particular poem plays off against the tradition of the elegy. But when we are reflecting on the poetry or poetic achievements of Eliot, Stevens, Williams, Mallarmé, Valéry, for instance, we implicitly employ general notions of the modern lyric, discussing their inflection of it or contribution to it. While it may be futile, as Wellek claims, to attempt to decide what the lyric in general does, poets, critics,

3. *Beyond Genre: New Directions in Literary Classification* (Ithaca: Cornell University Press, 1972), 79.
4. *Discriminations: Further Concepts of Criticism* (New Haven: Yale University Press, 1970), 251–52.

and readers cannot avoid having views on the question, so that in abandoning this level of focus one risks ignoring concepts that play a major role in the production and reception of poetry.

If one thinks of genres as sets of expectations, notions of tradition which guide reading and writing, then the question of what is the modern lyric is tied up with interpretations of Baudelaire. Though it would be possible to read Baudelaire in the context of French or European romanticism, criticism has preferred to see him as the founder of modern poetry: *Les Fleurs du Mal* is the pivot on which the lyric turns toward the twentieth century. T. S. Eliot called Baudelaire "the greatest example of modern poetry in any language," but the book whose claims did most to animate and direct the critical discussion is Hugo Friedrich's *Die Struktur der modernen Lyrik*, which identifies in Baudelaire the qualities characteristic of the twentieth-century lyric, describing his work in terms that define the possibilities later poets will explore: "Fundamental Neues bringt die Lyrik des 20. Jahrhunderts nicht mehr, so qualitätvoll auch einige ihrer Dichter sind."[5] Twentieth-century verse, according to Friedrich, has brought us almost nothing new.

Claims about Baudelaire's modernity tend to focus not on formal qualities of his verse or on the lyric forms he uses but on modes of consciousness: the poems as embodiments of a quintessentially modern consciousness. Paul Verlaine perhaps said it first: "La profonde originalité de Charles Baudelaire est, à mon avis, de représenter puissamment et essentiellement l'homme moderne. . . . Aussi, selon moi, l'historien futur de notre époque devra feuilleter attentivement et religieusement ce livre, qui est la quintessence et comme la concentration extrême de tout un élément de ce siècle."[6] Whether Baudelaire embodies or portrays modern man—and there is some ambiguity in Verlaine's discussion—his poetry is seen as exemplary of modern experience, of the possibility of experiencing or dealing with what we have come to call the modern world. Erich Auerbach, in his notable essay "The Aesthetic Dignity of *Les Fleurs du Mal*," identifies Baudelaire's originality with the embodiment of a modern state of consciousness. His modernity comes from the fact that "he was the first to treat as sublime matters which seemed by nature unsuited to such treatment. . . . He wrote in the grand style about paralyzing anxiety, panic at the hopeless entanglement of our lives, total collapse."[7] Such experiences take on a new character when they are treated not as marginal or exceptional but exemplary:

5. *Die Struktur der modernen Lyrik* (Hamburg: Rowohlt, 1956), 140.
6. "Charles Baudelaire," in Verlaine, *Oeuvres en prose complètes*, ed. Jacques Borel (Paris: Gallimard, 1972), 599–600.
7. Erich Auerbach, "The Aesthetic Dignity of *Les Fleurs du Mal*," in *Baudelaire*, ed. Henri Peyre (Englewood Cliffs, N.J.: Prentice-Hall, 1962), 154.

Jonathan Culler

Tu le connais, lecteur, ce monstre délicat,
—Hypocrite lecteur,—mon semblable,—mon frère.[8]

Baudelaire's catachreses—"La Mort, planant comme un soleil nouveau," or "Quand le ciel bas et lourd pèse comme un couvercle"—drew new visionary power from unusual combinations and seemed, Auerbach writes, "the most authentic expression both of the inner anarchy of the age and of a still hidden order that was just beginning to dawn. In an entirely new and consummate style, this poet, whose character and life were so strange, expressed the naked, concrete existence of an epoch. For his style was not based on his personal situation and his personal needs; it became apparent that his extreme personality embodied a far more universal situation and a far more universal need."[9]

Walter Benjamin, whose discussion of Baudelaire has become increasingly influential, links Baudelaire's exemplary modernity with the fact that he wrote as one for whom urban experience had become the norm. "With Baudelaire, Paris for the first time becomes the subject of lyrical poetry. This poetry is no local folklore: the allegorist's gaze which falls upon the city is rather the gaze of alienated man. It is the gaze of the flâneur, whose way of living still bestowed a conciliatory gleam over the growing destitution of men in the great city."[10]

At stake in the interpretation of Baudelaire's lyrics, then, seems to be the question of how one can experience or come to terms with the modern world. As Friedrich writes, in the book which did most to set the terms of the debate, Baudelaire used the term *modernity*

to express the modern artist's special ability to look at the desert of a metropolis and not merely see the decline of mankind but also sense a mysterious beauty hitherto undiscovered. This was Baudelaire's own problem: how was poetry possible in our commercialized and technologized civilization? His verse points out the way, and his prose makes an exhaustive study of it. The road leads as far as possible from the banality of real life to a zone of mystery, but in such a way that the subject matter found in civilized reality is brought into this zone and thus becomes poetically viable. This new outlook touched off modern poetry, creating its corrosive but magical substance.[11]

Among Baudelaire's poetic techniques central to modern poetry, Friedrich emphasizes *depersonalization* (*Entpersönlichung*) and *making unreal*

8. Charles Baudelaire, "Au Lecteur," in *Les Fleurs du Mal*, ed. Antoine Adam (Paris: Garnier, 1961), 6.
9. Auerbach, "Aesthetic Dignity," 168.
10. Walter Benjamin, *Charles Baudelaire: A Lyric Poet in the Age of High Capitalism* (London: New Left Books, 1973), 170.
11. Friedrich, *Die Struktur*, 35.

depersonalization
The Modern Lyric *difamiliarization*

(*Entrealisierung*): "Baudelaire sparked off the depersonalization of modern poetry, at least in the sense that the lyrical word no longer derives from a fusion of the poetic persona and an empirical person." Unlike Victor Hugo, for instance, he does not date his poems so as to relate them to biographical events. There is a neutralization of the person, in the sense that "the poet pays scant heed to his empirical ego when he writes his verses. He writes out of himself only insofar as he considers himself a sufferer of modernity." The "I" which speaks in most of *Les Fleurs du Mal* is a depersonalized poetic voice which foreshadows the dehumanized voices of later lyrics. Moreover, imagination in Baudelaire is the process of transforming reality and making it unreal. Modern poetry, according to Friedrich, is characterized by the "dictatorial imagination," enemy of the reality, which imposes a transformation or destruction of the real world. Reality, dismembered or torn to shreds by the power of the imagination, becomes in the poem "a landscape of ruins."[12] *James*

But this *Entrealisierung* paves the way for an aesthetic recuperation: "In the refuse of urban centers, Baudelaire smells a mystery, which his poetry depicts as a phosphorescent shimmer." An "aesthetics of ugliness" works to endow the grotesque, the degenerate, and the trivial with interest and, *effect of poetry* at the same time, for Friedrich, to make it less real. "Extracted from banality, like drugs from toxic plants, the images are poetically transformed into antidotes for 'the vice of banality.'" The production of images generates mystery which embodies both "a craving for escape from reality and a powerlessness to believe in or create a substantially precise, meaningfully structured transcendence. . . . Baudelaire often speaks of the supernatural and of mystery. What he means can be comprehended only by refusing, as he does, to fill these words with any meaning other than absolute mysteriousness itself." The images that are devised by the imagination for representing and ultimately overcoming reality are the "attempt of a modern soul, trapped in a technologized, imperialistic, commercial era, to preserve its own freedom."[13] Images that make unreal what they represent, in other words, are a strategy of modern consciousness for coping with experience and recuperating reality in some way, endowing it with what Friedrich calls an "empty ideality"—in contrast with specific transcendental values of religions or spiritual systems. This empty ideality works to confer a value that depends, if not on the "freedom" of the mind, at least on its activity, so that a poem such as "L'Héautontimorouménos," with its "Je suis la plaie et le couteau," dramatizes and thus values the self-torture of a "vorace ironie."

Friedrich's claim that *Entrealisierung* confers a value of empty ideality

12. Ibid., 36, 37.
13. Ibid., 43, 49, 165–66.

has been taken up and modified in a series of readings of Baudelaire by Hans-Robert Jauss, who, seeking to harmonize Friedrich with Benjamin, to put it simply, argues that the forced idealization of modern poetry is produced above all by memory: "But now it is only remembrance from which the counterimage of the new and the beautiful arises in a solemn procession of evocations. The harmonizing and idealizing power of remembrance is the newly discovered aesthetic capacity which can replace the extinct correspondence of soul and timeless nature by the coincidence of present existence and prehistory, modernity and antiquity, historical now and mythical past."[14]

Friedrich, and with him Jauss, give us through Baudelaire a vision of the destiny of twentieth-century poetry: "Dissonant beauty, removal of the heart from the 'I' of poetry, abnormal consciousness, empty ideality, deobjectification, mysteriousness, all of which were produced from the magic powers inherent in language and from the absolute imagination and were brought close to the abstractions or mathematics and the curving motion of music, were used by Baudelaire to prepare the possibilities that were to be realized in future poetry."[15] What I shall return to later is the significant combination, in this account of the crucial features of the modern lyric, of stress on depersonalization ("removal of the heart from the 'I' of the poetry"), and the association of value with operations of consciousness, such as remembrance or the dictatorial imagination. But these accounts, while they may speak of lyric poetry or the modern lyric, have not explicitly asked what the lyric is or what we want a theory of genres to do. Our next step in considering problems of the modern lyric is to return to these questions.

In *The Three Genres and the Interpretation of Lyric*, William E. Rogers contrasts genre theories which provide a grid, a mapping of logical space in which individual works can be placed, with theories treating genres "as relational concepts constitutive of understanding."[16] The first approach seeks to group works according to similarities and differences and sees proper classification as an operation that depends upon and follows from prior understanding. The second approach, on the contrary, asks what is

14. "Sketch of a Theory and History of Aesthetic Experience," in Jauss, *Aesthetic Experience and Literary Hermeneutics*, trans. Michael Shaw (Minneapolis: University of Minnesota Press, 1982), 84. In this passage he is extrapolating from remarks on Baudelaire's "Le Cygne."

15. Friedrich, *Die Struktur*, 58.

16. *The Three Genres and the Interpretation of Lyric* (Princeton: Princeton University Press, 1983), 41 and chap. 1 passim. Rogers's argument about the status of generic concepts is exemplary, though one might disagree with the terms in which he defines the genres, properly conceived as interpretive models: "To interpret a work as epic, then, I shall argue, is to interpret the relation between the mind and the world in the work as one of substance and accident; to interpret a work as dramatic is to interpret the relation in terms of causality; to interpret a work as lyric is to interpret that relation as one of community" (49).

1+2 can't be separated. all genre thing depends to some degree m pon in knowledge

involved in understanding a work as belonging to a particular genre and in effect treats generic concepts as conventions for producing or interpreting works. The first approach, witness Hernadi's *Beyond Genre*, seeks a definition of the lyric or lyrical that will enable it to classify works according to the presence or absence of these qualities. The second looks for assumptions and interpretive strategies that lie behind poetic production and its interpretation.

When one takes up the problem of the modern lyric one finds oneself repeatedly encountering, in various ways, models of poetry: models to which critics appeal, models of the modern poem which they actively promote, implicit models that underlie and make possible their interpretation of individual poems and poets. If one is to bring any clarity to this domain, one finds that one must in effect ask what have been the important and effective concepts of the lyric. One finds that discussion of modern poetry, criticism of modern poetry, and the reading and writing of modern poetry have not generally focused on narrowly conceived poetic genres—the sonnet, the ode, and the elegy, for instance. There has been debate about the long poem—the possibility of the long poem in the modern age, the kind of unity to which it might aspire, the reduced, nonepical role which it will or would doubtless play—and then there has been discussion about what one can only call the lyric, the most apt name for what writers, critics, and readers are thinking of when they talk about modern poems and poetry. We need to ask, therefore, what conception of the lyric, what model of reading, is or has been at work. The difficulties of defining lyric should not prevent one from investigating generic models.

For instance, though René Wellek rejects the conception of the lyric as the expression of *Erlebnis*, he does not mention an influential book in the Anglo-American tradition, Robert Langbaum's *The Poetry of Experience*, which emphasizes not the biographical or psychologically intense experience of authors but the experience dramatized in poems. Arguing that the desire to overcome subjectivity and achieve objectivity "has determined the direction of poetic development since the end of the Enlightenment," Langbaum claims that the essential idea of poetry in this period is

the idea of experience—the doctrine that the imaginative apprehension gained through immediate experience is primary and certain, whereas the analytical reflection that follows is secondary and problematical. The poetry of the nineteenth and twentieth centuries can thus be seen in connection as a poetry of experience—a poetry constructed on the deliberate disequilibrium between experience and idea, a poetry which makes its statement not as an idea but as an experience from which one or more ideas can be extracted as problematical rationalizations.[17]

17. *The Poetry of Experience: The Dramatic Monologue in Modern Literary Tradition* (Harmondsworth: Penguin, 1974), 23, 28.

lyric poetry - primacy of experience over analysis or reflection useful for *lullabies* (handwritten)

immediacy of lyric experience (handwritten, left margin)

The point here, one should emphasize, is not that a biographical experience of the poet's gets recollected and presented in the poem but that the poem has a dramatic character and presents itself as an event—the experience of a mind investigating, recollecting, being modified by circumstances with which it interacts—not as idea distilled from intense past experience. The notion of experience thus need not necessarily lead to the kind of psychologism that Wellek finds it easy to reject without argument, just by asserting that it has nothing to do with poems as aesthetic objects. The sort of lyric in question communicates not as truth or assertion but as dramatized experience of a consciousness and affords the reader an experience rather than a truth.

Yeats's "Among School Children," for example, would be interpreted, by this model, not as a protest against the imposition of discipline—

> Labour is blossoming or dancing where
> Body is not bruised to pleasure soul
> Nor beauty born out of its own despair,
> Nor blear-eyed wisdom out of midnight oil

—nor as a statement about mortality or any of the other subjects it touches on but as the drama of a mind attempting to come to terms with the relations between youth and age and the values or ideals ("Presences / That passion, piety, or affection knows") adduced in human strivings. Cleanth Brooks develops at length the argument that this poem "is a dramatization, not a formula; a controlled experience which has to be experienced, not a logical process, the conclusion of which is reached by logical methods."[18]

vague → (handwritten) Examples of this sort help to clarify the role of generic concepts. Instead of articulations of a logical space in which literary works can be placed, according to the qualities they manifest, genres are in effect treated as models that function within a particular culture to generate readings. The key question, as in this example, is what is involved in reading something as a lyric, or as a tragedy, as an epic. To work on generic codes is to try to elucidate the models that guide interpretation. In this case, to read a work as a lyric is not to extract a propositional lesson (that would be a different genre) nor to identify an intense biographically locatable experience to which the poet is referring but rather to describe the movement of a consciousness attempting to come to terms with fundamental aspects of the human condition, as embodied in the situation confronting it. This approach to genre is more closely related to

18. "Yeats's Great Rooted Blossomer," in Brooks, *The Well Wrought Urn* (New York: Harcourt Brace, 1947), 190.

ask students + instructors to examine why they/we read as we do

pedagogy than to scientific taxonomy, involving not the discovery of objective similarities and differences between forms but elucidation of the models by which people are taught to interpret.

If one thinks about the genre of the lyric in the twentieth century, one will, pace René Wellek, find oneself confronting the category of experience. Paul Hernadi's useful map of lyric possibilities consonant with his general map of generic space takes the lyric as "enacted vision," which seems to focus on the dramatic character emphasized by Langbaum's concept of the poetry of experience. Now Langbaum, having put forward this notion of the fundamental idea of post-Enlightenment poetry, proceeds to identify an important late nineteenth-century poetic form, the dramatic monologue. He recognizes the danger that, once one focuses on dramatic monologue, "every lyric in which the speaker seems to be someone other than the poet, almost all love songs and laments, in fact . . . , become dramatic monologues."[19] He takes steps to avoid this expansion of the genre, but once one has described the model of a poem conveying not a truth but an experience, there is a strong temptation to see poems in this light whenever possible and in effect to treat them as dramatic monologues.

Once this orientation was joined to the New Critical insistence on separating speaker from poet so that interpretation would be based on the words on the page rather than knowledge of the poet's doings at the alleged time of composition, then the way was open to see all lyrics as dramatic monologues. I submit that in Anglo-American criticism at least, this has become the most influential view, supplanting the older view of the lyric as a brief poem in which the poet intensely proclaimed his or her feelings. Pedagogical handbooks which once had promoted lyric as the expression of author's most precious emotions had, by the postwar years, made it a basic principle, in the words of Laurence Perrine's popular textbook, *Sound and Sense*, "to assume always that the speaker is someone other than the poet himself."[20] Students learned that the task of interpreting lyrics involved working out what sort of person was speaking, in what circumstances, and with what attitude. The operative conception of the lyric seemed to be modeled on the dramatic monologue. As Ralph Rader writes, in an article which seeks to make distinctions, "The most distinctive and highly valued poems of the modern era offer an image of a dramatized 'I' acting in a concrete setting. . . . The power and beauty of such poems seem intimately connected with the fact of their dramatic integrity and autonomy, and we have all been taught, in analyzing them,

19. Langbaum, *The Poetry of Experience*, 69.
20. *Sound and Sense* (New York: Harcourt Brace, 1963), 21.

shift from def. of lyric as intense procl. of poet's feelings to lyric as dramatic monologue to refer to a 'speaker' existing independent of the poet and to avoid the 'intentional' and 'biographical' fallacies."[21]

There are several factors that contribute to this model of the lyric:

(1) The fundamental organicist assumption of post-Enlightenment literature, which Langbaum calls the priority of experience over reflection but which also emerges in the idea of the concrete universal, the preference for symbol over allegory, the assertion that "a poem should not mean but be." This underlying presumption, which leads to a preference for something other than a message, affects the results of the other factors.

(2) The model of prose fiction, which increasingly exploited limited point of view and invited interpretation that focused on identifying implied narrators and showing how description manifested their character and attitudes. As novels and short stories became the literary genres most widely studied in schools and universities, they came to serve as the implicit model of literature and pedagogical approaches attuned to their compositional techniques became the norm.

(3) Modernist poets' claims to produce an impersonal, "objective" poetry, in contrast to the "subjective" poetry of the romantics and the Victorians. Examples are imagism's desire for direct treatment of the thing, the exact rendering of particulars, Eliot's emphasis on "objective correlatives" of emotion, or other modes of impersonality—masks and personae. "Upon the establishment of Yeats's mask, Pound's personae, Frost's monologues and idylls, and Eliot's impersonal poetry," writes one critic, "it became a point of dogma among sophisticated readers that every poem dramatized a speaker who was not the poet."[22]

(4) The insistence by Anglo-American New Criticism that interpretation focus on "the words on the page" rather than adduce biographical information to solve interpretive problems. Poems came to be treated as artifacts rather than statements of a poet, but concern with attitude and tone made it indispensable to posit a speaker to whom they could be attributed. As Wimsatt and Brooks put it in their history of criticism, "Once we have dissociated the speaker of the lyric from the personality of the poet, even the tiniest lyric reveals itself as drama."[23]

(5) The traditional conception of the lyric as utterance overheard, reinforced by such authorities as T. S. Eliot and Northrop Frye. For Frye the basis of generic distinctions is the "radical of presentation," and lyric is "preeminently the utterance that is overheard. The lyric poet normally

21. "The Dramatic Monologue and Related Lyric Forms," *Critical Inquiry*, 3, 1 (1976), 131.

22. Herbert Tucker, "Dramatic Monologue and the Overhearing of Lyric," in *Lyric Poetry: Beyond New Criticism*, ed. C. Hosek and P. Parker (Ithaca: Cornell University Press, 1985), 239.

23. W. K. Wimsatt and Cleanth Brooks, *Literary Criticism: A Short History* (New York: Knopf, 1957), 675.

pretends to be talking to himself or someone else: a spirit of nature, a Muse, a personal friend, a lover, a god, a personified abstraction, or a natural object."[24] Now, when we overhear an utterance that engages our attention, what we characteristically do is to imagine or reconstruct a context: identifying a tone of voice, we infer the posture, situation, intention, concerns, and attitudes of a speaker.

What happens when notions of a poetry of experience and lyric as overheard utterance come together is a new emphasis on speech as action and the speaker as a character, whose situation, attitudes, and values, as dramatized in the poem itself, must be interpreted. This is roughly the approach to the lyric expounded and exemplified by the New Criticism, which sees the lyric as characterized in part by what is left out and must be inferred: "It leaves out so much of the accustomed context and consequences of feeling that it can speak in a pure, lucid, intense voice."[25] Interpreting a lyric is thus a matter of working "to conceive of the kind of situation that might lead a speaker to feel thus and speak thus."[26]

To interpret a poem as a lyric, by this model, is to attempt to identify with an act of consciousness on the part of a constructed speaker. Consider Robert Frost's "Spring Pools":

> These pools that, though in forests, still reflect   A
> The total sky almost without defect,   A
> And like the flowers beside them, chill and shiver,   B
> Will like the flowers beside them soon be gone,   C
> And yet not out by any brook or river,   B
> But up by roots to bring dark foliage on.   C
> The trees that have it in their pent-up buds   D
> To darken nature and be summer woods—   D
> Let them think twice before they use their powers   E
> To blot out and drink up and sweep away   F
> These flowery waters and these watery flowers   E
> From snow that melted only yesterday.   F

I choose this poem because it is not obvious that it should be read as anything like a dramatic monologue. It could be taken as somewhat whimsical descriptive poetry. The current conception of the lyric, I am claiming, is such that to read this as a lyric (and thus to take it seriously as poetry, given our modern hierarchy of genres) we must focus on a speaker and see the poem as a drama of attitudes. In that case, what we

24. *Anatomy of Criticism* (New York: Atheneum, 1965), 246.

25. Barbara Hardy, *The Advantage of Lyric* (Bloomington: Indiana University Press, 1977), 2.

26. Barbara Herrnstein Smith, *On the Margins of Discourse* (Chicago: University of Chicago Press, 1978), 33.

Jonathan Culler

must concentrate on is the speaker's relation to the natural world and thus the relation between the images selected (the pools that chill and shiver) and the tone—call it a certain colloquial bluster—of the last lines ("Let them think twice"). How does that colloquialism balance with the formal chiasmus of "these flowery waters and these watery flowers"? These are not the same questions one would concentrate on if one were using another model of the lyric.

What this model does is to focus attention on speakers and consciousness, even in spare imagist poems which may aspire to direct portrayal of the thing itself. Interpreting Pound's "In a Station of the Metro"—

> The apparition of these faces in the crowd;
> Petals on a wet black bough.

—critics imagine a person seeing the faces and making a connection expressed in the natural image and thus take the poem to be about the imagination's ability to transform reality and confer on it values associated with trees and flowers more than with mass transport. Imagist poems which might seem to consist of discrete observations and aspire to objectivity are, by this model of the lyric, made subjective, as interpretation inexorably posits a speaker and a consciousness—albeit a depersonalized one—and interprets their images as products of what Friedrich calls the dictatorial imagination: imagination which, as it makes unreal, endows the objects of perception with mystery and empty ideality.

The model of the modern lyric, which focuses on the drama of consciousness of a depersonalized speaker, has provided a powerful strategy for interpreting even the most refractory poems: the most bizarre and disconnected images can be read as signs of alienation and anomie or of a breakdown of mental processes brought on by the experience in question. When Friedrich declares that twentieth-century verse has brought us almost nothing new, this is perhaps as much a self-fulfilling prophecy as an empirical observation. Twentieth-century poems can be processed in this way. Since a linguistic sequence seems to imply a speaker or at least a consciousness, this recourse to a depersonalized consciousness is always possible. "No matter how enigmatic or arbitrary modern poetry may become," Friedrich declares, "it is always recognizable in its structure"[27]—a structure established historically by Baudelaire's poetic project.

This structure gives us a depersonalized subjectivity transforming reality by acts of consciousness. We have lost the old presumptions of lyric sincerity and the figure of the inspired or accursed poet, but as Herbert

27. Friedrich, *Die Struktur*, 140.

Tucker remarks in a fine essay, "the new dogma took (and in my teaching experience it takes still) with such ease that it is worth asking why it did (and does)."[28] What this structure does is promote the notion of a free subjectivity by assuming that language must come from and should be explained by a consciousness. Tucker speaks of "the thirst for intersubjective confirmation of the self," which has made the overhearing of a persona our principal means of understanding a poem," and of "that late ceremony of critical innocence, the readerly imagination of a self,"[29] by which, when looking at a piece of language, we establish a specular relation that works to confirm for us the originary autonomy of the subject we consider ourselves to be.

This generic model of the lyric has been extremely powerful, but at least two qualifications should be noted. First, although, as I have suggested, the widespread use of this model in the teaching of poetry has inexorably led to its extension to lyrics of earlier periods, when critics do explicitly adduce this model they generally claim it applies to post-Baudelairian poetry, not to all lyrics. Second, in asserting the dominance of this model there is no question of denying that in the modern period poets have made quite different claims about what poetry should do. Numerous manifestos have argued, for instance, that a new poetry does or should portray things themselves rather than thoughts about things. My claim is that despite manifestos setting forth different ideas of what lyrics are or do, we have come to read lyrics according to the model sketched here, as dramatizations of the encounter of a consciousness with the world. Indeed, the central feature of the model is not that lyrics are cut off from poets but that they are to be read as dramatizations of a consciousness's dealings with the world.

This has been, I maintain, the dominant model of the lyric, at least in the Anglo-American world, but there are grounds for questioning it. Though this model can be applied systematically and comprehensively, as Friedrich claims, there are many poems which resist it, some because their elaborate rhetoric forces one, when one attempts to "conceive of the kind of situation that might lead a man to feel thus and to speak thus," to posit, in uncomfortably circular fashion, a speaker who is waxing poetical, indulging in bardic flights. Others resist because their typographic or intertextual oddities prevent one from imagining any speaker and situation except that of a poet constructing the artifact.

More specifically, emphasis on a speaker's acts of consciousness and on the point of view that is revealed by a linguistic sequence in effect assimilates the lyric to prose fiction, depriving rhythm and sound patterns of

28. Tucker, "Dramatic Monologue," 240.
29. Ibid., 242.

[298]
Jonathan Culler

any constitutive role and reducing rather than augmenting the spectrum of literary possibilities. Generic models ought ideally, one might suggest, to counter reductiveness by increasing the array of reading strategies.

Above all, this orientation leads to neglect of potentially interesting features of lyrics, such as the patterning Northrop Frye calls *melos* and *opsis* or babble and doodle. We are enjoined by this model to attend to sound patterning when it can be seen as elucidating the attitude of the speaker and to interpret puns as wit, instead of exploring verbal echoes or word play without reference to a principle of consciousness. Moreover, poems, unlike speakers' utterances, give language a visible form, providing further dimensions of representation and possibilities of riddling that the reigning conception of the lyric misses. It is as though in operatic arias one were supposed to attend only to that which contributed to understanding of a character.

Lyrics can also be seen as intertextual constructs, writing produced as variants of prior texts, and, as Michael Riffaterre would have it, as the periphrastic transformation of cliches and descriptive systems. This intertextual patterning is often missed by a model which, to attend to it, must give it a psychological significance, such as regret for another age, which is a weak and undiscriminating recuperative move.

Finally, and most important, the unquestioned acceptance of this model hampers investigation of the functioning of the lyric by obscuring its ideological basis. To assume that interpreting a lyric means identifying the speaker is to forget that the speaker is inferred from a voice, which is itself a figure here; but once one begins to consider the figure of voice, the question arises of how far the intelligibility of lyric depends on this figure and whether the generic model or reading strategy of the lyric is not designed to maintain the notion of language as the product of and therefore sign of the subject. Paul de Man, who had begun to explore this problem before his death, describes in the following terms the ideology which criticism should explore and contest: "The principle of intelligibility, in lyric poetry, depends on the phenomenalization of the poetic voice. . . . No matter what approach is taken, it is essential that the status of the voice not be reduced to being a mere figure of speech or play of the letter, for this would deprive it of the attribute of aesthetic presence that determines the hermeneutics of the lyric."[30] Investigation of implicit models of the lyric should cast light on this model of intelligibility and the disruptions that might follow from focus on the play of the letter or other formal patterning that resists recuperation as an exteriorization of consciousness.

30. Paul de Man, "Lyrical Voice in Contemporary Theory," in *Lyric Poetry*, ed. Hosek and Parker, 55.

The Modern Lyric

There are discontinuities in modern lyric poetry, but it may well be that investigation of continuities, especially continuities that play a central role in critical notions of modern poetry and the lyric genre, will help us to grasp both the function of genres as models of intelligibility and the potentially disruptive role that literary texts themselves can play. The comparative perspective here should enable one to investigate genres as models of reading and to explore the complicated relations between historical claims about changes in poetry itself and structural models that determine the interpretation of poems and suffuse our pedagogy.

[19]

Kafka and the Sirens: Writing as Lethetic Reading

CLAYTON KOELB

Near the beginning of book 12 of the *Odyssey*, Circe gives Odysseus some famous advice:

Your next encounter will be with the Sirens, who bewitch everybody that approaches them. There is no homecoming for the man who draws near them unawares and hears the Sirens' voices; no welcome from his wife, no little children brightening at their father's return. For with the music of their song the Sirens cast their spell upon him, and they sit there in a meadow piled high with the mouldering skeletons of men, whose withered skin still hangs upon their bones. Drive your ship past the spot, and to prevent any of your crew from hearing, soften some beeswax and plug their ears with it. But if you wish to listen yourself, make them bind you hand and foot on board and stand you up by the step of the mast, with the rope's ends lashed to the mast itself. This will allow you to listen with enjoyment to the twin Sirens' voices. But if you start begging your men to release you, they must add to the bonds that already hold you fast.[1]

The hero carries out these instructions exactly, and he is able to experience the marvelous enchantment of the Sirens' song, to let himself in fact be overwhelmed by it, without having to suffer the terrible consequences that befell those who went before him: "The lovely voices came to me across the water, and my heart was filled with such a longing to listen that with nod and frown I signed to my men to set me free."[2] Instead of setting him free, the men do as they have been instructed and tighten his bonds while the ship continues past the islands. Only when they are well out of earshot do they release their captain.

1. Homer, *The Odyssey*, trans. E. V. Rieu (Baltimore: Penguin, 1946), 190.
2. Ibid.

Kafka and the Sirens

Franz Kafka wrote his own story based on this famous adventure, apparently in late October of 1917, but he never published it. Max Brod, Kafka's friend and literary executor, found it in one of the octavo notebooks Kafka had left and included it in a collection of fiction from Kafka's *Nachlaß* which appeared in 1931. Kafka had not given it a title, and Brod, evidently thinking to draw attention to the story's most surprising feature, called it "Das Schweigen der Sirenen" ("The Silence of the Sirens"). In Kafka's version, the Sirens indeed do not sing: "Now the Sirens have a still more fatal weapon than their song, namely their silence."[3] This is the weapon that they use against the wily hero from Ithaca.

Kafka's Odysseus overcomes this formidable enemy, however, because he "did not hear their silence."[4] In Kafka's story of the encounter with the Sirens, not only had Odysseus had himself bound to the mast, but he, too, has stopped his ears with wax, as the second sentence of the narration tells us: "To protect himself from the Sirens Ulysses stopped his ears with wax and had himself bound to the mast of his ship."[5] This alteration of Homer's story, this wax in Odysseus's ears, is, I contend, a far more significant change than the substitution of silence for singing. It is possible to write a story about the Sirens' silence that is on the whole faithful to the spirit of the Homeric original and can be read as a version of the adventure from the *Odyssey*. As soon as you put wax in Odysseus's ears, however, you leave the *Odyssey* completely, you forget it, as it were, and embark on a different narrative project altogether.

Homer's story has two essential features. First, it tells how the Greek sailors were able to pass the island of the Sirens without falling victim to the deadly song, and, second but equally important, it explains how Odysseus was able to accomplish the feat of both hearing the Sirens and escaping them. This section of the *Odyssey*, we remember, is not narrated directly by the poet but is part of a long quoted discourse by Odysseus to the Phaeacian king Alcinous and his court. The story of the Sirens is therefore part of a first-person narrative embedded in the poem, where the point of view belongs exclusively to the hero. He can tell us only what he has experienced. Odysseus is able to recount to the Phaeacians exactly what the Sirens sang to him as his ship passed and to make their song a part of his story only because he heard it himself. Odysseus's unstopped

---

3. I cite Kafka in English from Franz Kafka, *The Complete Stories*, ed. Nahum N. Glatzer (New York: Schocken, 1971), abbreviated as *CS*; and in German from Franz Kafka, *Sämtliche Erzählungen*, ed. Paul Raabe (Frankfurt a.M.: Fischer, 1970), abbreviated as *SE*. In most cases, as here, I will give a translation in the text and the original in a footnote: *CS* 431, *SE* 305: "Nun haben die Sirenen eine noch schrecklichere Waffe als den Gesang, nämlich ihr Schweigen."

4. *CS* 431, *SE* 305: "hörte ihr Schweigen nicht."

5. *CS* 430, *SE* 304: "Um sich vor den Sirenen zu bewahren, stopfte sich Odysseus Wachs in die Ohren und ließ sich am Mast festschmieden."

Clayton Koelb

ears are an essential feature of the tale, then, not only because of what is
revealed about the hero's character but also because they are the absolute
narrative prerequisite of the story.

Odysseus plays the role of witness. If the story does nothing else, it
establishes him as the single mortal authority on the Sirens. He alone
among living men knows what the Sirens sing and what effect their song
has. The central section of the *Odyssey*, wherein the most fantastic of the
tales are related, depends entirely upon the witness role of the hero and is
in a sense *about* nothing so much as this role. The poet does not ask us to
believe *him*; he gives us an eyewitness whose stature within the fiction is
such that it encourages, though it does not guarantee, belief. Everything
we know about the Sirens comes from Odysseus; we must either accept
what he says or reject it and, if we reject it, reject along with it a substantial
portion of the entire poem.

The most fundamental feature of the Homeric version of the tale, then,
is the unique authority it ascribes to the narrating voice of Odysseus
himself. One could change various elements of the story and still be true
to the basic Homeric structure, so long as Odysseus himself retains his
position as unique witness. One could even change the Sirens' song into
silence and still remain within the basic tradition established by Homer, as
long as it was Odysseus himself who testified to their silence. This is
exactly what Rilke did in the poem "Die Insel der Sirenen" ("The Island of
the Sirens"), written one decade before Kafka's story, in 1907:

> Wenn er denen, die ihm gastlich waren,
> spät, nach ihrem Tage noch, da sie
> fragten nach den Fahrten und Gefahren,
> still berichtete: er wußte nie,
>
> wie sie schrecken und mit welchem jähen
> Wort sie wenden, daß sie so wie er
> in dem blau gestillten Inselmeer
> die Vergoldung jener Inseln sähen,
>
> deren Anblick macht, daß die Gefahr
> umschlägt; denn nun ist sie nicht im Tosen
> und im Wüten, wo sie immer war.
> Lautlos kommt sie über die Matrosen,
>
> welche wissen, daß es dort auf jenen
> goldnen Inseln manchmal singt—,
> und sich blindlings in die Ruder lehnen,
> wie umringt

Kafka and the Sirens

von der Stille, die die ganze Weite
in sich hat und an die Ohren weht,
so als wäre ihre andre Seite
der Gesang, dem keiner widersteht.⁶

Although Rilke revises the Homeric account in a surprising way here, he remains faithful to the basic structure of the classical version. The danger is still the Sirens' song, but now that song is perceived only indirectly: the sailors know that singing is sometimes heard coming from these islands, and the expectation of song conditions their experience of silence so that it is transformed into "the other side" of an irresistible singing. More important than this, though, is Rilke's reliance on Odysseus as the reliable witness. It is through Odysseus that the reader learns about the island of the Sirens and about the silence that is the other side of song. Like the story from the ancient epic, Rilke's poem focuses as much on the situation of the telling as on the story itself. The first stanza, for example, has nothing at all to do with the Sirens but rather is taken up with setting the scene of Odysseus's report, with explaining why and how he delivered himself of it. One might even suspect that the poem is meant to be as much about the storyteller himself as about the matter of his story. This suspicion is confirmed when we notice that the word *still* is used to describe how the hero "reported" (*berichtete*), the very same lexeme that appears later in substantive form (*Stille*) to describe wherein lies the danger of the islands. Odysseus's "song" is thus no different from what-ever it is that emanates from the island of the Sirens. It is a form of "quiet" that contains vast spaces ("die die ganze Weite in sich hat") and that may be as dangerous to the hospitable (*gastlich*) Phaeacians as any tales full of "Tosen und Wüten" (ranting and raving).

Rilke's poem essentially uses the authority of the Homeric text to authorize the alterations it makes in that text. We are not asked to take the word of some unknown, faceless narrator that the Sirens did not actually sing: Odysseus himself, whom Homer has told us was actually there and

---

6. Quoted from *Der Neuen Gedichte Anderer Teil* (Leipzig: Insel, 1919), 6. Here is a prose translation with no pretensions but which seeks to reproduce the ambiguities and syntactic complexity of the original: "When he quietly reported to those who were hospitable to him, late, after their day was done, since they asked about his journeys and dangers: he never knew how they frighten or with what abrupt word they turn, that they, like him, would see in the blue, becalmed sea of islands the gilding of those islands whose appearance makes the danger shift; because the danger is not in ranting and raving, where ever it was. It comes soundlessly upon the sailors, who know that singing is sometimes heard on those golden islands—and they lean blindly on their oars, as if surrounded by the silence that has all fullness in it and that blows about their ears, as if its other side were the song that none can resist."

Clayton Koelb

actually heard whatever it was that came from that island, Odysseus the eyewitness, revises the story. Rilke remains well within the main current of the tradition, even while he questions one of the prominent features of the tradition, because he accepts the fundamental structure of the Homeric narrative situation. One could even say that Rilke basically accepts the central point of the classical story by retaining Odysseus as narrator and sole medium through which we learn what it was the Sirens did; for that central point is not that the Sirens sang this or that song or that they sang at all but that, whatever it was they did, Odysseus was able to observe it and yet come away alive.

For these reasons, then, I would call Rilke's poem an alethetic reading of the Homeric story. An alethetic reading, as I have detailed elsewhere,[7] is one that assumes that the text being read essentially tells the truth, no matter how incredible or full of error that text may appear to be. Such reading assumes that texts have an outside and an inside, or a surface and a depth, and that an incredible surface can be opened up to disclose a depth worthy of belief. Rilke's "Die Insel der Sirenen" reads the *Odyssey* alethetically in that it assumes that the basic import of the epic is true and correct, even if its surface has been distorted by the replacement of an "actual" silence (as the revision would have it) with the imagined song which is its "other side." Homer's story of the Sirens matches Rilke's version if it is read as a certain kind of allegory wherein the song that Odysseus reports hearing is understood as the mythic fleshing out of the vast space (*Weite*) encompassed by the mysterious silence. In this reading, the words that Odysseus ascribes to the Sirens—words full of flattery ("flower of Achaean chivalry") and promises ("we have foreknowledge of all that is going to happen")[8]—are his own desires projected into the emptiness around him. There is no incompatibility between Rilke's and Homer's accounts as long as we presume that texts do not always say directly what they mean, a presumption fundamental to all alethetic reading.[9]

When we turn to Kafka's story, however, we are faced with a radically different situation. The narrator is no longer Odysseus himself but in-

---

7. See Clayton Koelb, *The Incredulous Reader* (Ithaca: Cornell University Press, 1984), 32–40.

8. Homer, *The Odyssey*, 194.

9. For another imaginative and extremely rich alethetic reading of the Homeric story of the Sirens, see Maurice Blanchot, "The Sirens' Song," in *The Sirens' Song: Selected Essays by Maurice Blanchot*, ed. Gabriel Josipovici (Bloomington: Indiana University Press, 1982), 59–65. Blanchot's sketch, first published in 1959 in *Le Livre à venir*, is in many ways very relevant to the topic of my essay, not only because it almost certainly derives in part from Blanchot's reading of Kafka but because it deals as well with one of Rilke's themes, the transformation of "the real song into an imaginary one" (64). Only considerations of space prevent me from treating Blanchot's piece in the body of this essay.

stead a nameless and characterless voice whose chief claim to authority is his knowledge of tradition, but now a tradition in which Odysseus has no role as witness. This narrator knows things that Odysseus does not and cannot know, including the potential meaning or meanings of the adventure. Odysseus's role as witness is erased from the outset with the announcement that he not only bound himself to the mast but stopped his ears with wax as well. With that announcement the story detaches itself completely from the tradition and sets off on a course entirely its own.

Kafka's "The Silence of the Sirens" is therefore a "lethetic" (that is, forgetful or oblivious) reading of the epic tale.[10] Lethetic reading takes place when the reader acts as if he or she does not believe the text being read and thus deliberately ignores what the text seems to be trying to say. It is not a naïve misunderstanding but an intentional radical reshaping of the materials out of which the text is made; it assumes, in fact, that the text being read is nothing more than a gathering of such materials, a storehouse of signifiers to be exploited at will. Reading in the lethetic mode is not interested in what a text means, only in what it says—or rather *that* it says. Where alethetic reading sees the text as, say, a house whose structure is sound and whose organization of internal space is excellent, even if its external appearance makes it look shabby or grotesque or even unstable and in need of substantial repair, lethetic reading finds in that same house a supply of building elements—windows, doors, staircases, valuable things of craftsmanship or materials perhaps no longer available—that can be used to make a new house with a completely different structure and internal organization. Rilke is an alethetic reader who does a brilliant alteration of the facade of Homer's magnificent old house; Kafka is a lethetic reader who plunders the old building for its scarce, virtually irreplaceable, ready-made architectural elements.

Before examining Kafka's lethetic reading of the *Odyssey* in detail, it is instructive to look at another text where we find elements Kafka has plundered from his reading of a classic. The short prose sketch that Max Brod published under the title "Das Stadtwappen" ("The City Coat of Arms"), probably written in late 1920, displays in its first sentence the characteristics of a text produced by lethetic reading: "At first all the arrangements for building the Tower of Babel were characterized by fairly good order; indeed the order was perhaps too perfect, too much thought was given to guides, interpreters, accommodations for the workmen, and roads of communication, as if there were centuries before one to do the work in."[11] The first few words, with their reference to the

10. For more on oblivious reading, see *The Incredulous Reader*, 143–57.
11. *CS* 433, *SE* 306: "Anfangs war beim babylonischen Turmbau alles in leidlicher Ordnung; ja, die Ordnung was vielleicht zu groß, man dachte zu sehr an Wegweiser,

Clayton Koelb

"building of the Tower of Babel" (in the original, "babylonischen Turmbau," that is, "Babylonian tower-construction") conjure up the biblical
story with which we are so familiar. And, lest the reader suspect that this
"babylonischer Turmbau" might refer to some other construction project
undertaken by the Babylonians, Kafka later clarifies the matter definitively: "The essential thing in the whole business is the idea of building a
tower that will reach to heaven."[12]

It is hardly necessary to glance back at Genesis 11 to recall the central
issue of that story of the Tower of Babel, announced in the introductory
phrases: "Once upon a time all the world spoke a single language and
used the same words." The Genesis narrative presents the building of the
tower to heaven as the origin of the many, mutually incomprehensible
human languages. Whatever else it is doing, it is unquestionably explaining why, if Adam gave the proper names to all things in the Garden of
Eden (Gen. 2) and thus created the perfect language, there are now so
many different languages in the world. That is the fundamental meaning
of the story, what orders all the other elements.

Kafka shows in his first sentence that he is not interested at all in what
the biblical narrative means. He has not failed to understand that meaning—how could one miss it?—but rather has ignored it, acted as if it were
not there. If one were to take the story in Genesis seriously, one would
suppose that there was one profession that did not and could not exist
prior to the building of the tower: interpreter (*Dolmetscher*). By introducing interpreters into the work force of the tower builders, Kafka demonstrates that his story is not simply a different version of the biblical
narrative, it is a different story altogether. His story takes place in a
different world from the one presented in *Genesis*: this world is already
fallen, already thoroughly secularized, and already so full of division and
disagreement that no divine intervention is necessary in order to bring
about confusion.

For all its obliviousness to the intention of the story from the Old
Testament, "The City Coat of Arms" is still recognizably made out of
various elements taken out of the old tale and reordered into a new
structure. Kafka has not merely taken the notion of building a tower to
heaven and pasted it onto a story that has no relation to the biblical one;
on the contrary, he has taken many important features from the Old
Testament and fit them together in a surprising way. One of the key
features of Genesis 11, for example, is its opposition of order to disorder:

Dolmetscher, Arbeiterunterkünfte und Verbindungswege, so als habe man Jahrhunderte
vor sich."

12. *CS* 433, *SE* 306: "Das Wesentliche des ganzen Unternehmens ist der Gedanke, einen
bis in den Himmel reichenden Turm zu bauen."

the project begins with order but, because of divine intervention, ends in confusion. Kafka takes this fundamental opposition and, in typical Kafka fashion, makes it into a paradoxical unity. The order that exists at the commencement of the construction is *already* disorder; it is an order so complex that it is indistinguishable from chaos. The planners are so concerned with thoroughness in all their preparations that they never actually get around to working on the tower, while the preparations become chaotically complex. The chaos manifests itself quickly in the rivalries that develop among the various groups, engaged not in building the tower itself but in the preliminary work, building the construction workers' city: "Every nationality wanted the finest quarter for itself, and this gave rise to disputes, which developed into bloody conflicts. These conflicts never came to an end."[13] Kafka suggests the paradox in the very language of the opening sentence, where he refers to the order as "tolerable" ("in leidlicher Ordnung"). The word *leidlich* contains the morpheme *leid*, which carries a lengthy burden of negative meanings: "painful, disagreeable, unpleasant, bad," and so on. Thus the word Kafka has selected to inform us that the order was, as the Muir translation puts it, "fairly good," tells us at the same time that this order was fairly bad, painful, disagreeable, and unpleasant.

Another element of central importance to the Genesis narrative, divine intervention, is vital in Kafka's story as well. But Kafka has completely transformed the role it plays in his story, moving from the center of the reported action to a kind of appendix placed at the end of the description of the city, where it is cited as part of an apocalyptic prophecy: "All the legends and songs that came to birth in that city are filled with longing for a prophesied day when the city would be destroyed by five successive blows from a gigantic fist. It is for that reason too that the city has a closed fist on its coat of arms."[14] The role of divine intervention in "The City Coat of Arms" is thus radically different from that in the Old Testament story. In the Bible, God intervenes by introducing disorder for the purpose of halting a project that has, from the divine point of view, all too great prospects for success: "Here they are, one people with a single language, and now they have started to do this; henceforward nothing they have a mind to do will be beyond their reach" (Gen. 11:6). In Kafka's story, the project to build the tower has absolutely no prospect for success,

13. *CS* 433, *SE* 307: "Jede Landsmannschaft wollte das schönste Quartier haben, dadurch ergaben sich Streitigkeiten, die sich bis zu blutigen Kämpfen steigerten. Diese Kämpfe hörten nicht mehr auf."

14. *CS* 434, *SE* 307: "Alles was in dieser Stadt an Sagen und Liedern entstanden ist, ist erfüllt von der Sehnsucht nach einem prophezeiten Tag, an welchem die Stadt von einer Riesenfaust in fünf kurz aufeinanderfolgenden Schlägen zerschmettert werden wird. Deshalb hat auch die Stadt die Faust im Wappen."

since "the second or third generation had already recognized the sense-lessness of building a heaven-reaching tower."[15] Divine intervention, if it were to come, would not put a stop to a dangerous effort to achieve something like equal status with divinity; it would, on the contrary, bring a merciful end to a sick organism that is unable to put itself out of its own misery.

"The City Coat of Arms" is unquestionably a text that derives from Kafka's reading of the Old Testament, but his reading has been quite untouched by the meaning discoverable by any "serious" reader. To use one of Kafka's own metaphors of reading derived from the Old Testament, his reading has passed "through the midst of the book . . . as once the Jews passed through the Red Sea."[16] Just as the Jews following Moses were able to go through the very center of the Red Sea without being flooded by it, "through the sea on dry ground," as it is reported in Exodus 14, so does Kafka pass through this and other monumental texts of the tradition without being "influenced" (i.e., "flooded") by them. There is no doubt that he can do it quite as well with Homer as with the Old Testament.

As Kafka's oblivious reading of the tower story announces itself most directly in the introduction of the "interpreters," so is his lethetic reading of Homer most evident in the matter of the wax in Odysseus's ears. This is certainly an important feature of the classical version, but it is pointedly attached quite firmly to the ship's crew and not to Odysseus. Kafka takes this element from the epic, detaches it from its original context (as if it were some kind of free-floating signifier), and recombines it with another element, the hero, formerly the one character to whom this feature was forbidden. From the structuralist point of view, the *Odyssey* sets up a binary opposition between captain and crew on the basis of the presence or absence of wax in the ears, an opposition which Kafka quite cheerfully obliterates. Instead of allegorizing the Homeric tale, as Rilke does, Kafka simply treats it as a random collection of elements which can be realigned into new narrative units. We still recognize it as deriving from the *Odyssey*, of course, but it is no longer a version of the same story.

Kafka has reconfigured the elements found in the epic, but he has not taken all the elements that were available. The ship's crew plays a crucial role in the *Odyssey* but disappears altogether in Kafka's story. The only indication in "The Silence of the Sirens" that Odysseus is not completely

15. *CS* 434, *SE* 307: "schon die zweite oder dritte Generation die Sinnlosigkeit des Himmelsturmbaues erkannte."

16. *CS* 75, *SE* 251: "mitten durch das Buch, wie einmal die Juden durch das Rote Meer." For more on this and other metaphors of reading in Kafka, see my "'In der Strafkolonie': Kafka and the Scene of Reading," *German Quarterly*, 55 (Nov. 1982), 511–25; and especially my "The Margin in the Middle: Kafka's Other Reading of Reading," in *Franz Kafka and the Contemporary Critical Performance: Centenary Readings*, ed. Alan Udoff (Bloomington: Indiana University Press, 1987).

alone comes in the most indirect manner with the declaration that the hero "had himself" ("ließ sich") tied to the mast. In all other ways Kafka's narrative assumes that a solitary Odysseus goes forth to meet the Sirens, and imagining the presence of a crew can only complicate and weaken one's reading. One would have to wonder if the other sailors were also chained as well as deafened with wax; if they, too, failed to hear the silence but did see the throats, breasts, and eyes of the Sirens as Odysseus does; and if they shared his feelings of "bliss" at the prospect of overcoming the singers. All these issues are irrelevant to Kafka's story, where the focus of interest is entirely upon the confrontation between Odysseus and the Sirens. The Homeric tale, on the other hand, reminds us not only that the crew is present during the encounter but that they are a set of individuals whose lives hang in the balance and whose actions are essential for the stratagem to succeed. When Odysseus, overwhelmed by the power of the song, signals the men to set him free, "they swung forward to their oars and rowed ahead, while Perimedes and Eurylochus jumped up, tightened my bonds and added more."[17]

The only remnant of the Homeric crew in Kafka's story is precisely the wax in the ears. By some kind of conservation of narrative energy, however, all the importance that had attached to the crew in the epic tale now inheres in the wax, which becomes the central element around which all others revolve. The story told by "The Silence of the Sirens" derives entirely from the situation created by putting this wax in the ears not of the now-vanished crew but of Odysseus himself. It is the wax that makes it possible for the hero to fail to hear the silence of the Sirens and to make the erroneous judgment (i.e., that the Sirens are singing but that he cannot hear them) which, paradoxically, saves him from experiencing their power and suffering destruction. The wax thus transforms Odysseus from the reliable witness he was in both the *Odyssey* and Rilke's poem into the fortunate beneficiary of a set of circumstances of which he is himself blissfully ignorant. This change in turn necessitates the change in narrative format introducing the authoritative voice of an unknown reporter who, while not exactly omniscient, possesses far more knowledge of what occurs than the hero does.

This placement of Odysseus within someone else's narrative frame has important consequences for the reader's reception of the story. The Homeric strategy of making Odysseus the teller of his own story (in this central section of the poem) creates an effect of immediacy that has been long recognized and justifiably admired. The reader[18] is placed, as it

17. Homer, *The Odyssey*, 194.
18. I use the term *reader* to refer to Homer's audience as well as Kafka's in order to maintain the comparison. That this audience was originally a set of listeners rather than readers has been well established by the Parry-Lord proposal, and I do not intend my usage to connote any conflict with this widely accepted theory.

were, among the Phaeacians, hearing the adventures at first hand, from the lips of the adventurer himself. The epic admits to and acquiesces in the necessity of narration while it overcomes to a great degree the distancing effect of narrative intervention. Kafka, on the other hand, urgently wants this distancing effect. He wants readers who are acutely, even painfully aware of the process of mediation that stands between them and the events reported and who realize that the narrator may not have the last and best word on the subject. Not only do we not have the eyewitness Odysseus telling the tale; we do not have a witness of any kind: the narrator, by mentioning the existence of a "codicil" ("Anhang") that has been "handed down" ("überliefert"), places himself at the end of a tradition ("Überlieferung") that is not necessarily consistent or complete and of which he is only the latest compiler. Thus, while Odysseus of the stopped-up ears could never be in a position to accurately tell what happened, no one else has any much greater claim on possession of the "true" story. One potential set of witnesses, the crew of sailors, has vanished from the scene, and the narrator, for all his assumption of authority, unmasks himself as a latecomer far removed from events he describes.

Paradoxically, Kafka has inserted into his story another set of characters who might have been in a position to understand and accurately relate what happened: the Sirens themselves. In the *Odyssey*, it should be remembered, the Sirens do not appear except insofar as their song reaches the hero's ears. We know no more about them than what Odysseus knows, which is the words of their song. Kafka reverses the situation: his Sirens do not sing, but they do appear. Odysseus sees them and the narrator describes both their appearance and their feelings: "But they— lovelier than ever—stretched their necks and turned, let their awesome hair flutter free in the wind, and freely stretched their claws on the rocks. They no longer had any desire to allure; all that they wanted was to hold as long as they could the radiance that fell from Ulysses' great eyes."[19] Kafka was apparently familiar with the traditional depiction of the Sirens in painting and drawing, where they often "are represented as half women and half birds,"[20] and one could therefore say that his depiction of them follows classical precedent. But it is a precedent foreign to the *Odyssey*, where they are never described at all. In typical fashion, Kafka transforms a physical quality of these mythical creatures into a figure of desire: birds have claws capable of grasping (*erhaschen*) prey, and this

19. *CS* 431, *SE* 305: "Sie aber—schöner als jemals—streckten und drehten sich, ließen das schaurige Haar offen im Winde wehen und spannten die Krallen frei auf den Felsen. Sie wollten nicht mehr verführen, nur noch den Abglanz vom großen Augenpaar des Odysseus wollten sie so lange als möglich erhaschen."

20. *The Oxford Classical Dictionary*, 2d ed. (Oxford: Clarendon Press, 1970), 993.

grasping (the Muir translation uses the rather colorless word *hold*) is what they want to do with the "radiance" they see in Odysseus's eyes.

These Sirens, quite fully fleshed out as characters in Kafka's story, are in the best position of anyone to comprehend fully what is happening, and they would be ideal witnesses, save for one thing: they are not conscious beings. The lack of consciousness, the narrator tells us, is the only thing that saves them from being destroyed by Odysseus's escape: "If the Sirens had possessed consciousness they would have been annihilated at that moment. But they remained as they had been; all that happened was that Ulysses had escaped them."[21] This quality that saves them— another absence, be it noted—also renders them useless as witnesses. *Bewußtsein* means not only "consciousness" but also "knowledge" and "conviction." The Sirens are no more aware than Odysseus of what has occurred. They appear to experience it, but their lack of *Bewußtsein* cancels the experience in the very moment it takes place.

While Rilke found in the *Odyssey* a story of an experience so immediate, vivid, and penetrating that it nearly escapes language altogether, Kafka creates out of the broken shards of the epic a story that questions the possibility of immediate experience. Rilke tells of sailors who are "surrounded" ("umringt") by a silence so palpable that it "blows about their ears" ("an die Ohren weht"). They experience this stillness so intensely that it seems like the inversion of a powerful form of speech, a "song that none can resist" ("Gesang, dem keiner widersteht"). The silence of Rilke's poem is "Stille" (cf. also "still" and "gestillt"), a calm or quiet that is presented as a kind of presence, indeed a plenitude that contains something vast within it ("die die ganze Weite / in sich hat"). Kafka's story is about a different kind of silence, not "Stille" but "Schweigen," not the positive silence of "peace and quiet" but the negative silence of the withholding of speech, not a presence and a plenitude but an absence and a void. "The Silence of the Sirens" presents this negativity as the most powerful weapon the sirens possess, but this negativity is in turn negated by the wax in Odysseus's ears. He fails to hear their failure to speak. The hero emerges from his meeting with the Sirens unscathed, but he remains ignorant of what actually happened. What he believes he has experienced—his victory over the Sirens by means of his wax and chains—has not happened: "He thought they were singing and that he alone did not hear them. For a fleeting moment he saw their throats rising and falling, their breasts lifting, their eyes filled with tears, their lips half-parted, but believed that these were accompaniments to the airs which died unheard

---

21.*CS* 432, *SE* 305: "Hätten die Sirenen Bewußtsein, sie wären damals vernichtet worden. So aber blieben sie, nur Odysseus ist ihnen entgangen."

around him. And what has happened remains far beyond his experience: "When they were nearest to him he knew of them no longer."[22]

This skepticism about the possibility of immediate experience is only partially modified by the "codicil" appended to the body of "The Silence of the Sirens": "Ulysses, it is said, was so full of guile, was such a fox, that not even the goddess of fate could pierce his armor. Perhaps he had really noticed, although here the human understanding is beyond its depths, that the Sirens were silent, and held up to them and to the gods the aforementioned pretense merely as a sort of shield."[23] The story's conclusion thus restores some credibility to the notion of genuine experience by holding out the possibility that Odysseus somehow knew all along exactly what was happening. At the same time, however, the narrator confesses that, in this interpretation, Odysseus's behavior is not comprehensible by human understanding ("mit Menschenverstand nicht mehr zu begreifen") and thereby in a sense withdraws what the codicil offers. If Odysseus did know and did indeed merely pretend not to hear the silence of the Sirens, his ability both to know (how could he, with his ears full of wax?) and at the same time to resist (how could he, when "no earthly powers can resist" it?) passes beyond the human into something else. The narrator calls him a fox, obviously a commonplace trope for a particularly crafty person, but in Kafka's fiction such tropes never quite lose their literal meanings. It is also said that Odysseus possessed an "innermost self" ("Innerstes") into which the goddess of fate herself could not penetrate, a quality that would put him on a par with, or perhaps even above, the Olympian gods. Odysseus is inhuman on the side of the animals or the angels, and maybe it does not matter which. If he has had a genuine experience in his encounter with the Sirens, it would seem to be of a kind and in a form unavailable to us in our daily lives.

And yet this encounter with the Sirens as interpreted by the codicil does look very much like a kind of experience Kafka has discussed before, the experience of a certain kind of reading:

I was only going to say books are useful in every sense and quite especially in respects in which one would not expect it. For when one is about to embark on

22. *CS* 431, *Se* 305: "er glaubte, sie sängen, und nur er sei behütet, es zu hören. Flüchtig sah er zuerst die Wendungen ihrer Hälse, das tiefe Atmen, die tränenvollen Augen, den halb geöffneten Mund, glaubte aber, dies gehöre zu den Arien, die ungehört um ihn verklangen." *CS* 431, *SE* 305: "gerade als er ihnen am nächsten war, wußte er nichts mehr von ihnen."

23. *CS* 432, *SE* 305: "Odysseus, sagt man, war so listenreich, war ein solcher Fuchs, daß selbst die Schicksalsgöttin nicht in sein Innerstes dringen konnte. Vielleicht hat er, obwohl das mit Menschenverstand nicht mehr zu begreifen ist, wirklich gemerkt, daß die Sirenen schwiegen, und hat ihnen und den Göttern den obigen Scheinvorgang nur gewissermaßen als Schild entgegengehalten."

some enterprise, it is precisely the books whose contents have nothing at all in common with the enterprise that are the most useful. For the reader who does after all intend to embark on that enterprise (and even if, as it were, the effect of the book can penetrate only as far as that enthusiasm), will be stimulated by the book to all kinds of thoughts concerning his enterprise. Now, however, since the contents of the books are precisely something of utter indifference, the reader is not at all impeded in those thoughts, and he passes through the midst of the book with them, as the Jews passed through the Red Sea, that's how I should like to put it.[24]

This passage from the relatively early fragment "Hochzeitsvorbe-reitungen auf dem Lande" ("Wedding Preparations in the Country") (1907–1908), which I have already cited in part, presents an interesting analogue to the story of Odysseus and the Sirens as presented in the last paragraph of "The Silence of the Sirens." Once we realize that Odysseus has in fact passed untouched through a "text"—since the song/silence of the Sirens is presented as a particularly powerful form of utterance—with the potential to penetrate ("dringen") and to overwhelm him, the analogy becomes clearer. Odysseus is a man embarked on an enterprise with which the Sirens, their island, and their song, have nothing in common. To become involved with their text would be a disaster to his enterprise, and so, either because he does not perceive or, more interestingly, be-cause he ignores that text, he sails through the danger quite obliviously.

This story must inevitably remind us of another, however: the story of Kafka's encounter with the Sirens' text, the old epic tale of the Sirens as found in Homer. Kafka, the writer embarked on an enterprise altogether different from Homer's, has passed through Homer's text just as obliv-iously as Odysseus through the Sirens' silence or the Jews through the Red Seas. The Homeric tale, like the biblical narrative of the Tower of Babel, penetrated Kafka only as far as his enthusiasm to write; it stimu-lated him to many thoughts concerning his own project of writing and furnished certain materials he could use in furthering that project. But its point, its meaning, left him quite untouched. Kafka's writing of his story of the Sirens, a story that concludes by proposing Odysseus's oblivious reading of the potentially devastating text of silence, is the result of Kafka's lethetic reading of the *Odyssey*.

24. *CS* 75, *SE* 251: "ich meinte nur, Bücher sind nützlich in jedem Sinn und ganz besonders, wo man es nicht erwarten sollte. Denn wenn man eine Unternehmung vorhat, so sind gerade die Bücher, deren Inhalt mit der Unternehmung gar nichts Gemeinschaftliches hat, die nützlichsten. Denn der Leser, der doch jene Unternehmung beabsichtigt, also irgendwie (und wenn förmlich auch nur die Wirkung des Buches bis zu jener Hitze dringen kann) erhitzt ist, wird durch das Buch zu lauter Gedanken gereizt, die seine Unternehmung betreffen. Da nun aber der Inhalt des Buches ein gerade ganz gleichgültiger ist, wird der Leser in jenen Gedanken gar nicht gehindert und er zieht mit ihnen mitten durch das Buch, wie einmal die Juden durch das Rote Meer, möchte ich sagen."

Clayton Koelb

It remains only to indicate briefly why Kafka turned to lethetic reading, a mode so contrary to our usual notions of "good" reading that it has existed for the most part only as a minor subversive tendency within the orthodox tradition of alethetic reading. The most satisfactory explanation is to be found in Kafka's extraordinary sensitivity to some of the disquieting implications of that orthodox tradition. When, for example, in a famous letter to his friend Oskar Pollak in 1904, he tries to describe what "good" books and "good" reading are like, he has recourse to image after image of violence. He says that one does not read books in order to be happy but rather in order to be opened up, to be "wounded" and "stabbed" by books whose effect is like a natural catastrophe ("like a disaster," "like . . . death," "like being banished"). He concludes by insisting that a book ought to be an "axe" to break through the "frozen sea" within the reader.[25] This language may sound extreme, but it only carries through the logical implications of a rhetoric of alethetic reading which, since Plato, has insisted that a "good" reader let himself (or, actually more frequently, "herself") be opened up by the text so as to receive its imprint. Although Kafka always maintained a deep respect for this sort of alethetic reading, he obviously found it frightening as well.[26]

Kafka developed his own theory and practice of lethetic reading as a less violent alternative to the orthodox tradition. While he continued to practice and value alethetic reading, there were evidently times when he wanted to read only in furtherance of his own thoughts and projects, without being torn open and made into a vessel to be filled by the concepts of another. And when it came to reading that was to form the basis for writing, an author as stubbornly original as Kafka could not help but make use of the lethetic mode.

25. *Letters to Friends, Family, and Editors* (New York: Schocken, 1977), 16.
26. I have summarized very briefly in this paragraph a discussion carried out in detail in my "The Margin in the Middle."

[2 0]

Culture Criticism and
"Language as Such"

Juliet Flower MacCannell

What is creative in the use of language is a superstructure; rhetoric
forces us to realize that insofar as the basic structure of human discourse
is concerned, all had already been said before the first speaker had made
the first speech. . . . Speech would not approach reality—the referential
world—directly but only through [the *koinoi topoi*] so that they frustrated
the conception of referential content as the bedrock of speech and
thought.

Paolo Valesio, Novantiqua

Walter Benjamin's thesis that "the work of art in the age of mechanical
reproduction" is an art that no longer exists in the mode of the "aura" has,
like many double-voiced texts, generated opposing interpretations of
what his position on this loss is. Because it can go on tour, be dislocated,
"exhibited," the mechanically reproduced work of art loses—in contrast
to the traditional work—its "presence in time and space, its unique existence at the place where it happens to be."[1] Benjamin argues that a new
mode of perception of the work, a new form of consciousness, must
correspond to what is a very real change in artistic spatiotemporal coordinates. Even if we agree that this is evident, however, we may well be
confused as to how Benjamin evaluates such a change. We may, for
example, agree that art's unquestioned "cult" values (associated with what
he simultaneously calls distance *and* presence in a memorial mode) have
ceded to testable "exhibition" values in today's society; we may equally
find it easy to concede that art today has been torn out of an apparently

---

1. Walter Benjamin, "The Work of Art in the Age of Mechanical Reproduction," in
Illuminations, trans. Harry Zohn (New York: Schocken, 1969), 220. First published in French
in *Zeitschrift fur Sozialforschung* (1936). Hereafter abbreviated WA and cited parenthetically
in the text.

unique location: "imbedded in the fabric of a tradition" (WA 223). But we may not be prepared, any more than Benjamin is, to decide on the priority of one over the other.

I want to begin by setting forth the differences between "cult" and "exhibition" values for Benjamin. I use a model derived from his own sense of the importance of the addresser and addressee of the work of art, and I try to frame it within his explicit pronouncements on theories of language in "On Language as Such, and on the Language of Man," reiterated with emphasis in his Moscow diary. Finally, I think that his perspective on a new artistic reception/perception bears comparison with that of another peculiar Marxist aesthetician, M. M. Bakhtin. Bakhtin, who apparently wrote under two pseudonyms as well as in his own name, worked at specifying interesting new coordinates for art, what he called the chronotope. He also positioned the work of art just as he positioned the word: as a negotiation between speaker and addressee. The question of "who is speaking and to whom?" was, for him, the critical feature of any work.[2]

Cult values find their original expression, says Benjamin, in the failure to address the work of art to the contemporary audience (even to hide it from them), aiming it instead at an invisible third dimension: "The elk portrayed by the man of the Stone Age on the walls of his cave was an instrument of magic. He did expose it to his fellow men, but in the main it was meant for the spirits" (WA 225). As Lacan would have put it, what makes the value of an icon is that the god it represents is also looking at it, that is, that its main intended addressee is the Other, not the other. Linguistically, Benjamin describes any set toward this pole of the work of art as its "expressive" side and, at the limit, finds it leading to "mystical silence" on the part of the expresser: what could one articulate or utter in the presence of God?[3]

Exhibition values, in contrast, take the form of a communication relationship in the strongest possible acceptation of the term, that is, one characterized by a growing *proximity* between art and its contemporary,

2. See my discussion of his work in "The Temporality of Textuality: Bakhtin and Derrida," *Modern Language Notes* 100, 5 (Dec. 1985), 968–87. It is ironic that the two theories of literary language and artistic form most closely allied with "deconstructive" notions of the decontextualizing of the work of art—Walter Benjamin's allegory and Mikhail Bakhtin's intertextuality—are the work of supposedly neo-Marxist materialists. I think this may be so because of their respective understanding the inescapable necessity for analyzing the existence of social values in the very heart of literary and artistic form.

3. See his statement in the *Moscow Diary*, ed. Gary Smith, trans. Richard Sieburth (Cambridge: Harvard University Press, 1986), 47: "The development of the communicative aspect of language to the exclusion of all else in fact inevitably leads to the destruction of language. On the other hand, the way leads to mystical silence if its expressive character is raised to the absolute. Of the two, it seems to me that the more current tendency is toward communication. But in one form or another a compromise is always necessary."

nonspiritual audience. With his usual irony, Benjamin discovers that 'distance' is overcome primarily by *technological* means. What narrows the space between art and audience is, incredibly enough, what one ordinarily thinks of as a screen or obstaclelike *medium*, the "media" as they are called these days.

The lens of the camera entirely transforms, for example, the relationship of viewer to actor that once held on the stage. On stage, even though the audience and actor are literally face to face, even though he acts in person, the actor's performance—what Benjamin calls the "artistic" side of his job (WA 228)—forms an effective wall between the two. In film, on the other hand, the camera violates the actor's performance and delivers him up to the viewer-become-critic "with his whole living person, . . . forgoing its aura." Alienated, become a mere thing—a "prop" "inserted at the proper place" (WA 230) in the film—the movie actor is nonetheless more completely "seen" than he would be "live." He has been divested of his cult value, his aura of (staged) presence, which has fostered only a pseudoconsciousness in the spectator. By granting the moviegoer the status of a critic, Benjamin tends to establish a particular form of communication-relation, a critically *conscious* one between viewer and actor, in which distance is lessened but mediation is not annihilated.

In the "Work of Art" essay then, for Benjamin, distance has a more than spatial value. It is at least a Bakhtinian type of chronotope, positioning space in relation to time: the past to what is high or elevated;[4] the immediate to what is low. Distance is socially charged with value insofar as it bears the burden not only of a masquerade of presence but also of hierarchy and level. Thus Benjamin is neither vacillating between a nostalgia for a lost aura (which intimates the presence of a spiritual spectator) nor enthusiastically welcoming the advent of critical distance as a new closeness. What he is doing is showing the different degrees of consciousness of the *form of mediation* in the two poles of possible kinds of artistic activity,[5] especially insofar as these have parallels in linguistic models.

4. Bakhtin represents social evaluation as the center and the horizon of every genuine work of art: an orientation toward the contemporary audience is constitutive. As a "double-voiced" cocreation, the variable value is that of the distance between, and the degree of openness in, this dialogic relation. In the epic extreme case ("Epic and Novel," in *The Dialogic Imagination*, trans. Caryl Emerson and Michael Holquist [Austin: University of Texas Press, 1981]), distance between the poet and his contemporary audience is maximal: one sings of the *remote* and *higher* past. In the postnovelistic consciousness, distance is minimal, and the accent is on the contemporary. At the maximum distance is aura; at the minimal, dismemberment in carnival: "Laughter has the remarkable power of making a object come up close, of drawing it into a zone of crude contact where one can finger it familiarly on all sides, turn it upside down, inside out, peer at it from above and below, break open its external shell, look into its center, doubt it, take it apart, dismember it, lay it bare and expose it, examine it freely and experiment with it" (23).
5. Interpretations of aura and of Benjamin's nostalgia for it are not limited to those who see his project as retrospective and hermeneutic; even socialist critics like Fredric Jameson

Unmediated, "pure communication," like Bakhtin's artistic logic, has violence and destruction as its telos; "pure unmediated expression" dialectically becomes its inverse, silence.

If we want to find in Benjamin that the destruction of the aura is a backhanded triumph in the sense of distance overcome—"art" against "Art" as it were—we will be disappointed. We cannot conclude that any victory of the contemporary, any final annihilation of the mystic, Other addressee would be unqualified. There is in Benjamin a rhetoric of loss that certainly must be accounted for. If the third party is missing, so also is our sense of the collective or general subject a god is supposed to symbolize. Where Bakhtin, by contrast, makes the discovery of the chronotope into an apparently positive event, Benjamin's text lends a critically mournful, if not melancholic, sense to the solving of the puzzle of the aura as a mere linguistic effect of the positioning of addresser and addressee. (In fact, there is much of the same dialectic in Bakhtin, as in any careful analyst of communication events. Those who wish to deny the importance of a third dimension, or third party, to artistic communication, are usually the most subject to it.)[6]

Only if we can take communication and expression as variables—in a sense, as nonpositions rather than as oppositions—in Benjamin's thought can we begin to explain some of the positional and evaluative paradoxes we find here. "Distance" positions one both vertically, in relation to the gods, and horizontally, in relation to one's fellows, and their extremes meet: silence, destruction. Benjamin seems to be working toward redefining the formal terms for consciousness in *both* expression and communication, as conscious forms and forms of consciousness. If he is interested in the potential of the reproduced image for shocking and thereby creating critical consciousness in the viewer,[7] he is just as interested in the potential of distance, *ostranenie*, estrangement, for evoking varieties of critical mind.

---

and Terry Eagleton, who link the aura with the fetishism of the commodity, retain a nostalgia for an "authentic 'auratic' experience," that of "richly recollected inwardness" (Eagleton, *Walter Benjamin; or, Towards a Revolutionary Criticism* [London: Verso & New Left Books, 1981], 27). Christopher Norris's reading of the *Trauerspiel* in *The Deconstructive Turn* (London: Methuen, 1983), 119–22, tries to dispel the nostalgia factor that Benjamin's cleverly worked rhetoric implies and structurally denies.

6. See my "Temporality of Textuality," and my *Figuring Lacan: Criticism and the Cultural Unconscious* (London: Croom Helm, 1986, and Lincoln: University of Nebraska Press, 1986). The work of Emile Benveniste on the third person is seminal.

7. Benjamin used somewhat elastically Freud's myth in *The Pleasure Principle* of how consciousness is constituted as a "shield" because of the shocks of experience. Bakhtin argued in 1928 (P. N. Medvedev and M. M. Bakhtin, *The Formal Method in Literary Scholarship: A Critical Introduction to Sociological Poetics*, trans. Albert J. Wehrle Baltimore: Johns Hopkins University Press, 1978) against the "psychotechnical" bent of Russian formalism because it rendered the reader or viewer passive; Benjamin's "shock" is a means of activating critical reception and moves well beyond the scope of a unipersonal psychology.

Culture Criticism and "Language as Such"

By placing the work of art in the same coordinates Benjamin uses for the linguistic act, we can, I think, shed some light on his peculiar understanding of the workings of literary language. What is finally at issue is the status of both the other and the Other. That is, we must try to think through the nature of what the French call *le destinataire* in the case of both expression and communication as these are involved in any artistic communication. If in the case of the other, we find its most human condition as a film image, and if in the case of the Other, we find it most effective when it is least of all a guarantor of the value of Values, the code of the Code, then we are dealing with a peculiar thinker indeed, whose peculiarities, are not, nevertheless, mere idiosyncracies but radical attempts to rethink the forms of social consciousness for a new age—even what we now popularly call the nuclear age. More important than arguing over Benjamin's kinship to deconstruction, Marxism, Judaism, et al. is his rereading the concept of social value from a semiotic and comparative perspective. We live in an age (inside, as Fellini's suicidal intellectual in *La dolce vita* once put it, a nuclear frame) that makes everything we do seem no more serious or practical than if it took place within a work of art. It is not ultimately possible to say where literary analysis begins and sociological analysis ends. Why reading literature for access to social values and vice versa should provide a model for breaking that frame will, I hope, be clear by the end of this essay. Why it is imperative to break that frame will also, I hope, be made even clearer.

Reconciling a double focus of art in relation to social values is a redoubtable task. It is, I think, necessary in the case of Benjamin and equally so in Bakhtin. There is a great deal of critical confusion concerning certain aesthetic concepts—allegory in Benjamin and in Bakhtin both polyglossia and intertextuality (the interpenetration of time and space as the "immediate context of the work of art"[8]—provoked by the paradox. These may be partially resolved by setting things up as polarities of the undecidability of the positions of the addresser and addressee.

A comparative reading of Benjamin and Bakhtin, two marginal Marxists, brushing against Freud and lightly adapting the analysis of the psyche to their own peculiarly literary purposes, provides at least an eccentric and/or elliptical rather than circular viewpoint on the problem.

Distance, Alienation: The Sign as Form of Critical Consciousness

We have stressed the bridging of distance in the "work of art in the age of mechanical reproduction." We can now turn to forms of art in which

---

8. See MacCannell, "Temporality of Textuality," for a discussion of his definition of the immediate context of any speech event.

distance, gaps, unbridgeable abysses, are emphasized, as, for example, in allegory. What is at stake in allegory is always the repetition of a distance, as de Man has so clearly shown,[9] and it is at stake in all allegories, not only Benjamin's. Connections are what allegories make, but they are always tempered by the awareness that they are mediated connections, in a sense as radically false as they are true.

In Benjamin's linguistic paradigm we could read allegory as a radical liberation of art from immediate context, from the contemporary, and thus from any specific addresser and addressee: it is not a social event. To use Jakobsonian terms, in allegory such "contact" fails, there is no phatic function, and when channels are blocked, communication is interrupted, cut off. Perhaps relayed elsewhere (to an Other?), the disruption of the communicative function results in a crucial desemiotization so that, to use Jakobson's famous schema, the message function of art is undone. Art becomes a message sent only to itself and can no longer be classed as a means of communication. As a self-referential, self-focused entity, its central function seems to be purely to make its sign-character "palpable," as Jakobson put it, or, in Benjamin's frame, to evoke critical consciousness

---

9. J. Hillis Miller claims Benjamin for deconstructive allegory, the "classic" definition of which is in Paul de Man *Allegories of Reading* (New Haven: Yale University Press, 1979), 270. Paul de Man makes Auerbach's theory of figura the partial basis of his own allegorical approach in "The Rhetoric of Temporality" in his *Blindness and Insight: Essays in the Rhetoric of Contemporary Criticism* (Minneapolis: University of Minnesota Press, 1983 [orig. 1969]), 187–228. There is no systematic analysis of the differences between a Benjaminian and an Auerbachian allegoresis, though hints abound in de Man's work. One major distinction that de Man does not draw out seems to me to be that Auerbach's is a theory of figural meaning not allegorical value.

The reader will recall that Auerbach's "figural" method for interpreting the meaning or significance of a real event lies neither in the event itself nor in its proper context, but only (1) in relation to another text that "completes it," and (2) in relation to a totalizing code that provides a systematic, comprehensive interpretation of the beginning and fate of history.

Auerbach does indeed believe that such a code was once exemplified by Christianity, which supported the figure. In later times, only dialectical materialism, according to Auerbach in his book on Latin antiquity, could provide the comprehensiveness of system required for figural allegory.

If we believe, explicitly or implicitly, that there exists somewhere a complete, finalized, doctrine (a specified "vertical" referential code) for relating two different events or texts in order for there to be a meaningful, significant "figure" we open the way to transcendence, an *Aufhebung*—a cancellation/preservation—that works in the "favor" of one or the other of the two, despite all ethical claims to their equivalence. Once Eve becomes a "figure" of the Church, she is "supposed" to be transcended and canceled by the later and latter entity. The institutional form of such thinking will be hierarchical in practice, if not in theory.

Oriented explicitly around value, Benjamin's allegorical "code" does not exist a priori, apart from the totality of its (fragmentary) manifestations; we have either the realm of human-made values (exchange) or the ultimate nonvalue, death, and these alone "read" the allegorical figure.

I discuss the open and closed figure in my "Kristeva's Horror," *Semiotica* 62, 3/4 (1986) 325–55. See also Henry Sussman, "The Herald," *Diacritics* 7 (Spring 1977), 54, for a description of a "deconstructive" Benjaminian allegory.

expression eventually becomes mystic silence / God's word as value beyond worth

Culture Criticism and "Language as Such"

of its sign-character.[10] Paul de Man has written eloquently of this habit of thought in Benjamin, as Benjamin did of Baudelaire.[11]

Terry Eagleton (*Walter Benjamin*) has resisted equations among deconstruction, Bakhtin, and Benjamin while stating his intuition of their affinity. The alert reader might find in Eagleton hints of a metalanguage into which Benjamin might be best translated: semiotics. Semiotic terms are perhaps the most appropriate descriptive ones for Benjamin in the sense that they go beyond the ordinary acceptation of language as a verbal/oral/aural system—and so does he. They can provide ways of describing the peculiar relations among language, social value, and art as Benjamin understands them. Now it is true that in the writings we have by Benjamin on language, and they are extensive, we have practically no mention of the term *semiotics* (although he is quite aware of it).[12] In the few places where he does talk about semiotics it sometimes appears in terms of a contrast with Edenic or Adamic language: the language of signs is the language of communication, that which has fallen from the purity of the essential language of human mental being: the language of names. We begin here to recognize the polarities of communication and expression so succinctly stated in the *Moscow Diary*, which was, of course, a restatement of his essay "On Language as Such and on the Language of Man" (1916).[13]

Let me reiterate what it is that allows, in semiotic terms, the "message" to be "transmitted" from a "sender" to a "receiver": a common code. Benjamin's work hints always at a double encoding: the set toward expression implies (though I will argue that it remains only an implication) an ultimately religious, biblical code, God's word as a value beyond worth;

10. Such "narcissism" can cut two ways: either the self-involvement of the technically "fascist" aesthetic consciousness or a means of promoting the critical consciousness of the sign-character of all language, all 'art.' *// yes*

11. De Man, "Form and Intent in the American New Criticism," in *Blindness and Insight*, 35: "Many great writers have described the loss of reality that marks the beginning of poetic states of mind, as when, in a famous poem by Baudelaire, '. . . palais neufs, échafaudages, blocs, / Vieux faubourgs, tout pour moi devient allégorie. . . .' The critic who has written some of the most perceptive pages on Baudelaire, Walter Benjamin knew this very well when he defined allegory as a void 'that signifies precisely the non-being of what it represents.'"

12. Among the places where Benjamin displays his semiotic erudition is the essay "Problèmes de sociologie de la langue," in his *Poésie et révolution*, trans. Maurice de Gandillac (Paris: Les Lettres Nouvelles, 1971). Not only does Benjamin refer to Saussure, Piaget, Buhler, and the Russians Vygotsky and Marr (both cited by Volosinov-Bakhtin), but his thesis startlingly prefigures the advances Lévi-Strauss's understanding of myth and its distinction from history makes twenty-five years later. See also Benjamin's *Origin of German Tragic Drama*, trans. John Osborne (London: New Left Books 1977), 166.

13. Walter Benjamin, "On Language as Such and on the Language of Man" in his *Reflections: Essays, Aphorisms, and Autobiographical Writings*, trans. Edmund Jephcott (New York: Harcourt Brace Jovanovich, 1978), 314–32, hereafter abbreviated OLS and cited in the text.

Juliet Flower MacCannell

the set toward communication, implies, ultimately, the code of social and economic exchange and its values.[14]

We ordinarily experience code unconsciously: in the form of a language (whose grammatical code is at least preconscious for all but the linguist or teacher) or of a traditional history—"background"—common to us or in the form of the unstated social norms and rules by which we get through everyday life. Many things can awaken our awareness of these codes, can draw attention to them. Tradition, particularly in the modern world, appears sometimes as a excuse for its violation; we make grammatical errors or find difficulties in deciding things like how to express the third-person singular pronoun in a nongendered form. Punks are pointedly impolite.

Violations of code, deviations, serve, then, as means of enforcing the idea that a code exists: we did not know it was there until we [almost] lost it. But is it possible that no code exists? that either texts or human beings could attempt to communicate with each other in the absence of a common social code, a shared history—most concretely put, in the absence of a common language, a single speech community? If the idea of a code (semiotically and most crudely, the binary code of presence and absence) were radically supplanted by a mere array of differences between entities, how could one thing and an other (text or self) be compared and, more crucially, *evaluated*, given value?

We could never take seriously any attempt to read the artistic function as a means of communication in the absence of a "communication context" in which messages would actually get delivered.[15] Or could we? Some have argued that if there is no clear, knowable master text that forestructures their significance, texts can exist, but not under the rubric of the communication of messages. Semiotic relations require not only a text but also a language, so that the artistic work considered alone, without any cultural context, without a definite system of cultural codes, is an alienated, deconstructive form known as *écriture*.

14. The early structuralists tended to think of norm and value as collective, coercive, and rule-stabilized. Jan Mukarovsky, for example, in *Aesthetic Function, Norm and Value as Social Facts*, trans. Mark Suino (orig. 1936; Ann Arbor: University of Michigan, Michigan Slavic Contributions, 1979), 25, puts its succinctly: "Value [is] the ability of something to assist in the attainment of some goal. . . . the establishing of the goal and the striving toward it depend on some individual." Norm would be the collective agreement, more or less contractual, on the sum of individual values. In someone like Bakhtin, quite a different idea of norm and value emerges, characterized by much more *unruliness*, dialogue, and vocal contestations. See Medvedev and Bakhtin, *The Formal Method*, xiv.

15. On the questions of meaning and intention, of addresser and addressee of messages, it is true that, as Derrida once put it, a letter can always *not* arrive at its destination, i.e., it can always exceed the circuit and break code (see "Signature, événement, contexte," in his *Marges* [Paris: Seuil, 1972], 381). The circulation of textual fragments, the absence of a master code, is greatly emphasized in deconstruction. However, On the question of *value* in deconstruction, however, "message" is exceeded by code.

Culture Criticism and "Language as Such"

Benjamin's "work of art," however, would suggest that cult values—the ritual and symbolic formulations of a common social code that informs and forms the interaction of its adherents—cede to an entirely new modality fashioned according to a severely displaced value set, called exhibition. By placing the work in this new context, which is independent of any fixed codification, Benjamin is asking a radical question of it: Is communication possible among those who live in the absence of an ex- plicitly or implicitly, open or closed, shared code?[16] It also remains to be argued, moreover, whether the "spirit," the final *destinataire*, or ad- dressee, of all our (prayerful) words, is, for Benjamin, lost definitively. Since no pronouncement that one could ever make on the topic would not be subject to being heard and read as a form of sacrifice of the real for the symbolic, that is, as a gift to God (Heidegger argues the impossibility of Nietzsche's enunciation "God is dead"), we would have to be able to read in a nonverbal mode for such an event to occur.

That such a "final" *destinataire* does exist for Benjamin as, overtly or covertly, a party to every human act is without doubt. But the extent to which this god is a representation (and therefore merely an ideologized form of ordinary social values) or whether it is beyond representation, existing as a wholly Other, remains an open question for our reading of Benjamin.

I think we can begin to see how he thought of responding to this question by turning our attention directly to his work on the linguistic code, on language as such. As a paradigm for the other codes—religious and socioeconomic—that Benjamin uses as the coordinates of his analysis of culture his linguistic work is complex, to be sure, but so is Benjamin's intense appreciation for language's capacity to support insupportable contradictions, to lay them bare.

Economic and Linguistic Value

Benjamin occasionally appeared to champion the retrieval of the lan- guage of human beings from the language of things, apparently from an ethical bias in favor of retaining a communicational, social-exchange model at the center of artistic production. Our reading of this bias has to be tempered by how this triumph of communication is expressed, always against the backdrop of loss of aura, of cult values, of some kind of

16. Only careful attention to the form of the form of communication will begin to account for the vast accumulation of paradox in Benjamin's treatment of language and the work of art. Susan Buck-Morss has been kind enough to discuss with me her exciting discovery of Benjamin's "commodity code," which, when she publishes it may modify my analysis here. It would differ a great deal from the ordinary sense of what we see as code in both traditional and modern semiotic terms.

encoding vis-à-vis "the spirits." The melancholia of allegory would express the ambivalence of wishing to do away with "the spirits" by an obsessive mourning for their loss.

In his model of allegory, Benjamin is most directly concerned with attacking the "Goethean" notion of the symbol. Allegorically seen, the work of art is the experience of a positive loss of the social norms and institutions that guide our interpretation both of it and of our fellow creatures, just as the critical camera lens and the audience's identification with the camera strips the actor of his artistic performance. Symbols bestow on human beings and their works "meaning," that is, a sense of the union of their materiality with a spiritual significance beyond the material. Symbols traditionally depend on an ideal order—linguistic, spiritual, Hegelian, or other *code*—for their operation. A third-party guarantor—the code (or for Lacan the Other who is there to hide the code)—is required to uphold the value and significance of what they imply. To say "God is dead" is to try to state our loss of access to each other through a collectively held or shared symbolic form. Is allegory an alternative form for simultaneous collective experience?

We usually (since the romantics) want to class allegory among those fleshless, immaterial modes, in which the real undergoes destruction. For Benjamin allegory is less the scene of the crime in which the thing is murdered than the guilty scene in which a god has been done away with. Its signs are the signs of a catastrophic loss of a shared (ultimately universal) code. Like the quotations that loom up in a text like highwaymen to rob the readers of their idle convictions, the quotational mode of allegory is inimical to accepted codes.

In the "Task of the Translator," Benjamin writes of the ultimate foreignness of languages to each other,[17] such that linguistic universals are radically denied existence. What is most interesting, and pertinent for both the literary and the linguistic avenues we have been pursuing here, is that to Benjamin's highly dialectical mind, this overt and conscious admission of loss of code, the memorial marking of the death of the universal, has as the consequence of its extreme alienation the marking not of a silence, an absolute and final distance and separation, but of a knowledge of "kinship."

Social values ("simultaneous collective experience" [WA 234]) are com-

---

17. Languages for Benjamin are "kindred" because the feeling one has that a language is one's own is shown to be an illusion the moment one encounters translation: all the values that surround the word in one's "own" tongue are revalued by its translation into another idiom, as in his example of *Brot* and *pain*; or in Saussure's of *mutton* and *mouton*. See "The Task of the Translator," (orig. 1923) in *Illuminations*, 69–82, and Paul de Man, "The Task of the Translator" in *The Resistance to Theory* (Minneapolis: University of Minnesota Press, 1986), 73–105.

ing to be exhibited for Benjamin in the form of the (mechanically reproduced) artwork; in literature they are exhibited through language, the formal medium of literature. If language exhibits social as well as aesthetic and symbolic values, then prose is the heart of poetry, and ordinary language is the basis of literary language.[18] The dual value of language as at once social and aesthetic places under enormous pressure those of Benjamin's texts that appear to criticize the bourgeois view of language as biased in favor of the communicational.

Benjamin often appears to be following the same line as Georg Lukács—and of his own peers in the Frankfurt school—in becoming a critic of the degraded values of modern bourgeois life, symbolized most clearly in its debased version of language.[19] The spiritual emptiness of language, its loss of essence, makes it the analogue of Benjamin's description of the photograph of a deserted Paris street: the absence of the human countenance—and, more important, of its aura—reveal it to be the "scene of a crime" (WA 266). Bourgeois language is undeniably *guilty* of murdering nature (the bourgeois arbitrarily designates things by means of signifiers that can be detached from those things, that therefore would have no intimate or necessary connection with the things they name) and of murdering the gods or replacing them with its own system of values. *see DH Lawrence, The Death of the gods*

For Benjamin, the communicational view of language is in fact by no means limited to the bourgeois case: the language of the enlightened classes is only a kind of low point in what has been our linguistic lot since the Origin and the Fall; it is also not without some social value. In its bias away from the theocentric and toward communication between self and other, guilty of murdering its gods as it may be, certain compensations—the rights of humanity, so to speak—are gained in it.

The idea of "degraded" language is, finally, too easy a mark, and Benjamin hardly stops in this essay to give it a second critical glance. What

18. Literarily, Benjamin is coming to be classed as a late romantic of a critical-idealist and protodeconstructionist sort and, like some of the adherents of these trends (Schlegel, for example), as erasing the boundaries between prose and poetry. See Irving Wohlfarth, "On the Messianic Structure of Walter Benjamin's Last Reflections," *Glyph* 3 (1978), 148–212, and "The Politics of Prose and the Art of Awakening: Walter Benjamin's Version of a German Romantic Motif," *Glyph* 7 (1980), 131–48.

Nevertheless, recent criticism such as Eagleton's, suspecting a similarity between Bakhtin and Benjamin (from their Marxism and their supposed religious mysticism), has offered a clue as to why Benjamin has recently become the focus of intense interest from a theoretical point of view that has modified the Marxist-Freudian Frankfurt school's interpretation of his work. A modified "Frankfurt school" approach to him can be found in Susan Buck-Morss, *The Origin of Negative Dialectics: Theodor W. Adorno, Walter Benjamin, and the Frankfurt Institute* (New York: Free Press, 1977), 136–50. Buck-Morss carefully details Adorno's debate with Benjamin, finding a kind of stylistic and ideational collapse between them in Adorno's *Minima Moralia*).

19. See Buck-Morss, *Origin of Negative Dialectics*, 146–50.

does seem to disturb Benjamin in the communication tendency of modern language is that, from the expressive perspective, it is debased, uninteresting: creativity, the kind of creativity associated only with God's word has fled to other regions. But then, perhaps, creation has only happened once . . .

Nevertheless, it is this creativity that Benjamin seeks out in language. And he also seeks the forms of expression possible in the realm of socially based (exchange) values, which operate as Saussure once reminded us, in the absence of a standard or transcendent criterion or code of codes. Benjamin becomes, in fact, the only one among the neo-Marxists to do what Marx had proposed in his theory: the concrete analysis of the signifying system of material things, of their value and significance under capitalism. When Benjamin does this type of analysis, he has no peer, except perhaps the later Roland Barthes.

no ideas but in things

An especially fine example is his unfinished work "Paris, Capital of the Nineteenth Century."[20] Here it is material objects that are the "epic" heroes of this world, in which people have been displaced from center stage. We see iron, for example, beginning, like Odysseus, in a strange place, alienated from its essence, merely sufficing to uphold and divide the showcase windows of the shopping arcades. Its duty here is to be not itself, not iron, but glass (P 147). Several sections later, we encounter iron again, but now not only has it lost its most salient "natural" quality—resilient strength—and come into its own as a purely plastic medium. It has achieved the replacement of its natural by its cultural essence in becoming a flower, an art nouveau post (P 155). According to Benjamin, art nouveau attempts to win back functional construction for Art.[21]

And how much more life and excitement for the career of iron than for the career of the bourgeois in these pages, who find themselves displaced from the spacious arcade to the cloistered apartment, who lose even the token sense of belonging to the commonplace, such as the flaneur, wandering in the traffic of the street, had managed minimally to find. The flaneur's actions are perverted: as he goes out to see he also goes out to be seen. Only in the objects he collects to decorate his apartment does the residue of public life—in the sense of communication with other human beings—remain for the bourgeois, but solely in muted form. For "collecting" claims "inwardness" and individual subjective "nostalgia value"—everything but use value—for objects (P 154–55), while the objects themselves have worked out their own system of communicating their formal integration of art and function. The iron flower is neither iron nor a

20. "Paris, Capital of the Nineteenth Century," in his *Reflections: Essays, Aphorisms, and Autobiographical Writings*, trans. Edmund Jephcott (New York: Harcourt Brace Jovanovich, 1978), 146–62, hereafter abbreviated P and cited in the text.

21. Benjamin wants to reverse the equation and win art over to functional values.

flower, it is an art-thing, or in Benjamin's terms from "Language as Such," a "language-thing."

Roland Barthes, writing in the 1960s, gave a latter-day account of this phenomenon of late capitalist culture from a structuralist viewpoint, and he insisted that only through the linguistic model could we hope to analyze the significance, the "what" of the communications obviously offered by things these days, things that have no prosaic quality at all: "Culture is a general system of symbols all governed by the same operations. . . . Culture in all its aspects, is a language. Therefore it is possible today to anticipate the creation of a single unified science of culture, which will depend upon diverse disciplines, all devoted to analyzing on different levels of description, culture as language."[22] I cite Barthes to bring out the differences between his notion of culture as a logical code in which any fragment or item in it is made significant or meaningful in the light of a universal code (grammar) and the Benjaminian conception. Benjamin's approach differs in terms of how to deal with language-things. Barthes homologizes the structure of the sentence to the structure of culture: he gives the context, or cultural code, the same logical form as the completed sentence, wherein rhetorical deviation is the signifying face of ideology. Benjamin does not; for Benjamin, the coherency of system simply does not exist. Things like the iron-flower communicate themselves very clearly, and they do so in the absence of any single system by which they could be called meaningful: the art nouveau post has its artistic side obscure its functional side, just as its functional side "justifies" its arty side without reference to economics or aesthetics as legitimating code. The flower presents itself, that is, in the divided mode of the sign— as a trope, or negation of essence. "Things" like the iron flower are neither poetic nor prosaic, neither a purely aesthetic nor purely social/practical value.

Most interesting, Benjamin's analysis is neither antiideological nor anticultural. If objects do not stay in their place as things and take over the "human" function of signifying, this is a call for analysis, not for hostility: after the Fall no "pure" state can be restored. But perhaps things as they are can be revalued, repaired. Seen not as an entity or essence but as a fragment, this object, the iron flower, is no less than a concrete and real instance of a trope. It cannot be interpreted (in Benjamin's text) in the light of any such systematic theory of Art as Hegel's nor of economy, even orthodox Marxism: it does not even have the status of a commodity. And for Benjamin this aesthetic "freedom" is in marked contrast to the careers of people, who precisely are commoditized: the Parisian whore is "sales-

---

22. Roland Barthes, "To Write: An Intransitive Verb," in *The Structuralist Controversy*, ed. Richard Macksey and Eugenio Donato (Baltimore: Johns Hopkins University Press, 1970), 136.

woman and wares in one" (P 157) and is highly interpretable as a living example of human alienation, a human being having the ambiguous form of a trope-for-sale. The iron flower does not. As things become rhetorical or tropic in their development (or as Barthes once put it, we can only know the goodness of the wine and not the wine itself), the critical reaction is to resort to a purification—the search for real as opposed to cultural essence. I do not read Benjamin in this way because I think his notion of allegory—signifying intertextually in the absence of mastering code—is perfectly compatible with his goal of reappropriating communication, rhetoric, and poetry for people, who can actually learn from the example of things.

Thus if it appears Benjamin is critical of communicative language (the prosaic language of ordinary men and women under capitalism) it is so only insofar as all the creativity of expression lies on the side of material objects. His treatment of the careers of things demonstrates both the complexity and "artiness" of artifacts and the degradation—to the point of total absence—of "authentic" language, the language of man. It is this "language of man," modeled *on* language-things rather than opposed to them, which is the subject of his 1916 essay on the topic.

"On Language as Such and on the Language of Man"

Irving Wohlfarth has made a contribution to Benjamin studies by explicating certain structures (messianism and the schema of Origin, Fall, Redemption) of Benjamin's prose, and the peculiar temporal structure of the *Jetztzeit*, remembrance versus memory, etc., in his writing.[23] These structures alert us to the necessity, in reading a Benjaminian text, of looking closely for the peripeteia, the ironic reversal (what Buck-Morss calls the utopian turn)[24] that twists around and looks at what has been written in order to remark it, reevaluate it. This structure of reevaluation is the mechanism of allegory for Benjamin. With this stricture/structure in mind, let us turn for a moment to the essay where Benjamin speaks most critically of semiotics or of language as communication. "On Language as Such," has generally been taken by critics as a gnostic essay *opposing* the "language of naming" to that of the "language of things," or communication.[25] Benjamin writes early in the essay:

Every expression of human mental life can be understood as a kind of language, and this understanding, in the manner of a true method, everywhere raises new

23. Wolfarth, "On the Messianic Structure."
24. Susan Buck-Morss, lecture, University of California at Irvine, 1985. She sees the "deconstructive" reading of Benjamin as opposed to this utopian one.
25. See Peter Demetz's introduction to *Reflections*, xxii–xxiv.

questions. It is possible to talk about a language of music and of sculpture, about a language of justice that has nothing directly to do with those in which German or English legal judgments are couched, about a language of technology that is not the specialized language of technicians. Language in such contexts means the tendency inherent in the subjects concerned—technology, art, justice or religion—toward the communication of mental meanings. To sum up: all communication of mental meanings is language, communication in words being only a particular case of human language of the justice, poetry or whatever underlying it or founded on it. [OLS 314]

Benjamin contrasts this language with naming. By repeating the Adamic act, human beings take over God's original function of giving things their essence, even though the medium for such essence-giving, language, is not God's medium, but humanity's. Why is it also true that things have language, that they communicate? After all, the essay opens with a pronouncement as sweeping as any ever made by Peirce or Benveniste, that

the existence of language . . . is not only coextensive with all the areas of human mental expression in which language is always in one sense or another inherent, but with absolutely everything. There is no event or thing in either animate or inanimate nature that does not in some way partake of language, for it is in the nature of all to communicate their mental meanings. This use of the word "language" is in no way metaphorical. For to think that we cannot imagine anything that does not communicate its mental nature in its expression is entirely meaningful; the greater or lesser degree of consciousness that is apparently (or really) in such communication cannot alter the fact that we cannot imagine a total absence of language in anything. An existence entirely without relationship to language is an idea; but this idea can bear no fruit even within that realm of Ideas whose circumference defines the Idea of God. [OLS 314–15]

Benjamin concludes the section with the paradoxical tautology that all things are languaged because they express themselves and because expression cannot be thought except as a language: "All that is asserted here is that all expression, insofar as it is a communication of mental meaning, is to be classed as language. And expression, by its whole innermost nature, is certainly to be understood only as language" (OLS 315).

Benjamin establishes a very subtle distinction here—the critical one for him—between "the mental entity of a thing," which is *not* language, and "language itself." But he is *also* distinguishing between the mental entity of a thing, and the mental entity of Man, which *is* linguistic: "The view that the mental essence of a thing consists precisely in its language—this view, taken as a hypothesis, is the great abyss into which all linguistic theory threatens to fall,[26] and to survive suspended precisely over this

26. "Or is it, rather, the temptation to place at the outset a hypothesis that constitutes an abyss for all philosophizing?" (Benjamin's note, 315).

abyss is its task" (OLS 315). Moreover, Benjamin insists that the mental essence is not communicated *through* language but only *in* it: "Languages therefore have no speaker, if this means someone who communicates *through* these languages" (OLS 316). The mental essence that is communicated in language is the linguistic element in its mental being: "The answer to the question '*What* does language communicate?' is therefore 'All language communicates itself'" (OLS 316). And now we have the lamp again: "The language of this lamp, for example, does not communicate the lamp (for the mental being of the lamp, insofar as it is *communicable*, is by no means the lamp itself), but: the language-lamp, the lamp in communication, the lamp in expression" (OLS 316). Defending his statements against the charge of tautology, Benjamin goes on, "All language communicates itself. Or more precisely, all language communicates itself in itself; it is in the purest sense the 'medium' of the communication. Mediation, which is the immediacy of all mental communication, is the fundamental problem of linguistic theory, and if one chooses to call this immediacy magic, then the primary problem of language is its magic" (OLS 316–17). We have here the heart of Benjamin's thesis. First, the so-called problem of the referential status of language is here already present in the form of the linguistic fact. We have no primary or original (prelinguistic) experience of things in their essence (as distinct from what Lukács tells us Hegel wanted); we only have them as they present themselves to us, that is, in linguistic form. Therefore, any commentary on or analysis of things is already a reflexive enterprise, language about language. Language can no longer be conceived formally as a container or as content; it is both at the same time.

The question thus arises: what is the logic, the grammatical code of this "linguistic quality" of the entity in which the linguistic aspect of the thing's being communicates itself? Is there any? If we consider the iron lamppost, if we think about how we don't have lamps but only "language-lamps" here, how do we achieve the context for their interpretation? This is entirely unclear, for we only know that this amphibious creature, this language-lamp sits astride more than one code, and like Barthes's "mythic" entity, engages its interpreter by overcoding itself. Very much in the manner of Barthes's culturally mythified "things," Benjamin's "things" also communicate—with us. We are the specific addressee of the communication of things.[27]

What of the linguistic being of Man? Here the opposite is the case, for not only does man not have a prior code, he himself creates language as

27. See also Benjamin's essay on Goethe's *Elective Affinities*, in which the "mythic" power things have over us is, though not exactly denounced, rendered ominous enough to give us pause.

naming, as the code: "Man alone has a language that is complete both in its universality and its intensiveness" (OLS 319). He does this not to order the universe of things, to dominate them, but only in order to communicate himself in them to God.

Thus, in naming things, Adam did not intend his communication for a receiver among the realm of things, less so for other Men (as there were none), but voluntarily gave these signifiers up to that system of unknowability, the hieroglyphic system named God. 'Naming is that by which nothing beyond it is communicated, and *in* which language communicates itself absolutely." . . .
Name as the heritage of human language therefore vouches for the fact *that language as such* is the mental being of man; and only for this reason is the mental being of man, alone among all mental entities, communicable without residue. On this is founded the difference between human language and language of things. But because the mental being of man is language itself, he cannot communicate himself by it, but only in it. . . . Man is the namer, by this we recognize that through him pure language speaks. [OLS 318–19]

In naming, the Adamic figure attains to the knowledge of things as they are, a knowledge to which God is privy without mediation, that is, without need for language. But the only name in which no tropic misprision is possible, the only name without the ambiguous status of the language of things is, ironically, the proper name.[28] The proper name neither means nor signifies; it operates only as a sign of its own linguistic activity. The name parents give their children has no cognitive status, no etymological or metaphysical essence to which it refers. Thus the purest language of man, proper naming, lacks epistemological status. In sum, naming as "knowledge of things" is ambiguity, and "proper naming" has no cognitive or other value.

The Edenic state does not last long here. As in Umberto Eco's seriocomic essay on Edenic language,[29] a different kind of knowledge from that of things appears in the Benjamin text, in the form of judgment, the basis of a *moral* code: "The knowledge of things resides in name, whereas that of good and evil is, in the profound sense in which Kierkegaard uses the word, 'prattle,' and knows only one purification and elevation, to which the prattling man, the sinner, was therefore submitted: judgment. Admittedly, the judging word has direct knowledge of good and evil. Its magic is different from that of name, but equally magical. This judging word expels the first human beings from Paradise" (OLS 327). This 'Fall'

28. Saussure discovered the erasure of the proper name in his *Anagrams*; Lacan analyzed it as the mark of the dead father.
29. Umberto Eco, "On the Possibility of Generating Aesthetic Messages in Edenic Language," in his *The Role of the Reader: Explorations in the Semiotics of Texts*, Advances in Semiotics Series (Bloomington: Indiana University Press, 1979).

is the fall into the language of evaluation, that is, into a language in which it is no longer knowledge but opinion that is at play: "The tree of knowledge did not stand in the garden of God in order to dispense information on good and evil, but as an emblem of judgment over the questioner. This immense irony marks the mythical origin of the law" (OLS 328).

Benjamin finds that the fall of language from name and into opinion— a romantic topic—results in the formation of language as "mere sign" (OLS 328). Man, that is, by desiring to make language a means of knowledge, is given by language (in exchange for the immediacy of name damaged by the Fall) a new "immediacy": a sense of code, what Benjamin calls "the magic" of judgment.

But as an encoding device, judgment is the origin of abstraction, the loss of the concrete. Babel results as in the "Task of the Translator." The core or essence of language—naming—is definitively lost. And because judgment and moral codes are multiform, Man no longer names, in a God-like manner, things according to their *proper* names but only "from the hundred languages of man," or differentiated Babel. He "overnames" (OLS 330) things.

In this extreme of alienation we see the Fall, the crime of languages: the loss of the concrete. But equally (as in all Benjamin's intensively dialectical writings) redemptive reversal is also at hand. Since the "language of Man" can never name but only overname it can only find its essence in the margins between codes (or rather phantoms of codes). The "language of Man" radically depends on dialogue, on the word thrown across the abyss between codes—on a (failed) communicational intention—for its words to attain any status at all. Thus the language of Man (as distinct from the language of God and from Adamic language) is semiotic; its model is the language of things, not the language of God.

Benjamin expects a repairing of the brokenness of the original Code of Codes, by the means of this plurality, this overdetermination:

There is a language of sculpture, of painting, of poetry. Just as the language of poetry is partly, if not solely, founded on the name language of man, it is very conceivable that the language of sculpture or painting is founded on certain kinds of thing languages, that in them we find a translation of the language of things into an infinitely higher language, which may still be of the same sphere. We are concerned here with nameless, nonacoustic languages, languages issuing from matter; here we could recall the material community of things in their communication. Moreover, the communication of things is certainly communal in a way that grasps the world as such as an undivided whole. For an understanding of artistic forms it is of value to grasp them all as languages. . . . It is certain that the language of art can be understood only in the deepest relationship to the doctrine of signs. Without the latter any linguistic philosophy remains entirely fragmentary, because the relationship between language and sign (of which that between human language and writing offers only a very particular example) is original and fundamental. [OLS 331]

As to the question of decipherability and code, the ultimate code of language for Benjamin is nonlanguage: language by no means coincides with signs, and language, at the same time that it is "in every case not only communication of the communicable" (OLS 331), is also at the same time the "symbol of the non-communicable" (OLS 331). This unspoken language, ironically, is "the residue of the creative word of God," which is, as a "higher language," nothing more than, in Benjamin's words, a "translation of those lower" (OLS 331–32).

Benjamin eventually finds himself *within* the languages after the Fall, the languages of judgment and opinion, the languages that begin semiotically, as signs of judgment-in-lieu-of-knowledge—the absence of knowledge of essences. Despite the apparent disparaging of "prattle" or ordinary judgments there is no doubt that they are the "language of Man." For Benjamin this is true even in the very heart of poetry, artistic form. And the "codes" according to which this language is formed are multiple rather than singular, languages not "Language."

This position is exceedingly close, as Wohlfarth has pointed out, to the notion of *Kunstprosa* in Schlegel, an overcoming of the opposition of prose and poetic language as a false binary opposition.[30] The concept, the figure of judgment, is creative in character. (For Eco, too, it was the judgment of God against the apple "by an ambiguously phrased prohibition . . ." that "stimulates the birth of history.")[31] And if Benjamin voices what appears to be nostalgia for Adamic language, it is nowhere structurally included in the language of Man or, more important, in "Man's" artistic form. The essence of poetry, of sculpture, of literature is founded on thing-languages, that is, on things as they are already traversed by judgment and communicated as such.

Bakhtin on Message and Value

I have tried to show how Benjamin is able, by means of a revaluing of things as they are, to turn the negative aspects of language—its differentiation, its absence of meaning, its reliance on value judgments (what Lacan and the semioticians would call signifiers, marks of value as opposed to meaning), its focus on communication—not into "virtues" (that

30. Irving Wolfarth, "The Politics of Prose and the Art of Awakening: Walter Benjamin's Version of a German Romantic Motif," *Glyph* 7 (1980), 131–48.
31. Eco, "On the Possibility," 103.

would be banal) but into a new formal precondition for the work of art. His thesis on language would demand, in respect both to art and to everyday things, that we incorporate the framing of the means of communication, a theory of the form of the form, of the medium itself, into the structure of art. In this frame, his vision of language, of the language of Man, the mechanism of cultural, including literary, language, is laid bare: it is language about language. In this way, not only is allegory at the very origin of the "language of Man" itself, it is also necessary that from the beginning and at the start, it be a language that is social through and through. For language as communication only begins with the supposed fall into value distinctions (good/evil—the beginning of prattle, gossip, *Gerede*), that is, the fall into society. And since this language is about language, then social evaluations come into play in the very beginning of human language. Intertext would be its only code; each aesthetic message not only modifies the code; it is constitutive of it.

What is unusual in Benjamin's approach, however, is that he does not forget "Language as Such," the origin (and therefore telos) of expressive language in "God." Mystical, silent, speechless, this is the Other of communication, whose guilty denial and forgetting of it is also constitutive of it.

Here again Bakhtin's work bears comparison. Bakhtin appears to champion and emphasize communication sustained by socioeconomic codes. After all, his dialogism permanently attaches the semiotic question of "who is speaking and to whom?" to the work. But we should read closely the following diatribe against the philological/linguistic approach to understanding, an approach that removes a text from its social context:

Each monument carries on the work of its predecessors, polemicizing with them, expecting active, responsive understanding, and anticipating such understanding in return. The monument, as any other monologic utterance, is set toward being perceived in the context of current scientific life or current literary affairs, i.e., it is perceived in the generative process of that particular ideological domain of which it is an integral part. The philologist-linguist tears the monument out of that real domain.[32]

Bakhtin here appears to deplore the severance of the aesthetic (more important, the linguistic) work from its contemporary social scene. Yet for all his apparent emphasis on the contemporary and on communication in the work of art, this text is hardly without ambivalence. The work is part and parcel of "the generative process of that particular ideological do-

32. M. M. Bakhtin [V. N. Volosinov], *Marxism and the Philosophy of Language*, trans. Ladislav Matejka and I. R. Titunik (New York: Seminar Press, 1930), 72–73.

main of which it is an integral part," to be sure, yet the "real domain" of any utterance for Bakhtin is as wide-ranging in time and space as any context imaginable. He speaks of multiple generations, history, etc. as all part of the "immediate purview."

Tending toward what the French have named his intertextual transformation of dialogue at the textual level, Bakhtin turns his works of art into fragments, which address not contemporary social peers but other texts from other times and places. They circulate outside their immediate political and social economies, their initial value frames, their life contexts. But they take on a life (or afterlife) of their own which operates independently of ordinary social and historical life.

It may well be that, for Bakhtin, the work of intertextuality is to tear texts out of their genetic and social history, away from expected communicational responses as a means of promoting consciousness of their sign character, their arbitrariness, their link with the exercise of power.[33] Divorcing the work from a "communicational" mode and placing it in relation to another code produces for the text the same kind of positive alienating otherness that "God" does in Benjamin's "Language as Such." Like any human production, the work of art deserves freedom from the tendency toward automation, repression, and censorship inherent in any human code. Thus Bakhtin, like Benjamin, also reminds us of the double-voicedness of any utterance, which always includes a third party—its hero, god, or other guarantor of value—in its form: most explicitly in the essay, "Discourse in Life, Discourse in Art."[34] Like Bakhtin, Benjamin's little essay on language reminds us of the hidden addressee, the god it was meant for, in every speech event.

33. In this reading it is no accident that Bakhtin chooses current scientific and current literary activity over social context as what defines the code for understanding of the monologic monument, which in effect is attempting to impose arbitrarily a monologic self definition. In this sense, then, the alienation and distance, the fragmenting quality of intertextuality, even something of the elevation of aura would mitigate the overvaluation of the contemporary. Bakhtin rescues the present from domination by the past in "Epic and Novel"; he reverses the plot here in *Marxism and the Philosophy of Language*.

The question remains: is this deconstructive act a putting them into *another* kind of relation to each other than the traditional one? is an alternative social mode reconstructed out of this deconstruction? Works of art (like human beings) that are no longer "uniquely imbedded in the fabric of tradition," placed instead in a more arbitrary "allegorical" relationship with other like beings, would appear to be at an unbridgeable, abyssal, and abysmal distance from each other. But as we have seen in Benjamin with the camera lens, is this not also a means of overcoming another kind of distance—social, politically engineered distance, perceptions of relations that have been blocked by "official" consciousness, be it that of an established canon formation or a moral censor?

34. Appended to *Freudianism: A Marxist Critique* (New York: Academic Press, 1976) (under the name V. N. Volosinov).

Juliet Flower MacCannell

Form, Figure, Formalism

Let me return briefly to the question of formalism and the formalist reading of deconstruction as that which excludes meaning from literature, gives it over to the system of "inscriptions written in a foreign language," and delivers it from signification or, as Paul de Man once put it, into the "arbitrary power play of the signifier."[35] Language as the Adamic language of names is excluded from the post-Lacanian deconstructive system, forever canceled from it by the entrance into the world not of meanings and interhuman recognition but of values.[36] But the loss does not begin with deconstruction, and methodologically, deconstruction is among the first of the post-Kantian human sciences to make the languages of evaluation—the prose of the world—the object of serious and systematic study. For the prose of the world is quasi-poetic; it is ideologized. As Bakhtin/Volosinov wrote:

Any ideological product is not only itself a part of a reality (natural or social). Just as is any physical body, any instrument of production, or any product for consumption, it also, in contradistinction to these other phenomena, reflects and refracts another reality outside itself. Everything ideological possesses meaning: it represents, depicts, or stands for something lying outside itself. In other words, it is a sign. Without signs there is no ideology. A physical body equals itself, so to speak; it does not signify anything but wholly coincides with its particular given nature. In this case there can be no question of ideology. . . . Every sign is subject to the criteria of ideological evaluation (i.e., whether it be true, false, correct, fair, good, etc.). The domain of ideology coincides with the domain of signs. They equate with one another. Wherever a sign is present, ideology is present, too.[37]

Here Bakhtin weaves together the threads of value, intertextuality, and code. Benjamin—who went to Russia to visit with Asa Lajcis while Saussure was making his greatest impact on literature and artistic theory and while Bakhtin was writing—can be read "through" him here.[38]

In his essay "Reported Speech"[39] and in the Dostoevsky book Bakhtin makes of evaluation the heart of literature, albeit in an eccentric or decentered way. He points out that the manner of reporting the speech of

---

35. Paul de Man, *Allegories of Reading* (New Haven: Yale University Press, 1979), 296.
36. This is to be compared with Lacan's treatment of the "murder" of Booz by metaphor—and his transcendence and elevation, equally accomplished by the rhetorical form.
37. *Marxism and the Philosophy of Language*, 9.
38. I know no evidence that either critic was aware of the other, but as I am not a scholar of Russian I am unable to follow up on this intriguing possibility. Benjamin does not mention Bakhtin in the *Moscow Diary*.
39. Bakhtin, "Reported Speech," in *Readings in Russian Poetics: Formalist and Structuralis Views*, ed. Ladislaw Matejka and Krystyna Pomorska (Cambridge: MIT Press, 1971), 149–75.

another (heteroglossia) is always evaluative. But before being able to make this evaluation one must decide what the crucial determinant of the heteroglot "message" is. The sole essential characteristic of a message is that it be regarded by the speaker as "belonging to someone else." Even (and especially) if the message appears to proceed from the Other, the speaker's evaluative "reporting" of it becomes a means of reappropriating it, through emphasis and expression. The only means available to the speaker, who is already always deprived of his or her "own" language (and if Benjamin is right, all of us are), is the oblique and necessarily refracted expression, via form, of an evaluative judgment expressed solely by the manner of reporting the speech of the other. If there is any communication going on between this secondary speech act and an audience or reader, it must necessarily take the form of the utterance (more important than the content of the message) into account. "The reporting context"[40] is that which is communicated. Such is the basis of intertextuality and also the means of retrieval of the question "who is speaking and to whom?" which can be answered . . . but only as a *how*.

This approach to evaluation and communication differs essentially from a formalist approach such as that outlined by Mukarovsky: "[The] tendency of the aesthetic norm [is] to become absolutely binding. . . . The aim of the aesthetic function is the evocation of aesthetic pleasure."[41] Aesthetic norm as a striving for universality and validity is essentially foreign to both Bakhtin and Benjamin. The notion of the norm as a binding, rather than a continuously revaluing, collective agreement on aesthetic values is a crucial difference between theirs and the formalist approach. The capacity to reappropriate by revaluing is absolutely critical for the two "proto"-deconstructionists. Language always already belongs to someone else; it is rhetoric, but at the same time, it is possible to imagine, through reevaluation, through intonation in reporting the speech of the other, through irony, its reappropriation.

This amounts to no less than a reevaluation of rhetoric, of a rhetoric that has become detached in the course of history from being precisely that study of the sociality of linguistic forms. For it is in the common-places, the *topoi*,[42] that community—the community of values—is found,

---

40. Ibid., 153.

41. In Mukarovsky *Aesthetic Function*, 28, the aim of language is not communicatio, but the aesthetic function: the obtaining of "aesthetic pleasure" by collectively agreed upon means, e.g., agreements on the subordination or domination of elements that lead to aesthetic pleasure. For him, this is the source of *value* in the aesthetic: that which facilitates achieving this goal.

42. Paolo Valesio, *Novantiqua: Rhetorics as Contemporary Theory*, Advances in Semiotics Series (Bloomington: Indiana University Press, 1980), 34, writes of the rhetorical topic (commonplace; *koinoi topoi, loci communes*): "The positive side of this use of rhetoric lies in this: when appropriating a commonplace I shed my particularity in order to adhere to the

as it is in the commonplaces, the Kierkegaardian prattle, the chatter of Heidegger, that social evaluations occur. It is also in the work of art that transvaluations or revaluations occur. Deconstruction is just such a re-valuation of rhetoric, and to that extent it is ironic that in America deconstruction is widely held—like semiotics in some literature departments—to be a sterile formalism without relationship to the outside world[43] at the same time that (some of) the rest of the world[44] sees the "Yale school" as among the first in the United States academy to move toward transgressing the overnarrow limits of textuality. As Bakhtin wrote, "Ideological creation is not within us, but between us."[45]

---

general, in order to become generality. Not at all like everybody, but to be exact, to be the incarnation of everybody."

43. Paul de Man, "Semiology and Rhetoric," in *Allegories of Reading* (New Haven: Yale University Press, 1979), 3–19.

44. Pamela Tytell, "Lacune aux Etats-Unis," *L'Arc* 58 (1974), 79–81.

45. *Formal Method*, 8.

[2 1]

On the Superficiality
of Women

Susan Noakes

This essay is meant to be a contribution to a semiotically informed feminist hermeneutics. I take semiotics to be an inquiry into the implication of the fact that signs (for example, words or cultural rituals or entire texts) mean not in themselves but only by virtue of their relations to other signs and specifically by means of their differences from other signs. The particular semiotic terrain this essay explores is primarily what is currently understood to be literary, that is, belletristic, in the sense that eighteenth-century aesthetics radically separated especially fiction, poetry, and drama from other kinds of sign production; but the implications of this exploration extend outside this limited domain into the very broad area of sign production (and interpretation) as creator of society.

I understand hermeneutics to be an inquiry into the nature of interpretation. A semiotically informed hermeneutics emphasizes that the origin of the interpretative impulse in the urge to reduce a plurality of meanings to a single meaning takes as its end the attainment of an illusion. It further emphasizes the importance of investigating the diverse ways in which this illusion is pursued and the reasons motivating such pursuit.

A semiotically informed feminist hermeneutics explores the ways in which gender differences have been employed in accounts of sign production and of interpretation in order to make manifest the traditional exclusion of women from the hermeneutic process and thus to impel inquiry into the causes and consequences of this exclusion. I understand gender differences to mean those differences between the two biological

I gratefully acknowledge the support of the General Research Fund of the University of Kansas, which made possible the completion of this essay.

Susan Noakes

sexes which society creates and elaborates in order to carry out specific functions in the simplest and most efficient way possible. Those functions of Western culture which have to do with the transmission of values by means of written language, namely sign production and sign interpretation, have been made more efficient in part by the creation and elaboration of gender differences that make it appear that women and men by nature think, talk, write, and read differently from each other.

In this essay, I will treat only the last of these culturally created differences: reading. Specifically, I focus attention on a stereotypical notion, repeated over a long span of Western literary history, sometimes jocularly and sometimes seriously, about the way women read—that is, interpret—linguistic signs. This notion represents women as reading wrongly by giving signs a sense opposite to what they "really" mean or, superficially, by mistaking a part of the sign, what is described by Western tradition as its "external" form, for its meaning. The second kind of stereotype is much more widespread in Western literature. It associates with female readers an inability to "penetrate" words, that is, a habitual cessation of interpretative activity prior to arrival at a suitable endpoint (a hermeneutic defect) and a failure to comprehend the complexity of sign production (a semiotic defect). My title plays upon this stereotype of the superficial character of reading as practiced by women in an attempt to indicate that attention will be focused here on how the Western hermeneutic tradition can be said to build itself "on" the notion of "woman" as a mere form in order to avoid recognition of temporality as an essential component of semiotic and hermeneutic processes.

The most timely way to begin this essay may be by reference to key questions raised by feminist literary criticism and theory over the past twenty years. Even though there has been demonstrably less intercourse between the professional study of Comparative Literature and feminist criticism than between, say, the study of American literature and feminist criticism,[1] it is reasonable to assume that most readers of this volume will have some familiarity with those currents in French and American feminist theory which have asked whether women read differently from men.[2]

1. Comparative Literature has frequently (though not exclusively) been seen by its practitioners as emphasizing world masterpieces, with all the implied gender biases, and has thus perhaps even more than the national literatures tended to exclude women writers from its canon. Moreover, female scholars, who are already marginal because of their sex, have tended to find it harder to survive in a nontraditional field such as Comparative Literature, where the possibility of a career begun and maintained in lower-level undergraduate service courses (where women instructors are traditionally more acceptable) does not exist because such courses in Comparative Literature generally do not exist or are offered only in very small numbers. In addition, feminist critics (with a few notable exceptions) have preferred to focus their attention on single-language domains, which encourage careful contextual work but make certain kinds of conceptual development difficult.

2. In the wake of Kate Millett's groundbreaking *Sexual Politics* (Garden City: Doubleday,

On the Superficiality of Women 's Reading

Citing the observable differences in the lives of the two sexes as likely causes of variety in interpretation, some feminist critics have tended to welcome such hermeneutic variety as liberating all readers, women readers in particular.

This question of whether women read differently from men has a dark side that must be less welcome to feminists, however, and I would suggest that this side of the question be carefully investigated before the notion of a distinctly feminine reading style is eagerly embraced. Going back centuries before the current wave of enthusiasm for the notion of the female reader, a long tradition has asserted that women do indeed read differently from men in that women read less well. Among other things, this essay will plot key points in this powerful tradition, including a discussion of how Eve is represented in Christian theology as history's first *mis*reader.

The passages to be discussed here could, like other extracts from literary works, be read in a variety of ways different from the way I will read them. They might be read literally or allegorically, as examples of a curious little literary joke or as illustrations of historical conditions obtaining in those periods in which they were written. I will disregard the fact that all these passages are presented as somehow marginal by their authors because I am less interested in how they form parts of the works in which they appear than I am in the coherence of the tradition that transmits the stereotypical notions they contain over two thousand years of Western writing. I take this tradition to be a cultural "work" at least as important as any of the individual "works" in which it at various times manifests itself.

Before beginning the archeological excavation of this tradition, however, I want to emphasize that I am not attempting to contribute to the empirical study of women readers (or of their representation in literature); instead I am moving in a different and equally important direction. One begins to see this direction when one asks *why* there exists a tradition designating women as inadequate readers which goes on *without alteration* during periods of substantial change in the empirical situation of women readers, for example, when women with a high level of cultural sophistication begin to play a major role in the reading public (as in the late

---

1970), this question has been raised most vigorously by Judith Fetterley, *The Resisting Reader* (Bloomington: Indiana University Press, 1978), and Patrocinio P. Schweickart, "Reading Ourselves: Toward a Feminist Theory of Reading," in *Gender and Reading*, ed. Elizabeth A. Flynn and Schweickart (Baltimore: Johns Hopkins University Press, 1986), 31–62. The latter volume includes (289–303) a bibliography on the relationship between gender and reading, drawn predominantly from North American sources. For French feminist theory, it should be complemented by Toril Moi, *Sexual/Textual Politics: Feminist Literary Theory* (London: Methuen, 1985), 91–173, 182–95. Also influential is Jonathan Culler, *On Deconstruction* (Ithaca: Cornell University Press, 1982), chap. 1.2: "Reading as a Woman."

Middle Ages and early Renaissance).[3] The answer I will suggest here has to do primarily with the way Western civilization construes reading and only secondarily with the relative cultural positions of the sexes. Indeed, the traditional discrimination between male readers, who read well, and female readers, who read poorly, merely masks under cover of a gender distinction a dichotomy between "good" reading and "bad" reading which generates Western notions of what reading is and is not. The tradition linking men and women, respectively, to "good" and "bad" reading is thus nothing more than a product of metonymic association; there is nothing essentially male or female about either of them.

The most extreme form of "bad" reading associated with women readers by the tradition to be traced here would read into the text a meaning close to the reader's own concerns, while the ultimate "good" reading would focus on the author's concerns without reference to the reader's. These two extremes, to be sure, exist only as caricatures, for in practice, reading always and necessarily both draws upon the reader's concerns and seeks to grasp those concerns conceived to be the author's.[4] Nonetheless, because Western culture has failed to develop an adequate account of reading, these caricatures, often in male and female garb, continue to provide the governing image of it. The perceived difficulty of reconciling these two images, which, indeed, arises from the need to prevent their reconciliation in order to generate a (false) understanding of the nature of reading, is well expressed by the dichotomy that Western culture decrees can never be resolved into one: female versus male. On the other hand, divesting these caricatures of reading of their gender-defined dress, as I hope to do here, should help expose their weaknesses and thus contribute to the deconstruction of the inadequate theoretical model of reading which has long prevailed.

One of the most entertaining and (if not read literally) least offensive representations of a superficial woman reader appears in the *UR*-novel of the English-speaking tradition, Laurence Sterne's *Tristram Shandy*. Female readers of this book are stopped in their tracks by Shandy's direct address to the female reader in volume 1, chapter 20: "—How could you, Madam, be so inattentive in reading the last chapter? I told you in it, *That my mother was not a papist.*—Papist! You told me no such thing, Sir. Mad-

---

3. The increased visibility of the woman reader from about 1300, evidenced especially by the more frequent appearance in fiction of female fictive readers, must not be taken to mean that the educational situation of women was improved by Renaissance humanism. See, for example, Joan Kelly, "Did Women Have a Renaissance?" in *Women, History, and Theory: The Essays of Joan Kelly* (Chicago: University of Chicago Press, 1984).

4. Cf. Schweickart's discussion ("Reading Ourselves," 36–37, 49–50) of Culler's concept of the struggle between reader and text for control.

On the Superficiality of Women

am, I beg leave to repeat it over again, That I told you as plain, at least, as words, by direct inference, could tell you such a thing." Thus begins a passage in which Shandy orders the "lady reader" to "turn back . . . and read the whole chapter over again." While she is "gone," he continues his discourse with the "other" reader, who is a gentleman, complaining of the "taste" of many readers for "reading straight forwards, more in quest of the adventures, than of the deep erudition and knowledge which a book of this cast, if read over as it should be, would infallibly impart with them." When the lady returns and professes still not to have found a passage relating "that my mother was not a papist," Shandy triumphantly points out a phrase which, if interpreted in light of a pronouncement by the doctors of the Sorbonne (then cited and discussed for several pages), makes possible the indicated inference.[5] Sterne thus pokes fun at the Sorbonne, as Rabelais and many others before him had done. More centrally, however, he ridicules a tradition associated with scholastic hermeneutics which stresses the need for the reader to possess arcane knowledge that transforms seemingly simple phrases (for example, in the Bible) into complex doctrinal allusions. Sterne's satire, then, seems directed against that style of reading which seeks out hidden meanings. By implication, he celebrates the delight of the text's surface, while also urging the reader toward a quite different kind of "depth" from the one being ridiculed, a semiotic rather than a hermeneutic one.

Shandy's language about the superficial woman reader is remarkable, however, for the distance it maintains from the domain that is really of concern here, reading and writing, and its substitution of an entirely different domain, that of morality, specifically sexual morality:

This self-same vile *pruriency* for fresh adventures in all things, has got so strongly into our habit and humours,—and so wholly intent are we upon satisfying the impatience of our *concupiscence* that way,—that nothing but the *gross* and more *carnal* parts of a composition will go down:—The subtle hints and sly communications of science fly off, like spirits, upwards;—the heavy moral escapes downwards; and both the one and the other are as much lost to the world, as if they were still left in the bottom of the ink-horn.

I wish the male-reader has not passed by many a one, as quaint and curious as this one, in which the female-reader has been detected. I wish . . . that all good people, both male and female, from her example, may be taught to think as well as read.[6]

---

5. Laurence Sterne, *The Life of Tristram Shandy, Gentleman*, ed. Melvyn New et al., 3 vols. (Gainesville: University Presses of Florida, 1984), 1:64–65; the editorial notes mentioned later in the text of this essay appear at 3:102–6.
6. Ibid., 1: 66; my emphasis.

This last sentence, likely to offend women readers today, has more commonly, no doubt, been read as humorous: an attempt to pull the legs of readers of both sexes, not only women. It pokes fun at Christian theology and the Christian hermeneutic tradition, which insists, apropos of Scripture, that very arcane "meanings," accessible only to the most able readers, must be admitted to be patently clear by all readers who wish to be "saved." Yet its language must not be read as humorous alone, for it points to a contempt for women on the part of the liberal Sorbonne satirizer which is as powerful as the misogyny of the Sorbonne doctors themselves. Indeed, the language of sexual trespass Sterne adopts here raises a question that is not funny in the least: why did Sterne single out the "female-reader" as representative of a class of readers who read without thinking? Empirical explanations for this choice may be entertained (for example, that women who read novels in the eighteenth century were observably less reflective than men or that women were more prone to being bullied, as the author of the traditional kind of narrative being parodied here might be said to bully the reader), but they alone can never be satisfactory. Especially when the text in question is a parody, some literary precedent must be sought, for the meaning of parody intrinsically depends on allusion to an earlier text or texts. The editors of the recent University of Florida critical edition try to locate it, without success. They note more than once how much like Swift Sterne sounds in this chapter, much of which is reminiscent of the introduction to *Tale of a Tub*; Swift, too, laments the carelessness of readers, who, he writes, will not look beneath the surface. But Swift does not discriminate among readers on the basis of gender; rather, he directs his barbs against contemporary readers in general. The Florida editors point out that neither "male-reader" nor "female-reader" is recorded in the *OED*.

Nonetheless, although the precise term Sterne uses may perhaps be without precedent or legacy, the concept the term indicates lacks neither. Sterne's designation of the female reader as uninterested in the deeper meanings of books is part of a centuries-old tradition, the character of which is suggested by much of the language Sterne uses to describe the activities of the "female-reader" in the passage just quoted: "vile pruriency," "concupiscence," "gross and . . . carnal." This is language connected by long-standing cultural habit with woman as temptress, as disruptive erotic force in society. How does language tied to woman the seducer come to be associated with woman the reader? Such a transfer of qualities from one sort of activity to an entirely different one must be accomplished through the transformation of two terms that are merely *contiguous* (woman is seductive, and woman is a reader) into terms that are, more significantly, *like* each other (woman as seducer behaves like woman as reader; thus, woman reads in the same way she seduces). One must look, then, for instances in which tradition changes the basic metonymic relationship into a metaphoric one.

Such a transformation first enters the tradition with Plato, who transforms the facts about the female role in reproduction as they were understood in his time into a model of the female role in the reception of cultural tradition, that is, in reading.[7] He presents the author as male, implanting the seed, which is his thought, into the reader, presented as female. The father-author inscribes in her a *conceptus*, "that which is conceived," a concept. The mother-reader who reproduces the image of the father-author which has been implanted in her is, by definition, a good reader. If, however, she does not thus reproduce an image that closely resembles the author-father's thought, she is a threat to a society based on the principle of patriarchal inheritance. The *conceptus* to which such a mother-reader gives birth will be of "unknown" origin, in that a mother cannot be viewed as the origin, the legitimating parent: only a father-author can provide legitimacy. The concept to which such a mother-*mis*reader gives rise will always be a bastard concept, bearing the stigma of illegitimacy brought about by the mother-reader's misbehavior, her "vile pruriency" and "concupiscence."

To be sure, European tradition has not read this Platonic myth of the female reader literally, for it has been clear all along that men as well as women can "misread." The very purpose of this model of reading, indeed, was primarily to make the nature of misreading, "bad" reading, plain to men and thus to warn them away from it and toward "good" reading. The Platonic model effectively implies that all readers (male or female) possess "wombs"; it discriminates, however, between two ways these wombs may be used. Some readers will use them to support patriarchal society, producing from the text a concept resembling the author's and thus understanding the text "correctly." They will strive to identify the readings they produce with the ideas of the father-authors, an effort that is perceived as bringing them a share of the stature of the father-authors, despite their inferior status as readers—that is, beings playing the passive, female role. Adapting a term suggested by Sterne (by making the first element in his compound construction function as an adverb rather than an adjective), one might call such readers "male-readers," a somewhat oxymoronic coupling indicating readers who identify what they produce as readers as originating in the male role of the author. On the other hand, readers who use their wombs to threaten tradition by giving birth out of the text to concepts alien to the author can

---

7. A concise exposition of such Platonic imagery appears in Clayton Koelb, "*In der Strafkolonie*: Kafka and the Scene of Reading," *German Quarterly*, 55 (Nov. 1982), 511–25. My analysis partly parallels that of Luce Irigaray, "Plato's *Hystera*," in her *Speculum of the Other Woman*, trans. Gillian C. Gill (Ithaca: Cornell University Press, 1985), 243–364.

be said, according to this model, to misread the text. The readings they produce are identified with their own ideas and thus have no author-derived status; they are, consequently, ridiculous because of their lack of proper paternity, even monstrous because they result from a female attempt to play a male role. Such readers might be called, with some redundancy, "female-readers" to indicate that they identify what they produce as readers as originating in their own female, reader's role.

The discrimination between (good) "male-readers" and (bad) "female-readers" becomes crucial with the advent of Christianity, because Christianity is founded on a peculiarly complex way of reading sacred texts. The juncture between what Christianity designates as "Old" and "New" Testaments announces itself as a redefinition of what constitutes "good" reading versus "bad." As a radical rereading of the "Old" Testament, the "New" Testament must not, if it is to prove its claims, look like the product of a "female-reader," interested only in its own concerns and negligent of tradition, that is, of meaning perceived to originate with the "father-author." It therefore redefines this point of origin. The "father-author" is no longer separated from the reader by the passage of a great period of time or distinct from the reader by virtue of a superior and unattainable status; rather, the "new" reader of the "Old" Testament (especially such readers as Jesus and Paul) has a unique relationship with the author permitting the privileged reader to give birth to a *conceptus* implanted by the author but kept hidden from other readers until the privileged reader's advent. That is, the gestation of the Christian *conceptus* is unusually long, but the offspring is claimed to be for this reason not more suspect but rather more legitimate, more like the idea of the father-author than any earlier *conceptus*.

While it is not possible to explore here the rich development of the discrimination between male-readers and female-readers in Christian hermeneutics, one example will show both that gender-related terms continue to be used to designate proper and improper readers and that Christianity brings to the dichotomy male-reader/female-reader an increased complexity that tends to rigidify it further. One of the greatest doctors of the late medieval Church, Saint Bonaventure, recounts the story of the Fall as if it had occurred in a library rather than a garden:

These truths we should hold about the whole man residing in Paradise: that a double sense was given to him, an interior and an exterior—of mind and of flesh. . . . there is [also] a double book, one written within, which is the eternal art and wisdom of God, and the other written without, namely, the sensible world. . . . there has been prepared for man a double good: "one visible, the other invisible; one temporal, the other eternal; one of the flesh, the other of the spirit. . . ." Man was given a double sense and appetite with respect to the two books and the two goods . . . so that he could turn to either by reason of his freedom of choice; *woman* by giving ear to the suggestion of the serpent in the exterior book, *did not turn back to the interior book* . . . but yielded to the sensual in the exterior book and began to negotiate for the exterior good.[8]

Here, in a passage that could not be more dissimilar to Sterne's in tone, there nonetheless appears the direct ancestress of the female-reader whom Sterne introduces to such humorous effect. Bonaventure's Eve "did not turn back to the interior book . . . but yielded to the sensual in the exterior book," as Sterne's female-reader was guilty of "reading straight forwards, more in quest of the adventures." Eve looks to the book for what is "visible," "temporal," and "of the flesh," as Sterne's female-reader is motivated by "vile pruriency for fresh adventures in all things," "concupiscence," "the gross and more carnal parts." That is, the notion of the character of "bad" reading, to be associated with females and especially with female sensuality, remains consistent from (at least) the thirteenth to the eighteenth centuries.

The most important element in this enduring portrait of female-readers appears in the phrases "did not turn back" and "reading straight forwards," for everything is at stake, in Christian literature especially, in the notion that good reading is that which does "turn back" and does not go "straight forwards." That these contrasting notions both concern time, the past and the future, is evident; yet these temporal concerns are, in the eighteenth century as in the thirteenth, converted into physical ones, contrasting surface and depth rather than future and past. If Eve had been a good reader, she would have turned back to read what was inside, the interior book; if Sterne's female-reader had not rushed forward but instead had "read [the book] over as it should be," she would have found "deep erudition and knowledge." The religion of the "New" Testament had necessarily to elevate the status of readings that go "deep" above those that remain on the "surface," because its claim to validity was based on readings that would by no means be evident to literal readers of the "Old" Testament.

It is Christianity that stresses that superficial reading (for "adventure," plot, to find out "what happens") is not, as one might suppose today, merely stupid but, more important, morally wrong. The true meaning ("interior book," "deep erudition") has been, in this view, deposited by the author at a level the reader can read only by going *through* the surface. Readings that remain *on* the surface, on the other hand, engage the reader's desires rather than the author's ideas. "Bad" reading thus comes to be equated with superficial reading, and the superficiality of women

8. *Breviloquium*, trans. Erwin Nemmers (St. Louis: B. Herder, 1946), 72–74, 85–86, my emphasis. The Latin text is cited from *Opera Theologica Selecta*, 5 vols. (Quaracchi: Typographia Collegii S. Bonaventurae, 1934–1964), 5:61.

Susan Noakes

readers becomes a sign of both moral and intellectual deficiencies. The temporal character of "turning back" and "reading straight forwards" is never addressed.

It is addressed, however, in the most famous medieval representation of a female reader, which is not Bonaventure's Eve but Dante's Francesca.[9] Francesca is, to be sure, a kind of Eve figure, in that she is the "first sinner" with whom the pilgrim converses. She can be regarded as distinguished from her ancestress by her birth in the work of an author who, in the _Vita Nuova_, designates women readers as an important part of his lay, vernacular audience. Her depiction thus suggests something of how women readers were seen in the period of the rise of the vernacular literatures and of the lay reading public; the details of that depiction can be briefly summarized as follows: Francesca, as the style in which she speaks to the pilgrim makes clear, is an avid reader of the love poetry that Dante will later in the _Comedy_ designate by the name "sweet new style"; she is also, she tells the pilgrim, a reader of Arthurian romance. Both stilnovistic poetry and the version of Lancelot and Guinevere which Francesca gives evidence of knowing would have been designated by Bonaventure as having an exterior and interior meaning (had Bonaventure lived in the fourteenth century and thought vernacular literature worth commenting on). The poetry of the "sweet new style" had elaborated upon the convention of earlier vernacular love poetry by endowing it with metaphysical and religious content that made love an ennobling experience preparing man to love God, and the _Prose Lancelot_ depicted the illicit love of Lancelot and Guinevere as leading to spiritual devastation and public humiliation. Dante depicts Francesca as reading the "interior book" in neither case. She picks up the terminology of the "sweet new style" without learning from it to rise above physical love, and she crudely imitates, with her brother-in-law Paolo, the adulterous kiss of Lancelot and Guinevere. That the superficiality of her reading is the product of something more serious than mere shallowness or stupidity is clear from her damnation to eternal torment. Although, with the famous line "A Gallehaut was the book and the one who wrote it," she blames the author of the Lancelot romance for the punishment that is the aftermath of her superficial reading, Dante makes clear that the responsibility is hers when he places Francesca, not the _Lancelot_ author, in hell. This woman's superficial reading is, once again, linked to her moral failure. She takes surface elements of both stilnovistic poetry and Arthurian romance and makes of them what she wishes, rather than penetrating "deep" into the meaning

9. Further analysis of the character of Francesca's reading, particularly as it illustrates the substitution of a sexual for a temporal problem, together with a discussion of Francesca as a kind of Eve figure, is presented in my "The Double Misreading of Paolo and Francesca," _Philological Quarterly_ 62 (1983), 221–39.

authors have placed beneath the surface. Using the language of temporality rather than that of corporality, she misapprehends the temporal character of written language, believing that what has been written in the past can be acted upon in the present.

Although the rise of the vernacular literatures brought frequent explicit designations of women as important parts of the reading public, such designations were not necessarily accompanied by any notion that women were increasingly able to be more than superficial, concupiscent readers, reading "straight forwards" in quest of "adventures," rather than reading "deep" within the text. The fifteenth and sixteenth centuries saw the emergence of women authors, whose writings repeatedly and unequivocally demonstrated the ability of real females to read "beneath" the surface. Several even demonstrated their ability to read literary tradition in a sophisticated way by explicitly discriminating between literary topos and reality in, precisely, their treatment of the figure of the female misreader.[10] Nonetheless, because the critical spirit of the Renaissance did not extend to the criticism of long-prevalent notions of what constitutes "good" reading but rather reinforced them,[11] the topos of the woman reader who is corrupted by the "exterior book" continued to prevail. I have pointed out its presence in the eighteenth century in Sterne; it is employed much more prominently by Jean-Jacques Rousseau.

The very title of *The New Heloise* alludes to a woman both famous for her learning and notorious for her fall. To be sure, gender is not the only issue the book addresses. Nonetheless, from its beginning, *The New Heloise* focuses attention on reading as an activity on which gender has an important impact. In the preface, Rousseau explains his choice of title as motivated by his desire to warn girls away from the book.[12] Defining

10. What Christine de Pizan regarded as her first serious literary work is a step-by-step critique of the notion that women are unable to learn from the classical past and are therefore unsuitable moral and political advisers, as I have shown in a forthcoming book, *Timely Reading: Between Exegesis and Interpretation* (Ithaca: Cornell University Press, 1988); for Christine's treatment of this same problem in another work, see also Margaret Ferguson's essay in the present volume. The late fifteenth-century Italian humanist Laura Cereta addresses the issue in her letter to the no doubt fictitious Bibulus Sempronius, translated in *Her Immaculate Hand: Selected Works by and about the Women Humanists of Quattrocento Italy*, ed. Margaret L. King and Albert Rabil, Jr. (Binghamton, N.Y.: Center for Medieval and Early Renaissance Studies, State University of New York at Binghamton, 1983), 81–84. Marguerite de Navarre, *Heptaméron*, trans. P. A. Chilton (Harmondsworth: Penguin, 1984), story 12, takes as heroine a literate peasant girl, who correctly reads the seductive words of the prince who pursues her; more generally in the framing narrative of her stories, Marguerite relates interpretation by females to basic hermeneutic problems.

11. As I have argued in a chapter on Boccaccio's sacralization of literature in *Timely Reading*.

12. Ed. Michel Lennay (Paris: Garnier Flammarion, 1964), 3–4, translations mine, hereafter cited parenthetically in the text.

Susan Noakes

female readers as having quite limited abilities (implying that mature women are not up to reading philosophical works but must instead take their philosophy from novels), the preface suggests that younger women who do not read the title as a warning will be unable to grasp the significance of the plot.[13] Rousseau's preface places the power to choose good or evil in the reader rather than the text, echoing Bonaventure and Dante in ascribing to prior corruption in the reader any ill consequences of encounter with the book. Rousseau's text is much more ambivalent than those of such predecessors, however, for it asserts that a girl corrupt enough to open this book might as well finish reading it, since "she has nothing more to lose." The warning is, at best, perfunctory; Rousseau does not develop it as Bonaventure and Dante do. Whereas even Sterne jokingly provides some reference to the hermeneutic instruction ("go back," "read more carefully") that traditionally accompanies such a warning, Rousseau moves against this tradition by advising the lost young female reader to go forward with her reading.

In a gesture that mirrors this part of the preface, the heroine herself, after the moral conversion that coincides with her acceptance of a suitable marriage, comes to blame her youthful fall on her reading of something she should not have read, her tutor's first letter (251). This retrospective admission of readerly corruption is ironic not only because the book as a whole shows Julie to be a paragon of that new form of eighteenth-century virtue based on "sensibility" but, more particularly, in the light of the early exchange of letters on the plan proposed for the heroine's studies, after both lovers have declared their passion to each other but before they exchange their first kiss. In this exchange (letters 12–13) the tutor had recommended a new study plan ostensibly based on the contrast between those "who need to read a great deal and think little" and Julie, who "put[s] into [her] reading better than [she] find[s] . . . , and whose active mind makes of the book another book, sometimes better than the first" (29). The view of reading espoused here again mirrors that presented in the preface, in that it locates in the reader's preexisting character the power to derive good or evil from reading. But the context is rendered ambivalent by the tutor's role here as seducer, who flatters Julie with the idea that she needs to spend less time reading and more time talking with her tutor about what she reads. He proposes that the heroine develop her skills as an active reader by enticing her into still more compromising interchange with him. His success as a seducer can be seen as the result of Julie's superficial reading of his proposal, so that the woman praised by

13. A young noblewoman's unsuitable love for her tutor brings grief and turmoil to her friends and family, perhaps even hastening her mother's death; the heroine finds tranquility before her own untimely death only in the performance of familial obligations.

On the Superficiality of Women

Rousseau's character as a notably active or "deep" reader, a woman who indeed gives considerable evidence throughout the novel of moral and psychological "penetration," simultaneously appears to be yet another seeker after "surface good," at least in her youth.

That aspect of Rousseau's preface which appears to warn young girls away from reading novels becomes something of a cliche in eighteenth- and nineteenth-century fiction. The most famous nineteenth-century example of a woman brought low by reading superficially is, to be sure, Flaubert's *Madame Bovary*. While being "finished" in a convent, Emma, a farmer's daughter, immerses herself for six months in historical novels. But for her history is a "dark immensity" against which the heroines she comes to idolize stand out "like comets . . . all unconnected."[14] Like other female-readers, Emma is depicted as reading with her desire rather than with her mind: "she fell in love with," "had a cult . . . and enthusiastic veneration for." In sum, she fixes on surface details that do not even have any relation to each other ("guardrooms, old oak chests and minstrels") without understanding the meaning of what she reads. Flaubert's evocation of Emma as a young reader concludes with scathing irony as he points out that she "always" brought to her reading the memory of plates "glorifying Louis XIV," which she ate from while stopping at an inn for supper just prior to being deposited at the convent (25). This detail suggests that Emma brings to her reading not thought but instead bric-a-brac, and scratched at that.

Flaubert's emphasis in describing the superficiality of Emma's style of reading is on its disconnectedness; her vision of what she reads is unstructured because structure is to be found only within, not at the surface, where female-readers, according to tradition, remain. Emma, like Bonaventure's Eve and Sterne's Madam Reader, has a "nature . . . that had loved . . . literature for the passions it excites" (28). Once married to Charles Bovary, she continues to appropriate into her own life the exterior forms of her romantic readings: "She wanted to experience love with him. By moonlight in the garden she recited all the passionate rhymes she knew by heart . . . but she found herself as calm after this as before, and Charles seemed neither more amorous, nor more moved" (31). Yearning to visit Paris, she subscribes to two "ladies' magazines," which she studies until she "knows" such things as "the addresses of the best tailors" (41), even though her only knowledge of Parisian topography comes from a map she has bought. Her method of reading at this stage in her marriage is described as "dreaming between the lines" (43). Because Emma's reading feeds her tendency to live her life in a dream world, neglecting, to her

14. Trans. Paul de Man and Eleanor Marx Aveling (New York: W. W. Norton, 1965), 26, hereafter cited parenthetically in the text.

peril and that of those around her, the inescapable realities of her existence, Flaubert's novel gives the impression, as it moves from these early chapters toward her concluding disaster, that she might have been better off never reading at all.

It may well be objected that I have read these five texts superficially. All the passages singled out for discussion here play, to be sure, a more complex role in the masterpieces of which they form small parts. I have left unsaid much that might have been said about the conception of the reader which informs each of the five and how it manifests itself in the representation of women as "bad" readers. I have pursued the goal that interests me rather than attempt to provide a survey of a topos that would lay any claims to historical comprehensiveness. I hope I have shown, on the basis of the depiction in works by Bonaventure, Dante, Sterne, Rousseau, and Flaubert of women readers whose superficial reading is an indicator of moral deficiency, that the female misreader is indeed a full-fledged topos within the Western literary tradition.

At this point one might well ask why anyone should regard the existence of this topos as any more than a minor, if perhaps embarrassing, episode in the history of the Western literary tradition. I submit that the character of this topos has a great deal to tell students of hermeneutics, and especially of a semiotically informed feminist hermeneutics. To begin with, it exemplifies one of the ways gender differences have been employed in accounts of sign production and interpretation. This topos constitutes a compelling reminder that _reading itself is a sign_ rather than an objective, value-free, ahistorical activity. Because it is a sign, reading derives its meaning from the differentiation of one of its forms from another. Indeed, there exists a whole series of opposing terms that generate the European concept of reading, including the following: good reading/bad reading; active reading/passive reading; superficial reading/deep reading. Leaving aside for the moment the opposition between active and passive reading, I would recall, as I indicated early in this essay, that women have most consistently been associated with the negative pole in the opposition between readings that give words their "real" meaning and those that do not and between readings that seek out in words an inner form and those that remain on their surface.

The illustrations brought together here indicate that the elevation of reading into an objective, value-free, ahistorical activity depends upon the exclusion of all those features that the Western hermeneutic tradition associates with bad or superficial reading. Perhaps, if it is time to reconsider this elevation, it is first necessary to observe more closely how reading is actually practiced, as the proponents of "subjective criticism," most notably David Bleich and Norman Holland, have urged. But

On the Superficiality of Women

whether one cares to engage in such observation or not, the important thing to bear in mind is that *reading is a learned activity* (at its highest level as well as at the most elementary). To conceive of it as similar in kind to a natural activity, such as seeing and eating (as Western hermeneutic tradition has in fact done), is a serious error. Moreover, *reading is taught, and the discriminations on which it is based are inculcated with great passion*, not with any degree of calm neutrality. The norms that define the character of "good" reading are propounded with the same vigor as those that establish sexual taboos. In fact, as I have shown, the language of sexual transgression is frequently transferred wholesale to the description of reading. If hermeneutics is to move beyond its present impasse (I refer here primarily to Anglo-American literary theory and the conflict that has in the last decade divided the explorers of deconstruction from their critics), reading will have to be conceived of in a new way.

Because reading is a sign, it must always be understood as constituted by the differentiation of one of its forms from another. Rather than the differentiation of male-reading and all it implies from female-reading and all it implies, however, I would urge that *reading needs to be conceived of as generated by a temporal rather than a sexual or spatial (interior/exterior) distinction*. As I argue in *Timely Reading: Between Exegesis and Interpretation*, Western hermeneutics has evolved as an ongoing attempt to "overcome" time. (I mark this last verb with quotation marks to set apart this example of the martial and male language that frequently appears in the hermeneutic tradition and will similarly mark others. This particular example comes from Baudelaire and is treated in a chapter of *Timely Reading*.) Written language has been conceived as transmitting through time a meaning that remains always the same, being thus unaffected by time and specifically by the contingencies of history. Without such a conception, reading as it is traditionally conceived has no meaning. If a reader does not "recapture" the meaning words had for their authors or at least for the readers who were the author's contemporaries, by "penetrating" the structure of written words called a text, the reader is not conceived of as reading but rather as merely playing with a surface or using it narcissistically to mirror present concerns. This opposition between the reader engaged in penetrating the text and the reader who desires to enjoy the text's surface is a false one. All readers partake of both kinds of activity.

I submit that the opposition that in fact generates the Western hermeneutic tradition's concept of reading is between exegesis and interpretation. The exegetical mode of reading, which seeks to understand a text as it would have been understood by its author, and the interpretative mode of reading, which seeks to understand a text by reference to the concerns of the reader, are often presented in contemporary theoretical discourse

Susan Noakes

as opposed to each other. In fact, however, reading is constituted by the complementary functioning of both these modes, for all reading oscillates ceaselessly between them. To adopt the sexual hermeneutic language employed earlier in this essay, there are no exclusively male-readers or female-readers.

Yet the illusion that male-reading can approach the "true" meaning of the text, defined as a single meaning apparent to the author and available to all "good" readers, has been relentlessly pursued by what I would call mainstream applied hermeneutics: a pedagogical orientation that tends to class reading as more and more naïve the more closely it approaches the interpretative mode. Interpretative reading is a siren that lies under a taboo. The reason for this taboo, and for the celebration of male-reading, is the need to maintain as an ideal an authoritative voice. Indeed, the central function of written language in the Judeo-Christian tradition is to erect authorities from the past (Moses, the Founding Fathers) into forces fit to shape latter-day behavior and values.

The literary commonplace treated in this essay thus has much to say about how sign production and interpretation shape society. It brings to the fore discriminations found within accounts of reading which are dressed up in gender-specific apparel in order to make the transmission of the values of the past by means of written language more efficient. Only one message need be received if it can be made clear that the receipt of other messages is in itself an indicator of "vile pruriency," lack of thought, or ignorance. Guilt by association is a powerful principle in Western hermeneutics.

The Western hermeneutic tradition is built on the notion of the mis-reader, very often characterized as a woman reader. While focusing on this dependence, I have shown that there is a recurrent element in Western literature which insistently suggests to women while they are reading that they are unlikely to be reading well, or as well as men. This is deplorable; it cannot help but harm new generations of women readers unless it is pointed out to them that the topos of the female misreader is precisely a topos, not a reflection of reality.

Apart from this empirical concern, however, the existence of the topos treated here has several implications for literary hermeneutics. First of all, it shows that two kinds of readers one might intuitively think to be quite different, even opposites, are instead understood by long literary tradition to be but minor variants of the same type. The "passive" reader who is "swept off her feet" by an author's language, manipulated and seduced by a text, is no different from the "active" reader who willfully "alters" a text's meaning to bring it into conformity with the reader's own concerns. Both may be said to interact with the text exclusively as with a surface: while the "active" reader plays with that surface, bending words, phrases,

On the Superficiality of Women

and fragmentary images to serve her purposes (seduced, according to tradition, by her own desire for a good too narrowly defined), the "passive" reader, too, plays with such surface elements as sound and image in order to attain a goal which is no less the object of an act of will.

Second, it makes evident the Janus-like character of reading, which inevitably looks to both past and present: the past, in a search for the meanings of words that authors only appear to select, words that the reader can suppose to have meaning only insofar as she grasps that they have a past; the present, in a rummaging within the self for images (old dinner plates), connections, sounds, above all other words that will authorize, more than any author can, the sense that what is being read is indeed understood. Reading shifts continually between these two aspects and puts the reader always into a state of ambiguity.[15]

What has here been called female-reading (with *female* serving as an adverb rather than an adjective) is again and again punished by male authors,[16] whether through ridicule or, with telling severity, through depiction of the female-reader's disgrace, death, or damnation. This punishment is meted out, no doubt, in order to lead readers into the path of male-reading, in which a concept closely resembling the author's would be born. But because the latter can never happen to a degree that fully satisfies the demands of both author and reader, female-reading never passes out of the hermeneutic tradition. It remains a constant, to be exorcized again and again with every new literary generation. Indeed, no reader can ever be wholly a male-reader or a female-reader; both these figures are merely chimeras constructed to disguise, through simplification, a reality too incongruous to contemplate with ease. If the gender-determined garb could be removed from the polarities that generate reading as it is generally described in the West, it might be possible to focus further attention on their temporal character. For centuries, writers have inscribed on the bodies of women the same hermeneutic text, over and over again.[17] But this text is thus displaced; it should instead be written, over and over again, on the face of a clock.

15. The nature of this ambiguity, fundamentally temporal but disguised as, among other things, sexual, forms the topic of *Timely Reading*.

16. It is celebrated by such notable female authors as Christine de Pizan and Marguerite de Navarre. Space limitations unfortunately forbid any exposition of their development of a tradition counter to traditional Western hermeneutics. Recent French contributions to the concept of *écriture féminine* in some ways continue this countertradition.

17. For this image, cf. Koelb, "*In der Strafkolonie*."

[2 2]

On the Sign Systems
of Biography

Michael Riffaterre

All attempts at reducing biography to its defining principles have traditionally focused on three: biography must record the life of an individual;
this record must be truthful, both historically and psychologically; and it
must be a work of art. Of the three, the first seems so self-evident as not to
raise any question, and yet there are biographies in which the hero's life is
but a convenient narrative thread to put together vignettes of a society.
Such bastardized implementations of the principle suggest that it does
not suffice to separate biography from history. The truth principle seems
more useful, since indeed it differentiates biography from fiction. But it is
hard to see what biographical truth contributes to biography as art. On
the one hand, truth interests even when it is artless, in diaries for instance.
On the other hand, any but a chronological organization of the facts
threatens to visibly subordinate veracity to purpose (demonstrating a
thesis, privileging a viewpoint, etc.) or simply to the writer's subjectivity. It
is not that truth and art cannot go hand in hand. It is just that by
recognizing the facts of the text only inasmuch as they correspond to
categories deduced from these principles, we separate the facts from their
functions and cannot quite see how these work in harmony. At best we
can say they coexist, but we still cannot show how this coexistence takes
shape.

I propose to approach the problem from the opposite direction, not
from the principles but from the conditions of their actualization, from
the textual features the decoding of which eventually leads the reader to
invoke such principles or to question their relevancy. My starting point

A first version of this paper was read as part of a program arranged by the Division on
Comparative Literature on the theoretical implications of literary biography, under the
chairmanship of Ralph Friedman.

On the Sign Systems of Biography

handwritten margin notes: GW bio as parody of hagiography; all biography is moral or claims moral authority; biographer is an authority for a story w/ didactic authority or imputed authority; ✗ ✗

will not be the discrete components of biography as a genre, but the literariness of the biographical text as a whole. By *literariness* of literature is meant a consistent and repeatable reader response to a text, such that the form itself is perceived as inseparable from the message and that this perception is inseparable from value judgment. Accordingly, I would like to consider the mechanisms that control readers' perception of a literary life and make them see it as an interesting representation of an interesting person, justifying both the choice of the subject and the way the subject is depicted.

I shall propose a tripartite model to account for this response. The model is based on a distinction between three semiotic networks, three sign systems that, I submit, are always at work together in a biography. The first refers to the biographee as an extraordinary subject, the second to the biographee as an ordinary subject, the third refers to the biographer. The first is a hero-making system: it makes the human subject an exciting one. The second is the humanization system: it keeps the hero close enough to mere mortals so that the reader recognizes common frailties and empathizes. The third is the moral system: it presents the writer as an authority for his story, and the story as an authority for a lesson or a concept.

The first system is founded on a presupposition, built on narrative structures, and implemented diegetically. The second, the humanization system, is founded on referentiality, built on descriptive structures, and implemented mimetically. The third is founded on grammar, built on rhetorical and intertextual structures, and implemented metalinguistically.

These systems must be distinguished because they have separate functions, but they are inseparable within the actual text, where their functions are mutually complementary.

The first system, composed of those signs that indicate the unusual character of the subject, is free of any burden of proof because it derives from the very ethos of the genre. The mere title—*The Life of So and So*, or *So and So, a Biography*—is enough to presuppose the truth of the life story about to be told. The basic assumption that the individual here memorialized did exist automatically guarantees the actuality of whatever happened that made him or her worthy of attention, deserving to be remembered as an example to imitate or to shun. I must emphasize that this blanket assumption of truth is only one constituent of the semiotic system: it does nothing to make readers acquiesce to the lesson that might be drawn from events assumed to be true, nor does it make them find the story believable in terms of their experience. All it does is signal something so unusual in an individual that it would tax credibility if it were not for the genre-induced presupposition, if the story were found in any other text not covered by that presupposition. This unusualness may be exemplary of something good or bad, or it may simply be typical to the point of being exotic or picturesque. Exemplariness is found in its most extreme form in the early period of biography: in Antiquity, when the genre was essentially moralistic, as with Plutarch's *Parallel Lives* or Suetonius's *Lives of the XII Caesars*; in the Middle Ages, when biography merged with hagiography; later on, when a commentary on fate or on Providence would be found in the political tribulations of the mighty (for instance, Cavendish's *Life of Cardinal Wolsey*); and generally whenever it has been fashionable to eulogize the dead, as in Victorian biographies. But exemplariness need not be dramatic, so long as it makes the subject memorable. This is the case of Boswell's *Johnson*: even though a modern editor explains its effectiveness by the fascination of the uneventful, Dr. Johnson is extraordinary because of the powers of his mind, and even more extraordinary in that his uncouth appearance and behavior belie them. Without the genre-induced presupposition, he would be in turns idealized and grotesque, farfetched either way.

Presupposition thus legitimizes the telling of the unusual. It is, however, the unfolding of the diegetic sequence that actually represents the unusual: descriptions beget narrative consequences, and each abstract narrative structure in turn produces concrete descriptive scenes. These sequences are made at one and the same time exemplary and unusual, because narrative structures combine with diegetic models. However disturbing these models may be, they are also familiar because they come from the sociolect. The models are characterized by an oxymoronic grammar: every model pits against every other a component that is expected or appears acceptable and one that is unexpected in the context of the first one.

Diegetic models are structural invariants themselves, since they assume diverse shapes, organize a number of stories, and yet the reader understands them in terms of functions that remain unmodified from one actualization to the other. To take but one example, quite a few biographies offer variants of such a model for the subject's difficult beginnings in life. The circumstances of his birth or early youth impede his progress so as to give him an opportunity to display his ability to conquer—a handicap structure, as it were. Since a handicap is supposed to be overcome, this first hurdle entails the vaulting of it, a feat that serves to adumbrate the character's final success.

Thus, for the protagonist of André Maurois's *Life of Disraeli*, there is the onus of Jewish extraction in a Parliament of Christian gentlemen; in Boswell, the sad spectacle (his term) of Dr. Johnson's spastic ailment which causes new acquaintances to mistake this powerful intellect for an idiot in the literal sense; in Lytton Strachey's *Queen Victoria*, her being a

On the Sign Systems of Biography

Suspense comes through overdetermination of diegetic models — reverse reading for su...

woman. This last example is especially well developed. For the first two hundred pages or so of his magnum opus, Strachey focuses on the princess's femininity, of which each facet is a presumption of vulnerability. Impressionable, naïve, isolated by her mother and her governess from the real world (understand, the male world), she seems a malleable clay in the hands of protective father figures. But as the narrative progresses, every single sign for female inferiority is transformed into a sign for feminine resiliency: her ladylike poise changes into assertiveness, her coddled little-girlish whims into petulant authoritarianism, her naïveté into an ability to see that any emperor trying to get in her way has no clothes on. A series of parallel transformations, with a comical version of poetic justice for their common model, spells out the metamorphosis of the pliable princess into a self-willed monarch. Each of the successive mentors who taught her that the only legitimate defense for her was maidenly reserve (her mother, the Duchess, her uncle, the King, her Prime Minister), finds to his discomfiture that reserve has turned into a wall of stubborn independence. One after the other, they are made to feel like so many plotters hoist with their own petard.

This kind of overdetermination makes reading biography an exciting experience, if only because our familiarity with the diegetic models increases our expectations, creates a representation of suspense on the very point where the story by itself would have excluded actual suspense, since we generally know the outcome of a biography. Furthermore, these overdetermined signs make biography a moral genre since they change the accidental sequence of events, half luck, half the hero's hard work, into a teleological apologue. Every single event is transformed from a step in the narration into a morally meaningful proairesis, which reflects and dictates an interpretation. If birth may in reality allow for a certain biological predictibility, its mimesis transforms these indices into signs prophetic of a foreordained future. Biography translates predestination, the stuff of didactic and epic poetry, into biological code. The other pole of the biographical vector, death, elicits similar interpretive constructs. The intentionality with which Plutarch draws a loaded picture of a public speaker's debut by making his Demosthenes overcome a speech impediment, this same intentionality dictates that Boswell should show Johnson stricken with aphasia. There is in both instances a dramatic aptness in the visitation. It affects precisely the function or the organ most essential to the talent or technique that entitled the subject to be chronicled. No reader therefore can avoid finding a lesson or simply a symbolism in the fact that the greatest Greek orator and a great British conversationalist should be speechless. This kind of coincidence translates into a pathetic image, in which we may read the finger of fate or simply a felicitous literary device. Thus, narrative overdetermination, freed from the

further: idiot débil mental stutterer dreamer no education

finally, barreness (for women in cultures where maternity is ? simply biological exp.)

shackles of verisimilitude, able therefore to build ideal constructs, is a factor of literariness as well as a generic trait.

I am not unaware that Samuel Johnson actually suffered a stroke and that Boswell did not invent it for art's sake. But he does exploit it for art's sake. Beethoven's biographies offer similar reconstructions around the composer's deafness. The emphasis on the event, the dramatic buildup to it, the accumulation of letters quoted verbatim retracing by the hour Johnson's first realization of his plight, then his fight to keep his sanity and later to reconquer his power of speech, these are Boswell's. His ability to select the significant from among trivial occurrences, his sense of suspense, his stage director's instinct transform a jumble of facts into an epic of the mind's triumph over the flesh.

Were it not for the generic presupposition of truth, we would be apt to think that these episodes are too good to be true. The signs of this system therefore are dramatized and valorized mimetic units. But even though their semantic contents are representational, their semiotic function is tropological.

The second sign system of biography, contrariwise, has to be good enough to look true. It does not matter if what it represents is false factually, so long as it has the appearance of truth. Based on referentiality, that is, on the assumption that meaning can be tested against the outside world, this system has verisimilitude for its principal mechanism. It therefore rests on a network of stereotypes like the first system, but these are not valorized or polarized or extreme: they are a collection of vignettes stored up in language for our apprehension of and almost automatic allusion to everyday experiences of normalcy. They organize the space and time of our lives. For each instance they provide ready-made pictures that the word appropriate to circumstances (a lexical nucleus) suffices to conjure up: the picture implements through derivative words or phrases the semes constitutive of the lexical nucleus. All that is needed for verisimilitude to work, that is, eventually to substitute for truth, is that the textual signs respect the grammar of these habitual derivations.

Biography uses this second system for the telling details, the minor incidents that ring true instead of being presupposed so, for the atmosphere, for the background, for the bringing to life. Without verisimilitude's sensory input, settings and characters would remain the abstract narrative situations they are in the first system. The biographical subject would stay as flat as the paintings we may have of her or him. This is the aspect of a biography onto which critics latch to appraise its evocative power: critical comments typically and revealingly cluster around the biographer's ability to sketch a silhouette, a gesture, an inflection of voice. The effusive friendliness of King Henry VIII walking in Thomas More's

On the Sign Systems of Biography

garden, his arm thrown around the neck that he will have cut, Victoria's smile showing her gums, in Roper or Strachey.[1] But of course the writer does not choose them at random. They are selected because they are already in the sociolect, recognized and valid metonyms or synecdoches complete with their possible interpretations from which the writer cannot wander away. They leave the biographer no freedom, save that of choosing either their negative or their positive version. Linguistic usage sets definite limits to the deciphering of the human face as a text: a forehead leads to inferences as to spiritual or rational traits; a chin is an index of willpower. Cheekbones yield little beyond pointing to the femininity of a profile or a racial type, or connoting a meager diet. The gums rank below lips and teeth in the scale of facial esthetics: we conclude therefore that Victoria is not very pretty, but we also fill the gap left by our information; if the witness can see the queen's gums, it must be that she opens her mouth too wide, a lack of reserve no doubt in so wellbred a person; hence there is an inference of guileless enjoyment, the suggestion that behind the royal mask there hides a girl who does not watch herself when she is amused, a suggestion of naïveté. This prepares us to accept that she should fall under the spell of someone like Disraeli.

From my viewpoint, however, focusing as I do on the systemic features of the genre, these aspects of the verisimilitude system by itself are not defining features of biography. The use of descriptive details I have just outlined is nowise different from that of realism in fiction, or that of T. S. Eliot's objective correlative in poetry.

What *is* specific to biography is the relationship between the verisimilitude system and the hero-making system. Because the latter focuses on the difference that makes the hero worth writing about, the verisimilitude system privileges the subject's commonality, selecting signs that designate those facets of his personality that he shares with other people. Here again biography taps the sociolect's supply of stereotypes, this time those representing prevalent behaviors or pointing to social types. Instead of using them for the direct representation of the usual that we would find in a novel, biography systematically contrasts them with the narrative signs and diegetic models of the first system, as if verisimilitude in portraiture could succeed only by concentrating on these traits of the subject that are irrelevant to the moral implications of the narrative and to the subject's "biography-worthiness." Strachey tells us that Prince Albert, Victoria's consort, looked to the British like a foreign tenor. Later, His Royal Highness, getting older, began to look like a butler (154, 289). The detail as

---

1. William Roper, *The Life of Sir Thomas More*, ed. Richard S. Sylvester and Davis P. Harding (New Haven: Yale University Press, 1962), 208; Lytton Strachey, *Queen Victoria* (New York: Harcourt Brace, 1921), 91, 94, hereafter cited parenthetically in the text.

such brings home the dowdiness of the court, *but* in contrast to the sympathetic analysis of the prince's intellectual achievements, it has the impact of dramatic actuality. It underscores the bias Albert's foreignness cannot overcome. The comicality of the image also saves the portrait from the eulogizing conventions that had stultified English biography in the nineteenth century.

Aside from helping the reader relate to the subject, these contrasts define a mode peculiar to biography: surprise—surprise because the reader never tires of marveling at how homey the famous can be, how ordinary in whatever is not their claim to our interest, and how petty despite their greatness. Hence are two possible consequences. One is comic relief at rediscovering humanity in the enshrined subject. The other is an avatar of verisimilitude, based first on a belief in the subject's genuineness by virtue of the commonplace that a real being must be complex and contradictory. And second, verisimilitude is based on a cliche that truth is always what does not first meet the eye (the pattern of exposure is so strong that it has generated a subgenre: sensational biography). The contrasts also give rise to a form of suspense, or rather to a substitute for it, since the fact that we already know the issue defuses fictional suspense. Biographical suspense arises from a narrative of the errors of judgment eyewitnesses and contemporaries made about the subject. While contrasts lead the reader to a belief in the humanity of the subject, they have led contemporaries to a disbelief in his uncommon merit. Hence there occur a sequence of surprises that successively retrace the path of the subject toward recognition.

Lastly, the third system of signs consists in the explicit representation of the writer or in the writer's implied presence in the text. Explicit or implicit, this presence functions first as a mimesis of interpretation, a representation of the biographer's interpretive stance, and second as a guideline for the reader's eventual espousal of that interpretation.

The biographer's presence is made explicit by an actual representation of himself or herself in the text as an eyewitness or as a diligent collector of evidence—one more indication that the story is true. But the real import of establishing the interpreter as a character in the story, is that this presence points to an interpretation and bolsters the one he vouchsafes. Boswell is obviously an extreme case of this type, since he goes so far as to create situations in which Dr. Johnson can be prodded into self-display. Boswell's is an experimental biography in the sense we speak of Emile Zola's *roman expérimental*, testing a form of behavior or a psychological type in various environments.

Biographers intervene only implicitly, but their hand is felt just as keenly when they are represented only by grammar or by rhetoric or by intertextuality. In the first case, the uses of the third-person pronoun for the biographee presupposes that of the first for the narrator. The presupposed first-person pronoun warns the reader that the choice of materials and of examples reflects a purposeful point of view. Quotations from the subject, thoughts or words attributed to him or to other actors but recorded in free indirect discourse, halfway between the verbatim reproduction of the character's *dicta* and their integration into a historical narrative, signal ostensibly that evidence has been rearranged toward an end.

Resorting to rhetoric serves the same purpose. The use of tropes in biography would in itself give the discourse on the subject the sound and the voice of the narrator, but beyond this general reminder that the story is shifting from plain recording to commentary, tropes are used as buoys signaling the progress of change in the subject. When Lytton Strachey compares his young Queen Victoria to a "small smooth crystal pebble . . . so transparent that one can see through it at a glance" and notes four years and eighty pages later that the pebble has been corroded by "humanity and fallibility" around it, and that it seems "actually growing a little soft and a little clouded" (49, 128), the gap between the two passages emphasizes rather than weakens our perception that they participate in an extended metaphor. That metaphor redefines a posteriori every incident that occurred between its first proleptic form and its continuation. Every experience in Victoria's life that has been told in between has now to be revised analeptically under the new tags "soft" and "clouded," as a possible cue to the insidious growth of what the writer's metalanguage now makes explicit as "secret impulses of . . . self-indulgence." Every instance thus reexamined with the benefit of hindsight seems to corroborate the biographer's reading.

As the text borrows some of its early formulation for a new one, there takes place in the reader's mind an illuminating comparison that is properly intertextual. The second version of something said before signifies only if the reader, urged to read one through the other, realizes the mutual complementarity that makes the intertext the key to the text's interpretation. The example I have just given, a case of intratextual intertextuality, could perhaps fail to command attention if mistaken for a mere stylistic variation.

The impact of full-fledged outward-bound intertextuality, however, is inescapable. In that case, readers are left with a feeling of incompleteness, of a lack, unless they retrieve the missing intertext. This intertext is the text of the subject—either the subject's life taken as a text or a text in which the subject must have seen a commentary on his or her own experience or a metaphorical model for it. The biographer's interpretation, then, is a reading of the subject's reading of his or her life. The biographical narrative no longer represents a life directly. Rather it repre-

Michael Riffaterre

sents it indirectly, by presupposing a first, hypothetical text, the biographee's interpretation of his or her own acts and motives.

A case in point is Izaak Walton's *Life of John Donne*, a short biography
that presents a disconcerting imbalance. More than a third of it is devoted
to Donne's illness and to his obsessive preparations for death, told with a
wealth of detail totally missing from the first part, which hurries through
his life and his love and his poetry. We see Donne busy designing an
allegorical conceit of Christ for seals and rings to be distributed among
the friends he leaves behind. Walton lingers over the protagonist sitting
not on the sitter's stool but on a funerary urn for a life-size statue of
himself. First he undresses completely, then he tightly wraps himself in a
shroud, with only his face exposed, but with eyes closed, like a death
mask. Etc.[2]

This very imbalance, however, happens to be the device that changes
the narrative from an objective history into an artifact, whose aesthetics
are inseparable from its moral purpose. Indeed, disproportion in the
factual reading of the life history is an index pointing to equipoise in the
philosophical reading of that life. The reader suddenly realizes that Walton's narrative is not centered on life but on death. It now reflects the
concept of a Christian life, which has meaning only as a preparation for
death. It thus accurately evokes the abiding obsession of the subject, the
interpretation Donne himself willed unto his life.

If Walton were referring directly to Donne's uninterpreted acts and
documents, the reader might not perceive their significance. Intertextuality provides the interpretation, for the biographical narrative's sign
system of truth is effective not because it stands for facts but because it
stands for words that themselves have been chosen to organize the facts—
words rather than facts, because this second part of the biography is
entirely derived from one matrix sentence, a quotation from Saint Paul
(underscored by a quotation from Job). The Saint Paul passage is a very
short, effective oxymoron: "He dies daily" (41).[3] And this oxymoron will
now serve as a transformation rule whereby any event of what is left of
Donne's life can be translated into an image of death. As a direct reference to reality, as language, the text is a biography. As an indirect reference, through the intercession of the Pauline intertext, as metalanguage,
Walton's text is a thanatography.

This interpretation, this dual or indirect reading, would not be imperative and inescapable, however, if readers were left to their own devices.
But two further instances of intertextuality ensure the text's absolute sway

---

2. Izaak Walton, *The Life of John Donne*, ed. S. B. Carter (orig. pub. 1640; London: Falcon
Educational Books, 1951), 58–59, hereafter cited parenthetically in the text.
3. 1 Corinthians 15:31.

on their attention. They are linked together, since they function as the *incipit* and the *clausula* of a thanatography subtext. The *clausula* is another quotation, from Donne's motto, that foretold his life to come as an exercise in mutability (*How much shall I be changed Before I am changed*: every life event is but a deceptive change, before the true final one [60]). The *incipit* is the preface, in which Walton alludes to the death of Pompey, assassinated on the Egyptian shore, and compares himself to Pompey's solitary mourner and his life of Donne to Pompey's makeshift funeral pyre (5). The heavily symbolic finale of Plutarch's *Life of Pompey* is thus the intertext for Walton's idea of where we must look for the meaning of existence. This intertext packs all the more power because Plutarch already builds on an intertext, on Homer. The funeral pyre on a shore is in epic poetry a stage set for the commemoration of shipwrecked heroes. Intertextually this generates a symbolic code in which death is the significance of life's voyage.

Thus the signs of the third system are meaningful *and* literary because their truth is established through intertextuality.

This cursory survey of the sign systems of biography suggests that despite the name of the genre, a literary life does not record the life. It records rather a reading of that life. Verisimilitude displaces referentiality. Interpretation displaces representation, and the mimesis itself is only a means toward an evaluation. It would be wrong, however, to conclude that biography is condemned to hover between the two opposite rhetorical categories of encomium and vituperation. Either one is at best a contingent choice. Evaluation in biography, in its durable aspects irrespective of topical peculiarities, is an aesthetic transposition. To be sure, originally biography is a subgenre of the *exemplum*, the use of a life story as an illustration to a moral end. But in the past four centuries or so, biography has become a rhetorical transcoding. In this transcoding, life is transformed into a simplified and easily demonstrative linear narrative. Life's drama, its characters, its stage are made into variations on pretested, prevalorized models. The turning points of existence are made into tropes, its suspense into a set of antithetical conceits. The mimesis reflects not reality but an earlier mimesis. Biography is not the depiction of a subject and the life he led. It is a text referring to an intertext that the subject did use or could have used as a model.

Notes on the Contributors

A. OWEN ALDRIDGE, founder and editor of the journal *Comparative Literature Studies*, taught for many years at the University of Illinois and is now Will and Ariel Durant Professor of the Humanities at Saint Peter's College (1986–1987). He is the author of ten books, including *Comparative Literature: Matter and Method* (1968); *Early American Literature: A Comparative Approach* (1982); and *The Reemergence of World Literature* (1986).

STANLEY CORNGOLD earned his Ph.D. in Comparative Literature at Cornell University in 1969. He is now Professor of German and Comparative Literature at Princeton University and president of the Kafka Society of America. His books include *The Commentators' Despair: The Interpretation of Kafka's "Metamorphosis"*; *The Fate of the Self: German Writers and French Theory*; and the forthcoming *Franz Kafka: The Necessity of Form*. He is at work on a study of eighteenth-century German literature titled *Wit, Judgment, and Imagination*.

JONATHAN CULLER holds a B.Phil. in General and Comparative Literature from Oxford, where he also earned the D.Phil. in Modern Languages. He is currently Class of 1916 Professor of English and Comparative Literature at Cornell University. He is the author of six books: volumes on Flaubert (1974), Saussure (1976), and Barthes (1983); a collection of essays, *The Pursuit of Signs: Semiotics, Literature, Deconstruction* (1981); and two theoretical works, *Structuralist Poetics: Structuralism, Linguistics, and the Study of Literature* (1975) and *On Deconstruction: Theory and Criticism after Structuralism* (1982).

MARGARET W. FERGUSON, Professor of English and Comparative Literature at Columbia University, is the author of *Trials of Desire: Renaissance Defenses of Poetry* (1983) and many articles on sixteenth- and seventeenth-

[367]

century authors. She has coedited, with Maureen Quilligan and Nancy Vickers, *Rewriting the Renaissance: The Discourses of Sexual Difference in Early Modern Europe* (1986), and, with Mary Nyquist, *Re-membering Milton: The Texts and the Traditions* (1987). In 1986 she held a National Endowment for the Humanities Fellowship to work on a new book, *Limited Access: Studies in Female Literacy and Literary Production in Early Modern Europe*.

MELVIN J. FRIEDMAN is Professor of Comparative Literature and English at the University of Wisconsin–Milwaukee, where he has taught for the past twenty years. He has also taught at the Universities of Maryland, Wisconsin–Madison, Illinois, Marquette, and Colorado, as well as at universities in England, Belgium, New Zealand, and Germany. He is the author or editor of a dozen books; his most recent is *Critical Essays on Flannery O'Connor* (1985). He was the founding editor of *Wisconsin Studies in Contemporary Literature* and (with A. Owen Aldridge) of *Comparative Literature Studies*. His essay was delivered as a lecture at the International William Styron Conference held at Winthrop College, Rock Hill, SC, in April, 1986.

WLAD GODZICH is Professor of Comparative Literature and French Studies at the Université de Montréal, as well as Professor of Comparative Literature and Russian and Eastern European Studies at the University of Minnesota, where he also serves as director of the Center for Humanistic Studies. He codirects the "Theory and History of Literature" series at the University of Minnesota Press and has coedited *The Yale Critics: Deconstruction in America* (1983) and *Literature among Discourses: The Case of the Spanish Golden Age* (1986). He is the author of *The Emergence of Prose: An Essay in Prosaics* and (forthcoming) *The Culture of Literacy*.

Malaysian-born WOON-PING CHIN HOLADAY studied English and American literature at the University of Malaya, Cornell University, and the University of Toledo. Since completing her doctoral dissertation on Ezra Pound's Chinese History Cantos, she has published articles on aspects of East-West Comparative Literature, including the emergent literatures of Southeast Asia and Asian influences on American literature. She is a poet and a translator of Indonesian/Malaysian poetry and the recent coauthor of a book of translations of Malaysian aboriginal myths, *Tales of a Shaman*. She was Fulbright Lecturer in American and Comparative Literature at the University of Indonesia in 1979 and at the Shanghai International Studies University in 1983–1984. She currently teaches at Haverford College.

W. WOLFGANG HOLDHEIM was born in Berlin and came to the United States in 1947. He is now Professor of Comparative Literature and

Notes on Contributors

Fredric J. Whiton Professor of Liberal Studies at Cornell University. In addition to many essays on French and Comparative Literature and on literary theory, he has published *Benjamin Constant*; *Theory and Practice of the Novel: A Study on André Gide*; *Die Suche nach dem Epos: Der Geschichtsroman bei Hugo, Tolstoi und Flaubert*; and *The Hermeneutic Mode: Essays on Time in Literature and Literary Theory*.

CLAYTON KOELB, who studied Comparative Literature at Harvard University, has taught German and Comparative Literature at Purdue and Princeton and the University of Chicago, where he is currently Professor in the Department of Germanic Languages and Literatures and the Committee on Comparative Studies in Literature. He has published many essays on topics in European literature and literary criticism and theory. His books include *Thomas Mann's "Goethe and Tolstoy": Notes and Sources* (1984); *The Incredulous Reader: Literature and the Function of Disbelief* (1984); and, forthcoming, *Inventions of Reading: Rhetoric and the Literary Imagination*. He is coeditor, with Virgil Lokke, of *The Current in Criticism: Essays on the Present and Future of Literary Theory* (1987).

JULIET FLOWER MACCANNELL holds bachelor's and doctoral degrees in Comparative Literature and currently teaches in the Comparative Literature program at the University of California, Irvine. She is the author of *Figuring Lacan: Criticism and the Cultural Unconscious* (1986) and *Couplings: The Semiology and Rhetoric of Heterosexuality from Rousseau to Lacan* (forthcoming); and is coauthor, with Dean MacCannell, of *The Time of the Sign: A Semiotic Interpretation of Modern Culture* (1982). As director of the Focused Research Program in Gender and Women's Studies at UC Irvine she has undertaken to edit a volume on gender and representation for the Irvine Series in the Humanities.

ROBERT MAGLIOLA received his doctorate in Comparative Literature from Princeton University. He has taught at Purdue University, where he served as Professor of English and Comparative Literature and cochair of the program in Philosophy and Literature, and at Tamkang University, Republic of China, where he is now Distinguished Chair Professor in the Graduate School. He is the author of *Phenomenology and Literature* (1977) and *Derrida on the Mend* (1984), as well as many essays on literary theory, aesthetics, and Buddhology. He was a National Humanities Center fellow in 1979–1980 and is active in the Cercle International de la Recherche Philosophique.

LOWRY NELSON, JR., is Professor of Comparative Literature at Yale University. Among his published works are *Baroque Lyric Poetry* (1961) and *The Poetry of Guido Cavalcanti* (1986). He has edited *Cervantes* in the series

Twentieth-Century Views (1968) and coedited and contributed to *The Disciplines of Criticism* (1968) and *Vyacheslav Ivanov: Poet, Critic, Philosopher* (1986). From 1980 to 1986 he was chairman of Medieval Studies at Yale. Currently he is editing a volume of his own essays, translating Ivanov's poetry, and writing a book on the literary tradition of the Song of Songs.

SUSAN NOAKES, who studied Comparative Literature at Yale, has taught at the University of Chicago and the University of Kansas, where she is now Associate Professor of French and Italian and director of the Program in Women's Studies. She has published many essays on French and Italian literature, semiotics, and hermeneutics and is the author of *Timely Reading: Between Exegesis and Interpretation* (1988). She is coeditor, with Robert Kaster, of an edition of Tommaso Schifaldo's *Libellus de indagationibus grammaticis*.

MICHAEL RIFFATERRE is University Professor at Columbia University, where he has served as chairman of the Department of French and Romance Languages. He is director of the School of Criticism and Theory at Dartmouth College. He has written extensively on French literature and literary theory, focusing on text analysis, literariness, and the theory of reading. He is especially interested in questions of intertextuality. His books include *Le Style des Pléiades de Gobineau* (1957); *Essais de stylistique structurale* (1971); *Semiotics of Poetry* (1978); and *Text Production* (1979). He has also published many articles on poetics and literary semiotics in European and American journals.

ALDO SCAGLIONE has been Professor of Italian and Comparative Literature at the University of California, Berkeley (1952–1968), and then at the University of North Carolina, Chapel Hill (1968–1987). He is now Professor of Italian at New York University. In 1971–1972 he was Visiting Professor of Comparative Literature at the Graduate Center, City University of New York. His books include *The Classical Theory of Composition* (1972) and *The Liberal Arts and the Jesuit College System* (1986), in which he has attempted to bring together the history of the liberal arts and the history of literature, especially from the vantage point of theories of style and the theory and practice of literary criticism. He is also the author of many studies of Italian and French literature.

SUSAN RUBIN SULEIMAN is Professor of Romance and Comparative Literature at Harvard University. Besides many essays on modern literature and theory, her works include *Authoritarian Fictions: The Ideological Novel as a Literary Genre*; *The Reader in the Text: Essays on Audience and Interpreta-*

Notes on Contributors

tion (coeditor); and *The Female Body in Western Culture: Contemporary Perspectives* (editor).

Educated at Yale (B.A.) and Columbia, FRANK WARNKE is currently Professor and Head of the Comparative Literature Department at the University of Georgia. He previously taught at Yale, the University of Washington (chair of Comparative Literature, 1967–1975), Queens College, and the Graduate Center at the City University of New York. He has been visiting professor at the German universities of Munich, Münster, and Erlangen. His publications include *European Metaphysical Poetry*, *Versions of Baroque*, an edition of John Donne, a critical study of Donne, and the recent *Three Women Poets*, a volume of translations from Louise Labé, Gaspara Stampa, and Sor Juana Inés de la Cruz. He is an associate editor of the *Princeton Encyclopedia of Poetry and Poetics*.

SAMUEL WEBER has taught at the Johns Hopkins University, the University of Minnesota, and the University of Massachusetts, where he is now Professor of Comparative Literature. He is the author of *The Legend of Freud* (1982) and *Institution and Interpretation* (1986), as well as many essays. He is the coeditor of *Glyph Textual Studies*.

RICHARD WEISBERG, founding president of the Law and Humanities Institute, holds a Ph.D. in French and Comparative Literature from Cornell University and a J.D. from Columbia University Law School. He has taught French and Comparative Literature at the University of Chicago, has practiced law in Paris and New York, and is now Professor of Law at the Benjamin N. Cardozo School of Law, Yeshiva University. He has written many articles treating the interrelations of legal and literary texts and is the author of *The Failure of the Word: The Protagonist as Lawyer in Modern Fiction* (1984) and *When Lawyers Write* (1987).

ULRICH WEISSTEIN, Professor of Germanic Studies and of Comparative Literature at Indiana University and chairman of Indiana University's Comparative Literature Program, received the Ph.D. in Comparative Literature from Indiana. He has also taught at Lehigh University, Middlebury College, Stanford, the University of Wisconsin, and the European universities of Hamburg, Vienna, and Graz. He is the American secretary-general of the International Comparative Literature Association and was a member of the Executive Council of the Modern Language Association. He has published books on Heinrich Mann and Max Frisch, as well as *Introduction to Comparative Literature* (first published in German and since translated into English, Spanish, Japanese, Korean, and Chinese), and has edited *The Essence of Opera*. His most recent book is a collection of essays on Heinrich Mann and Bertolt Brecht, *Links und links gesellt sich nicht*.

PAULINE YU is Professor of Chinese Literature and a member of the steering committee of the Program in Comparative Literature at Columbia University. She received her Ph.D. in Comparative Literature from Stanford in 1976. Her publications include *The Poetry of Wang Wei* and *The Reading of Imagery in the Chinese Poetic Tradition* and many articles addressing issues in Chinese poetry and poetics from a comparative perspective. She was also a member of the American delegation to the first U.S.-Chinese Symposium on Comparative Literature, held in 1983 in the People's Republic of China, as well as to the second Symposium, held at Princeton University in 1987.

Index

Index

Index

Library of Congress Cataloging-in-Publication Data

The Comparative perspective on literature: approaches to theory and practice/edited and
with an introduction by Clayton Koelb and Susan Noakes.
      p.   cm.
   Includes bibliographies and index.
   ISBN 0–8014–2031–8 (alk. paper). ISBN 0–8014–9477–X (pbk.: alk. paper)
   1. Literature, Comparative. I. Koelb, Clayton, 1942–   . II. Noakes, Susan.
PN863.C597   1988   809—dc19   87–25062